PRAISE FOR *HONOR FLIGHT: A VISUAL JOURNEY*

"It is wonderful to see a community come together in such an extraordinary way. *Honor Flight: A Visual Journey,* like the film that came before it, does a stunning job of capturing what makes this country great and is an incredible reminder of how blessed we are to live in this great land. So tonight when you go to sleep – and say your prayers of gratitude for those who served so many years ago in World War II – remember, too, that at this moment there is a young man or woman half-way around the world, sitting alone in the dark, waiting to go out on patrol. They may be tired, and even a little scared – but every day they put on that uniform, and they lay their lives on the line for each of us."

—Former President George H.W. Bush
41st U.S. President and World War II Veteran

"Honor Flight is a tremendous organization dedicated to honoring our nation's true heroes – those who risked their lives to preserve our freedom by serving during World War II. Countless World War II veterans have visited *their* national memorial in recent years, thanks to the generosity of Honor Flight. This book of photographs captures the essence of the Honor Flight journey for future generations – further honoring the legacy of these brave American men and women."

—Senator Bob Dole
U.S. Senate (Retired) and World War II Veteran

"It's so gratifying to see members of the Greatest Generation revisit their difficult days as warriors and honor their buddies who didn't make it back. This handsome book is a moving tribute to the sacrifices they made and how Honor Flights are an important tribute from succeeding generations, thanking them for the lives we enjoy."

—Tom Brokaw
Broadcast Journalist and Author, The Greatest Generation

"My grandfather was a veteran of World War II and served in the Navy in the Pacific. He died before having the chance to visit the National World War II Memorial in Washington, D.C. I regret not making that happen for him. He, like so many others, served and sacrificed. We all owe them so much. This book, *Honor Flight: A Visual Journey*, gives us all a chance to take this trip of a lifetime with our treasured WWII veterans. With each page turn you can see and feel the respect of a grateful nation and you will feel like you have a front-row seat on the Honor Flight. There is no better way to respect their service than to give these veterans the chance to visit their memorial."

—Mark Kelly
NASA Astronaut (Retired) and Captain, U.S. Navy (Retired)

"So much of what we enjoy today is due to the astounding courage, sacrifice and commitment of our World War II veterans. These heroes left their homes, as volunteers, and fought for freedom around the globe, some of them gone for years, too many of them never to return. We acknowledge their sacrifice today through Honor Flight. I have had the privilege of meeting some of these remarkable men and women at their memorial in Washington, D.C. Unforgettable experience for me. The photographs in this book capture that so well."

—Timothy J. Keating
Admiral, U.S. Navy (Retired), Former Commander, U.S. Northern Command and NORAD

"Watching the World War II veterans at the airport early in the morning – all pumped up like a bunch of kids going off to summer camp – and then seeing them just as excited when they return late at night is a real thrill. Thank you to Stars and Stripes Honor Flight for giving these heroes a once-in-a-lifetime experience!"

—Governor Scott Walker
State of Wisconsin

"Thank you, Stars and Stripes Honor Flight, for honoring Wisconsin's servicewomen of World War II and recognizing their contributions to the nation. Some 400,000 women served during WWII. They left the safety and comfort of their homes and did things and went places many American women had never done or seen before. They changed America and the world. After the war, they went back home and went about the business of life. Regrettably, for the most part, their service was lost to history – seldom addressed in our history books, frequently denied by our veteran organizations and, until recently, left out of our memorials. Thank you for giving them the trip of a lifetime – for letting them finally see and experience the gratitude of the nation and the memorial that pays tribute to their service – and with the release of *Honor Flight: A Visual Journey*, giving these American heroines back to the nation and to history."

—Wilma L. Vaught
Brigadier General, U.S. Air Force (Retired) and President, Women In Military Service For America Memorial Foundation

"*Honor Flight: A Visual Journey* is a poignant tribute to our veteran heroes. Those of us who have been on the playing field stand in awe of all those who have served and who continue to serve on the field of battle. Read this once-in-a-generation book; reflect upon the incredible photographs and know again, the debt of gratitude we owe to all of our veterans."

—Bart Starr
Retired NFL Quarterback, Green Bay Packers

"*Honor Flight: A Visual Journey* is a remarkable tribute to our veteran heroes. Even better, the proceeds from this book will ensure that Fisher House Wisconsin becomes a reality and that Honor Flight continues to fly and honor those who have sacrificed more than most of us can imagine. These amazing photographs will rekindle your sense of humility and gratitude for this nation's hard-won freedom and for all who serve."

—Aaron Rodgers
NFL Quarterback, Green Bay Packers

"Born and raised here in Wisconsin, with a multi-generational family legacy of military service, the Leinenkugels are proud to support our men and women in service to our nation. My father, Bill, served as a Marine in WWII in the South Pacific and my brother Jake and I were proud to serve as Marine officers. Jake's sons, Matt and CJ, both enlisted and served in the Marines. We are grateful to Stars and Stripes Honor Flight for their work in allowing members of our Greatest Generation to witness the memorial in their honor first hand. And we thank WE Energies for their generous support of this book to allow Fisher House Wisconsin to build its caring place for veterans and their families on the grounds of the Milwaukee VA Medical Center. Semper Fi."

—Dick Leinenkugel
Business Development Manager, Board Member, Jacob Leinenkugel Brewing Company and Board Member, Fisher House Wisconsin

"*Honor Flight: A Visual Journey* is everyone's story, our nation's shared history of parents, grandparents, siblings and children who have served their country proudly. The beautiful photos in this book allow us to reflect on the enormous courage of these reluctant warriors as they take you on a journey that will stay with you long after turning the final page. This is a poignant, heartwarming tribute to our aging military heroes that should be shared with the entire family."

—Lee and Bob Woodruff
Co-founders, the Bob Woodruff Foundation (bobwoodrufffoundation.org)

"The Honor Flight experience is filled with so many decisive moments. Many are dramatic, like the arrival at the World War II Memorial or the joy of the Homecoming celebration, but so much of what makes Honor Flight special are the small, often unseen moments of reflection throughout the day. Veterans looking out the window of the bus, sharing an emotional memory with an escort or fellow veteran, or simply sitting on a bench soaking up the experience. All of those moments are perfectly captured by the VIP team in this remarkable photography book. It's another powerful testament to the service and sacrifice of these World War II heroes."

—Dan Hayes
Founding Partner, Freethink Media and Director, documentary film Honor Flight

"I grew up in a family where military service was important. I have a grandfather who was a paratrooper in the U.S Army. I had another grandfather who was on the USS *Honolulu* in Pearl Harbor on that fateful morning of December 7, 1941. My Pearl Harbor grandpa died before the World War II Memorial was finished. I think of him every time a Stars and Stripes Honor Flight takes our veterans to see their memorial. *Honor Flight: A Visual Journey* beautifully captures our nation's shared pride and gratitude for all that these brave men and women have done. I look forward to the important work of Fisher House Wisconsin as they care for the men and women and their families who fight for our freedom."

—John Mercure
Host, Wisconsin's Afternoon News, *Newsradio 620 WTMJ*

"My grandfathers were both veterans but neither one lived long enough to visit their memorial. Their generation sacrificed so much and it was an honor to accompany another veteran on an Honor Flight. When I look back on that trip, more than anything else, I see their faces. I will never forget the look on the faces of our veterans when they landed in Washington, D.C., and were received like royalty. Then it was their faces as they opened letters during mail call. That same night it was again their faces as thousands gathered at the airport to greet them and thank them for their service to America. This book, *Honor Flight: A Visual Journey* reminds me of the faces I will never forget and serves as a beautiful tribute to the humble heroes who survived to see their memorial and witness the long-overdue homecoming they all deserve."

—Molly Fay
Host, The Morning Blend, *TODAY'S TMJ4*

"We cannot visit George Washington's monument with the men who served with him at the Battle of Trenton, and only ghosts remain in the fields of Gettysburg. But visiting the World War II Memorial with the men and women who served in that war ranks as the most humbling day I've had in journalism. To hear their stories and see their tears reminds us of what makes America great. It is our collective thank you to these selfless troops. Those of us who came after them should be dedicated to making sure every willing veteran boards the Honor Flight."

—Ted Perry
Anchor, WITI Fox 6 News

"Bridging the past and present, reuniting families and veterans, rekindling memories and emotions all while inspiring a new generation, this is what the Honor Flight program accomplishes. *Honor Flight: A Visual Journey* invites the reader to contemplate the cost of freedom and deeply appreciate those who have served, especially all who have experienced war."

—Bill Michaels
Host, Bill Michaels Sports, *Bill Michaels Radio Network*

"I would not have thought it possible, but the Stars and Stripes Field of Honor event managed to give Wisconsin veterans the incredible thank you they deserve. The crowd shots in this book are amazing and speak to the success of the SSHF program, but please study the faces of the veterans. These were normal people who did incredible things in order to preserve our freedom. Buy this book and share it. One hundred percent of the proceeds will be divided between Stars and Stripes Honor Flight and a new Fisher House."

—Jay Weber
Host, The Jay Weber Show, *WISN 1130*

Published by Stars and Stripes Honor Flight, Inc.

Text © 2013 Stars and Stripes Honor Flight

Photography © 2013 Visual Image Photography unless otherwise credited

All rights reserved. No part of this book may be reproduced or transmitted in any form or by any means, electronic, mechanical, including photocopying, recording, or by an information storage and retrieval system – except by a reviewer who may quote brief passages in review – without permission in writing from Stars and Stripes Honor Flight.

Printed in the United States of America by Quad/Graphics

Book Pages Printed on Appleton Coated – U1X® Silk Text

Manufactured in Wisconsin with Green Power

Minimum 20% Post-Consumer Recycled Fiber, FSC© – Forestry Stewardship Council certified fiber, Green-e® Certified Power. Acid Free, pH neutral for archival use. Enhanced elemental chlorine free, Lacey Act compliant.

ISBN: 978-0-9899031-0-3

Front cover photo/interior photos: Visual Image Photography

Front/back cover/interior design: Meghan Blaney   Back cover photos: Visual Image Photography

HONOR ★ FLIGHT
A VISUAL JOURNEY

"EVERY DAY

IS A BONUS."

—JOE DEMLER
WWII veteran and POW survivor
Stars and Stripes Honor Flight alumnus

Dedicated to our World War II heroes and all our nation's veterans, past and present

Contents

★ ★ ★ ★ ★

12   INTRODUCTION

14   THE BIRTH OF A MOVEMENT

18   THE STORY OF STARS AND STRIPES HONOR FLIGHT

36   WHY WE FLY

40   EVERY DAY IS A BONUS

43   THE FACES OF HONOR FLIGHT

59   REVEILLE — 0500 HOURS

87   D.C. ARRIVAL — 1000 HOURS

121   THE MEMORIALS — 1200 HOURS

223   ARLINGTON — 1630 HOURS

241   MAIL CALL — 1900 HOURS

267   HOMECOMING — 2100 HOURS

335   EPILOGUE

336   SOMETIMES THANK YOU IS NOT ENOUGH

341   ACKNOWLEDGMENTS

Introduction

★ ★ ★ ★ ★

GALE E. KLAPPA
Chairman and Chief Executive Officer
Wisconsin Energy Corporation

The night was filled with energy and emotion. The crowd at Miller Park swelled to nearly 30,000. And together, we watched the debut of an amazing documentary called *Honor Flight*.

On that warm August night, this book was born.

Joe Dean, the visionary behind Stars and Stripes Honor Flight, approached me with the idea for a book about the Honor Flight experience. My reaction was, "When do we get started?"

I've been involved with Stars and Stripes Honor Flight (SSHF) for several years and I'm continually moved by its mission. How do you repay an entire generation a debt of freedom? You can't. You just have to say thank you – humbly and with your whole heart – and that's what SSHF does each and every flight.

The stockholders of Wisconsin Energy and our utility, We Energies, are proud supporters of the Stars and Stripes Honor Flight program and of Fisher House, which provides a home away from home for the families of veterans receiving medical care. Presented with the opportunity to raise additional support for these two great organizations, it was easy to say yes. You see, for us, it's personal.

While the country was engaged in World War II, We Energies played a special role on the home front. Back then, we provided electric trolley service. Many young men and women rode our trolleys and passed through our transportation depot as they embarked on their military service. At war's end, our trolleys carried many back home to their loved ones.

We actively supported our troops during the war. We hosted numerous USO dances, orientation sessions, and military award ceremonies at our Public Service Building in downtown Milwaukee. Ads on our trolleys urged Americans to buy war bonds.

And even more important, during World War II, more than a thousand of our own employees answered the call of duty. They left their jobs and their families to fight for our freedom. Sadly, some did not return, but many did and dutifully resumed the work of serving our electric and gas customers.

We're proud of our history and we're proud to be a part of this project.

Over the past few years, I've had the opportunity to talk with many veterans who have traveled on the Honor Flights, including several of

> *Winston Churchill may have said it best: Never in the field of human conflict was so much owed by so many to so few.*

our employees who served as guardians. All of them say the journey is profoundly moving — and that they wish others could experience it, too. Well, now you can.

It's my privilege to help share the Stars and Stripes Honor Flight experience with you through this book. The photographs beautifully illustrate the emotional journey — a day-long adventure filled with laughter, tears, and reverence for those who paid the ultimate sacrifice.

Only through the perspective of time and the prism of history can we truly understand the enormity of the challenge, the magnitude of the sacrifice, and the valor of the young men and women who fought fearlessly for our freedom during World War II.

Winston Churchill may have said it best: "Never in the field of human conflict was so much owed by so many to so few."

This book is a fitting tribute to the Greatest Generation, and I'm certain that it will be a cherished addition to your personal library. For me, it's a special reminder of the price of freedom and of those who proved that America IS the hope of the world.

Gale Klappa (in red shirt) visits the WWII Wisconsin Pillar of Honor at Coal Dock Park in Port Washington, Wisconsin, with three WWII veterans featured in the documentary film *Honor Flight*. This exact replica of the Wisconsin Pillar from the National WWII Memorial was built on the site of the former coal storage area for the We Energies generating station. From left, Julian Plaster, Harvey Kurz, and Joe Demler. *(photo/Visual Image Photography)*

The Birth of a Movement

★ ★ ★ ★ ★

EARL MORSE
Founder, Honor Flight, Inc.
Co-founder, Honor Flight Network

Everybody loved Leonard Loy and vice versa. Leonard was as jovial and kind-hearted as they come. The only people who didn't like him were the ones who hadn't had the privilege of meeting him yet. Within minutes of talking with him you sensed that he had a pure love for life that was infectious. Before I give you the wrong impression about Leonard, let me also say that if Santa Claus had a younger, mischievous brother who barely stayed out of jail, it would have easily been Leonard. As a child growing up, Springfield Police here in Ohio thought that he would never turn his life around. By the age of 17, it appeared he was headed for the pokey. "One of the best things that ever happened to me was when the judge told me to join the military or go to prison," reflected Leonard decades later. He joined the Navy – and it was no picnic.

Leonard served on the USS *Lyons,* a troop ship that transported thousands of G.I.s to Europe. He worked in the engine room, but during invasions he operated the cranes that lowered landing craft from the deck into the water. Troops would then climb down cargo netting, board the landing craft and head for the beaches. After the invasions, he would hoist the battle-damaged boats back on deck to make the necessary repairs for the next invasion. He endured three invasions in Europe, then sailed past our friendly shores, on through the Panama Canal, and straight out into the Pacific and on to two more invasions on the other side of the planet. Our world was at war and the United States had a big bull's-eye painted on her back.

Something happened to him during the war that transformed him from a juvenile delinquent to a caring, optimistic and lively person you enjoyed spending time with. It was my privilege to care for him at the Springfield VA Clinic during his most senior years. In the summer of 2004 we had a lot to talk about.

On May 29th our nation finally dedicated the long-awaited World War II Memorial. That was the topic of conversation among my senior warriors for weeks before and after the ceremony. I congratulated all of them on their memorial. I often heard, "I'm glad we finally got one!" Others would say, "I wish my friends had lived long enough to see it." I would shoot back and ask, "Well what about you? When are you going to see it?" They often replied, "I'm sure I'll head out there sometime. My kids will probably take me," was a frequent response. "I'm pretty sure my VFW Post will put something together," was another reply.

I was so happy for all of them. They had waited about 60 years for a national landmark to recognize their service. This newly created

WWII Memorial was America's long-overdue "Thank You!" But I also knew most of these men and women didn't travel very often and all of them were on fixed incomes. Many came to our VA clinic because their life savings were gone, so, too, their houses. Many had to decide things like, "Do we eat or pay for our prescriptions this month?" Now things were different. I could see it in their eyes. Finally having their own memorial gave them back a sense of dignity and worth many hadn't felt for several years. In the summer of 2004 we all had high hopes this memorial would lift a lot of spirits and honor some long-overlooked heroes.

Summer turned into fall then fall painfully marched into winter – the worst season for the elderly. The cold often has a crippling effect on them. Shut-ins don't make it outside and succumb to boredom, depression and muscle wasting. Remain stationary and pneumonia will insidiously start to creep in. In December I was seeing many of those same WWII veterans I had seen in May. I asked each one of them if they had gone out to visit their memorial. Remarkably, not one of them had made the trip. When I asked why, most would look at the ground and say, "Well, we don't get around like we used to" or "My wife's been kinda sick" or "The kids have been real busy." The saddest part of their reply was the self-realization that they would never be able to visit their memorial. If they survived the winter they certainly weren't going to be any younger, richer or more capable of traveling to Washington, D.C., next year or the years after that. In the winter of 2004, I quit asking the question. It was too painful to watch them mentally process the reality that it wasn't going to happen – ever.

That irritated me like a slowly developing, gnawing ulcer. The more I thought about it, the worse the sickening feeling I had in my stomach. World War II veterans collectively and literally saved the world. They are the most appreciative, stoic, genuinely patriotic and humble people I have ever met. They waited 60 years for a memorial they will never get to see? This was wrong.

I started exploring options. A three-day bus or car ride round trip from Ohio wouldn't work because most elderly people can't travel for that long and no 80-year-old would leave his 80-year-old spouse for three days. A flight to Washington, D.C., on a small airplane appeared feasible. I could rent one for about $600 to $800 for the day. The Piper or Cessna seats four. I would need a copilot to split the aircraft rental cost

above: Leonard Loy (center) became Honor Flight's pioneer WWII veteran in May 2005. He is shown here before his flight with Honor Flight, Inc. founder Earl Morse (right) and pilot Chuck Daily. *(photo/Paul Sharp)*

HONOR FLIGHT FOUNDER

Earl Morse, founder of Honor Flight, is a retired Air Force captain and private pilot who currently works as a physician assistant at the Department of Veterans Affairs in Springfield, Ohio. From that first flight in May of 2005, Morse expanded the program into the Honor Flight Network with the help of co-founder Jeff Miller. The Honor Flight Network now has 120 hubs nationwide.

above: Earl (far right) on the inaugural Honor Flight. Six small planes flew out of Springfield, Ohio, taking twelve WWII veterans to visit their memorial in Washington, D.C. *(photo/Paul Sharp)*

and flying duties because that certainly would be a long and emotional day. Take off at sunrise, three-hour flight over the Appalachian Mountains, land, get a cab ride into D.C., visit the WWII Memorial, back to the airport, fly home another three hours and land before sunset. My father agreed to rent the plane with me and we were all set. I just needed to find a WWII veteran.

World War II veterans collectively and literally saved the world. They are the most appreciative, stoic, genuinely patriotic and humble people I have ever met. They waited 60 years for a memorial they will never get to see? This was wrong.

The first week of 2005 I returned to the Springfield VA Clinic with a renewed sense of optimism. Instead of avoiding conversations with WWII veterans about their new memorial, I planned on having a big conversation about it. In walked Leonard Loy just as bubbly as ever. At the end of his appointment I asked if he had ever made it out to Washington. Like all the other veterans, he said he hadn't. "Well, do you have any plans to make it out there this year?" I asked. Then, sadly, he looked down at the floor and talked about how there were no plans, how expensive it would be, how he doesn't drive very far, and several other reasons. I listened and then asked him a key question. "Leonard, have you ever flown in a small plane – and I mean a very small plane?" His face lit up and he said, "Yeah! My Uncle Phil had a Piper Cub and he would take me up every once in a while. I loved it!" His response could not have been any better. "Well Leonard, my dad and I are going to rent a plane. My dad's a Vietnam vet and he's never seen the Vietnam Memorial. We're going to fly out to D.C. for the day, then fly back that evening. There will be two seats in the back. If you want to go, you can ride along for free. It won't cost you a dime. While we're there, we'll also walk down to the World War II Memorial. Do you want to go?"

I watched his face and waited. I was ready for an enthusiastic "Yes!" or "Let me discuss it with my wife." I wasn't ready for him to start crying. He then said he would really appreciate it if he could go with us. He gave me his phone number and I told him I would get back with him in the spring for the flight. As we left my office, the staff watched as Leonard headed down the hall still trying to compose himself. As Leonard turned the corner, office staff quickly and quietly asked if everything was OK, fearing that I had given him some tragic medical news. (Did I mention that everyone loved Leonard?) I assured them that he was fine. Those were tears of joy. Once I explained what the conversation was about, they were relieved and very happy for him.

That conversation took place on the 3rd of January, 2005. On May 21st, Leonard became the first veteran to take off on the first Honor Flight to Washington D.C.. Since then, I've discovered that America is filled with tens of thousands of Leonards and Lynettes. The Honor Flight Network has now transported more than 125,000 WWII veterans from all the United States and we're still going strong.

Leonard died two years ago and while I know there will never be another Leonard, I can still see him on every page in this book. I can still see that half-crooked smile, the gleam and twinkle in the eye, the tears of joy, and the mischievous squint of Leonard in the facial expressions of so many of the wonderful veterans in this book. Photographs do a wonderful job of capturing moments, brief seconds in time.

Since starting Honor Flight, I can say that some of the most meaningful and important seconds in the lives of these veterans and their families have been captured beautifully on these pages. You can almost hear the hum of the plane, the cheers, the band, the applause, the children, the sobs and sniffles. I would encourage you to soak in the images of these priceless moments when the full measure of a person's emotion, relevance and significance are captured in the moment as they are surrounded by a grateful loved one, family, community and nation. I hope you sense the overwhelming love and joy veterans and families experience through these pages. America is a great country. The men and women on these pages still believed she and all of us were worth fighting for. They have earned their memorial, their Honor Flight trip and the eternal gratitude of our nation.

The Story of Stars and Stripes Honor Flight

★ ★ ★ ★ ★

JOE DEAN
Chairman and Founder
Stars and Stripes Honor Flight

IN THE SHADOW OF 9/11

Before Stars and Stripes Honor Flight, there was a dream. Before that, in fact seven years prior, I stood with the finest men I have ever known on board the USS *Alabama*. Even with all flights grounded in the wake of 9/11 – we had all traveled to Alabama by car, some of us nearly 20 hours – these 80-year-old heroes of Land Invasion Operation Navy (LION) would not be denied their last reunion as WWII shipmates.

"Nothing happens unless first we dream."

— Carl Sandburg

Standing next to my father, watching CNN footage of the aftermath at Ground Zero, the still-smoldering Pentagon and the carnage in Shanksville, Pennsylvania, my dad's Navy buddy, J.T. Daniels, leaned into me and said, "I thought we had taken care of all this in 1944." Sadness turned to resolve in the LIONs as they talked about freedom and vigilance. But there was also a weary recognition that we live in a dangerous and troubled world – so often beautiful, yet too often brutal.

One day led to another in Alabama and the reunion took on an upbeat tone. Spouses joined the guys and with them came healing. Stories and laughter soon followed. I was honored to deliver the keynote speech at the event. Using dusty photos and memorabilia I had found in my father's footlocker in the attic of his Wauwatosa, Wisconsin, home, the aging warriors watched and were amazed at this new "PowerPoint thing," with digital pictures and streaming video. After a final tribute from the U.S. Navy, several other dignitaries and a salute from me on behalf of my generation, the men of LION headed for the bar and I wandered outside.

"Chips" (so named for his South Pacific card-playing prowess), a big-hearted war buddy of my father, joined me as I stood beneath a towering tree. Being careful not to spill his Brandy Manhattan, he stooped down and picked up an acorn. Handing it over to me, Chips said, "Son, from the smallest seeds grow mighty oaks. What you just did in there means the world to these guys . . . I'm not sure where you go from here, but I know this, you are not done."

THE LION KING

My dad had rallied for this trip and driving home it was clear he had peaked. I was thrilled to have joined him at this summit. Yet, driving in the car from Mobile to Milwaukee, it became clear that dad's Alzheimer's had turned a terrible corner. All too soon, he joined so many other WWII heroes. Dad died.

So, seven years later when I saw Earl Morse on TV and heard the brief segment about a new program called Honor Flight, I did what so many of us do: I absent-mindedly wished someone else would start a program just like that, close to home. That night I dreamt of U.S. Navy teenagers in the throes of an island poker game. Upon waking, I thought, "Darn it, I know who should do this." I decided to go all in.

Coincidentally, as an Ozaukee County Supervisor, I attended a meeting that morning with fellow elected officials, some of whom were WWII and Vietnam veterans. I ad-libbed a presentation for this group and to my delight the message touched a nerve. On the way home, speed dialing, I began recruiting the busiest people I knew. I naively told them it would be easy. I spoke truth too, telling them it would be extremely meaningful and that "no" was simply not an option. Subsequently, these generous friends became the nucleus of Team Stars and Stripes Honor Flight and the rest, as the saying goes, is history.

opposite: David Dean, Joe Dean's father. *(photo/courtesy of Joe Dean)* **left:** Cornelius Hatchell, Joe Dean's father-in-law. *(photo/courtesy of Peter J. Hatchell)*

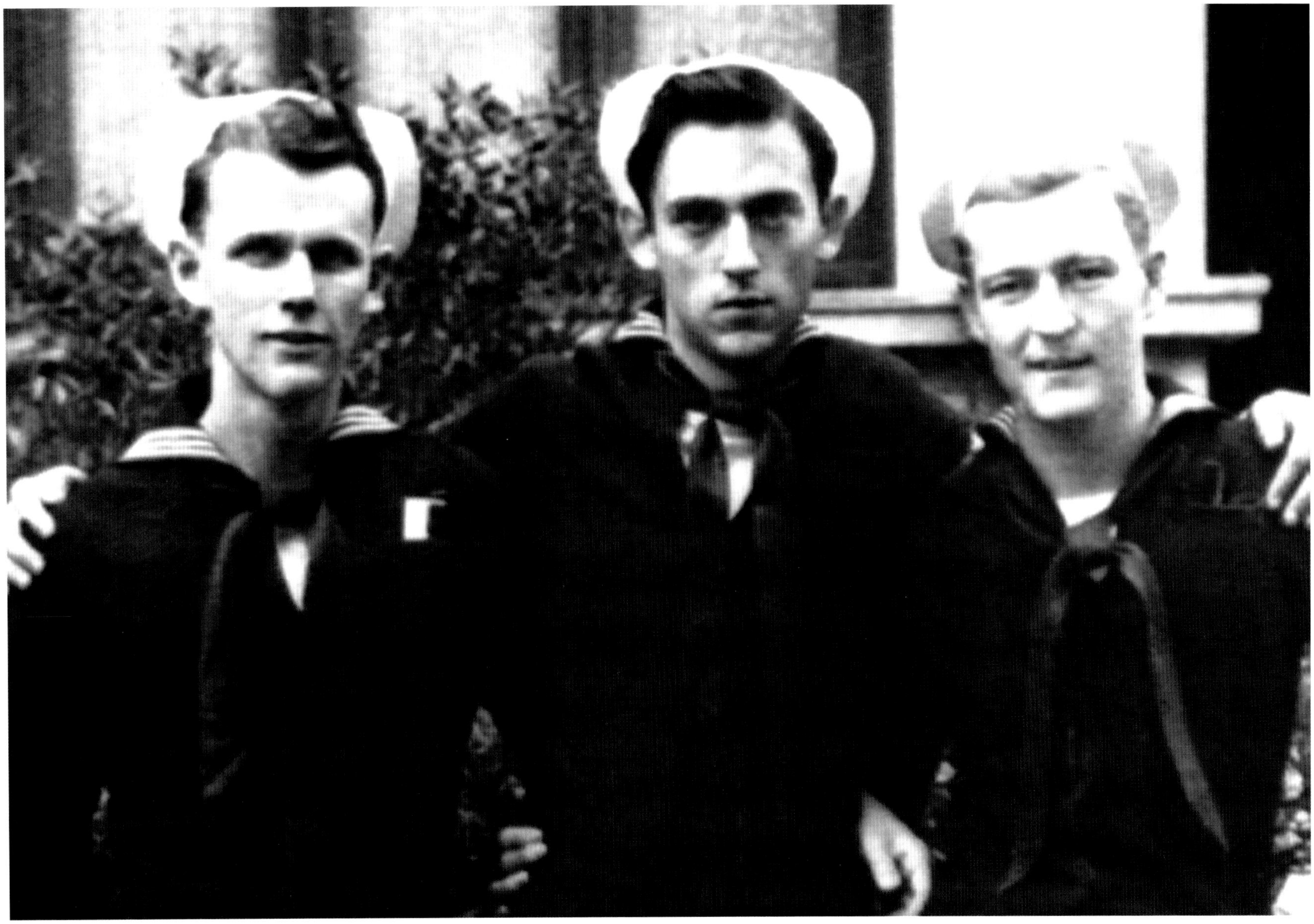

BUT FIRST THIS

Pacing and nervous in the parking lot outside of a local supper club before our first official fundraising presentation, I phoned Steve Deutsch who would soon become VP of Logistics for Stars and Stripes. Deutsch coached me up, saying something about "just tell them stories," so I did. Ten minutes in, I was distracted by all the heads nodding in support, a few people in tears, all of them in agreement. Clearly, this was our shared history. The proverbial hat was passed, $600 was raised and I couldn't leave that evening without hearing one after another, after another and yet another war story.

Within days, fellow Board member, Dr. Doug McManus, suggested I meet with Joe Demler, a POW from the Battle of the Bulge. From there, in a divinely inspired bank-shot we met Iwo Jima veteran Harvey Kurz bagging groceries at the local Pick 'n Save. Harvey and Joe joined us for our first brat fry (hey, only in Wisconsin!) and we raised another $250. Emboldened and a bit crazy but wildly committed, our team decided to book our first plane to Washington, D.C. The good people at We Energies soon met Harvey and Joe and to this day Gale Klappa and crew at Wisconsin Energy Corporation are our largest contributors and dearest friends.

People have often asked me if I ever imagined Stars and Stripes Honor Flight would grow to the movement it has become. "Actually yes," I tell them. "I could see this coming." As anyone who participated in those first days will tell you, it quickly became clear that this was everyone's story. All we really needed to do was get the word out.

OPERATION RESOLVE

Following an early flight, we recruited Renee Riddle as our PR director. Renee described her first trip with us as "magical," and reached out to her friends in the media. On Veterans Day, Milwaukee radio talk show host Charlie Sykes invited me to a "phoner" interview and we soon fell into a comfortable conversation about this emerging group of volunteers and a story that seemed to be capturing the hearts of our community. Following the call, I rushed to the WTMJ radio studio and hand-delivered a book of pictures from our most-recent trip along with an invitation for Charlie to join us on a future flight. My cell phone rang on the drive home. It was Charlie. "Joe," he said. "Whatever it takes, let's fly these guys!"

Within weeks our little grass-roots group was growing exponentially as veterans started signing up in droves. After one Board meeting, a

opposite: (l–r) David Dean and his LION buddies, William Deem and Clifford James. *(photo/courtesy of Joe Dean)* ***above:*** Joe Dean (in red shirt), with Stars and Stripes Honor Flight pioneer veterans Harvey Kurz (left) and Joe Demler, both of whom were featured in the documentary *Honor Flight*. *(photo/Visual Image Photography)*

few of us dropped by a local pub and began discussing our new, wonderful dilemma: Before we truly knew what hit us, our sign-up list had grown to more than 700 veterans, with an average wait time of 18 months. We talked, as only Team Honor Flight can, about other seemingly impossible missions, including the moon launch and President Kennedy's now famous words: "We choose to go to the moon … and do other things, not because they are easy but because they are hard." I flipped over a napkin and drew up a logo with the first words that came to mind: "Operation Resolve." Gunny Sergeant and Board member Mark Grams simply said, "Goosebumps." With that serving as our complete market test and focus group, we launched Operation Resolve – and booked a 747, the largest plane we could find.

We started receiving a remarkable amount of support from the community. To this day, my favorite donation is the one from a 94-year-old grandmother who had heard about Operation Resolve. She was the widow of a WWII pilot and used to sit on the roof of her childhood home, watching planes fly over and thinking about her sweetheart, soon-to-be husband, deployed overseas. Her letter said, "I have very little money left but I have lived a good life, I would like you to have this in honor of my husband." The check was made out for $7.47.

Months later we had booked not one, not two, but three 747s. We never looked back.

GOT FREEDOM?
They are our fathers and mothers, grandparents and great-grandparents. Day by day they are becoming our ghost soldiers. Now you see them, now you don't. Brace yourself as you embrace this book and know that the men and women shown here harbor amazing stories. Some were starving. Trying to bide time, they would eat sawdust as they prayed for liberation while clinging to one more day in the putrid labor and revolting decay of the Nazi prison camps. Many huddled together in foxholes on the beaches of Normandy or in the volcanic ash beneath Mount Suribachi on Iwo Jima. Others have told me of long days and nights sweating, under fire, in the sweltering rains and mosquito-infested South Pacific while across the globe entire battalions were freezing, mired in ice and muck at the Battle of the Bulge.

One 90-year-old Honor Flight veteran – a teenager at the time – told us this story about being stranded in the dark Philippine Sea after his ship, the USS *Indianapolis*, had been torpedoed: "In order to keep my sanity, I held fast to the medal of St. Anthony that my mother had given to me. Funny, how so many of us, tough as we thought we were, just wanted our moms. For each of those four long days and nights in the water, we clung to each other, telling jokes and stories while the sharks circled our group." When nighttime came, the words of encouragement turned into screams as one after another of the 900 men succumbed to the shadows below. "Sea monsters and nightmares remain . . .," he said, his voice trailing off to a whisper. "But freedom is worth it, isn't it?"

Another guy, a pilot in the European theater and a war brother of the man who would become my father, kept his shattered plane aloft long enough for his crew to parachute to safety. He spun out of control and crashed, killed instantly. This, on the very day his son was born. His grieving mother gave her newborn son, my cousin, two names: one to honor his dad, the other to honor mine. Paul David, newly born in the reflection of a Gold Star window, serves as a daily reminder that freedom is not free.

The women of WWII were equally remarkable. Women like Dr. Lucy Cohn who at 18 years old was struck by the screaming as she walked the halls of a psych ward near the front lines in a makeshift hospital in Germany. She describes her first patient as a boy. "He was so young and he had a gaping head injury," she said. "I held his hand as they wheeled him into surgery and asked him if he had written to his mother." He told her no, that since getting hit, he had "forgotten how to write." Lucy walked beside the gurney as they wheeled the boy into surgery, certain he would not survive. "Don't worry," she told him. "When you come out of this operation, you talk and I'll write for you." She felt bad lying to him, but recalls that "even false hope was better than no hope." But the young man survived and he and Lucy teamed up to send daily letters back home. A small victory, she would say, in a ward full of wailing, crying men. Men who were still raw with the terror of what they had seen and done. But Lucy was of a generation that refused to quit. Instead, she used the experience to come home and dedicate her life to serving those with mental illness. She met the love of her life while overseas, the two of them becoming quiet philanthropic pillars in our community. Lucy passed away as this book was coming together. She died doing what she did best, ministering to those around her in hospice.

Not all the WWII stories are grim. In fact, many of the men and women pictured in this book have shared with us stories of simple pleasures juxtaposed with deep poignant moments of humanity. Miraculously,

opposite: WWII veteran Lucy Cohn at the Vietnam Women's Memorial. During her Honor Flight, Lucy visited her husband's grave at Arlington National Cemetery. *(photo/Visual Image Photography)*

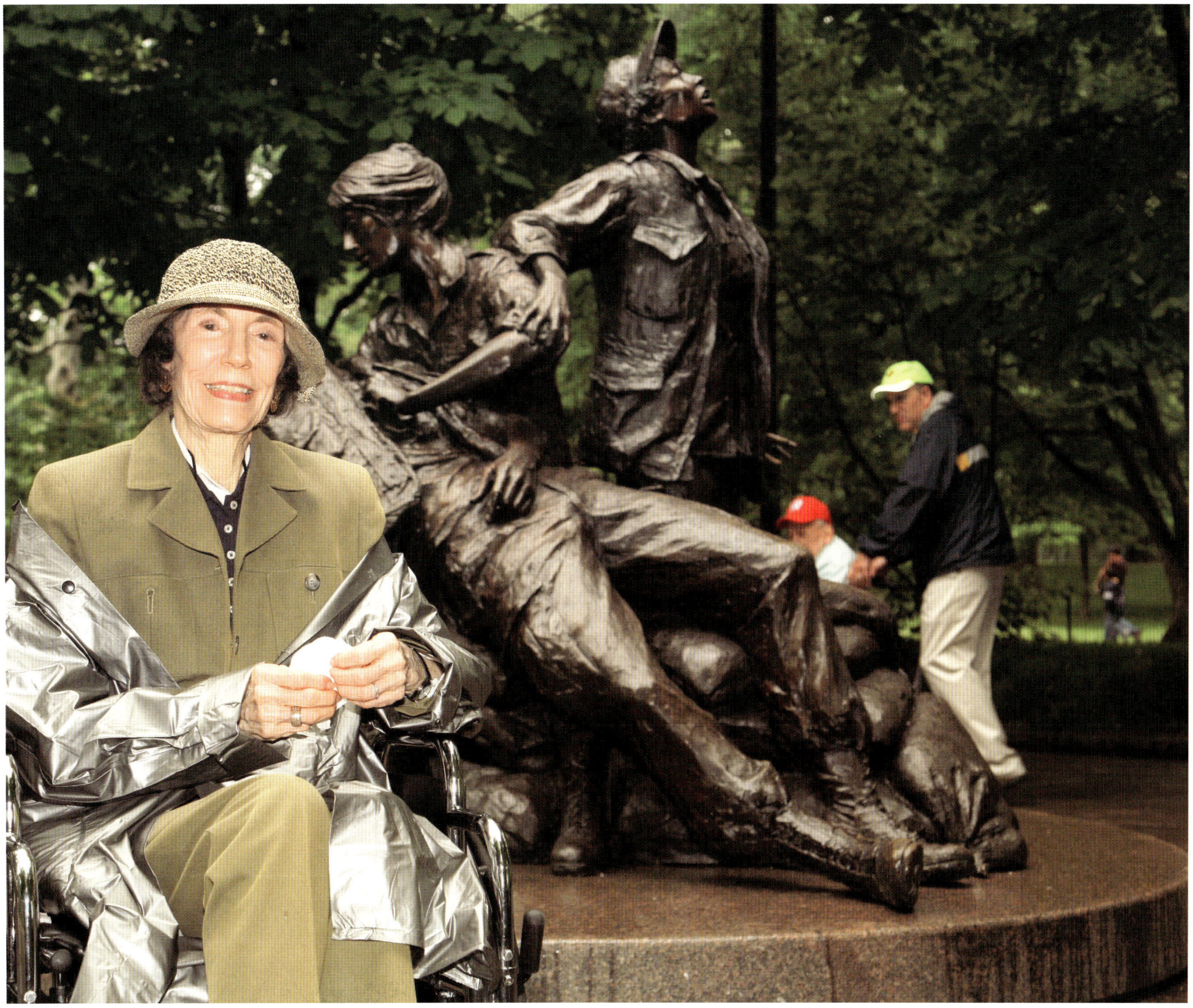

STARS STRIPES
HEROES
LABEL OTHER END
LABEL OTHER END
UNITED STATES POSTAL SERVICE
U.S. MAIL
UNITED STATES POSTAL SERVICE
FLAT MAIL TRAY
U.S. MAIL
UNITED STATES POSTAL SERVICE
UNITED STATES POSTAL SERVICE
FLAT MAIL TRAY
UNITED STATES POSTAL SERVICE

they often found humor and laughter in spite of the circumstances. This strength of spirit in the midst of the chaos and the terror stands as a remarkable tribute to the men and women of WWII.

Never did the members of the Greatest Generation ask for a thank you. Instead, they returned from war, set their duffle bags in the back hall of modest homes and farms, hugged their moms and dads and set about creating our communities and building our families. They never talked about the war again. That is, until Honor Flight.

A DAY IN THE LIFE OF HONOR FLIGHT
With an 0500 reveille, we welcome these heroes to Mitchell International Airport. The day begins with the singing of the national anthem and other songs, followed by a preflight prayer. One of these prayers was led by Father James Ernster, who was on the front lines of WWII himself when he vowed that if he got out alive, he would dedicate his life to the priesthood. Seconds after making that promise, a bullet hit the tin-plated Bible James kept in his chest pocket. The bullet lodged in the Bible – and James got religion.

By 0730, the veterans and their guardians have all boarded and following a water cannon salute, the highest honor for a military pilot's last flight, we are airborne and off to Washington, D.C. There is really no describing the deplaning process and the welcome we receive on the tarmac and in the terminals at Dulles, Baltimore–Washington and Reagan International Airports. Strangers stand on chairs to cheer and get a better view: Boy Scouts, Girl Scouts, cheerleaders and volunteers converge on these airports to be sure the men and women of WWII receive their first thank you in 70 years. Bands play and tears flow. Then we board our buses and, with an escort of Vietnam veterans on motorcycles and the U.S. Park Police, the heavy freeway traffic parts before our eyes as our caravan proceeds to the U.S. Marine Corps Memorial (more familiar to some as the Iwo Jima statue), Arlington National Cemetery, several other memorials and ultimately, the highlight of the day: a tour of the National World War II Memorial.

All too soon, at 1730, we are heading back to the airport. Inevitably, the young guardians who accompany our veterans use this time to nap. Almost inexplicably, the WWII men and women – inspired by this fountain-of-youth day – rally and use this time to swap stories as if they were 19 again. Witnessing this transformation, hearing the healing, difficult and cathartic stories continues to be one of life's greatest blessings and most memorable moments.

Back on the plane, one more surprise awaits our veterans. Well before the day of the flight, family, friends, schoolchildren and even strangers have secretly written letters reminiscing and thanking our heroes for their service and for our freedom. Flying through the night sky, our plane comes to life as flight attendants and other volunteers jump in, calling each veteran's name as the captive crowd whoops and grins, watching us run the aisles to deliver the mail.

When the plane lands in Milwaukee, the veterans' arms are full of mail, their hearts content and filled with gratitude. As we assist them from the plane, bagpipes play and there is a distant rumbling in the corridor. No words can properly describe the Homecoming celebration, but the pictures in this book and the scenes in our movie *Honor Flight* come as close as possible to capturing the magnitude of this long overdue thank you and welcome home. Once back in the loving arms of family members, the magic really begins as we often hear that for the first time in their lives, these veterans begin to open up and find a way to communicate the war stories that shaped them and an entire generation.

WAR. HELL.
Dwight D. Eisenhower once said, "I hate war as only a soldier who has lived it can, only as one who has seen its brutality and stupidity." In the movie *Honor Flight*, we describe war as the "abject failure of the human condition." Thus, with a heavy and careful heart we have asked many of the members of the Greatest Generation featured in this book about their enormous bravery and service. More precisely, we have invited them to share their secret. In the midst of the hell, which is war, how did they do it? The closest they come to explaining it is this: "We were attacked. Our country needed us. Nearly everyone sacrificed or served."

These soon-to-be warriors came from families shaped by the Great Depression. Raised in the echo of the "war to end all wars," World War I, they worked shoveling coal, milking cows or delivering newspapers. Many will tell you that death was a constant companion due to widespread epidemics such as polio and the great influenza. As children, they managed their young lives with few expectations. They were simple kids and truly free. They were tough, rub-some-dirt-on-it guys and girls who were set loose each morning to find their way. By and large, their parents gave them three rules: work before play, be nice and come home when it gets dark out.

opposite: Each Honor Flight veteran is surprised with a packet of mail from family, friends, neighbors and even strangers during Mail Call on the flight back to Milwaukee. The mail – enough to fill nine suitcases! – is sorted just prior to the flight in a local middle school cafeteria. *(photo/Joe Dean)*

So when war came, these boys and girls packed up, signed up and served. Through it all most of them were optimistic, dignified and selfless. A Greatest Generation friend recalls a classic example: "There was this guy, a brother really, who whistled the entire time while we amputated his leg at our makeshift hospital on Manus Island. Later, to ease the pain, the amputee was sharing a swig from our Seabees-built, island still, and he told us he whistled because he could see how hard it was for his fellow corpsmen to begin the sawing. As he lay on that cot, with his femur sticking out and gangrene setting in, he wanted us to feel better and he wanted us to know it was going to be okay."

The men and women pictured in this book will tell you the real heroes are the ones who didn't come home. I beg to differ and I ask that you beg to differ as well.

Together, all of them – as citizens of this great experiment, the United States of America – worked at home and abroad, coalescing around a common mission and they saved the free world. They are quiet and humble. They are fountains of endless stories and we are losing them at the rate of 900 each and every day. Taken together, they are the seven-decades-old echo of the time when freedom met evil in our world gone mad. Thanks to them, freedom won.

JOIN THE JOURNEY

Now they are our 80- and 90-year-old neighbors. Bent and often spent, they came of age in the most compelling, awful, heroic, beautiful and terrible of times. They were steeped in traditional values and they worked hard trying to pass those values on to each of us. They are the heroes next door.

They bag our groceries. They have delivered our mail and taught Sunday school. Some led our Girl Scout Troops, others formed Lions Clubs. They are Rotarians and Kiwanians. They were not perfect, but their sacrifices and bravery call us to lives of gratitude, patriotism and community. For far too long and far too often we have walked past these heroes in our neighborhoods and nursing homes. Worse, in our busy lives, we have taken them for granted. Right smack in the midst of raising our own children, we ignore these living history lessons, at our peril. Our children, who are the direct beneficiaries of this hard-won freedom and the remarkable courage of all of our veterans, deserve to know their stories.

Since the first National Honor Flight in 2005, communities across the U.S.A. have responded. Nationally, thus far, Honor Flight has flown more than 125,000 Greatest Generation heroes to Washington, D.C. More than 5,000 of those heroes, thanks to our sister hubs across this state, are from Wisconsin. The images in this book are of our Wisconsin veterans, but this is really the story of all our WWII heroes and their Honor Flight experience. Through *Honor Flight: A Visual Journey,* you can stand beside them before the Wall of Freedom, where each star among the 4,048 stars represents 100 men and women – teenagers really – who paid the ultimate price for you and for your children.

opposite: The visit to the National WWII Memorial is a profoundly moving experience for our heroes. *above:* The Freedom Wall holds 4,048 gold stars, each representing 100 American service personnel who died in WWII or remain missing. *(photos/Visual Image Photography)*

Through the photos and stories here, you can join the band of Honor Flight volunteers and our aging, youthful heroes as pulses quicken, tears flow and conversation ceases. Join the 70-year-old dream as it comes to fruition and our moms and dads, our grandfathers and grandmothers, press their noses up to the glass of our chartered, air-conditioned buses. Lean in with them. Grasp the significance of what they did and be better for the experience.

You hold in your hands, by design, a heavy book. It is not to be taken lightly. It requires your active meditation on freedom. These pictures need to stay with you long after turning the last page. Breathe life into this story and make it your story for yourself and for generations to come, as we all work toward a more peaceful world. On behalf of our Board of Directors, I ask that you internalize this experience, knowing in your soul that it is personal. Please, take courage from our veterans and our shared history, steeped in the knowledge of the cost of freedom and recommitted to the challenge of our time: We dare not live trivial lives.

above: Honor Flight serves to honor our WWII heroes – and engage a new generation in understanding the sacrifices they made for our freedom. *(photo/Joe Dean)*

OUR JOURNEY – FROM BRAT FRY TO "FLY BOY" BUSH

"Like our veterans themselves, Stars and Stripes Honor Flight had humble beginnings. Our first fundraiser – a traditional Wisconsin brat fry (pictured) – brought in $250. But in just five years, thanks to this community and 600 volunteers, we have flown thousands of WWII veterans to see their memorial.

Along the way, we were so moved by the veterans and their stories, that we helped make a movie documenting the Stars and Stripes Honor Flight experience. After premiering the film *Honor Flight* before a record-setting crowd, we were invited to show the movie at the U.S. Capitol. In 2013, we attended a screening of the film in Kennebunkport, Maine, hosted by former President and "Fly Boy" George H.W. Bush, pictured above with his wife, Barbara, and SSHF Board Members (l-r) Renee Riddle, Joe Dean, Steve Deutsch and Jane Dean.

The Stars and Stripes Honor Flight founding mission, Operation Resolve, has been resolved, as we have flown all WWII veterans in our service area to see their memorial. As we move into the second phase of Stars and Stripes Honor Flight, and begin flying our Korean War veterans – and hopefully our Vietnam Veterans one day – we are proud to support Fisher House Foundation, which also serves to honor our nation's veterans and their families. The Honor Flight story continues to be one of, for and by the people."

—Joe Dean

above, left: The first Stars and Stripes Honor Flight fundraiser. *(photo/Jane Dean)* *right*: Before the screening of *Honor Flight* for former President George H.W. Bush and his wife Barbara. *(photo/PRNewsFoto/SnagFilms)*

FIELD OF HONOR

Nearly 30,000 veterans from World War II and our nation's other conflicts were joined by their families, friends and community members for the premiere of the documentary film *Honor Flight* at Miller Park, home of the Milwaukee Brewers. The day-long Field of Honor event on August 11, 2012, started with a tailgate party in the parking lot and culminated in the showing of the documentary – to a Guinness World Record-setting crowd of 28,442, topping the former record set for the Brazilian premiere of a soccer documentary.

A SALUTE TO THE GREATEST GENERATION

Associated Bank
JOURNAL SENTINEL
pepsi
IT'S Miller TI
FIELD
YOUR LEGACY
Club Goodwill
KOHL'S
CHEVY
FIELD of HONOR
A SALUTE TO THE GREATEST GENERATION
8:53

19
4
50
ONOR
CREATING BUILDING
ENVIRONMENTS
THAT INSPIRE
CHAMPIONS
Johnson Controls
Lite
PALERMO'S
US Cellular
Time Warner Cable
TOYOTA
TERRITORY
OUR FREEDOM
HIGH LIFE
ATI
8:53

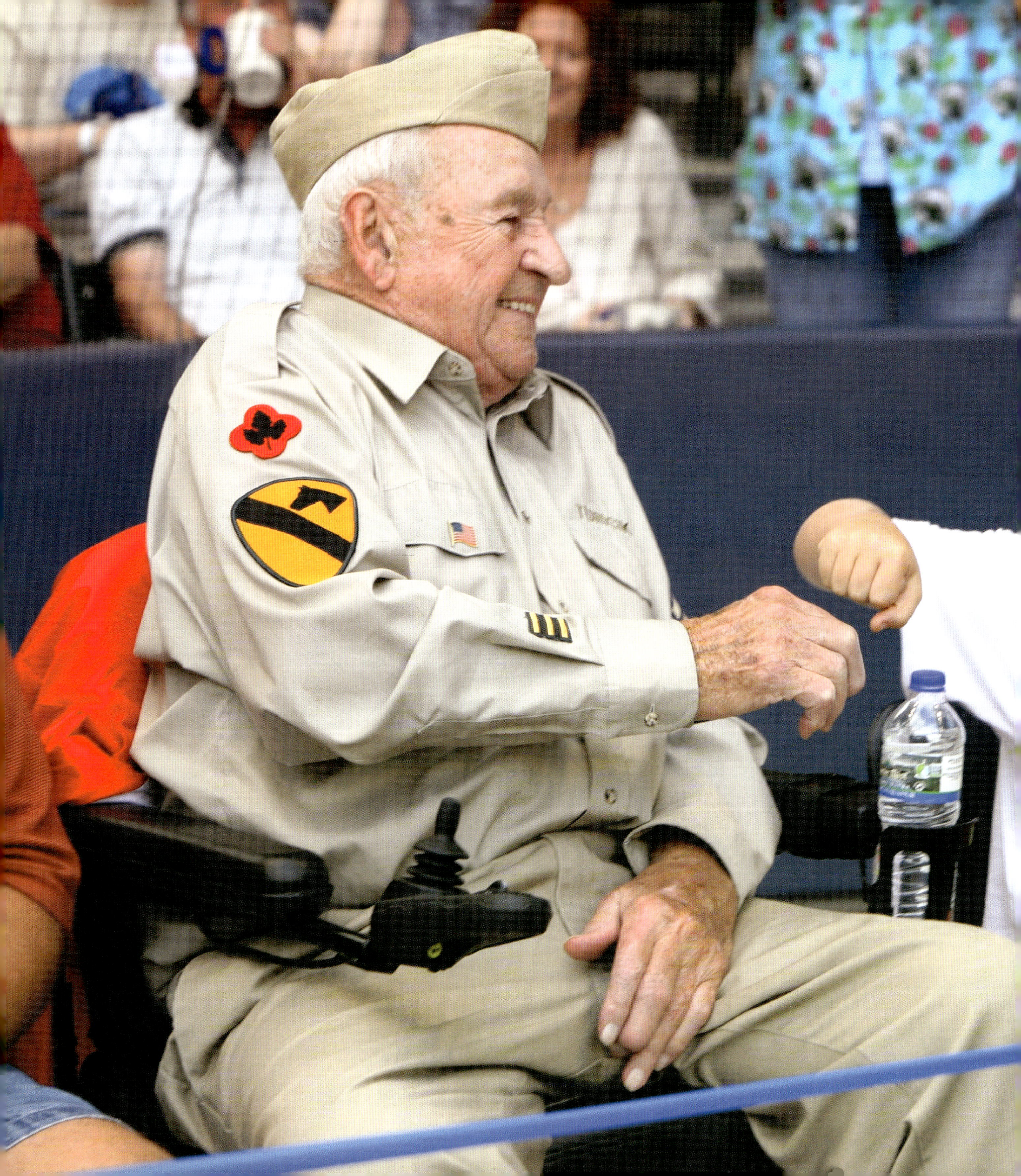

I FEEL LIKE A KING!

When WWII veteran Joseph Turicik was interviewed about his November 2009 Honor Flight experience for the documentary film, *Honor Flight,* he said, "I feel like a king!" That soundbite was used in the original film trailer making Joe one of our most memorable veterans. We were thrilled to see him again three years later at the Field of Honor event at Miller Park. Still wearing his U.S. Army uniform, just as he did on his Honor Flight, and still "feeling like a king" he is shown here fist-bumping his great-grandson before the movie premiere.

Why We Fly

★ ★ ★ ★ ★

CHARLES J. SYKES
Host
Newsradio 620 WTMJ

They are always surprised. No matter how much they may have heard about the flight – the memorials, mail call, the Homecoming, they are still surprised by the day and the outpouring of gratitude and enthusiasm. Perhaps that is because they were the unentitled generation; they never asked for this and never expected it, certainly not seven decades later.

The truth is that many of these men thought of themselves as being on the shelf; some had been retired for 20 years or more. In our youth culture, with its cultivated historical amnesia, we were perfectly happy to ignore them, and they had gotten used to that.

For the most part they didn't want to talk about the war. In the 1950s, they worked hard to build their lives, raise their families, and spare our generation from having to endure the privations they had experienced. In the '60s and '70s, they watched as the boomers rebelled against their values and proclaimed themselves the brightest, most compassionate generation ever. In the '80s and '90s, they retired, and began to watch their brothers begin to slip away. For too many, the WWII memorial came too late.

Then something changed. Not in them, but in our culture and in our generation. We started to remember who the Greatest Generation really was (hint: it wasn't us). We also began to realize that time was slipping away and that we had serious unfinished business. There were things to be said, commitments to be honored, debts to be paid.

I had paid only sporadic attention to the push to create the National WWII Memorial, but I knew that it was important to my mother, who

above: Charlie Sykes at the WWII Memorial during a 2010 Stars and Stripes Honor Flight. *opposite:* Charlie interviews veterans for his 620 WTMJ radio show. *(photos/Visual Image Photography)*

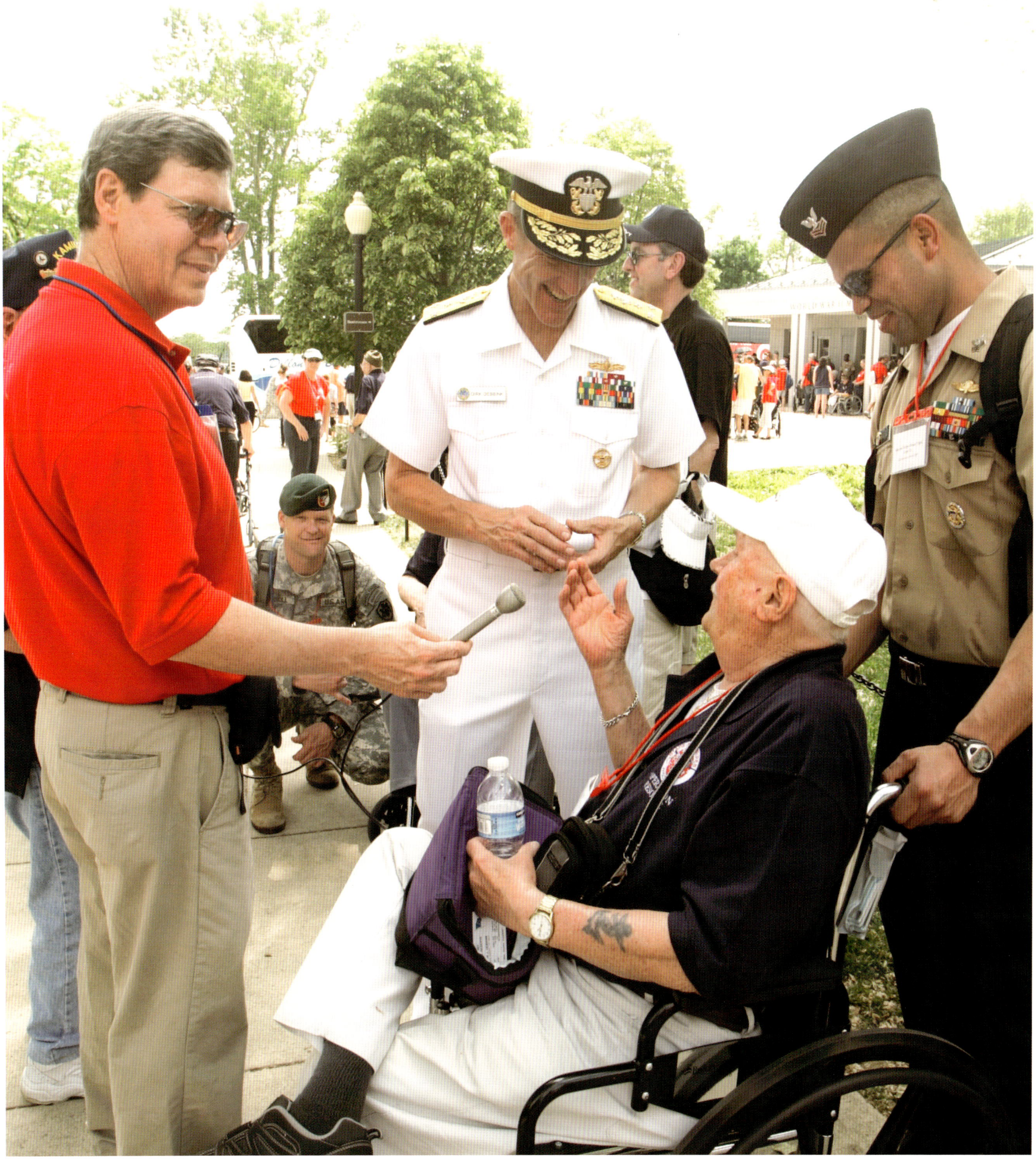

FROM THE MOVIE *HONOR FLIGHT*

"By the time we land back in Milwaukee, these guys are very tired – a lot of them are in their 80s and 90s. They know there is going to be a homecoming. But they have no idea what it's going to be.

So you walk along with them. In the distance you can begin to hear this sort of rumbling. It's not distinct at first; something is out there, but you can't hear it from the corridor.

I was walking next to one of the guys and he said, 'This is like heaven.' And I said, 'What do you mean?' And he said, 'It's like seeing all the people you loved and you cared about. It's like having your whole life before you and realizing that what you did mattered. That it was actually worth it. To see my grandkids and my kids . . .' That is a powerful moment.

This is a precious legacy that we have gotten from these guys. We cannot squander it. We can't waste it.

You guys were good dads. You were good moms. You sacrificed for us. You took care of us. And we never told you when we had a chance. This is the vehicle where we get to say thank you. You mattered. We remember you. Thank you. You deserve this."

— Charles Sykes, from the documentary *Honor Flight*

> *"We also began to realize that time was slipping away and that we had serious unfinished business."*

began writing small checks to the foundation and sending me updates on the campaign. Only after she died in May 2007, however, did I understand how much it meant to her. I found a metal box in which she had kept every record of her first husband's military service.

Lambert Hruska was her childhood sweetheart and she kept every piece of paper – from his enlistment papers to his medals (he was awarded the Bronze and Silver Stars) – to the telegram she received after he was killed in action in Sicily in 1943. She was 24. This wasn't ancient history; this was my mother's life. After the war, she married my father, who had also served in Europe during the war. He died in 1985. Neither my mother or father ever got to see the National WWII Memorial.

Maybe that's why something clicked in me when Joe Dean and Renee Riddle showed me the pictures from an early Honor Flight. You could see how moved and grateful the veterans were, and how genuinely surprised they were to be treated like kings for a day. They never asked for it, but it was obvious that the Honor Flight was a defining moment in their lives. You could see something else too: the excitement of those 19-year-old boys who once saved the world in places like Iwo Jima and Normandy.

I still remember the day in late 2009, when I walked down the hall of the WTMJ studios and asked our broadcast group's operations manager, Tom Land, if we could make this our cause. He surprised me by immediately saying yes. We didn't need to form a committee, or run it past other departments. We were in.

And I knew we were in over our heads. The original goal was to raise $150,000 to lease a 747 to send 300 veterans to Washington, D.C. That was far more than I had ever raised on the air and, as much as it meant to me personally, I certainly couldn't be sure we'd be successful. If we failed, the plane wouldn't fly and the veterans, who had so little time, would be left waiting. Then on the morning in January 2010, when we were set to announce the campaign Operation Resolve, I was told that we actually needed to raise $250,000. It seemed impossible.

But not only did we raise enough money for one 747, we raised enough to send three 747s. Since that first 747 in May of 2010, Stars and Stripes Honor Flight has organized 15 additional trips. Since its inception in 2008, that's a total of 20 missions and close to 3,000 veterans flown to their national memorial.

So, how did we do it? First we told the stories, then more stories. Joe Demler and Harvey Kurz and others came on my show and talked about their experiences, their lives, and how much Honor Flight meant to them. Veterans who had never talked about their service, began sharing their stories with their families for the first time.

And then Wisconsin responded. Dramatically. We'll never know if something like this could have happened a decade earlier, but the campaign touched something in the community. Churches, civic organizations, Girl Scouts, school groups, even local taverns adopted the mission.

Everyone, it seemed, had a reason for getting involved. For some, it was fathers and grandfathers who had never gotten their homecoming; for others, it was the fathers and grandfathers who never would.

Over the next three years, Wisconsin embraced a generation of heroes who would never again be forgotten. And then we saw their faces.

At the Homecomings, thousands of people have gathered on the concourse of Mitchell International to greet the Honor Flights on their return, but for the veterans, the experience is intensely personal. Whole families – sometimes two or three generations – come together to welcome them home from this final mission, many of them holding signs and pictures for their veteran.

It is impossible to capture the power of the moment when a 91-year-old man, walking slowly into the terminal, already overwhelmed by the day and the size of the crowd waiting for him, catches sight of his grandchildren in the crowd waiting for him.

This is why we fly. For these heroes.

opposite: Stars and Stripes Honor Flight veterans give a group salute at the Marine Corps War Memorial. *(photo/Joe Dean)*

EVERY DAY IS A BONUS

In 1944, Joe Demler was an 18-year-old track athlete at Port Washington High School in Wisconsin when he was drafted into the U.S. Army. Within two months, Joe was in the thick of the Battle of the Bulge.

"A tank round hit the farmhouse we were in and I was thrown up into the second story. The next thing I knew, I was captured and loaded onto a train. We were packed like cordwood; for four days we stood in this railcar without food or water or bathroom facilities … the guy next to me died." As a prisoner of war, Joe endured the horrors of a Nazi prison camp, including the daily rumors that Hitler had ordered the men to be killed by flame throwers. Upon his liberation, Joe was near death and weighed just 69 pounds.

When he was rescued, he said, "From now on, every day is a bonus." Joe tells us that he also learned to pray in that POW camp. "I still pray for those guys I served with every single day," he says.

Joe Demler helped raise funds for the first Stars and Stripes Honor Flight and continues to be an active volunteer and an inspiration to us all. Joe and his story are featured in the documentary film *Honor Flight*.

In honor of Joe Demler, Stars and Stripes Honor Flight adopted the phrase "Every Day is a Bonus," which is embroidered on the backs of all SSHF jackets, shirts and hats as a reminder that we dare not live trivial lives.

41

The Faces of Honor Flight

★ ★ ★

Norbert Radtke was 89 years old the day of his October 2011 Stars and Stripes Honor Flight. Norbert passed away just three months later, one month after his 90th birthday. His wife of 63 years, Charlotte, says Norbert would only talk about the good times during his four years in the Navy. He stayed silent about the rest of his service.

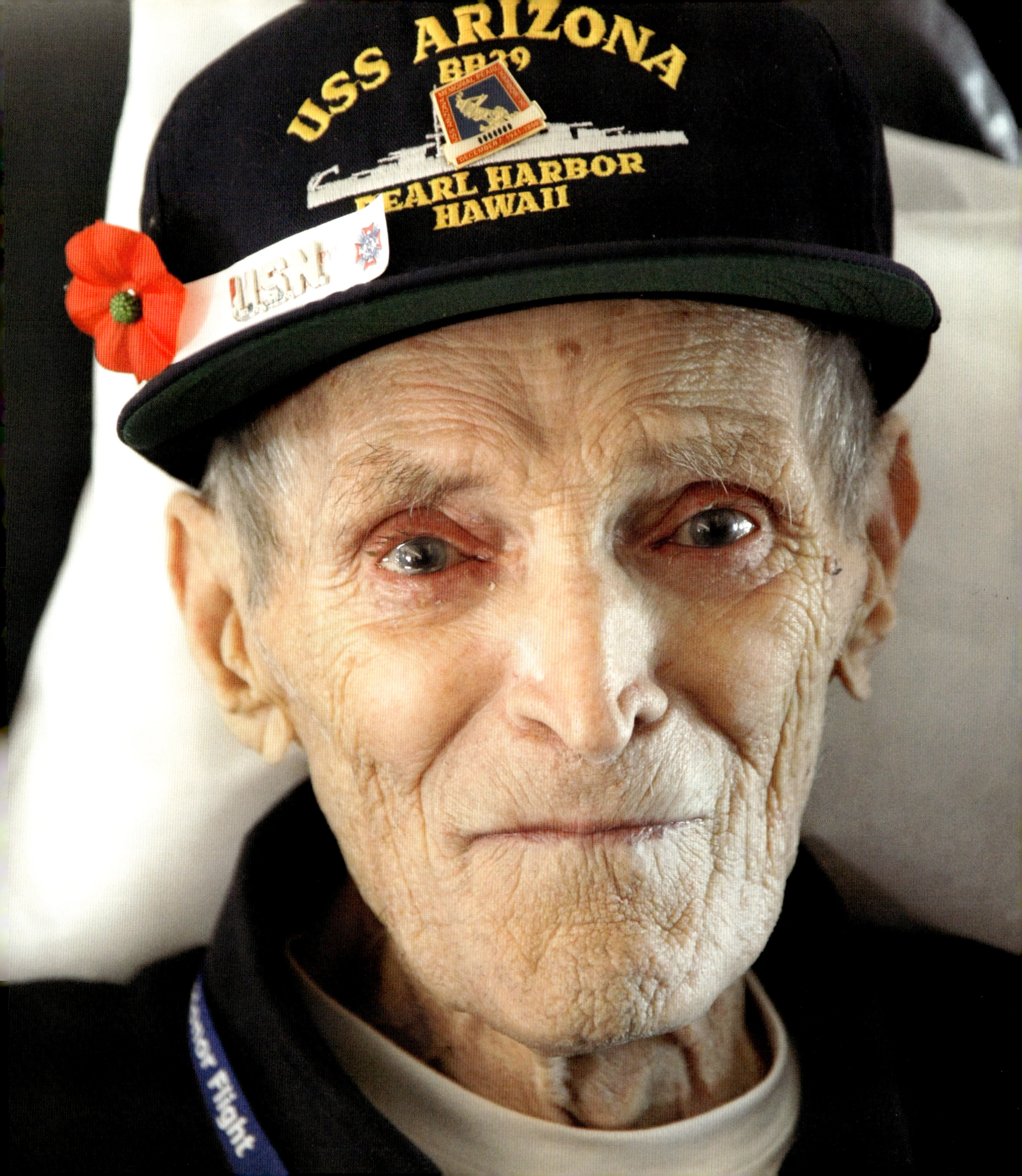
USS ARIZONA
BB39
HAWAII
USN
Flight

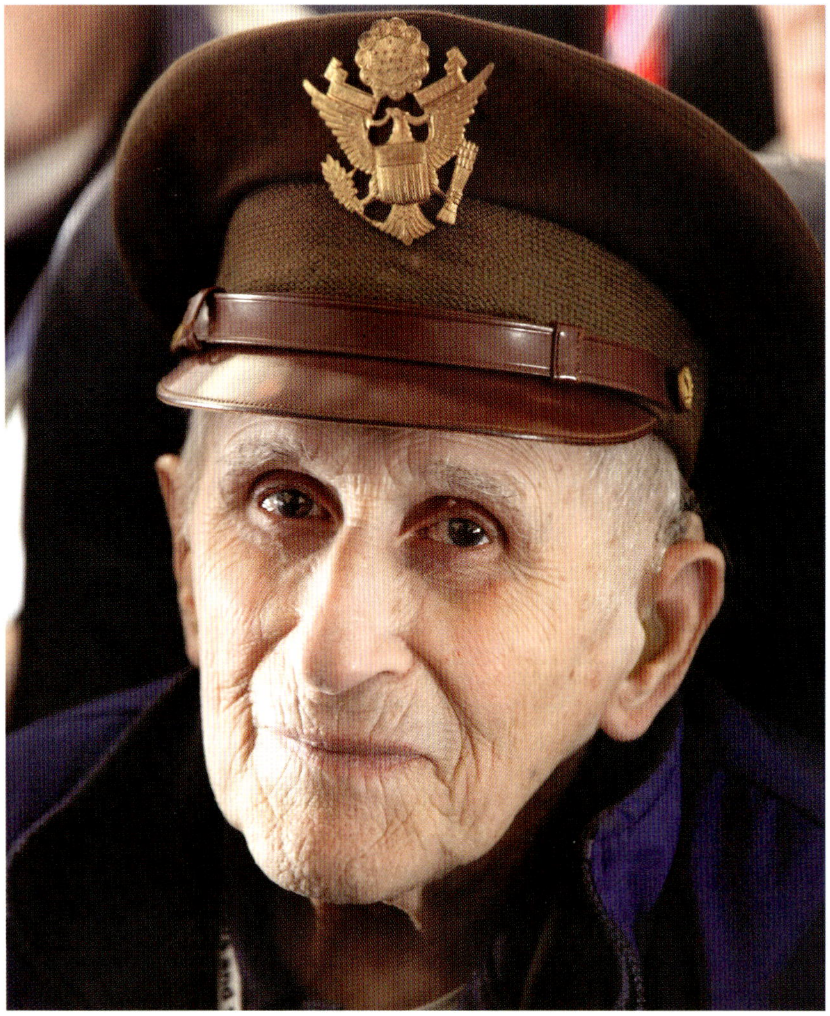

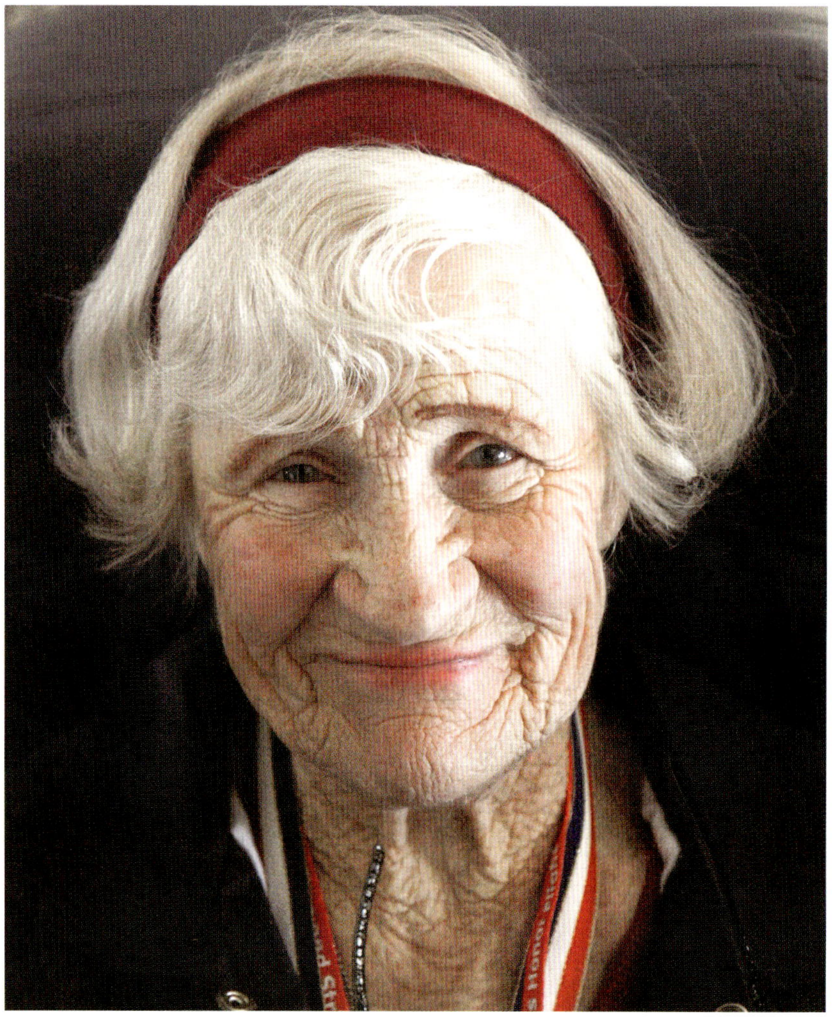

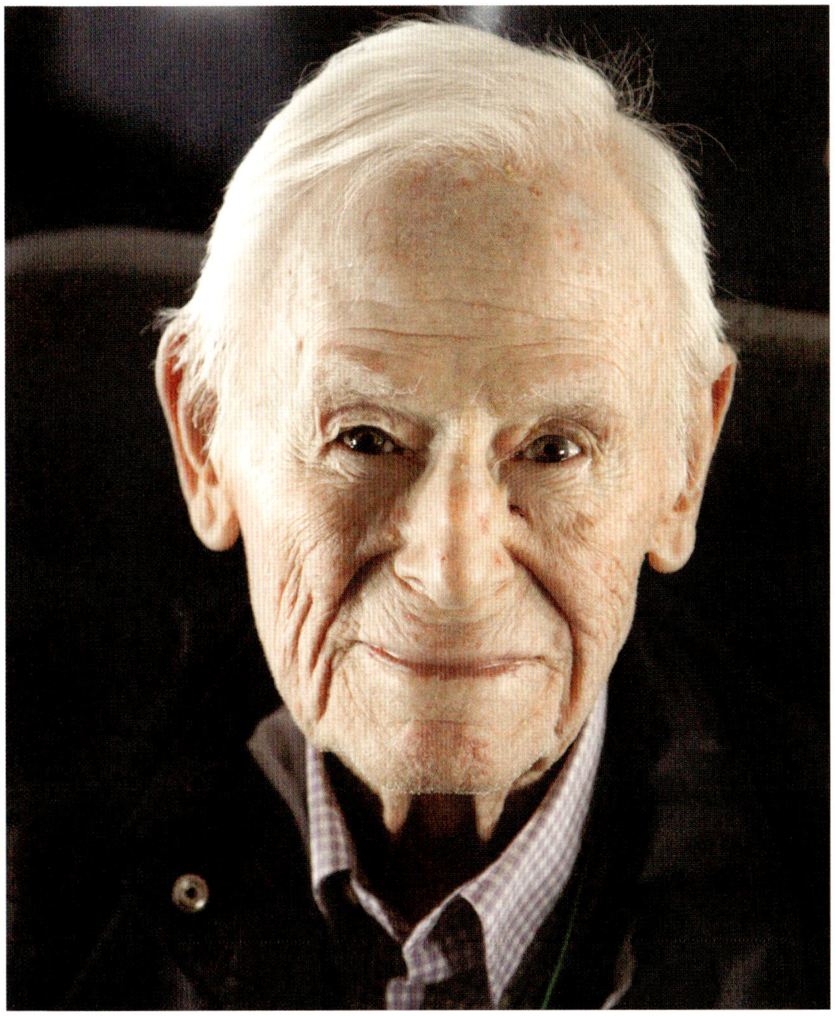

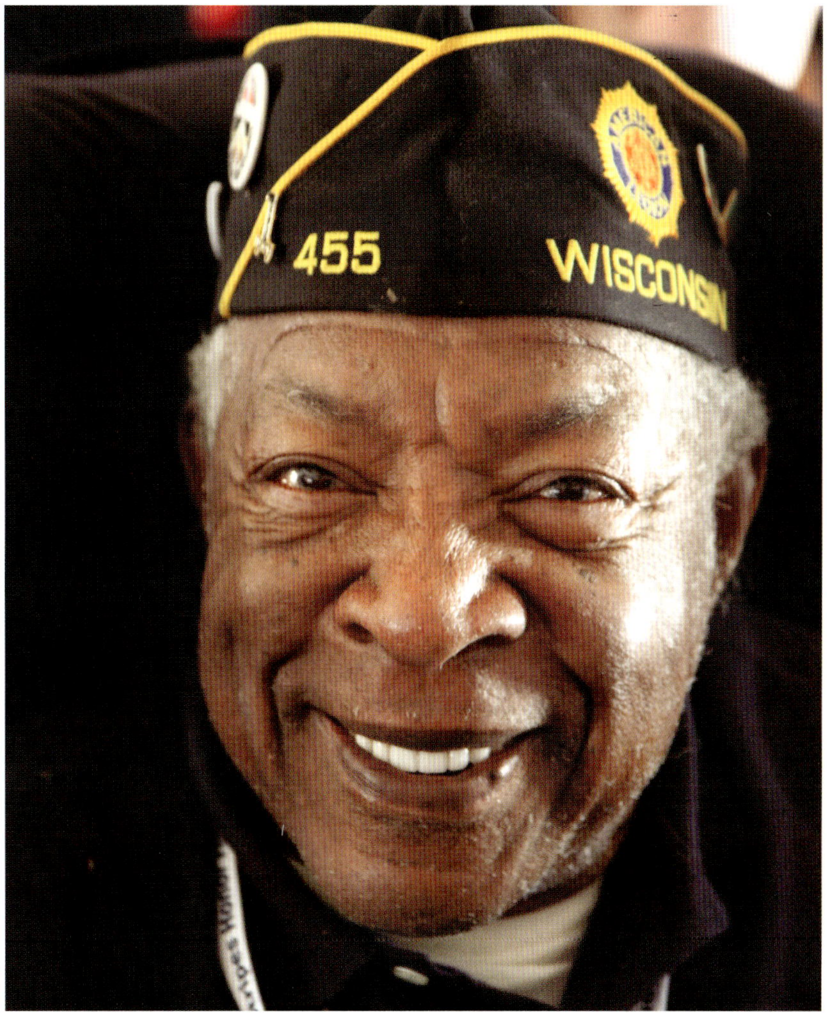
455
WISCONSIN

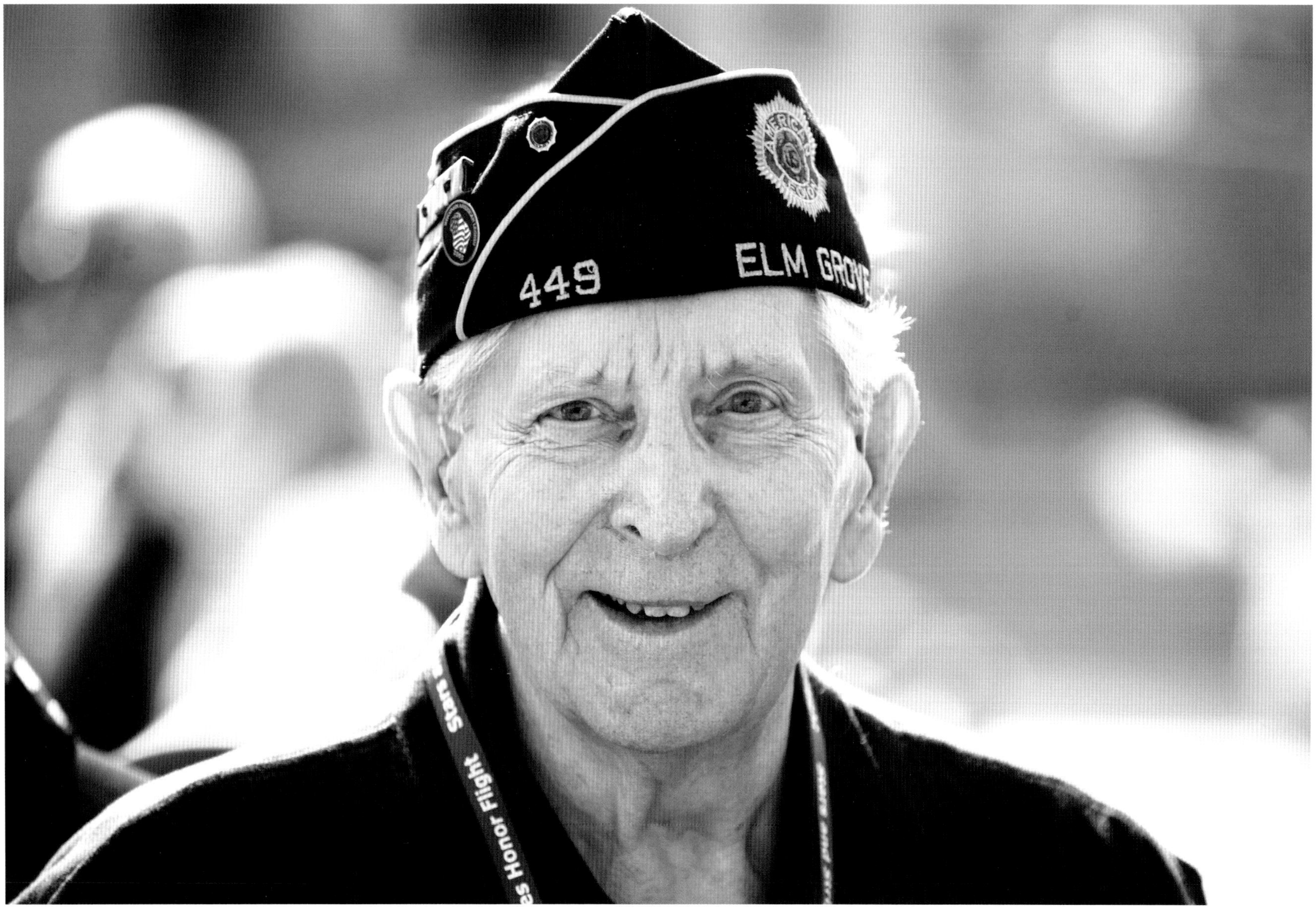
449
ELM GROV
Honor Flight

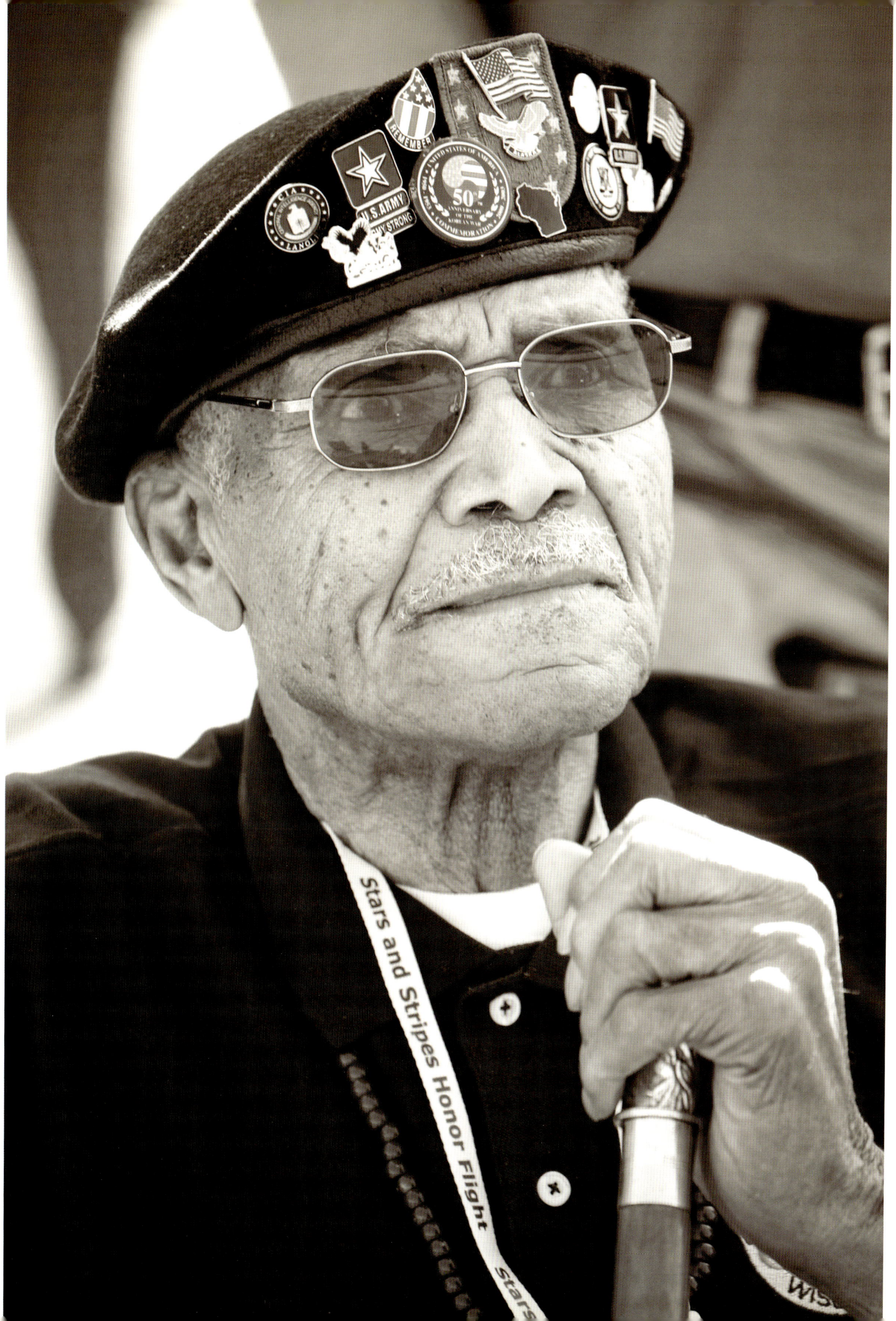
REMEMBER
U.S.ARMY
Stars and Stripes Honor Flight

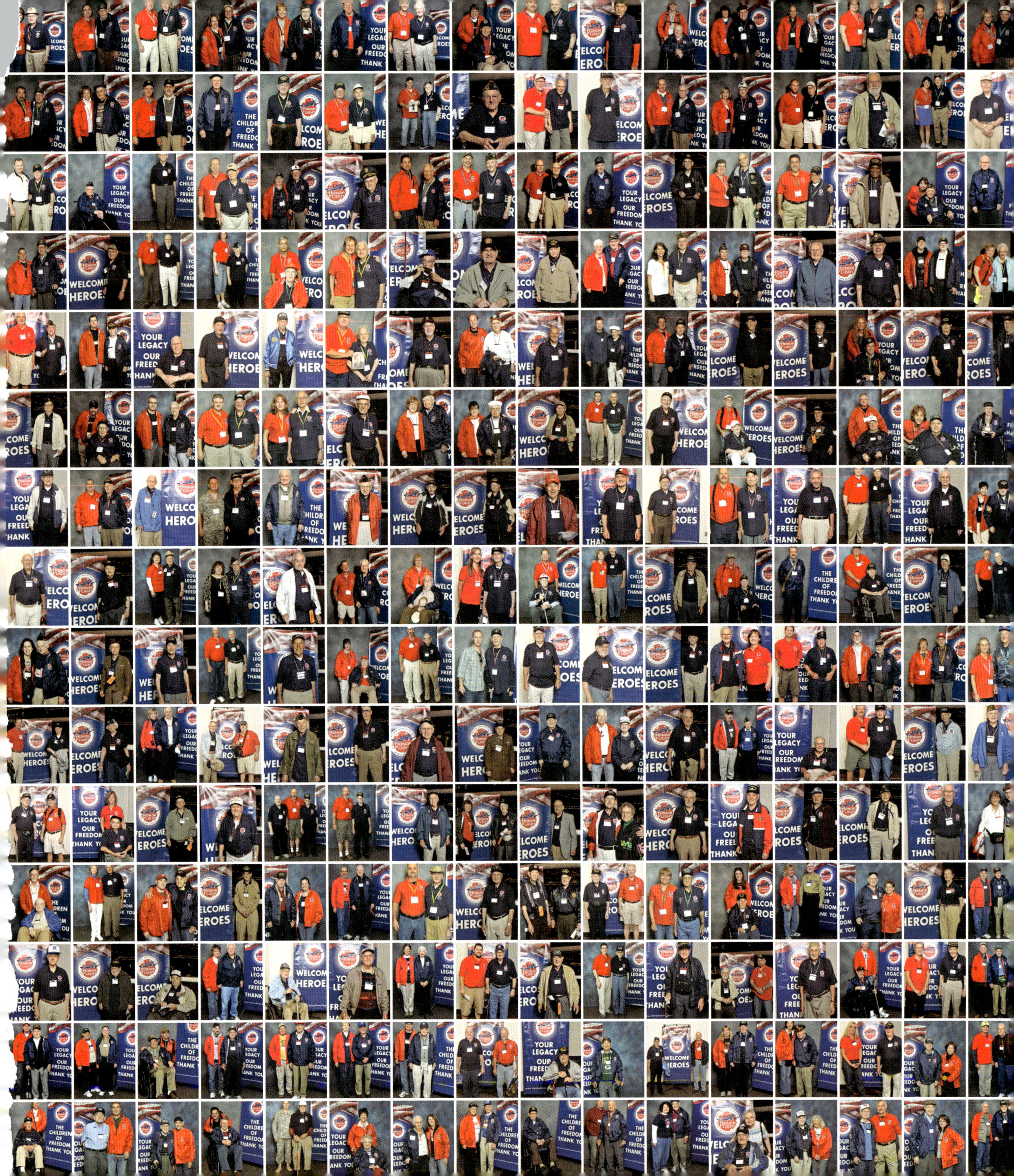
WELCOME HEROES

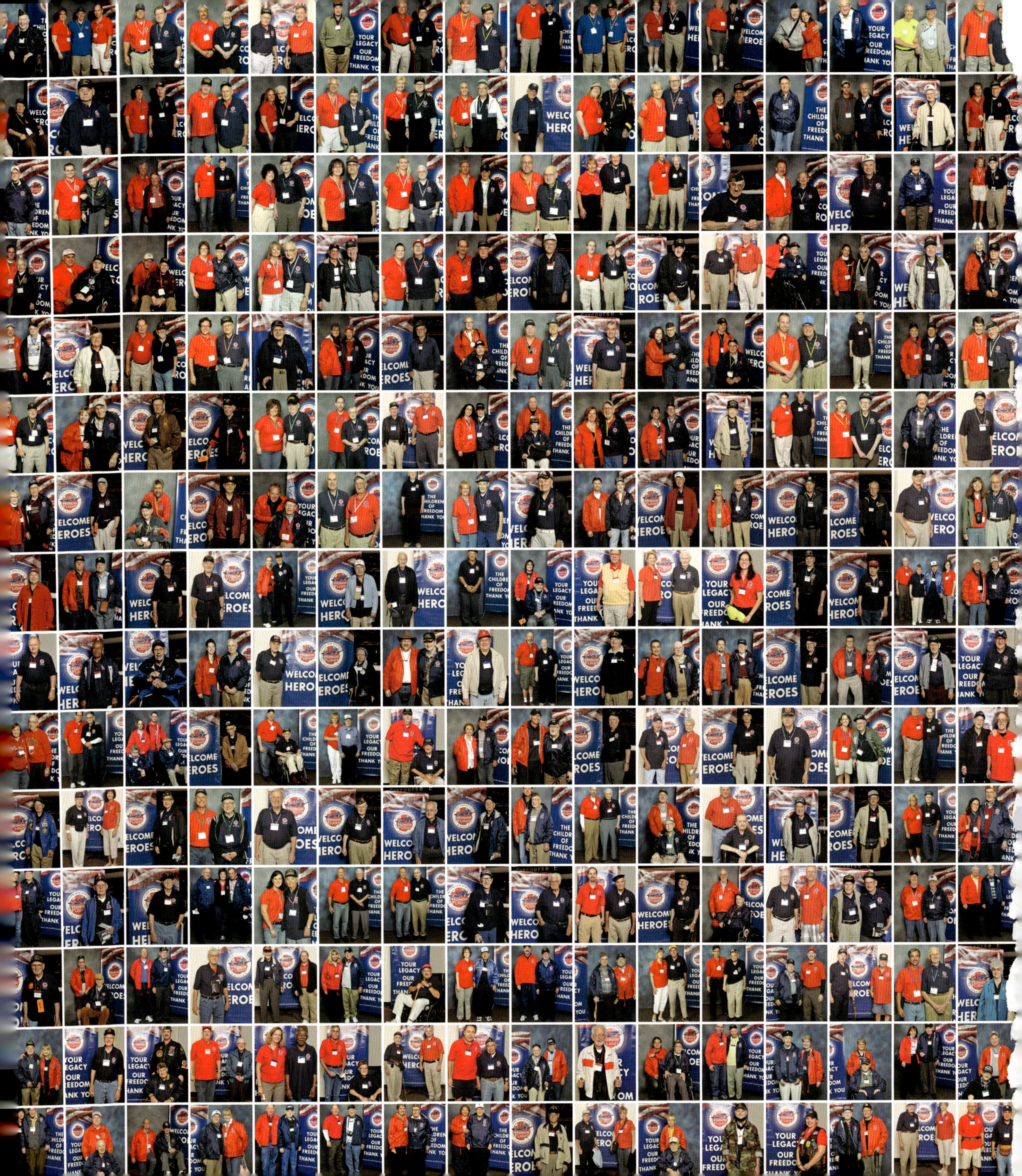

THOUSANDS OF VETERANS

ONE MISSION

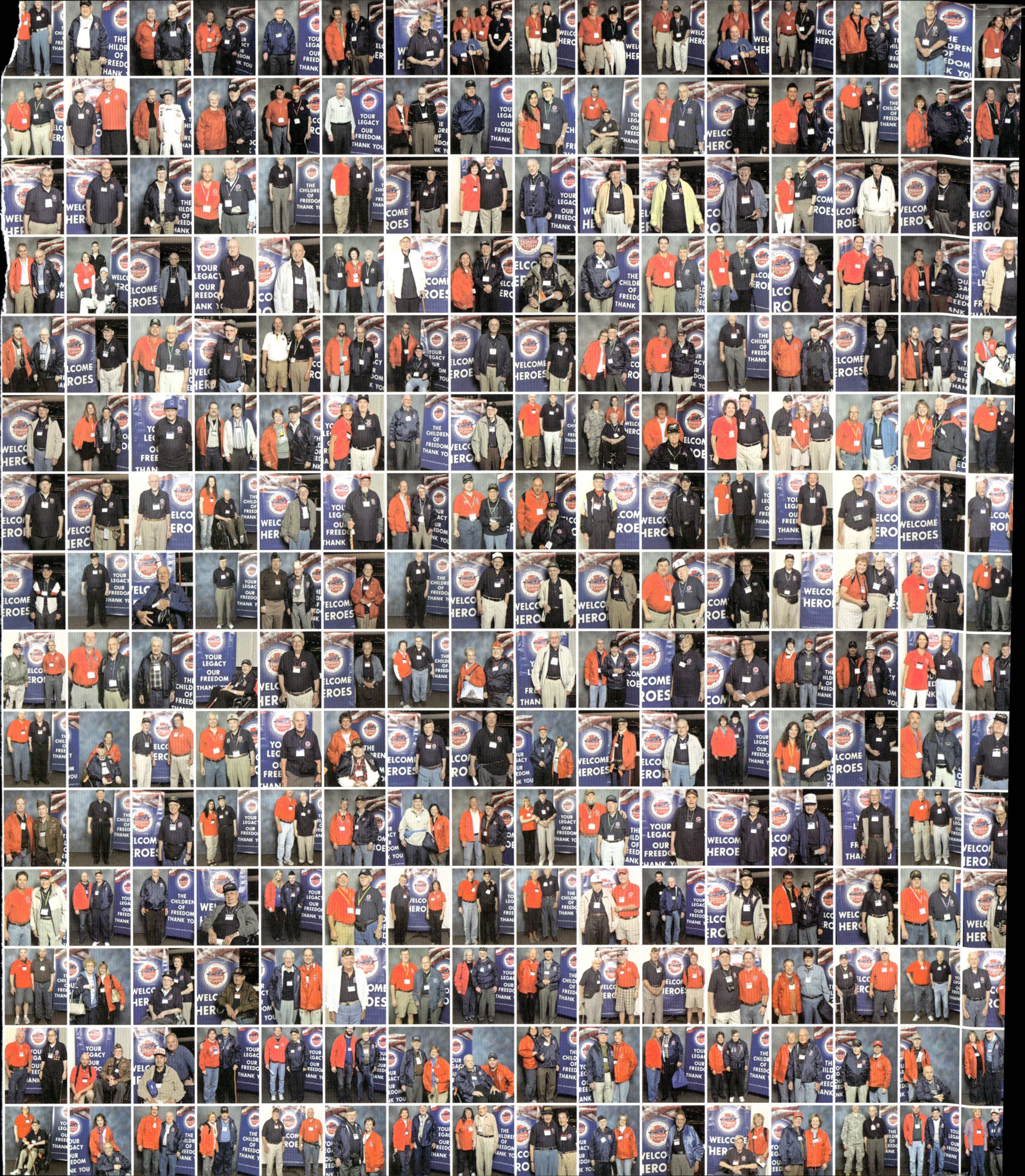
YOUR LEGACY OUR FREEDOM THANK YOU
WELCOME HEROES

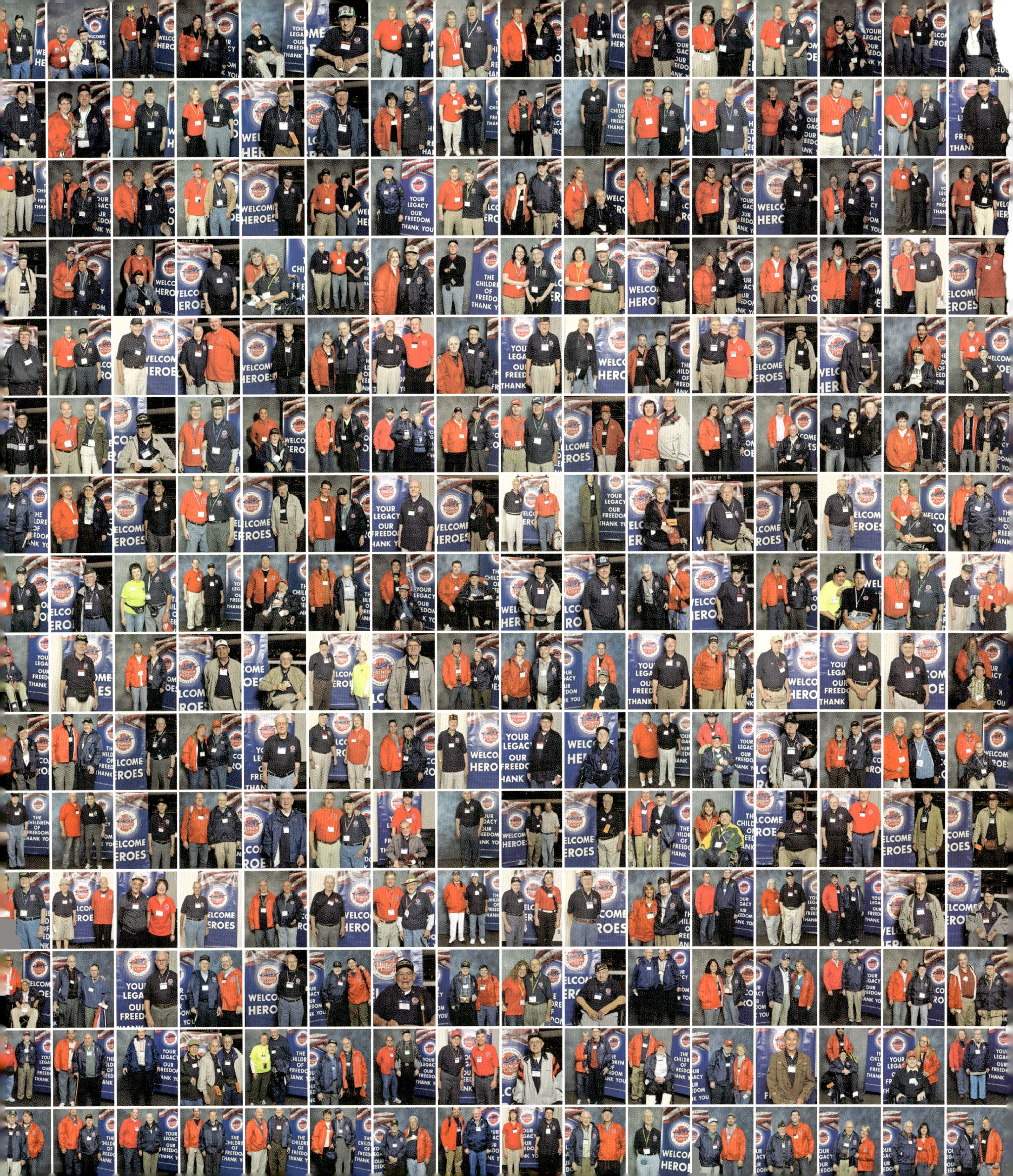
WELCOME
HEROES
YOUR
LEGACY
OUR
FREEDOM
THANK YOU

U.S. Army veteran Dorothy Hanson took her Honor Flight in November 2011 and said it was one of the best days of her life. During the trip, Mrs. Hanson showed off her spunk, which served her well when she was among one of the first waves of women to serve in the Women's Auxiliary Army Corps, from 1942 to 1947. Mrs. Hanson said it was hard doing a "man's work," but she was extremely proud to serve her country.

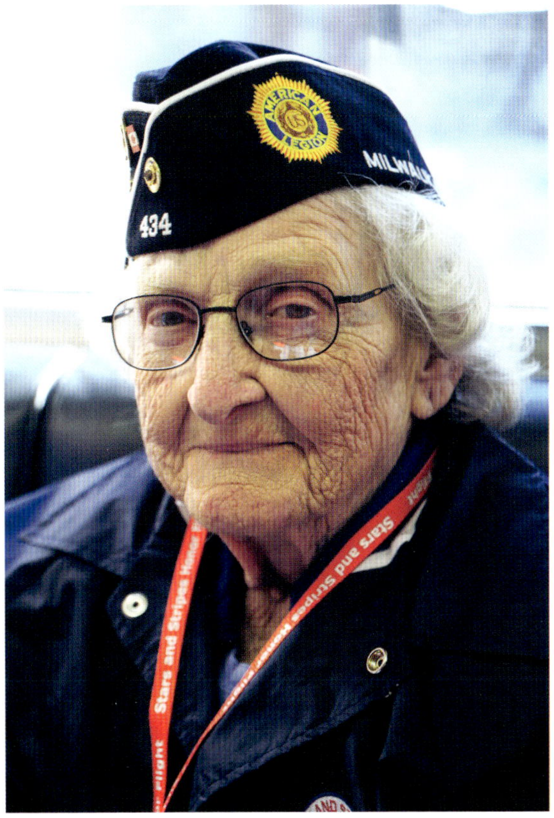
434
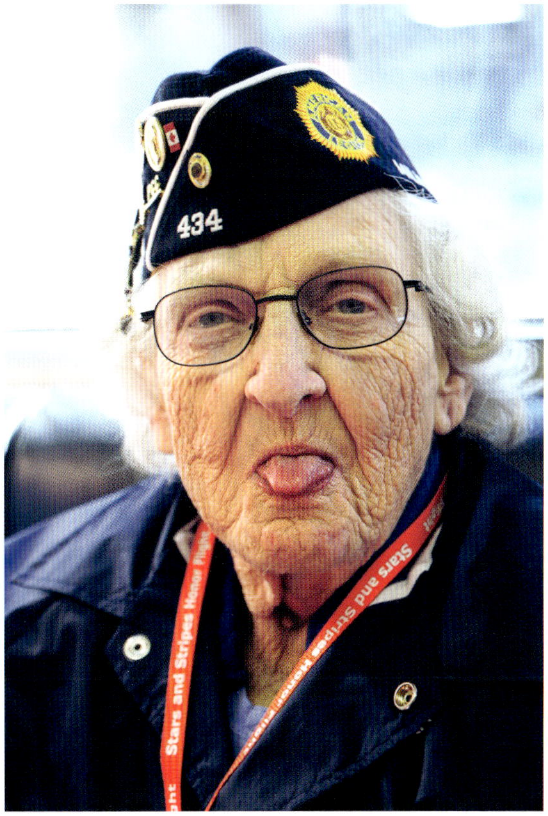
434
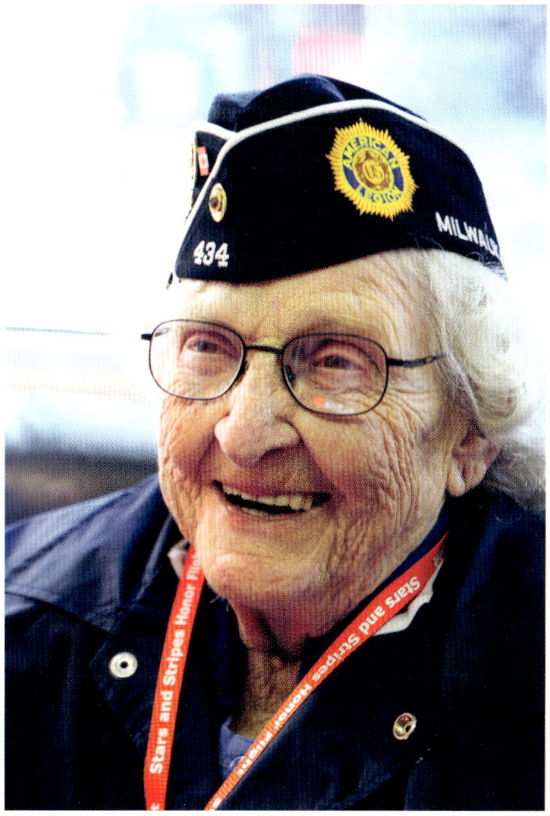
434

Reveille

★ ★ ★

0500 HOURS

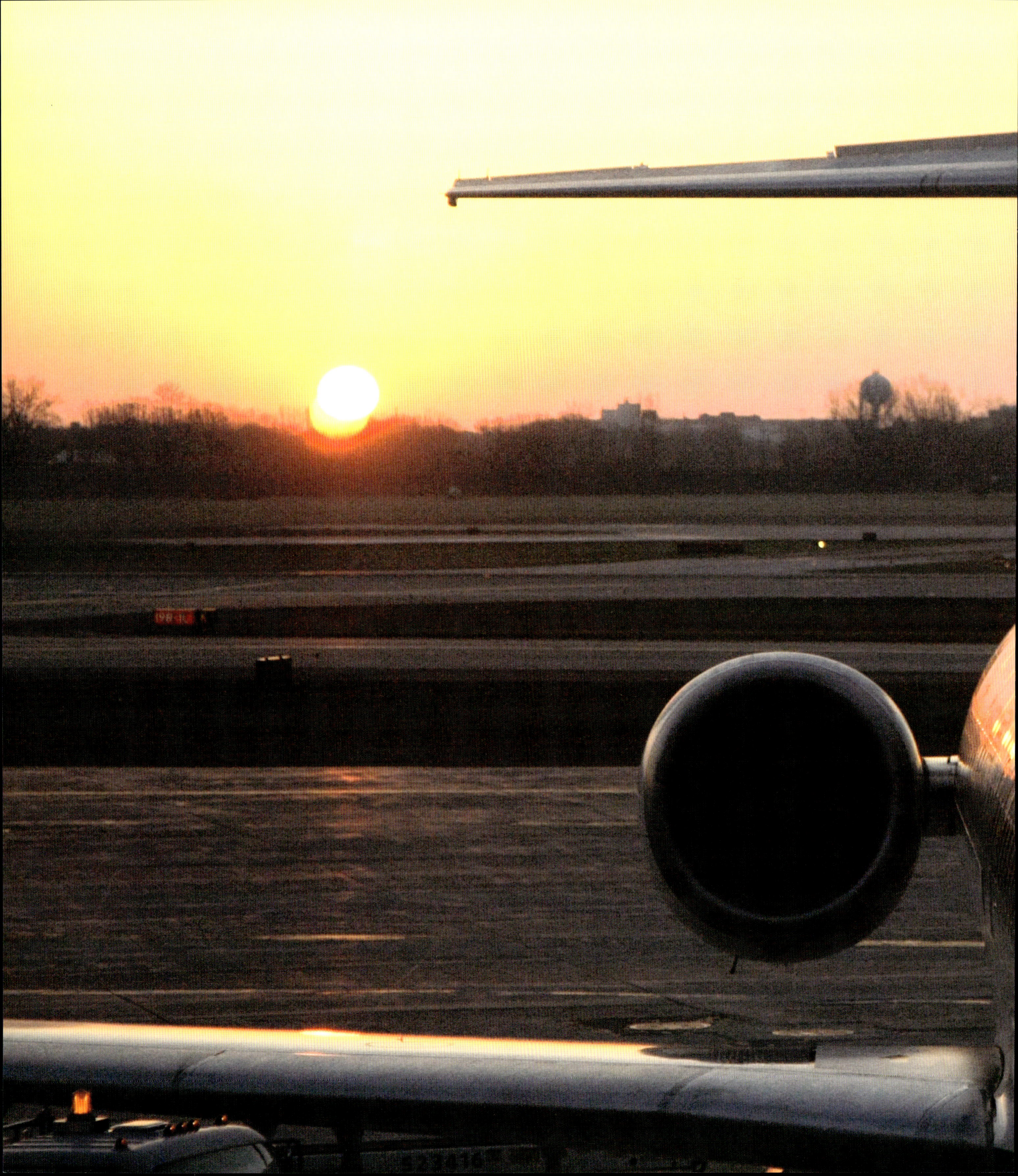

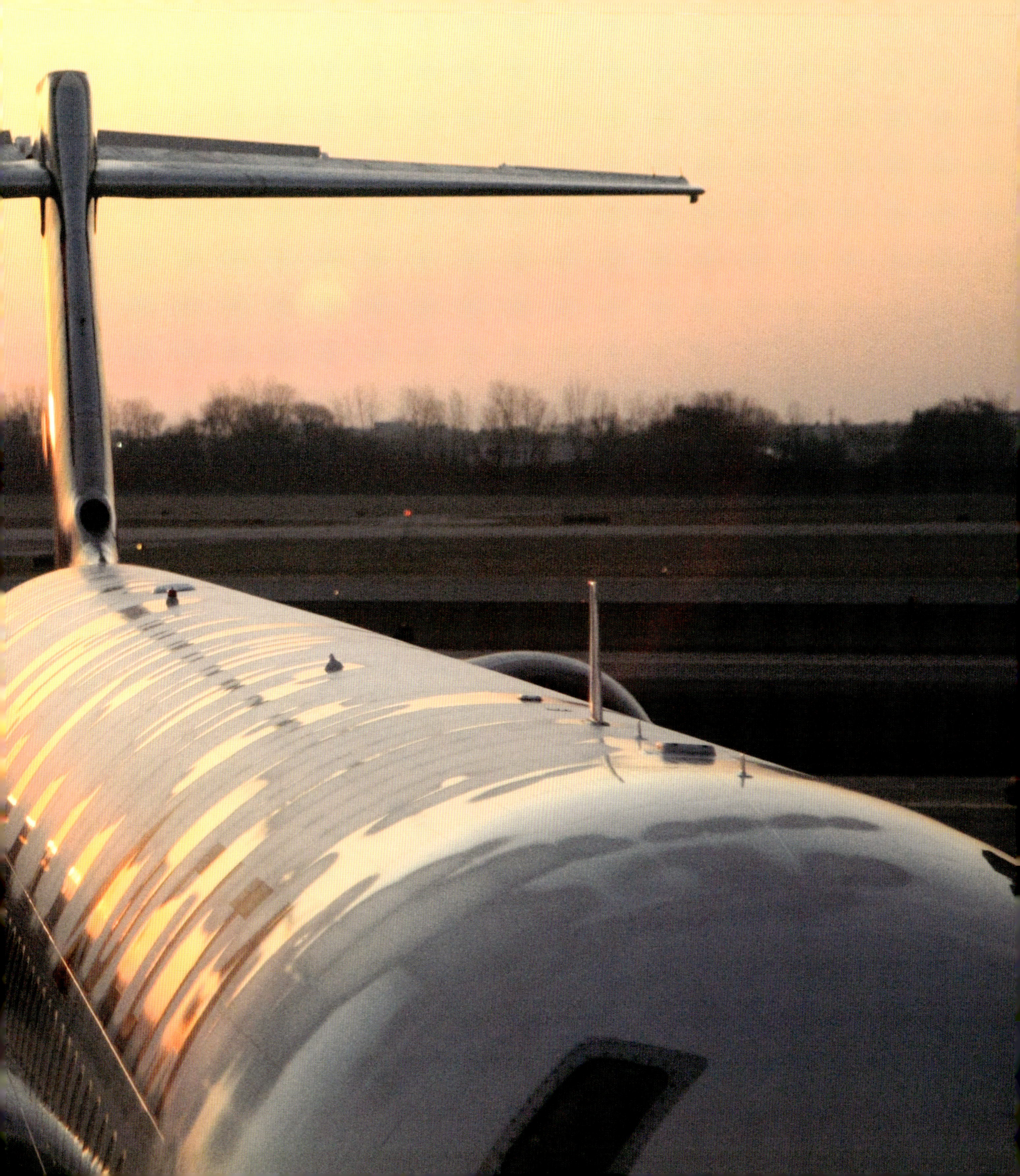

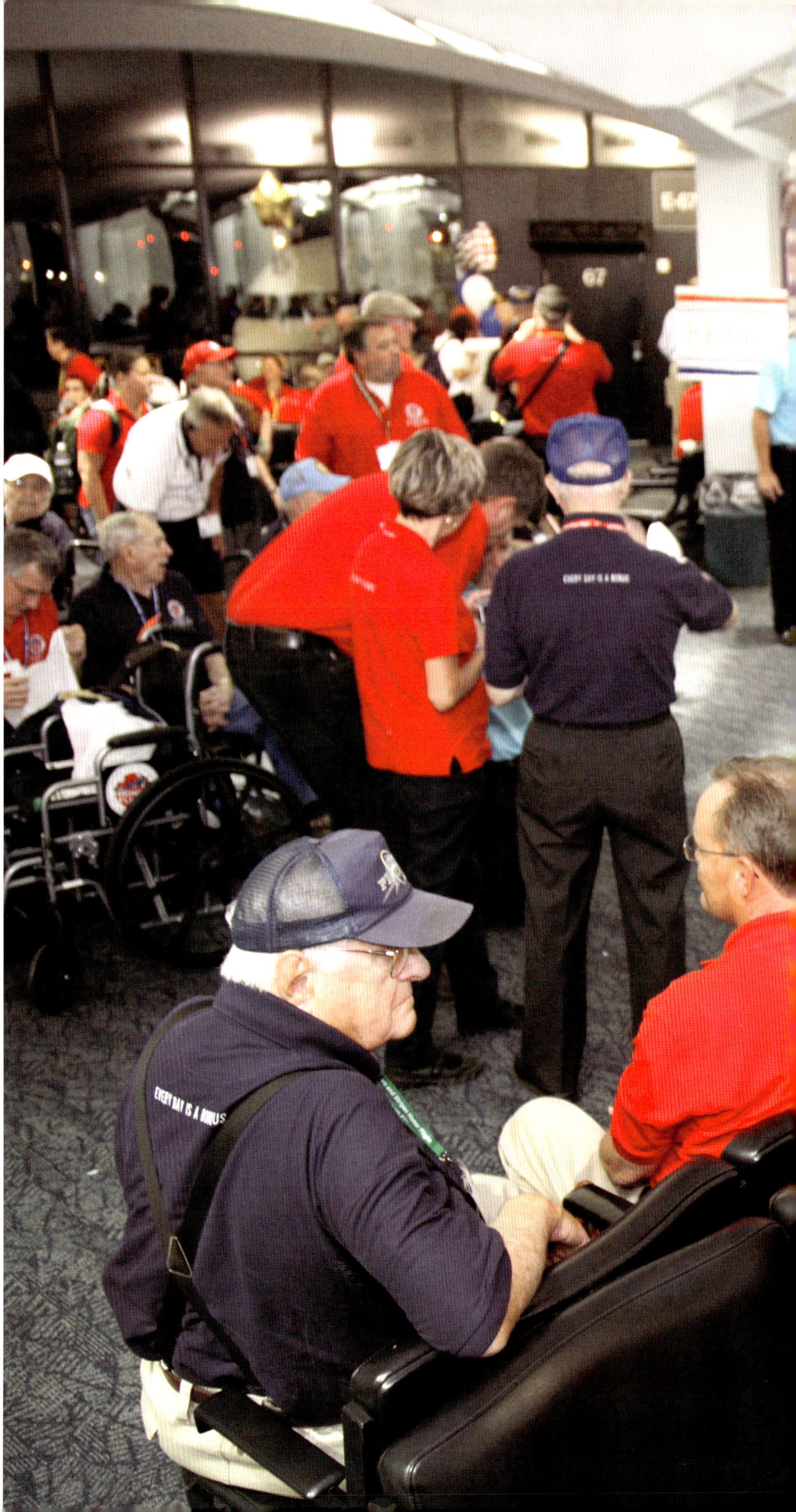
67
EVERY DAY IS A BONUS

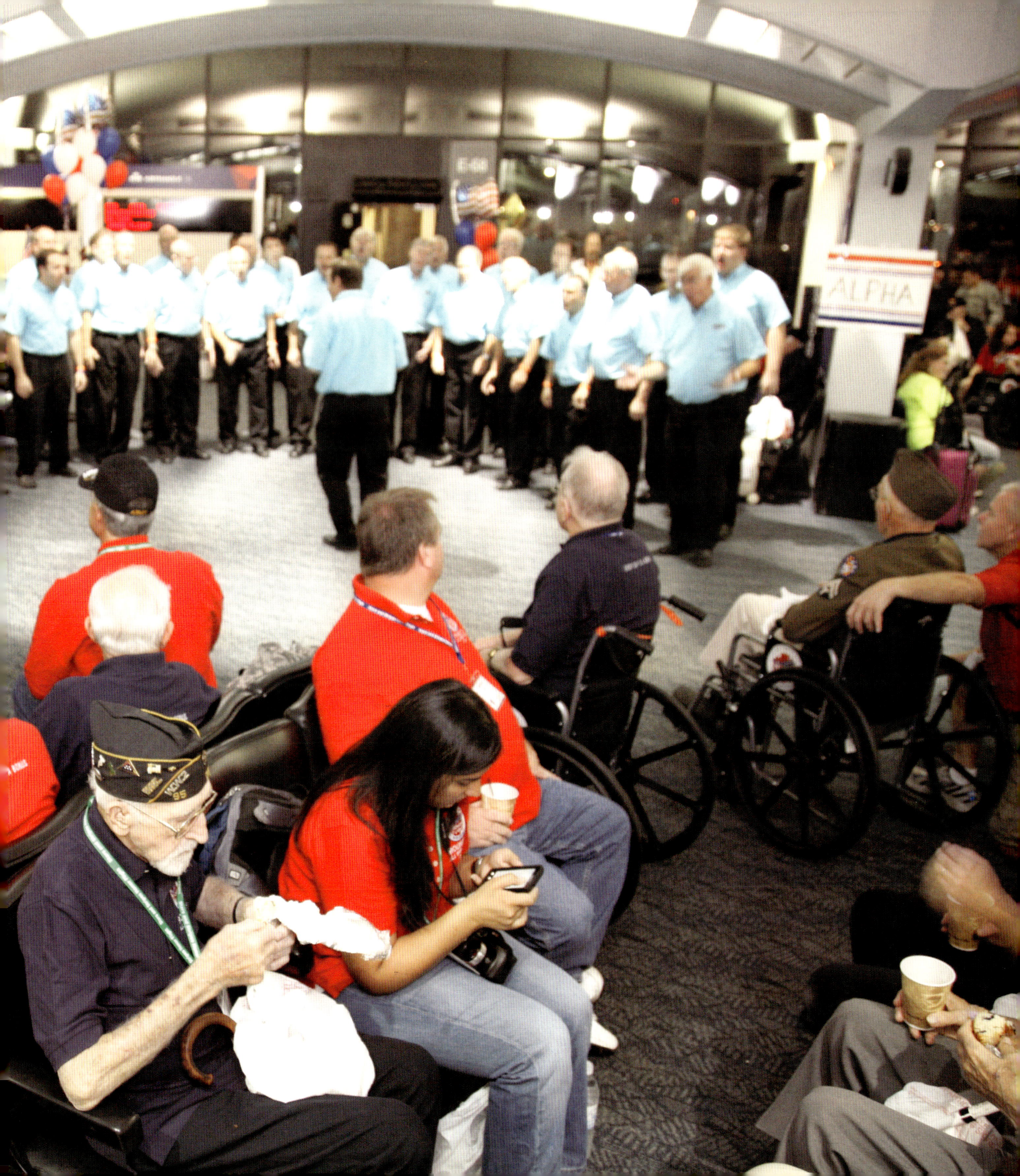
ALPHA

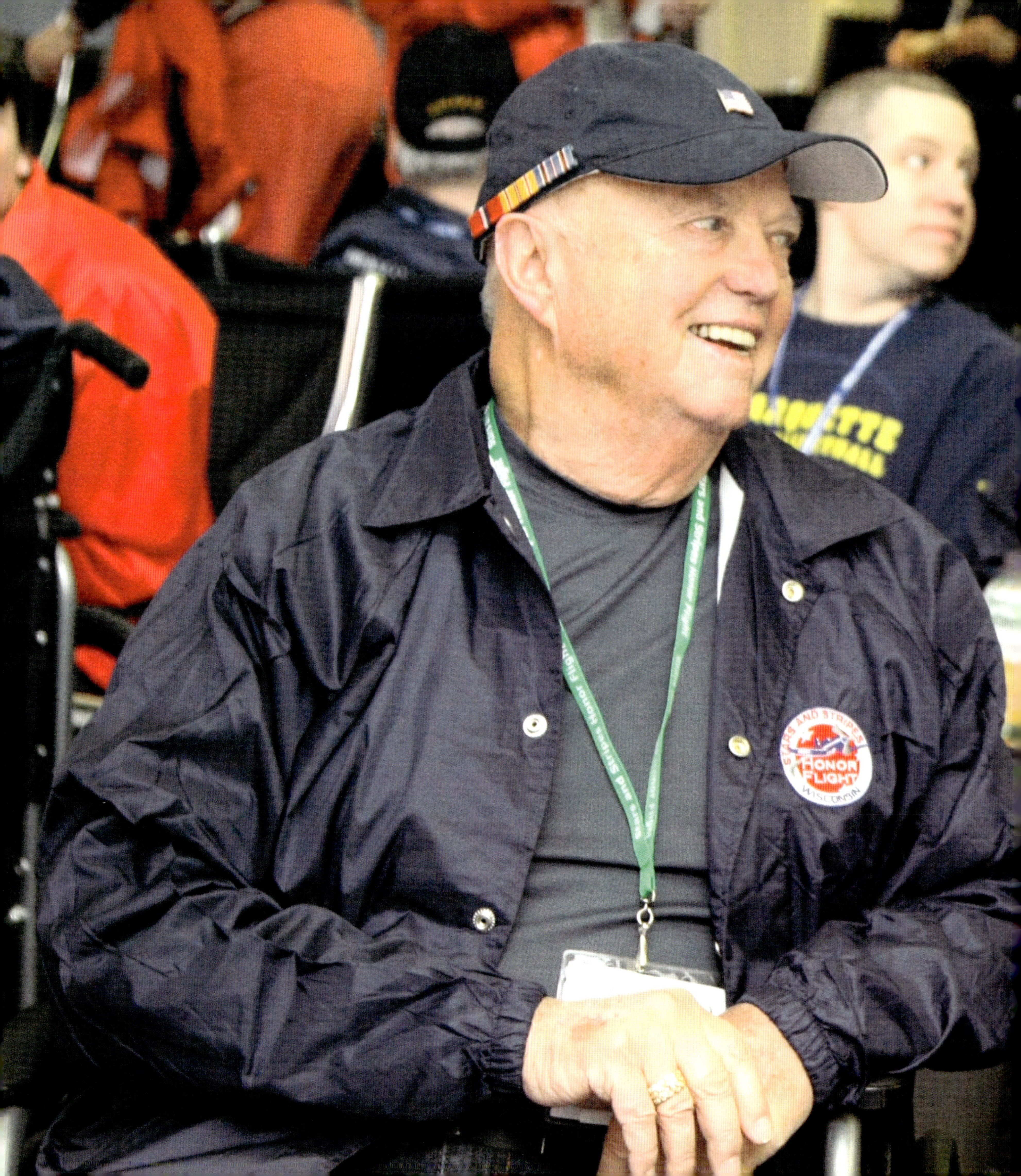
STARS AND STRIPES
HONOR FLIGHT
WISCONSIN

MENOMONEE FALLS
WISCONSIN
STARS AND STRIPES
HONOR FLIGHT
WISCONSIN
Stars and Stripes Honor Flight
Wilfred

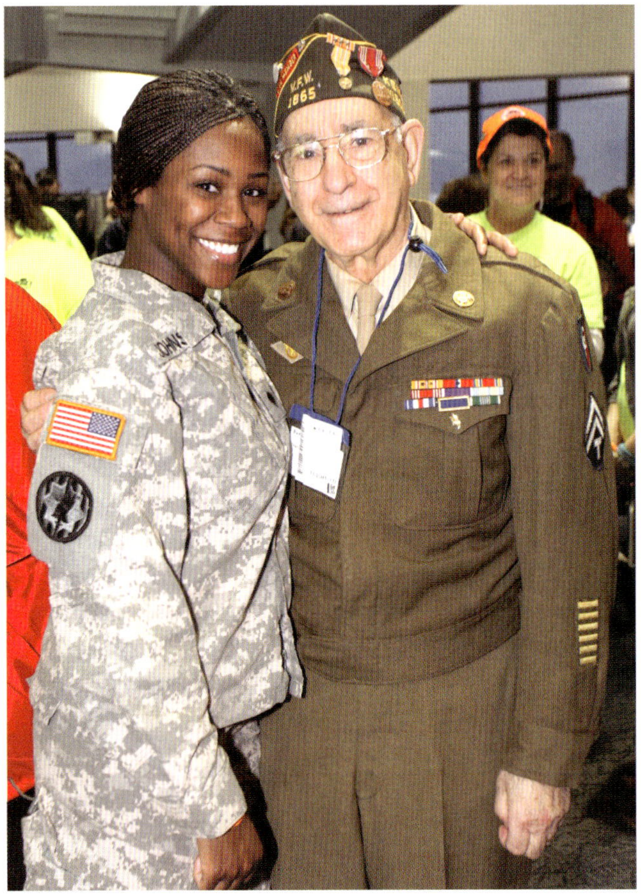

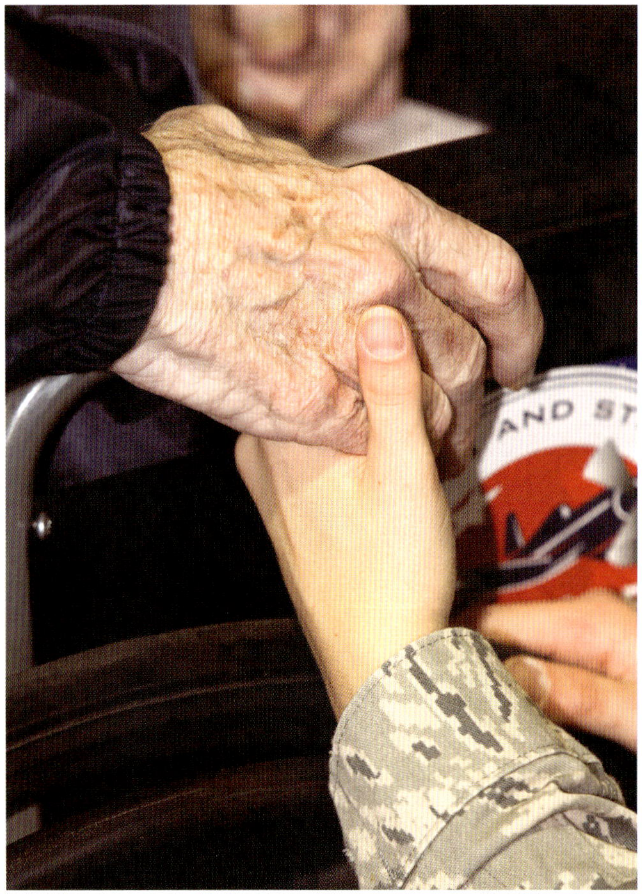

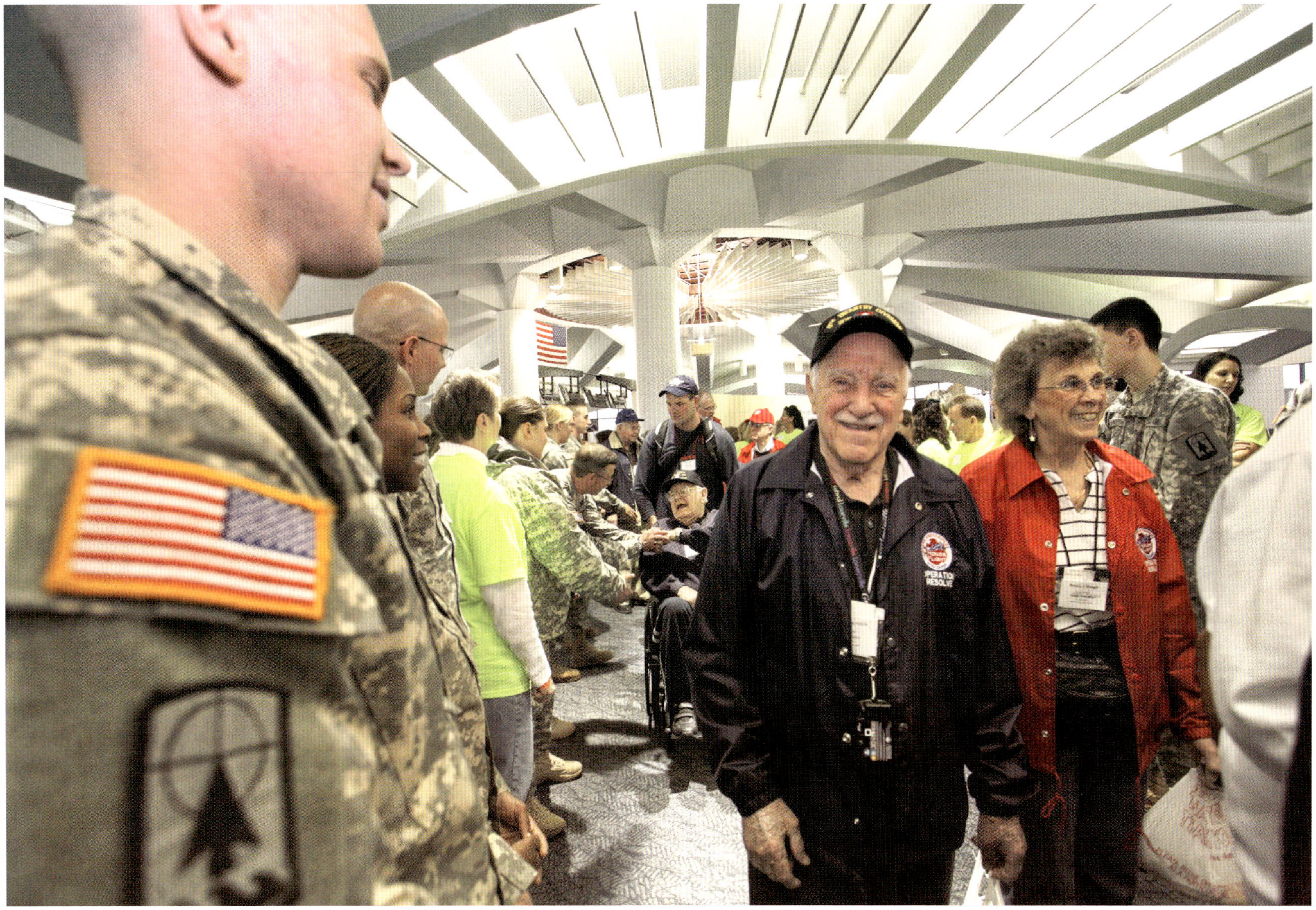

Many veterans carry special photos with them on their Honor Flight, like the veteran who was one of five brothers to serve in WWII (above, left), or the guardian who brings a photo of a loved one (center), or the veteran who brings a photo of their younger self from their service days (right and opposite).

68

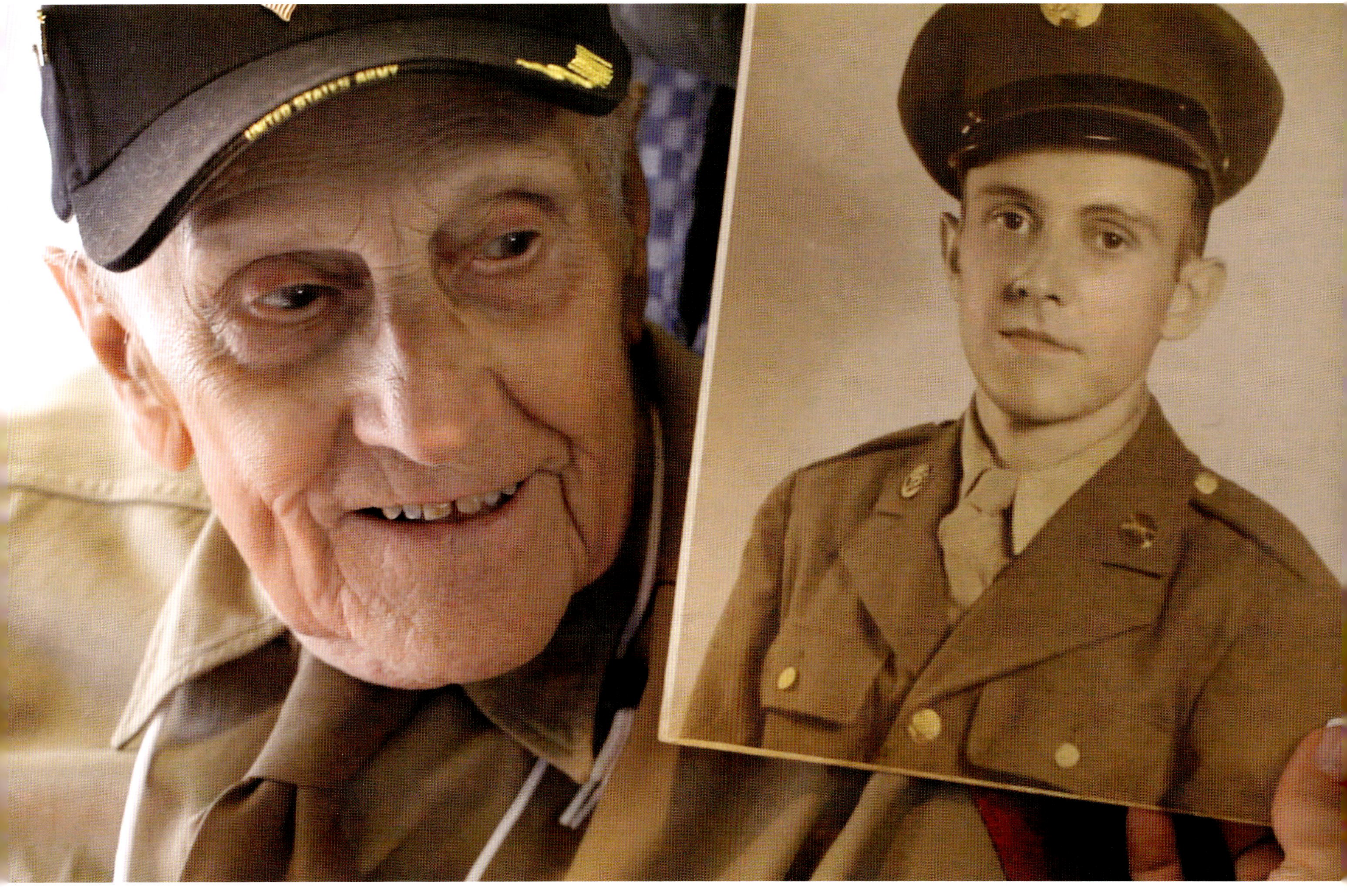
UNITED STATES ARMY

Despite the early-morning roll call at the airport on the morning of his 2010 Honor Flight, 87-year-old Walter Roob (above) was moved to play a few bars on his harmonica. Walter served from 1943 to 1945 as a photographer in the U.S. Army Air Corp in Europe. When he returned home after his tour of duty, he remembers thinking, "Holy cats, God. You got us back and we're still alive. What a feeling to be alive."

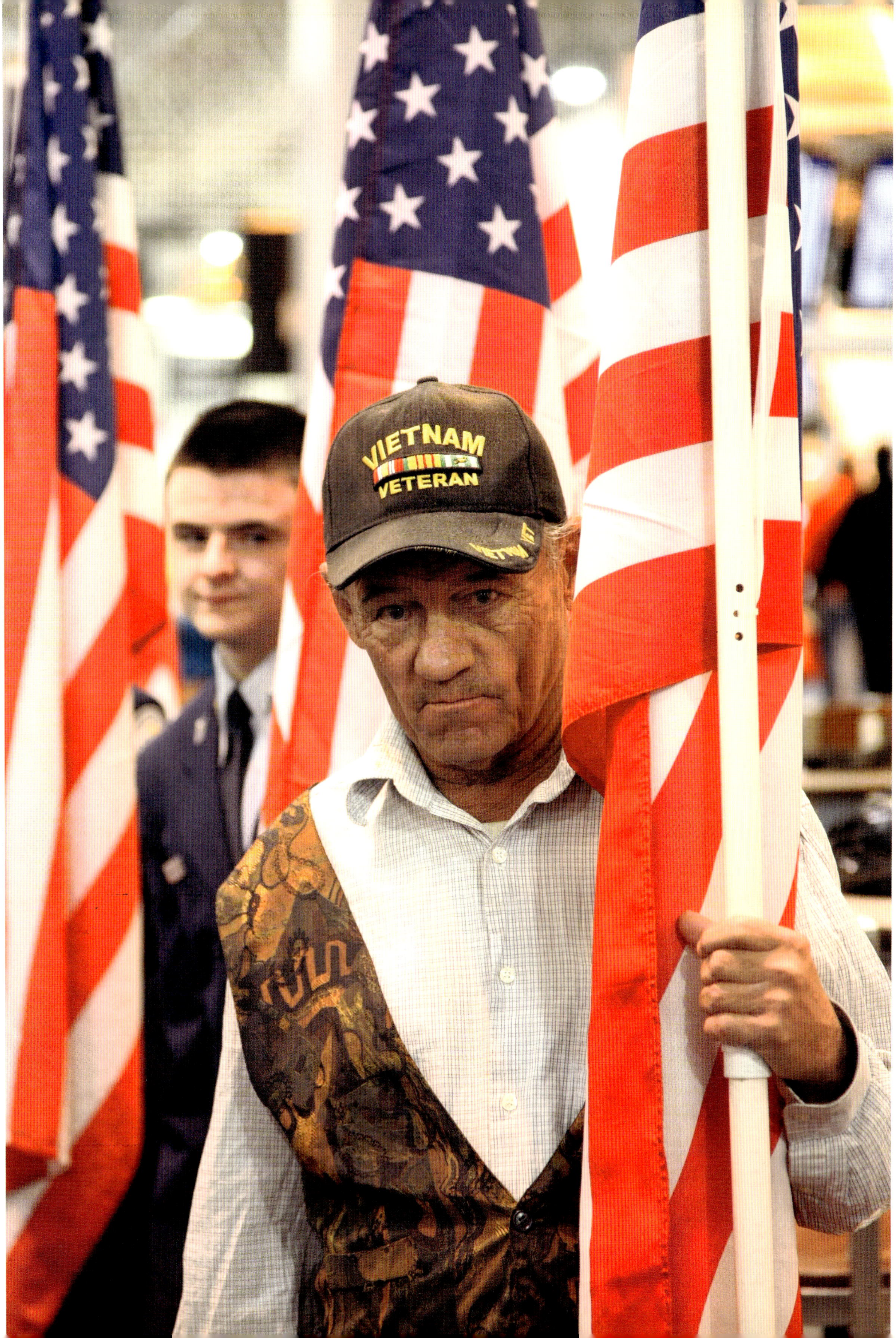
VIETNAM
VETERAN

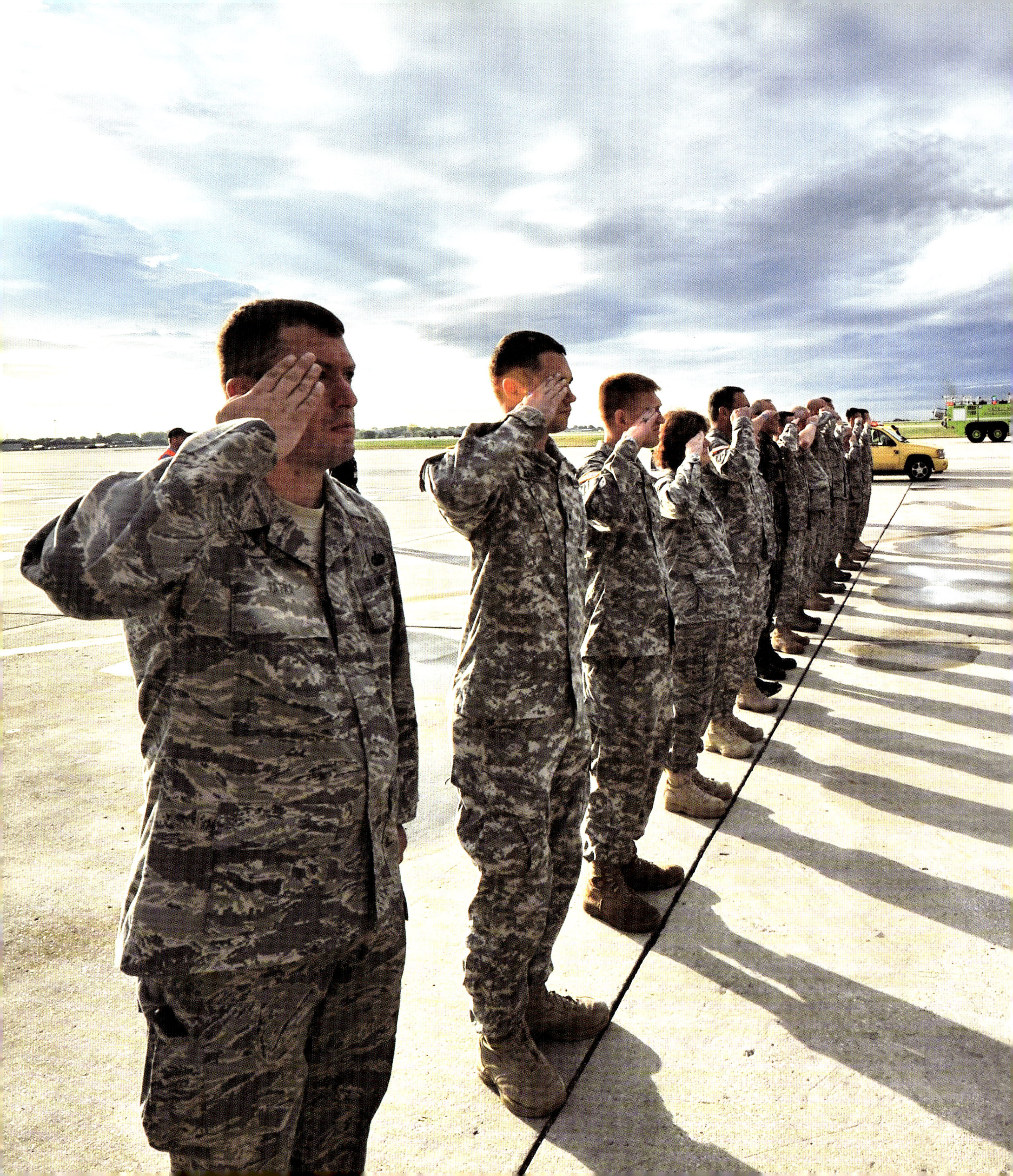

Active duty soldiers line the tarmac at General Mitchell International Airport in Milwaukee to salute an Honor Flight as it departs for Washington, D.C.

Every Stars and Stripes Honor Flight plane is sent off and greeted by a water cannon salute, a high honor originally used to mark the retirement of a pilot.

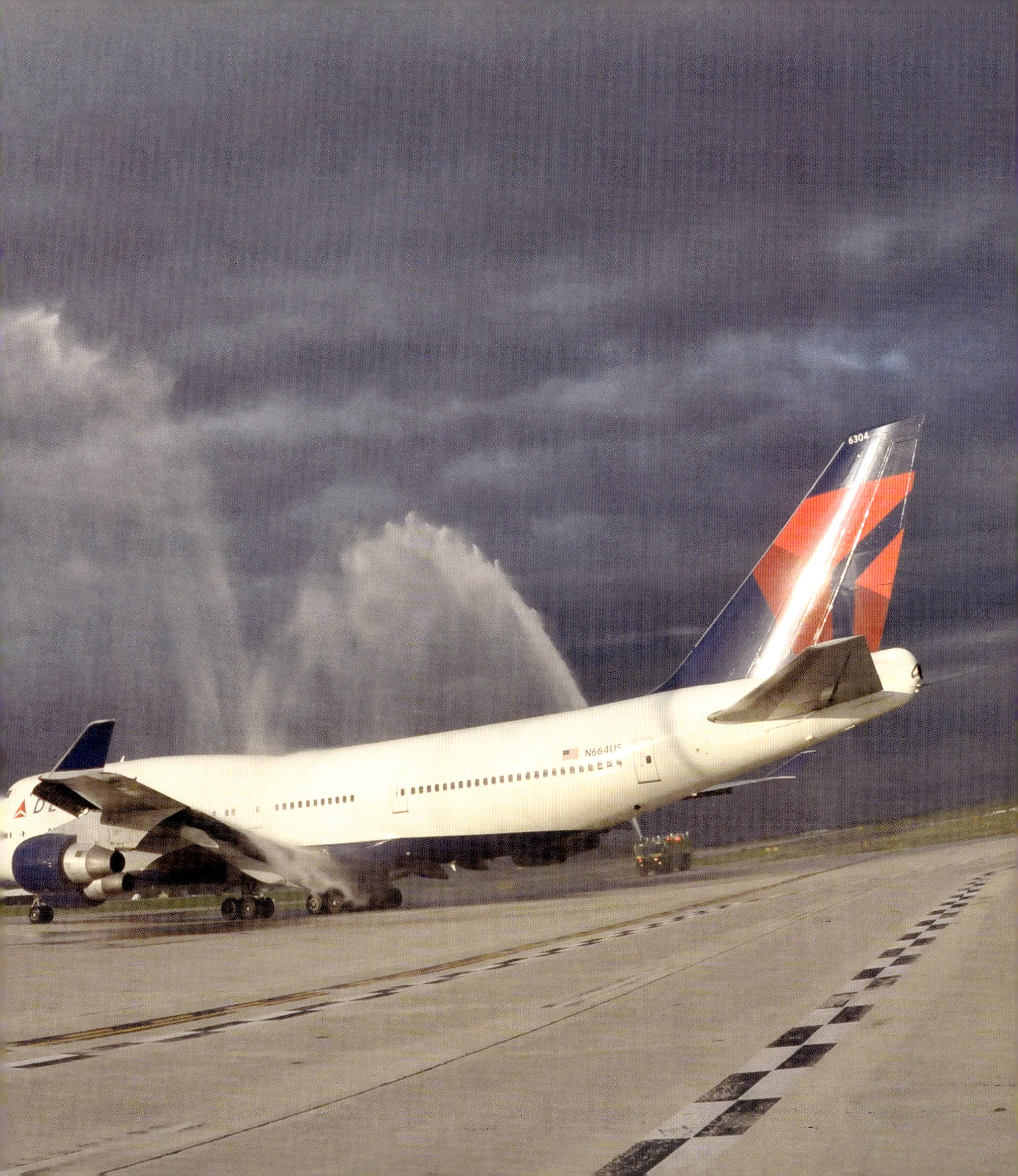
6304
N664US

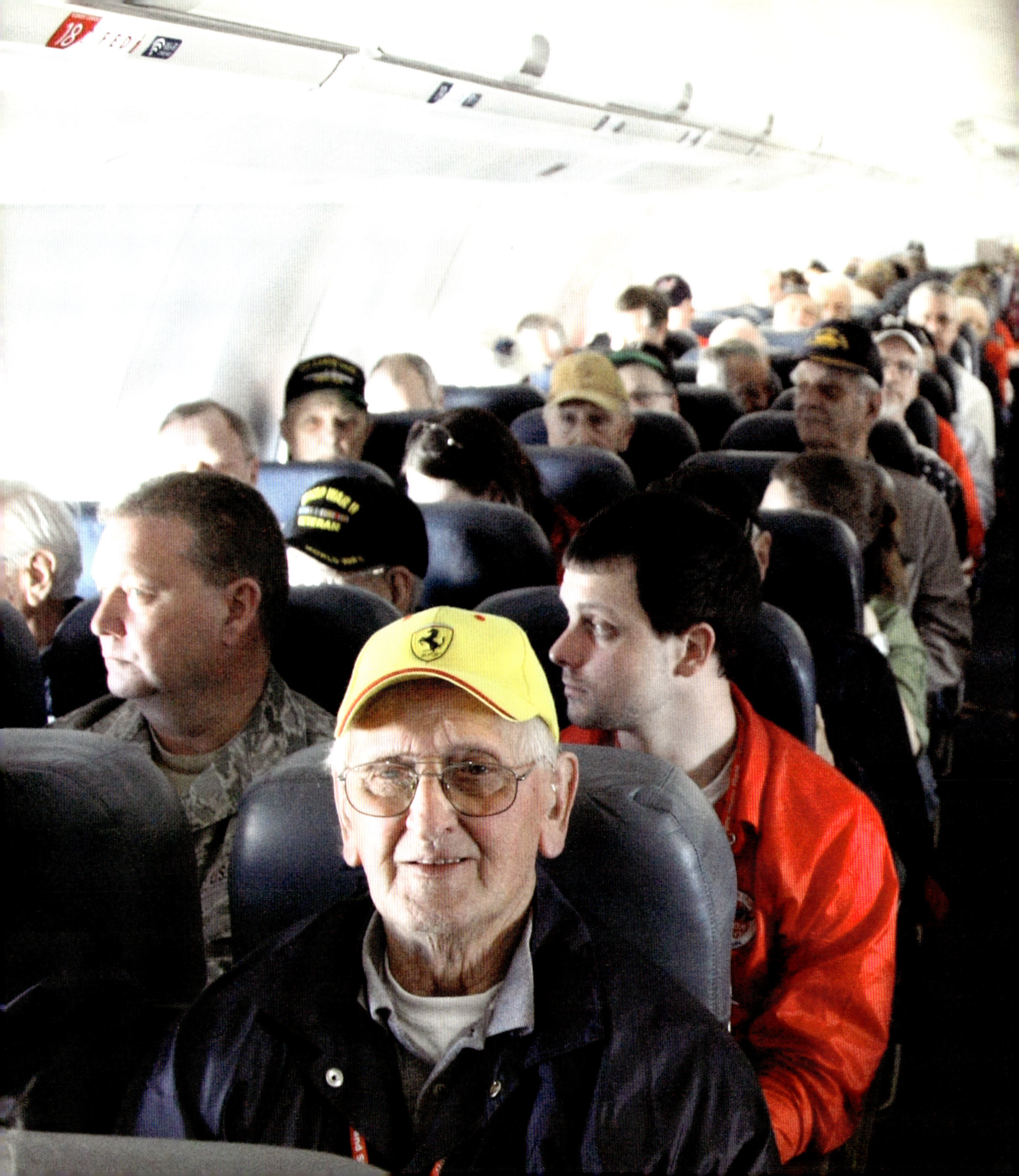
18

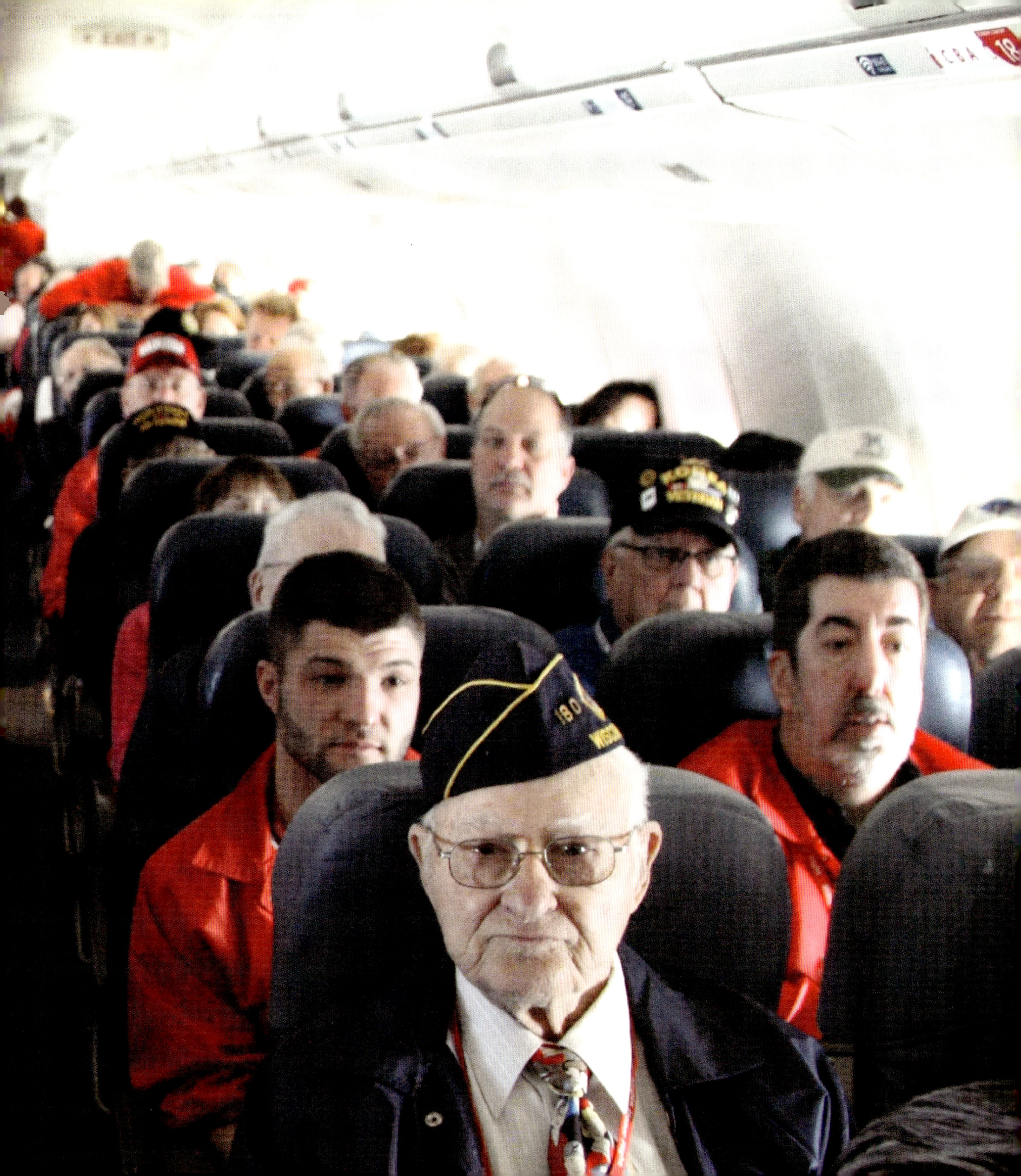

HONOR FLIGHT
OPERATION RESOLVE
STARS AND STRIPES
HONOR FLIGHT
WISCONSIN
OPERATION RESOLVE
Stars and Stripes Honor Flight
Louis (Louie)
Udovich
Stars and Stripes Honor Flight

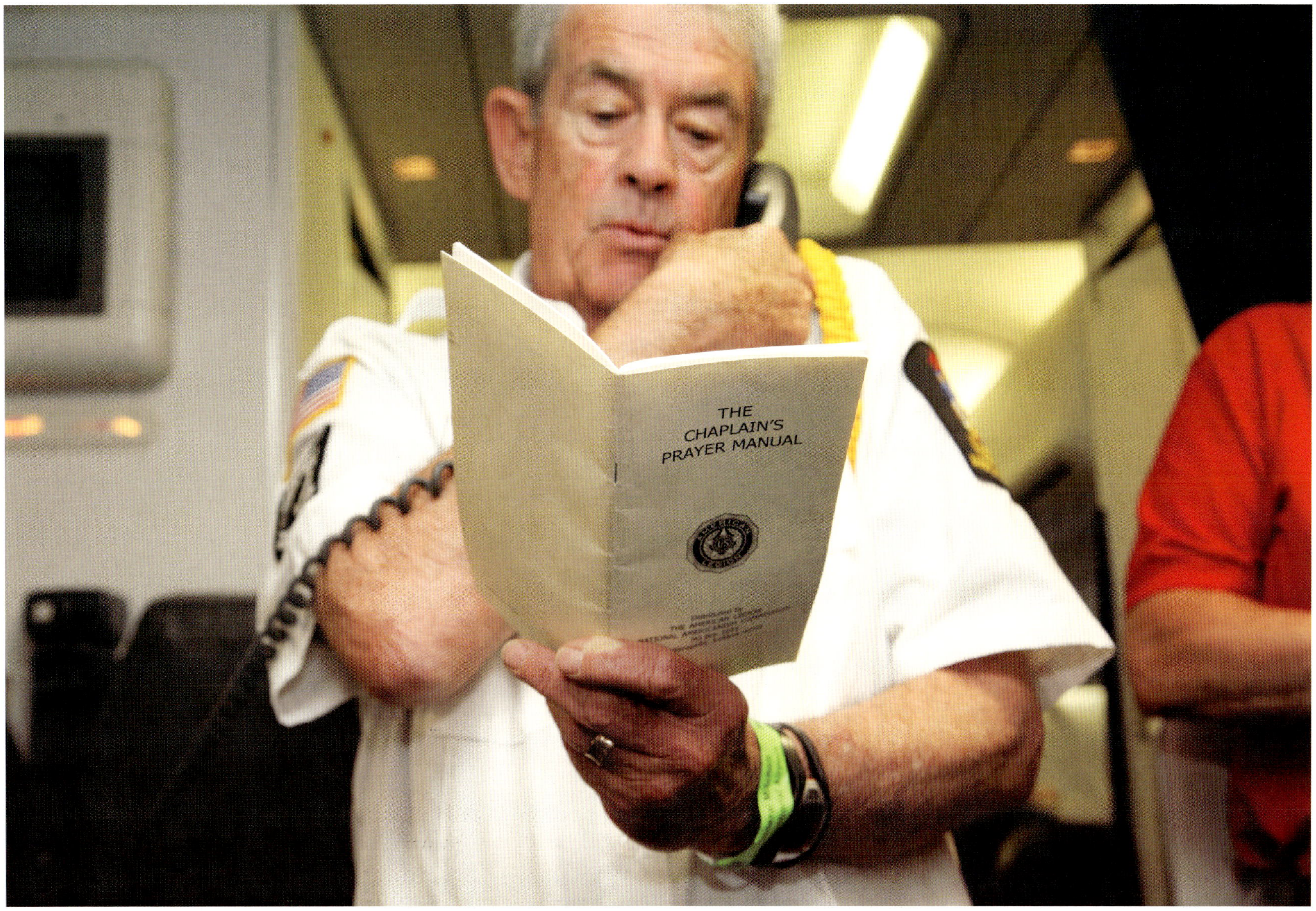
THE
CHAPLAIN'S
PRAYER MANUAL

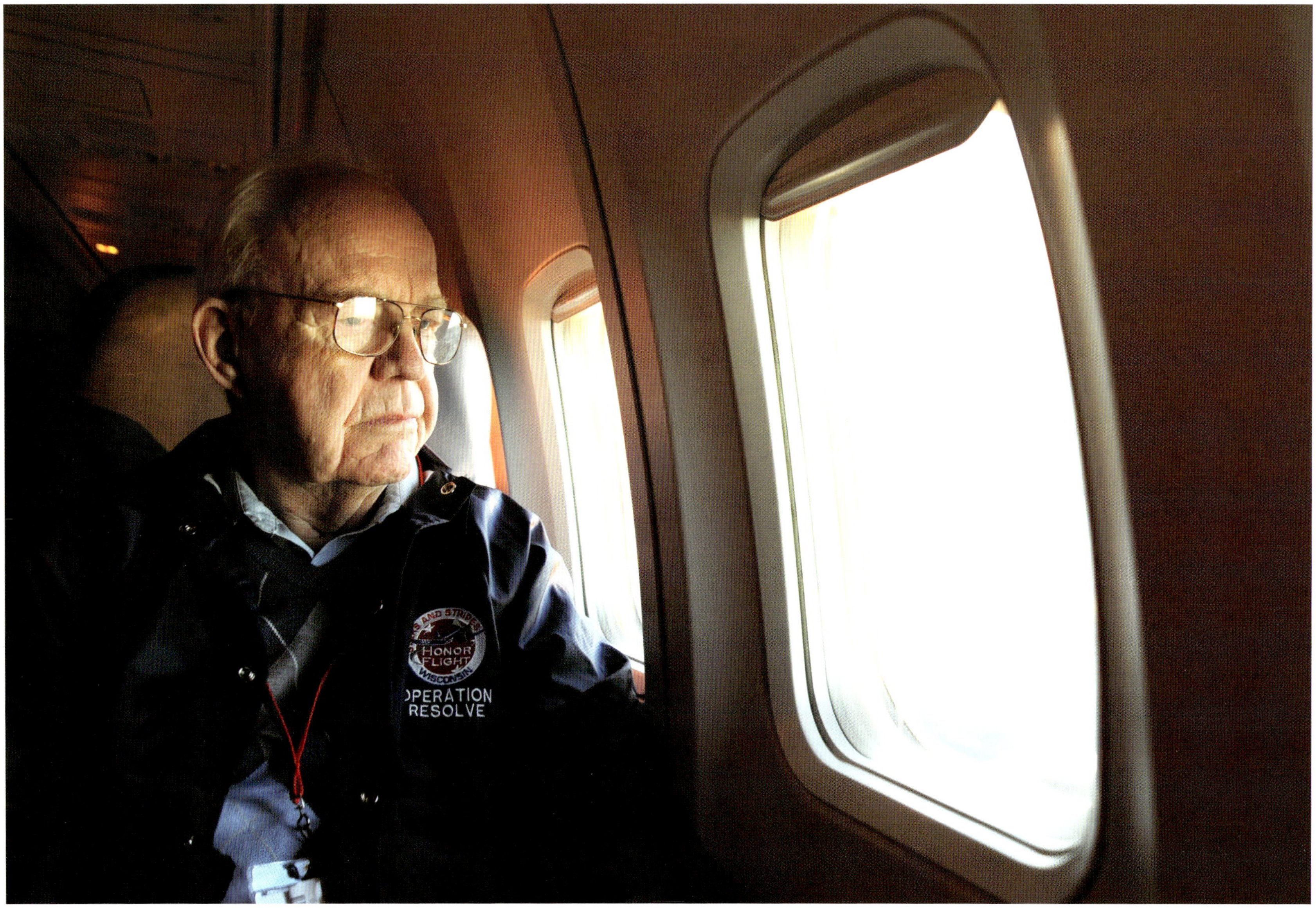
HONOR
FLIGHT
WISCONSIN
OPERATION
RESOLVE

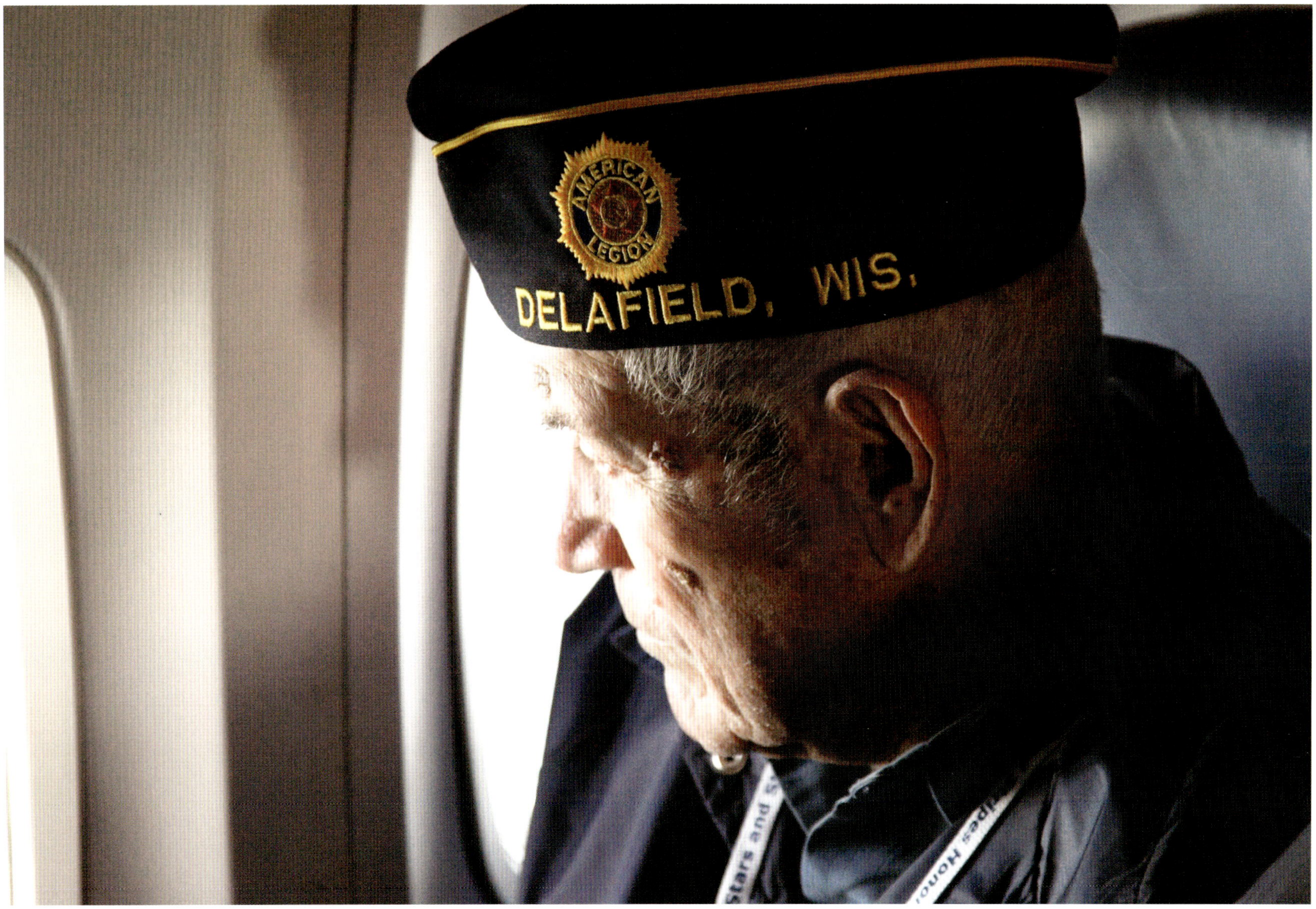
AMERICAN LEGION
DELAFIELD, WIS.

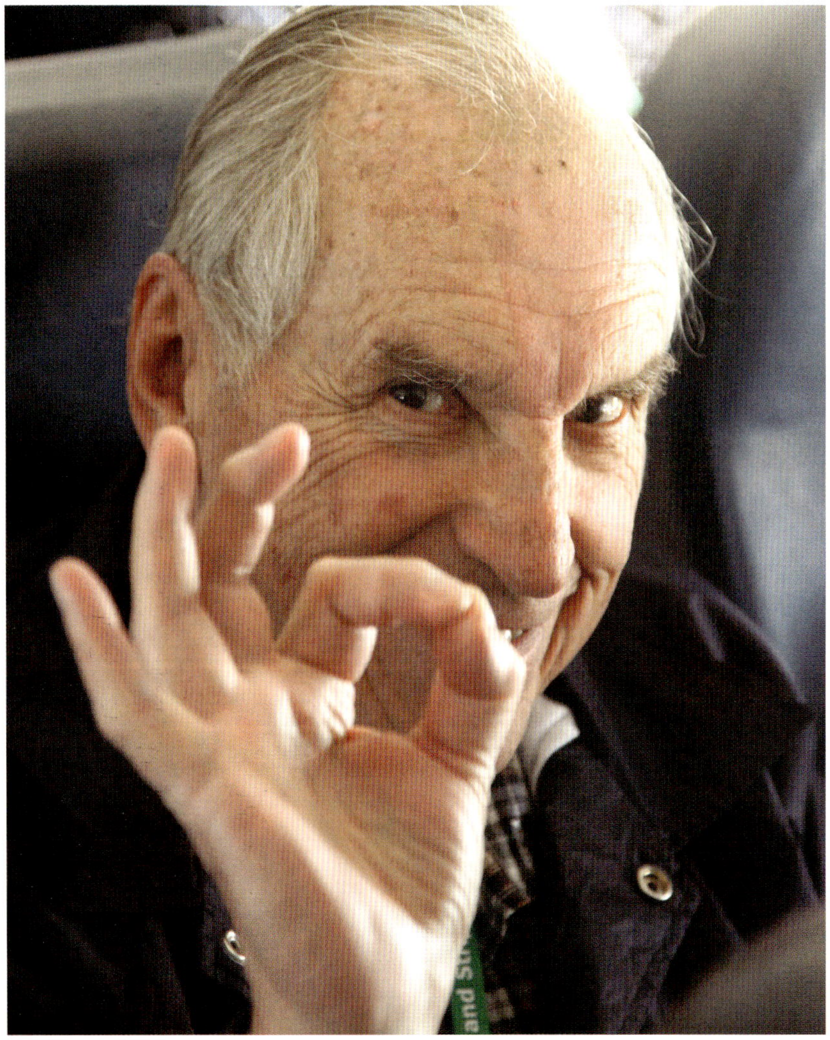

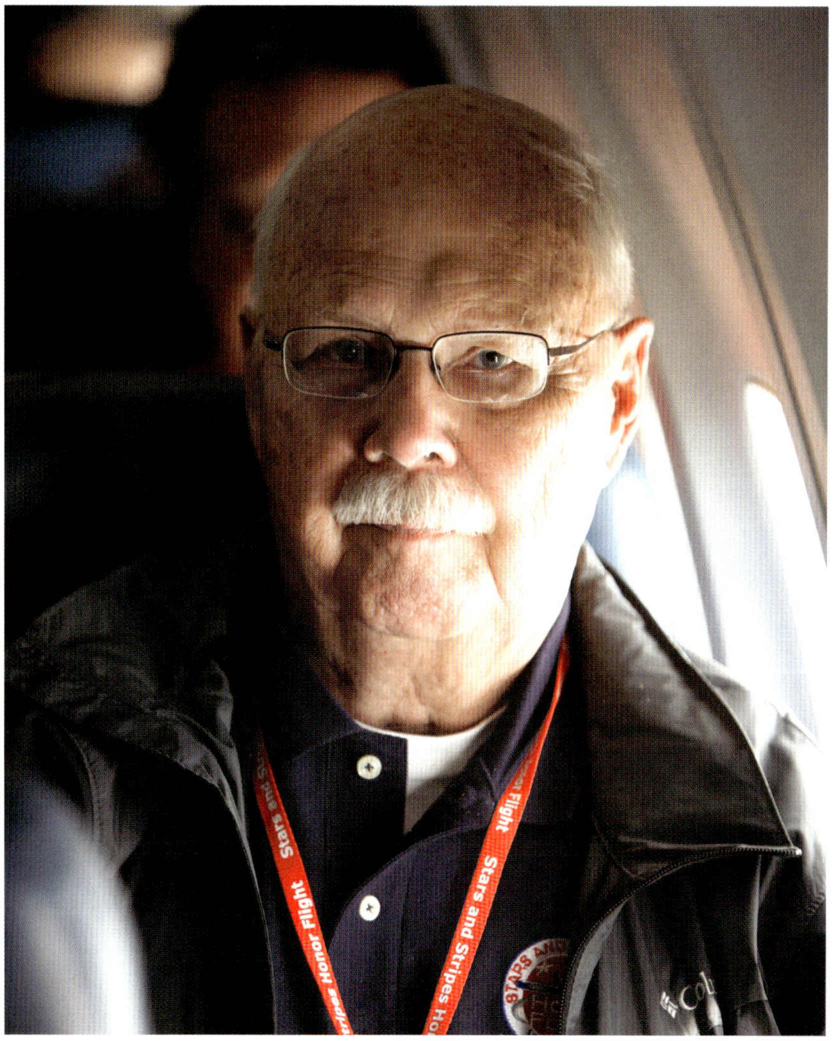
Honor Flight
Stars and Stripes

VFW
10892
Stars and Stripes Honor Flight
HONOR FLIGHT
OPERATION
RESOLVE

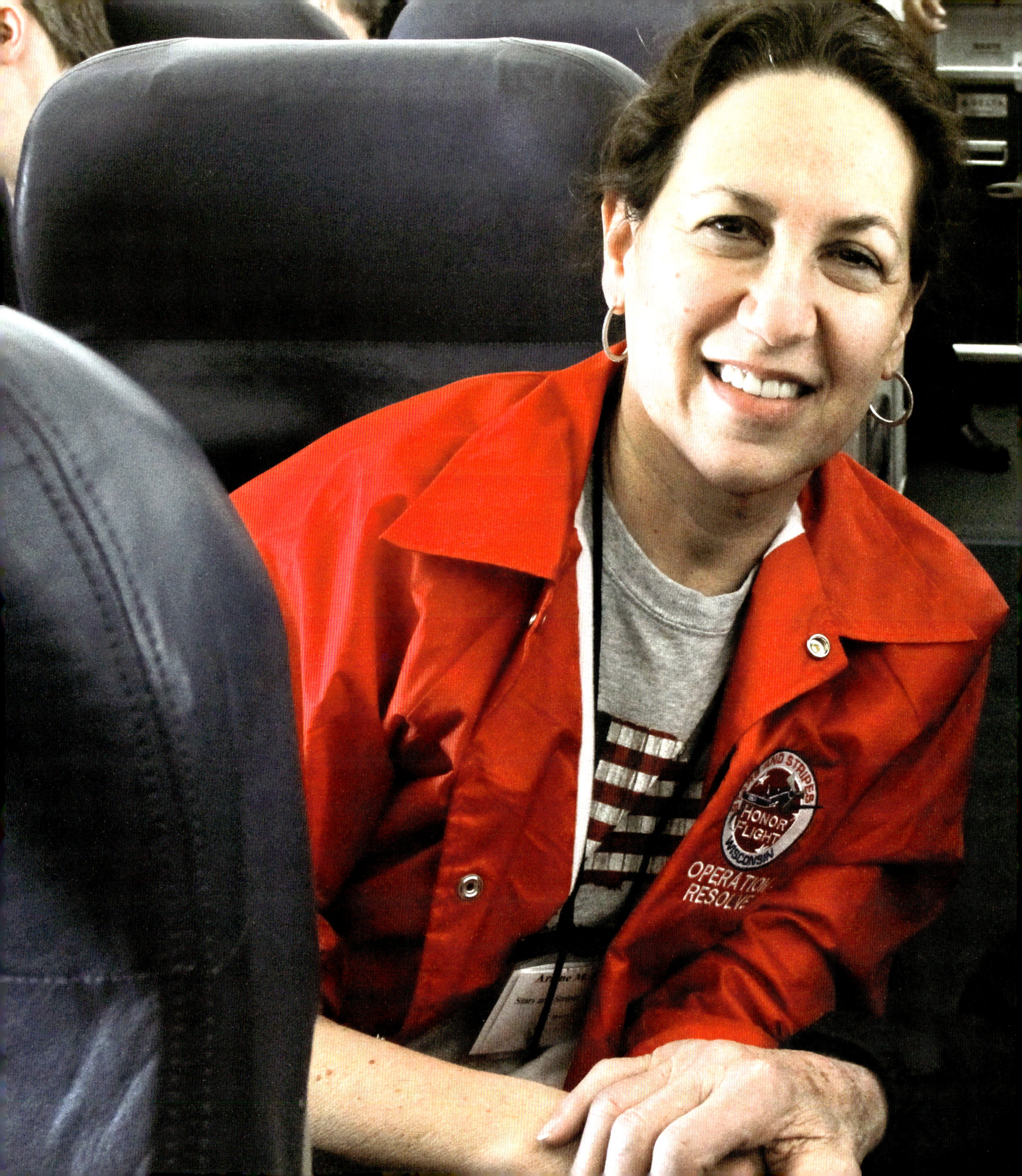
HONOR
FLIGHT
WISCONSIN
OPERATION

STANLEY
BOARDING PASS
D. Margolis
and Stripes Honor Flight
Bravo 5

D.C. Arrival

★ ★ ★

1000 HOURS

Welcome to D.C.! The Honor Flight Network has an incredible volunteer base which organizes groups to greet every Honor Flight plane that arrives from all over the country throughout the spring and fall flying seasons.

DELTA
HONOR FLIGHT
OPERATION RESOLVE
HONOR FLIGHT
Operation Resolve

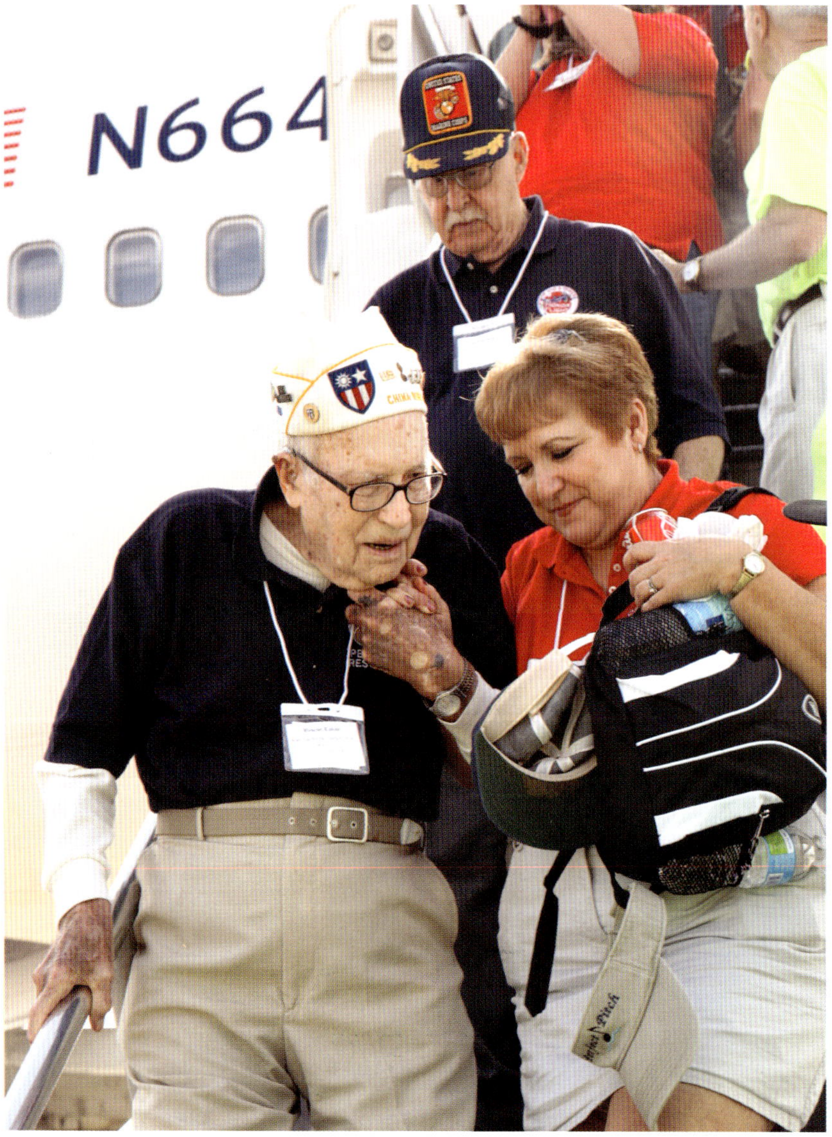
N664

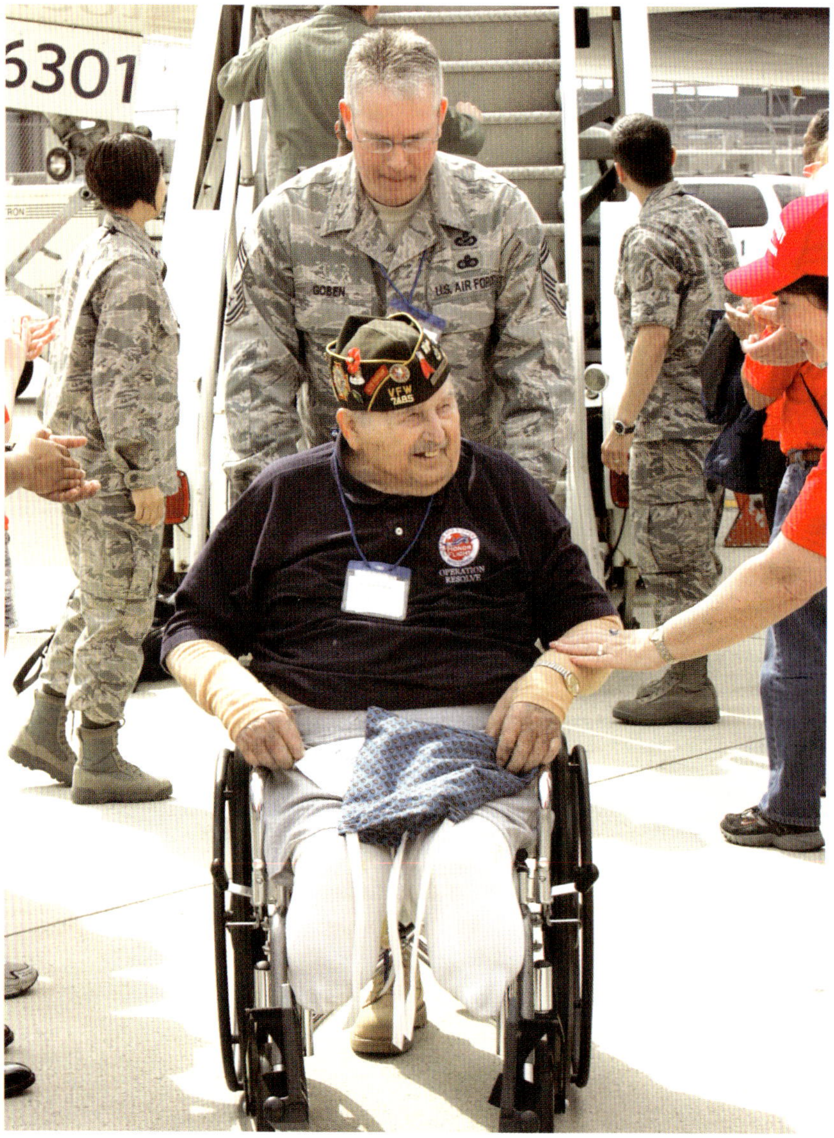
6301

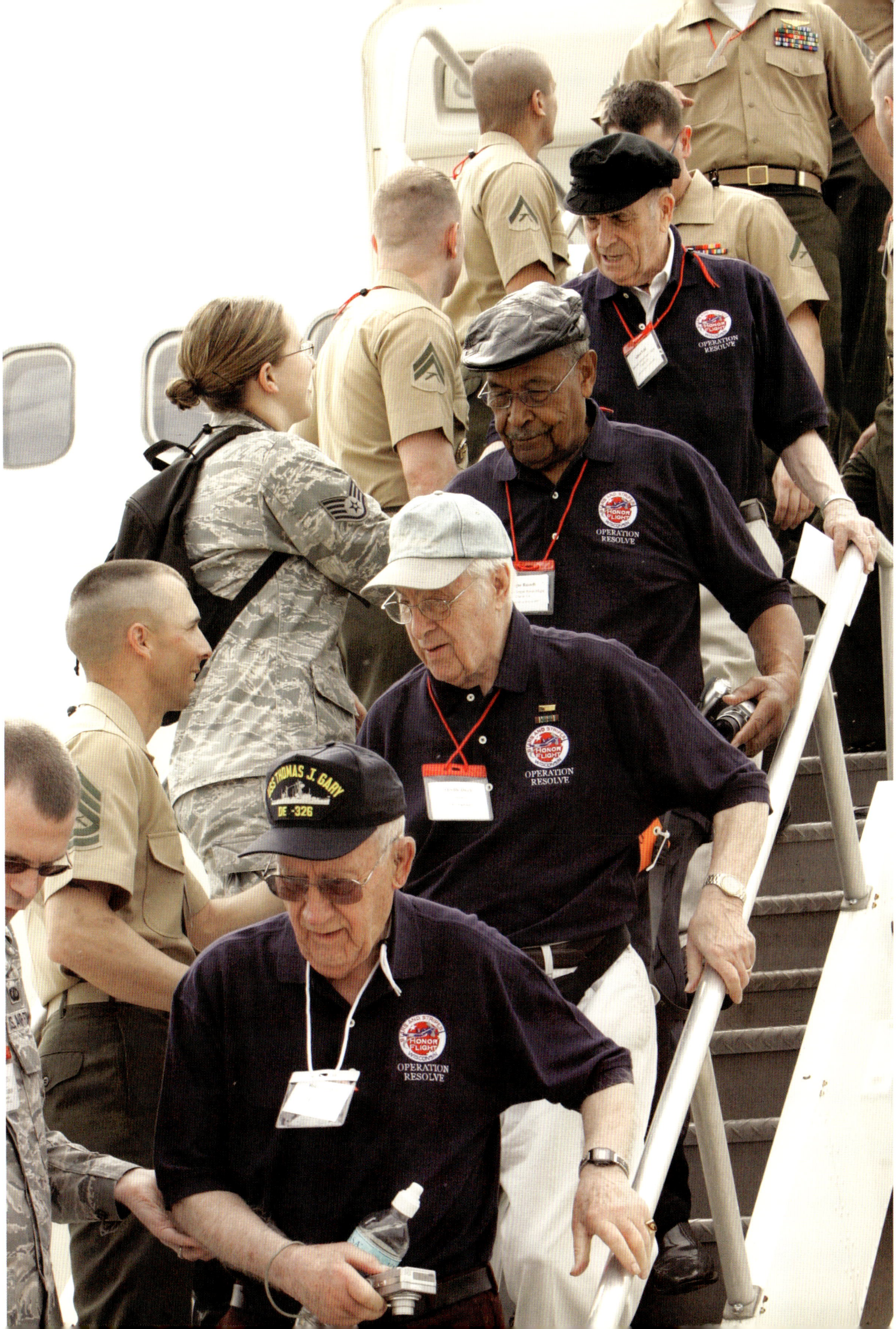
USS THOMAS J. GARY
DE -326
HONOR FLIGHT
OPERATION RESOLVE

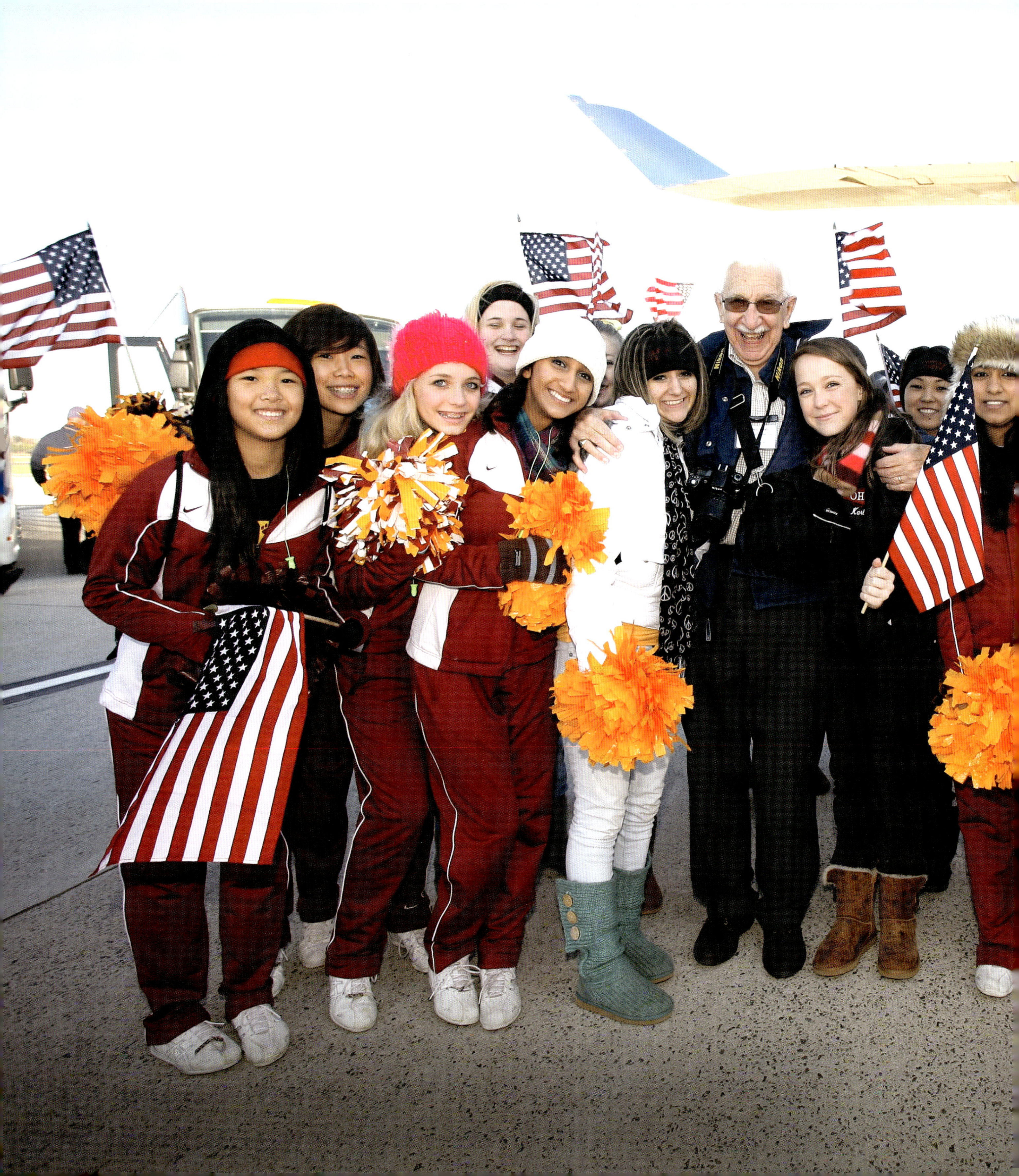

Milwaukee veteran Eugene Schulz received a warm welcome from the entire Oakton High School (Vienna, Virginia) cheerleading squad. Eugene's Honor Flight experience inspired him to finish a book about his war years. *The Ghost in General Patton's Third Army* documents Eugene's eyewitness account of the first Nazi concentration camp discovered by American troops.

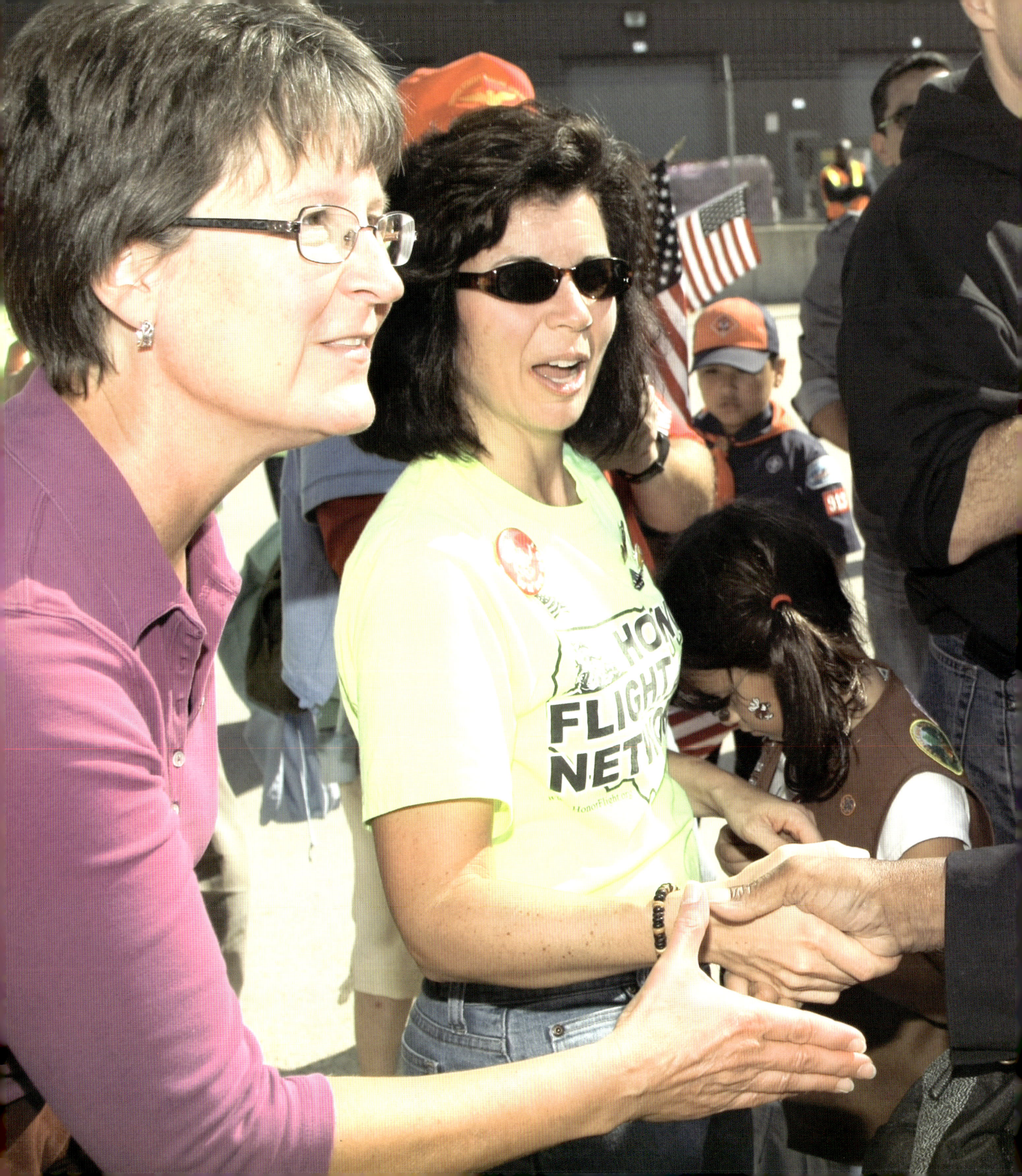
FLIGHT
NETW

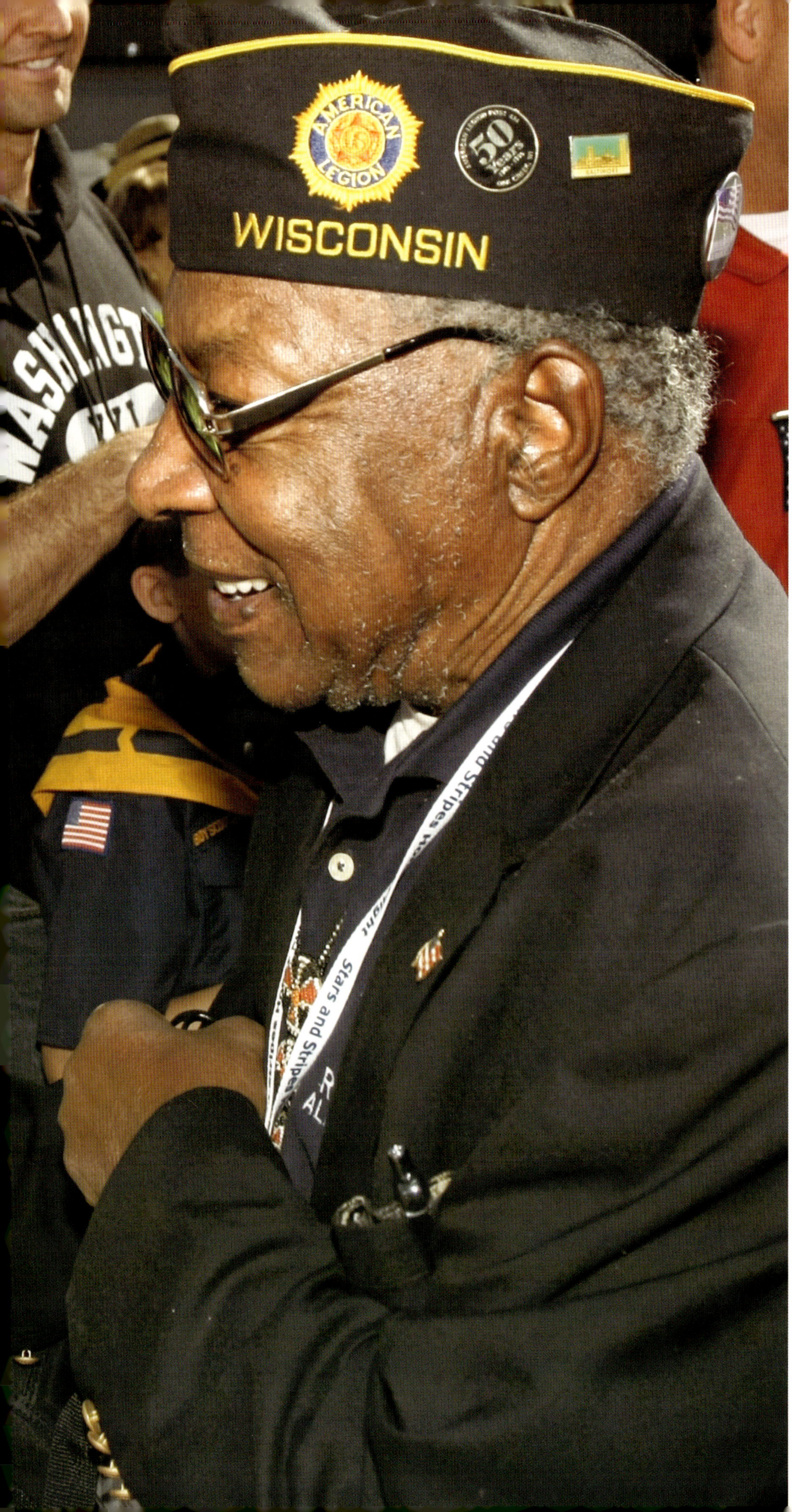
AMERICAN LEGION
WISCONSIN
Stars and Stripes

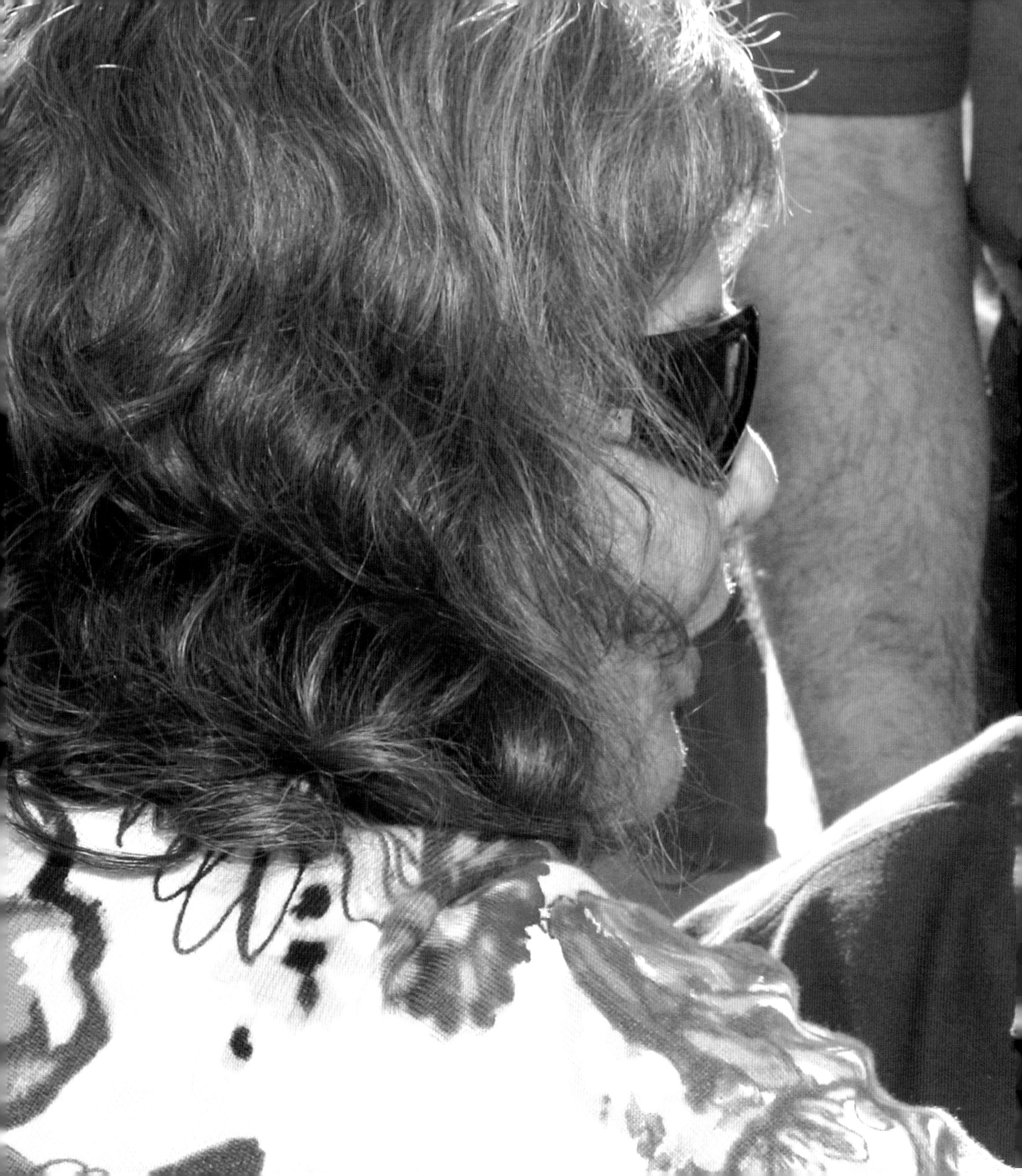

FREETHINK MEDIA PRESENTS
HONOR FLIGHT
ONE LAST MISSION
'Enormously moving."
LA Times
WINNER BEST OF FESTIVAL DOCUMENTARY FEATURE RICHMOND INT'L FILM FESTIVAL 2013
WINNER GREG GUND MEMORIAL STANDING UP COMPETITION CLEVELAND INT'L FILM FESTIVAL 2013
GUINNESS WORLD RECORD LARGEST FILM SCREENING 2012
WINNER BEST DOCUMENTARY AUDIENCE CHOICE OMAHA FILM FESTIVAL 2013
WINNER BEST OF FESTIVAL DOCUMENTARY FEATURE GI FILM FESTIVAL 2013
FREETHINK MEDIA PRESENTS "HONOR FLIGHT" DIRECTED BY DAN HAYES PRODUCED BY CLAY BROGA EXECUTIVE PRODUCERS KMELE FOSTER TED BALAKER
EDITOR HAWK JENSEN CINEMATOGRAPHY BY BENJAMIN GASKELL DAN HAYES COMPOSERS JOSH CHRISTIANSEN ALEX MAAS
PRODUCER - WISCONSIN ERIC SCHROEDER CO-PRODUCERS HAWK JENSEN CHANDLER TUTTLE
PARENTAL GUIDANCE SUGGESTED PG EMOTIONAL THEMATIC ELEMENTS, SOME WAR-RELATED DISTURBING IMAGES, BRIEF SMOKING AND MILD LANGUAGE
Some Material May Not Be Suitable for Children
SnagFilms
www.HonorFlightTheMovie.com
freethink

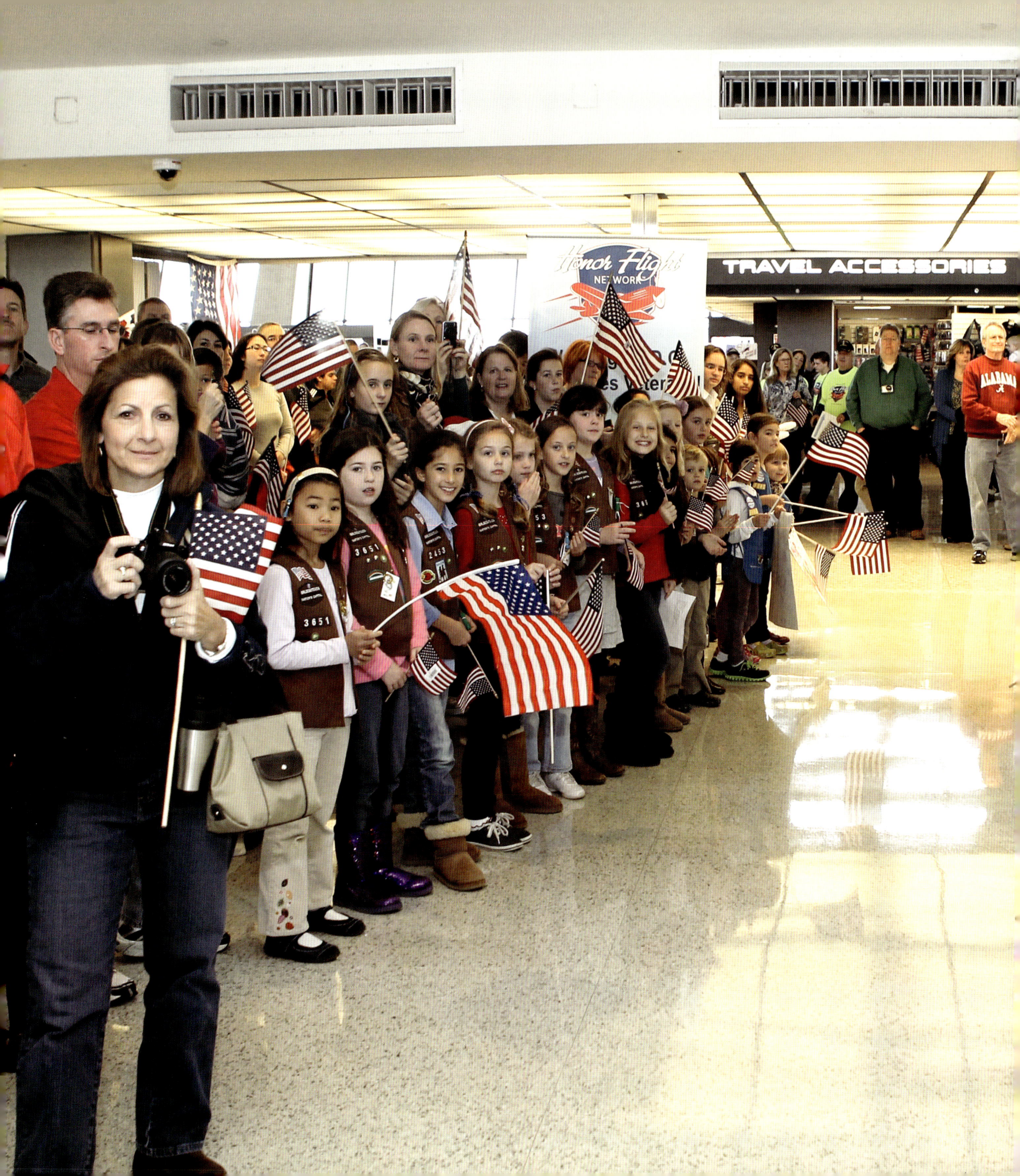

Honor Flight
NETWORK
TRAVEL ACCESSORIES
ALABAMA

This scene greets our veterans upon their arrival at the Washington's Dulles International Airport. While the veterans have some notion about the homecoming that awaits them in Milwaukee at the end of their day, few of them expect so many people to welcome them to Washington. Most Honor Flight greeters have no connection to the veterans who land in Washington – they simply turn out to welcome them and thank them for their service.

101

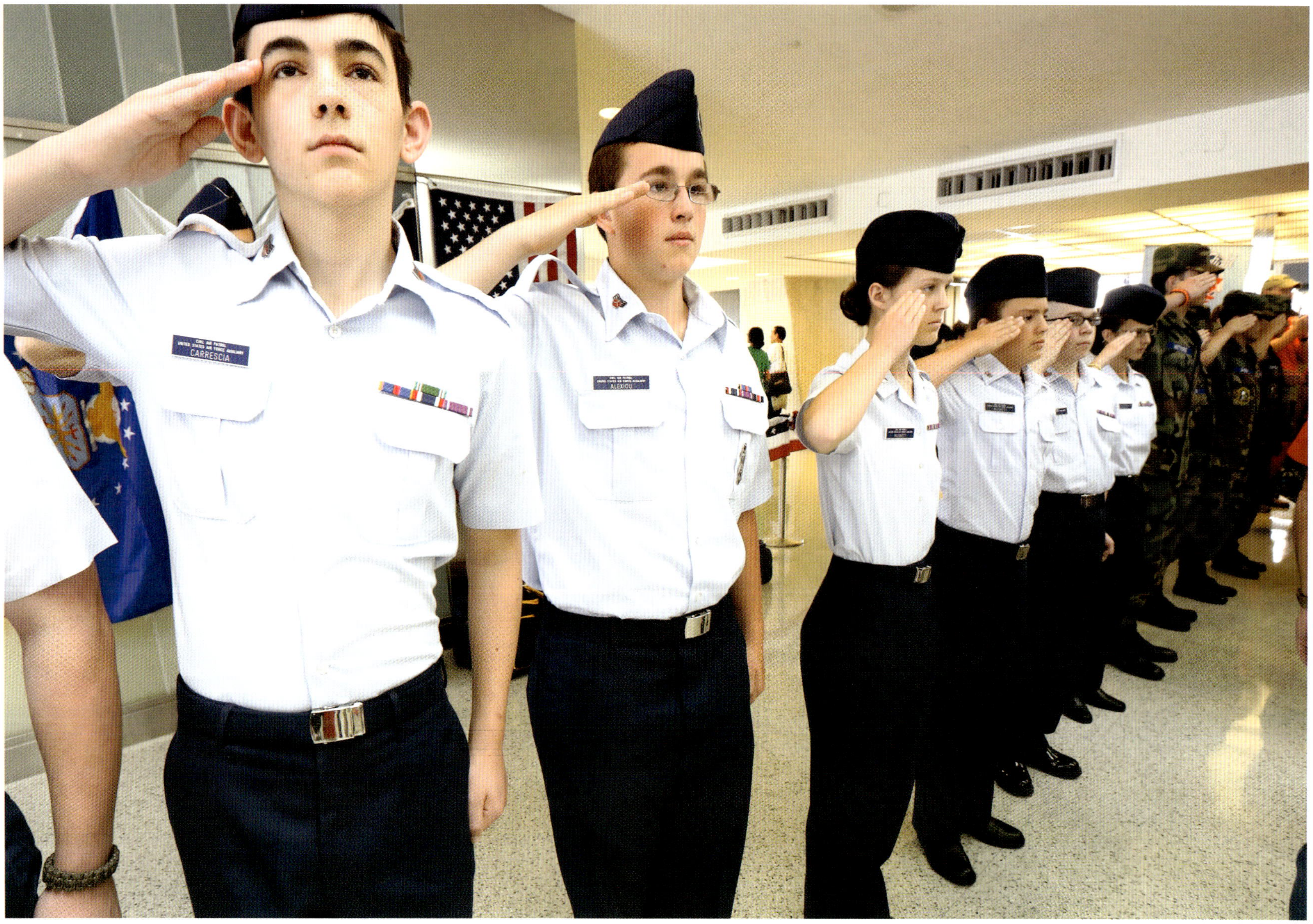
CARRESCIA
ALEXIOU

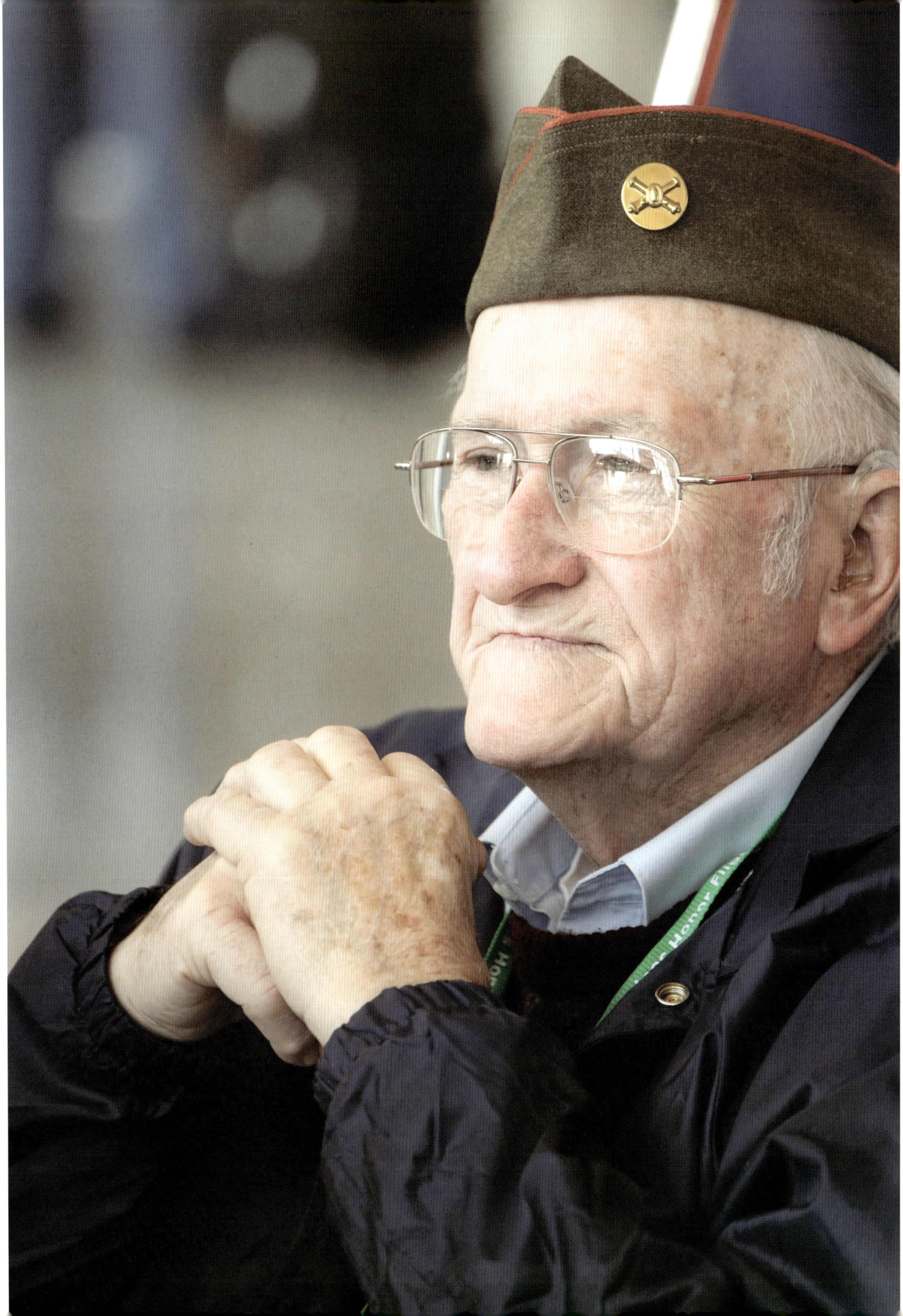
Honor

WELCOME, HERO
♡ DePreter
♡ Flatley
♡ Goss
xxoo Sue

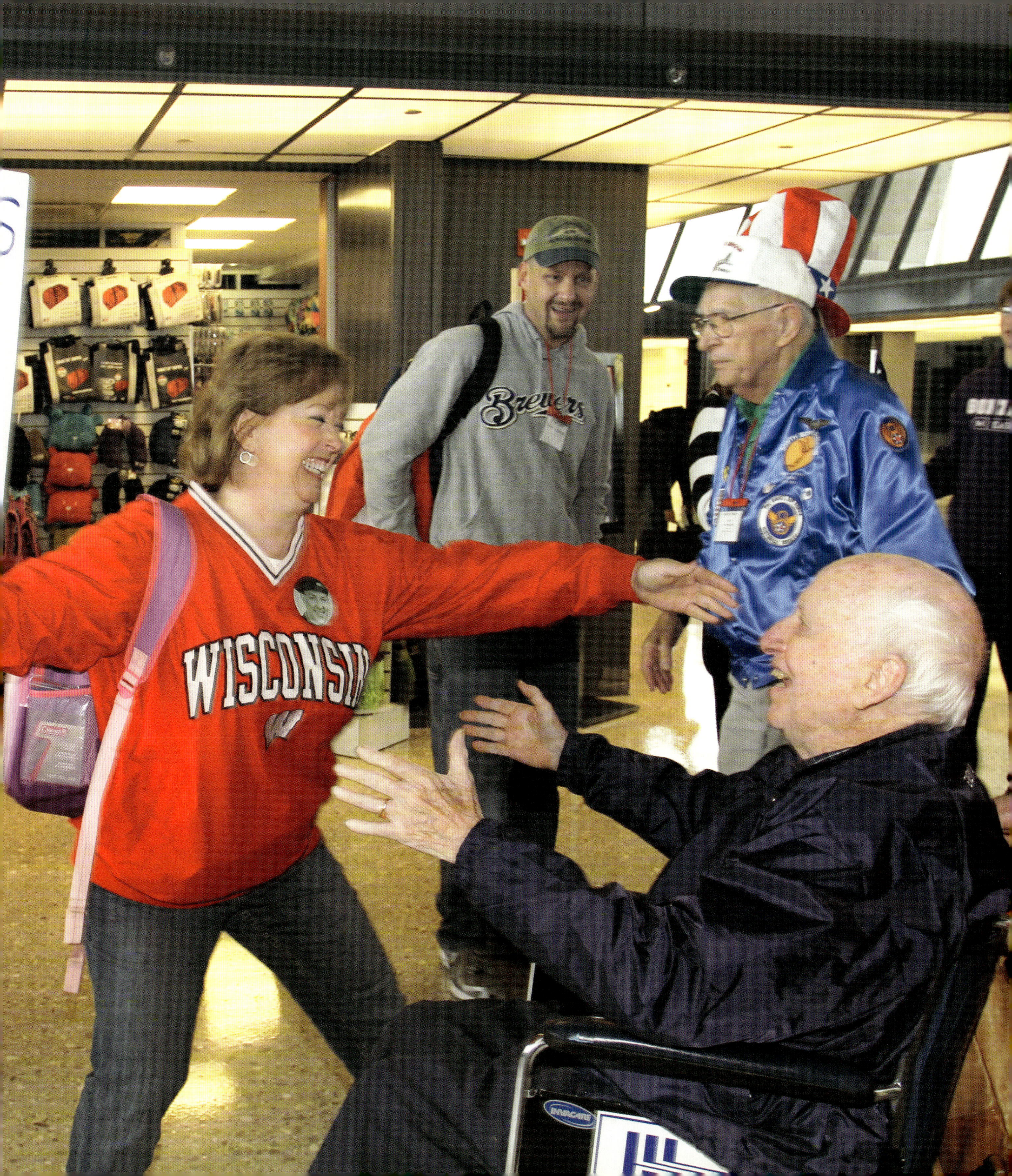
Brewers
INVACARE

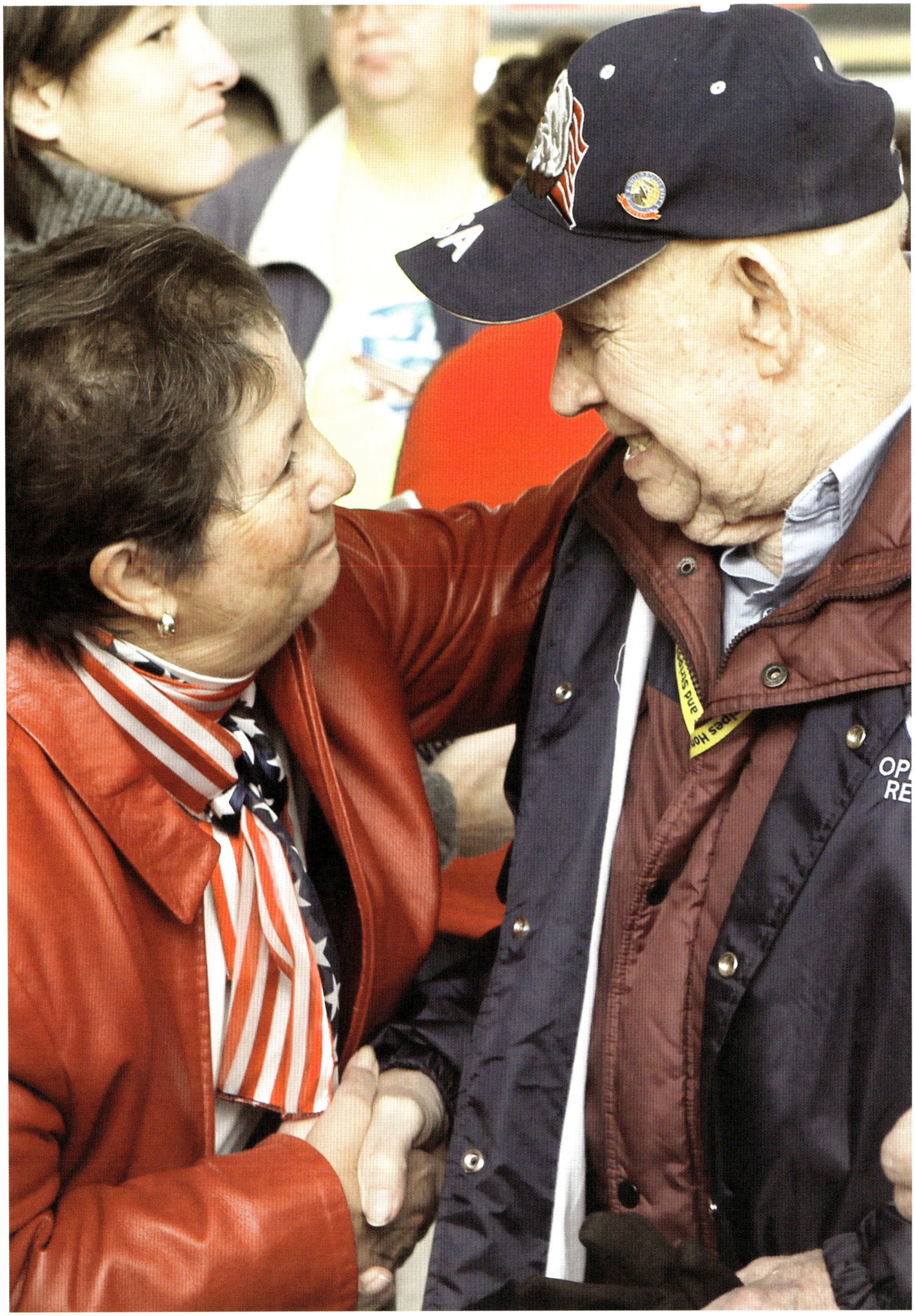

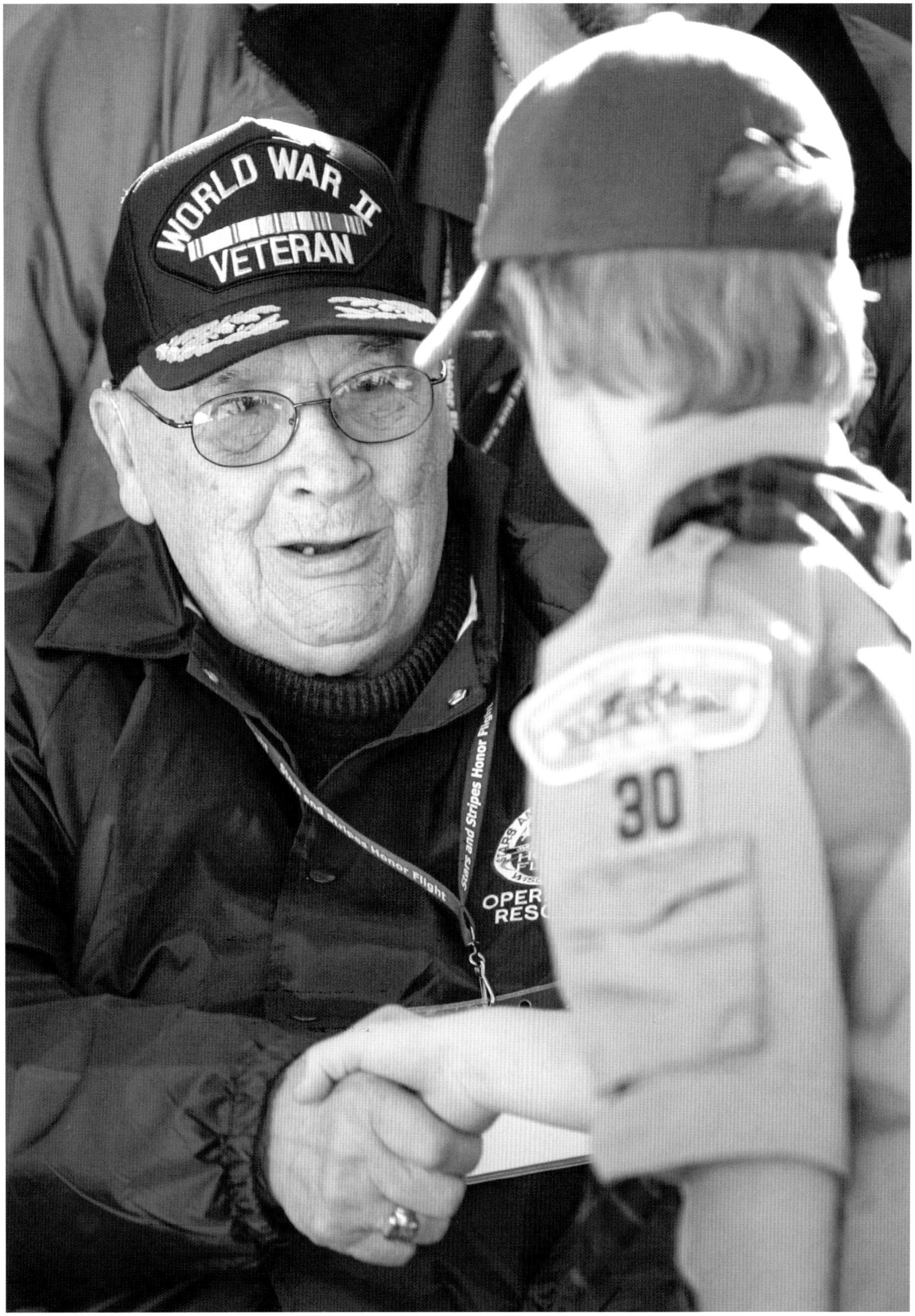
WORLD WAR II
VETERAN
Stars and Stripes Honor Flight
30

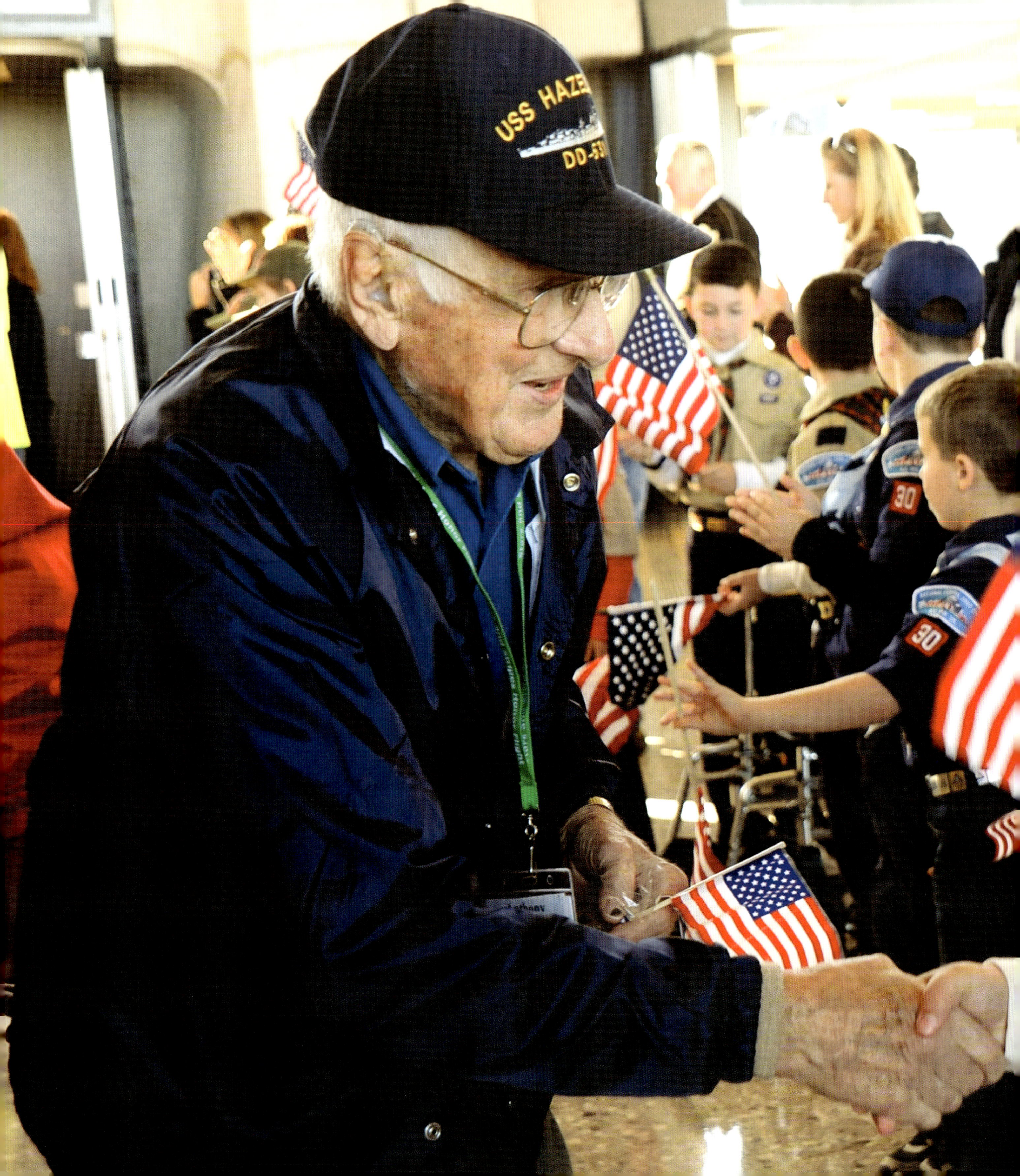
USS HAZE
30

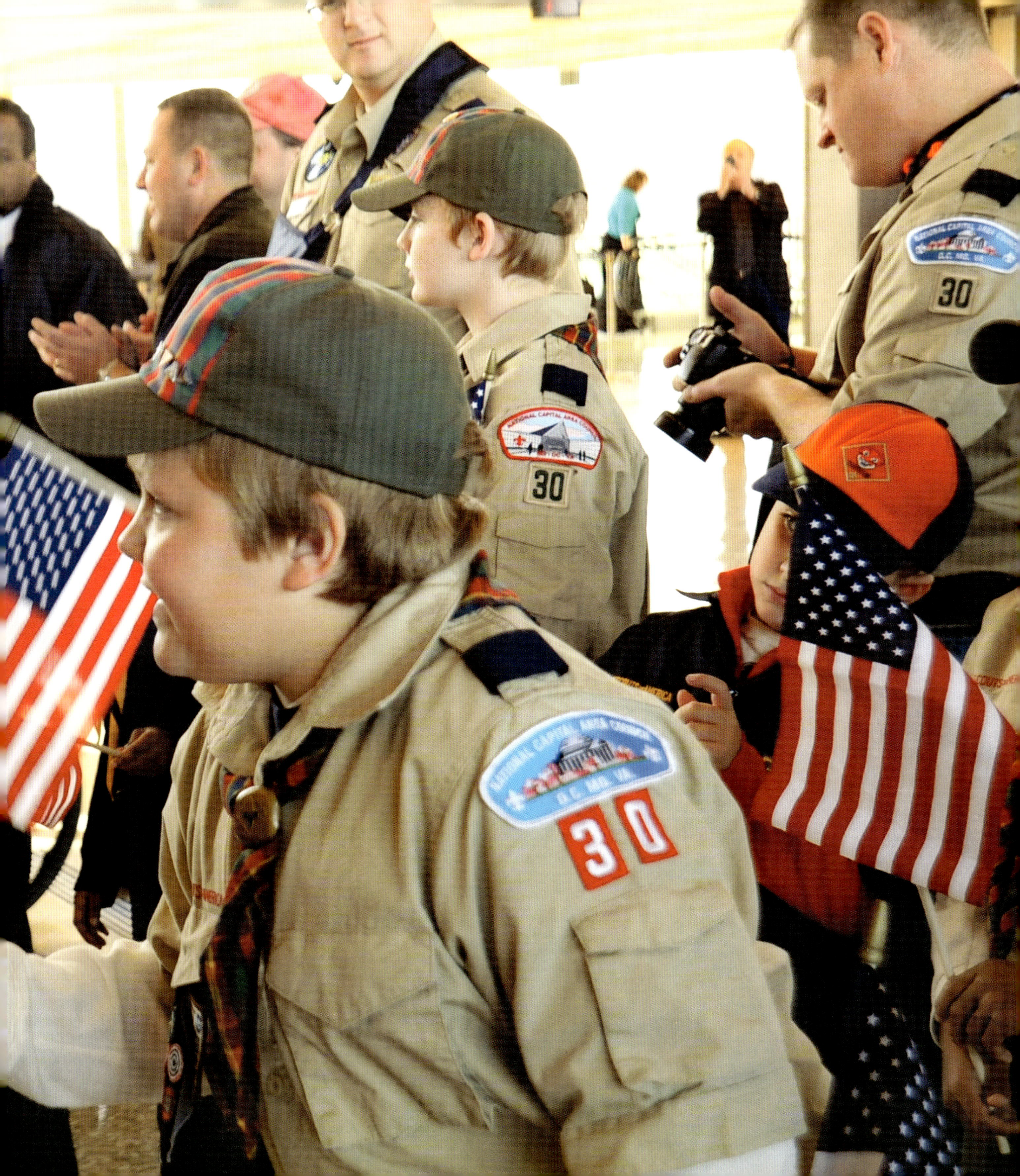
NATIONAL CAPITAL AREA COUNCIL
D.C. MD. VA.
30
30
30

110

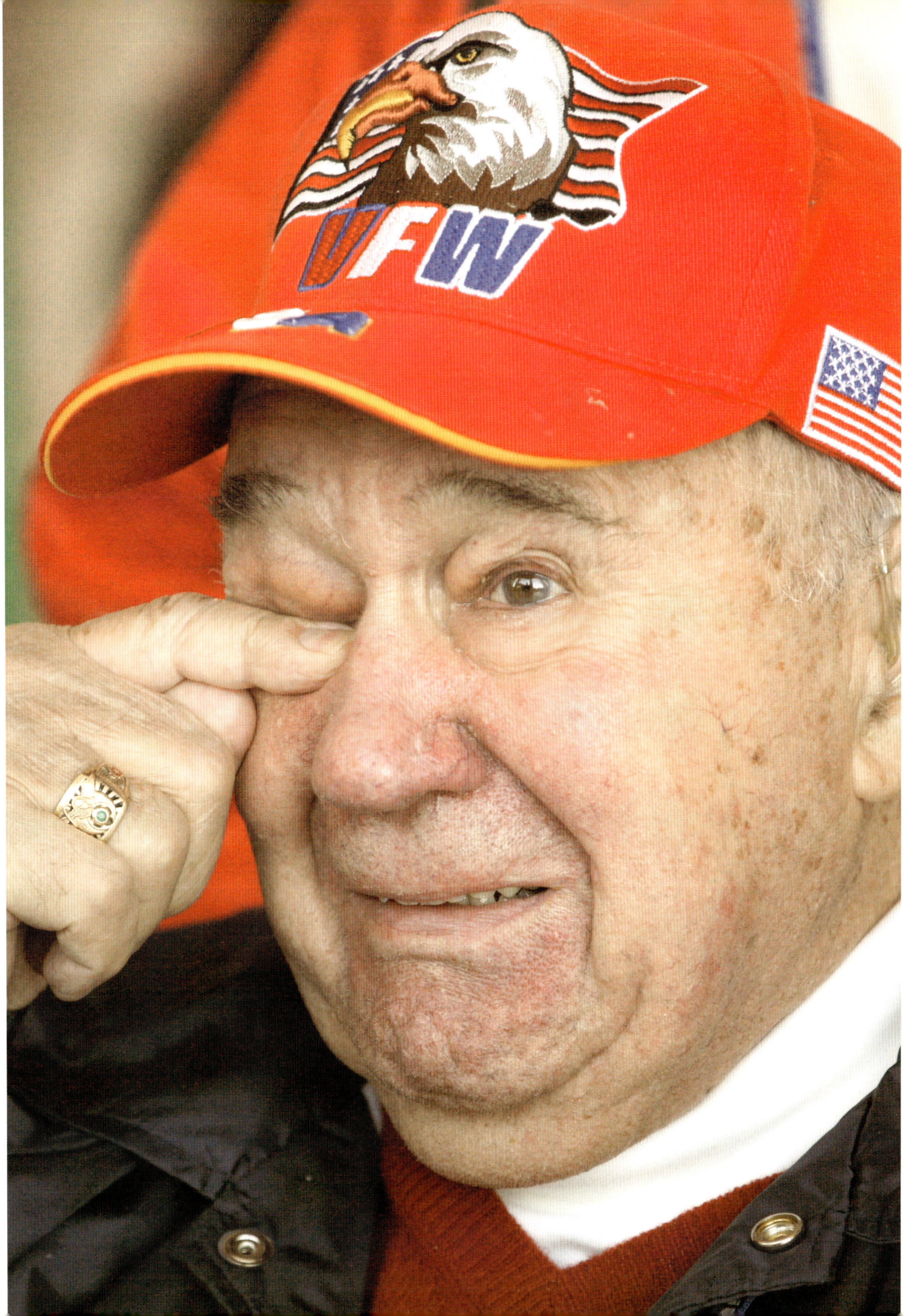
VFW

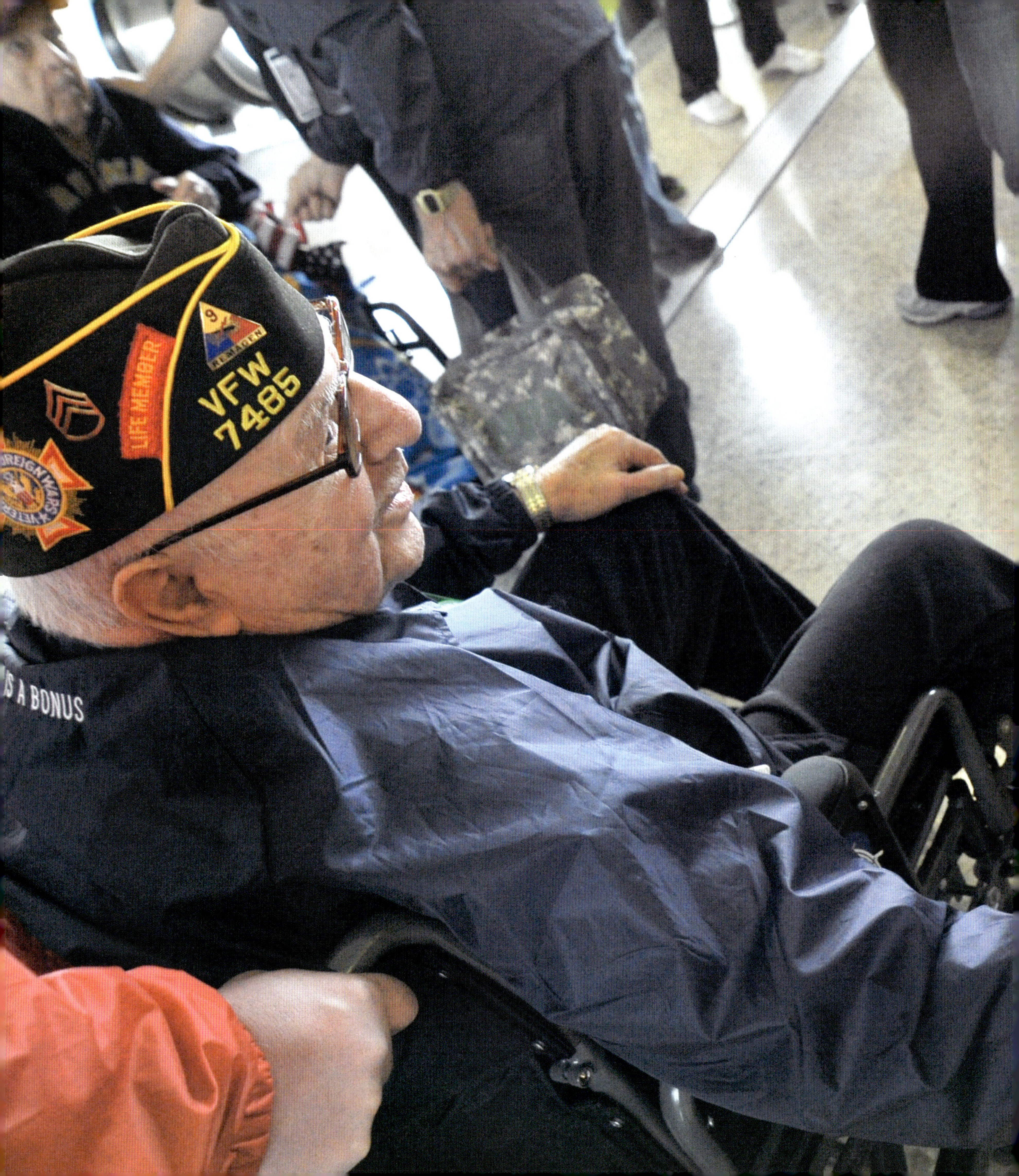
LIFE MEMBER
VFW
7485
REMAGEN
S A BONUS

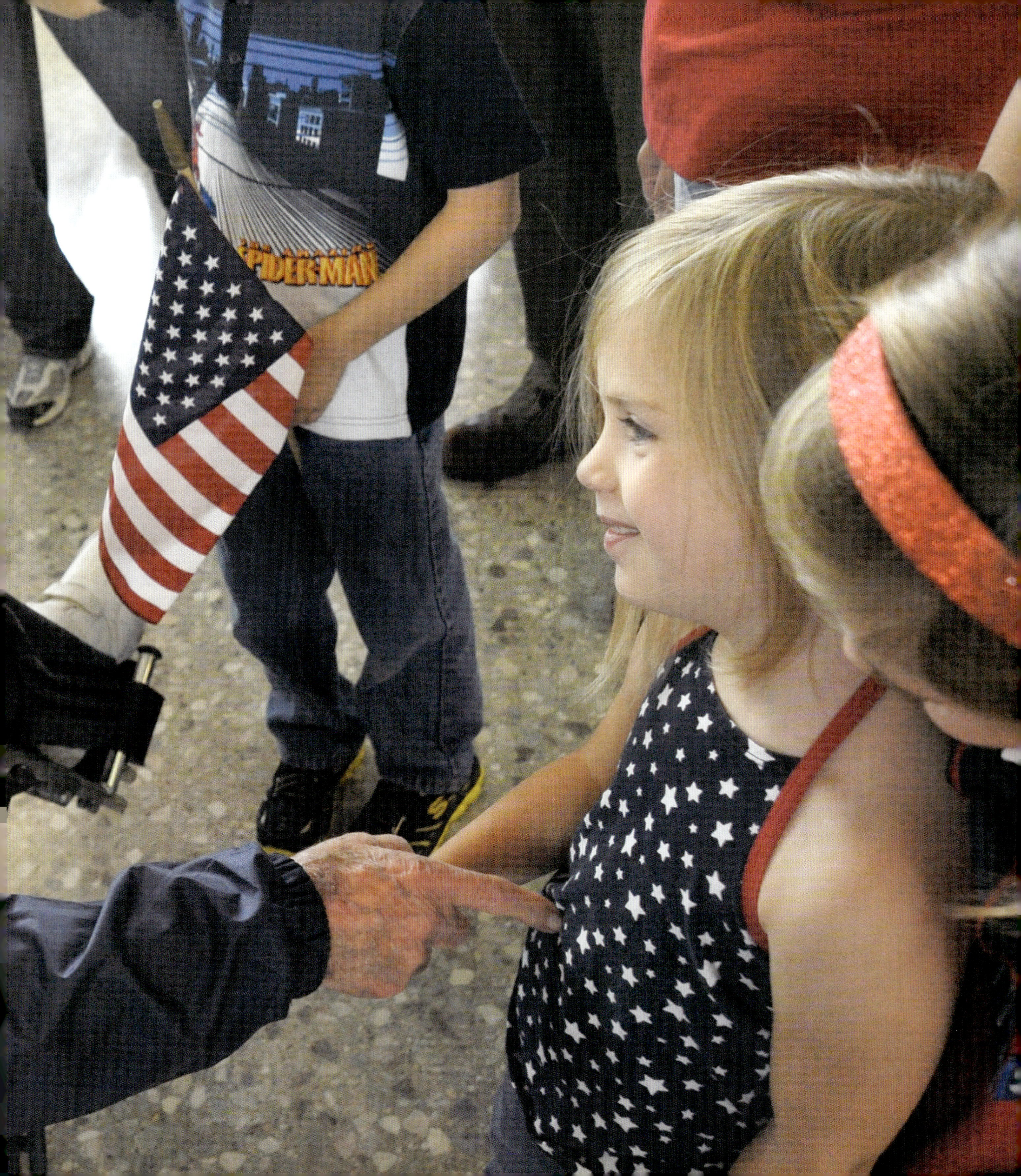
SPIDER-MAN

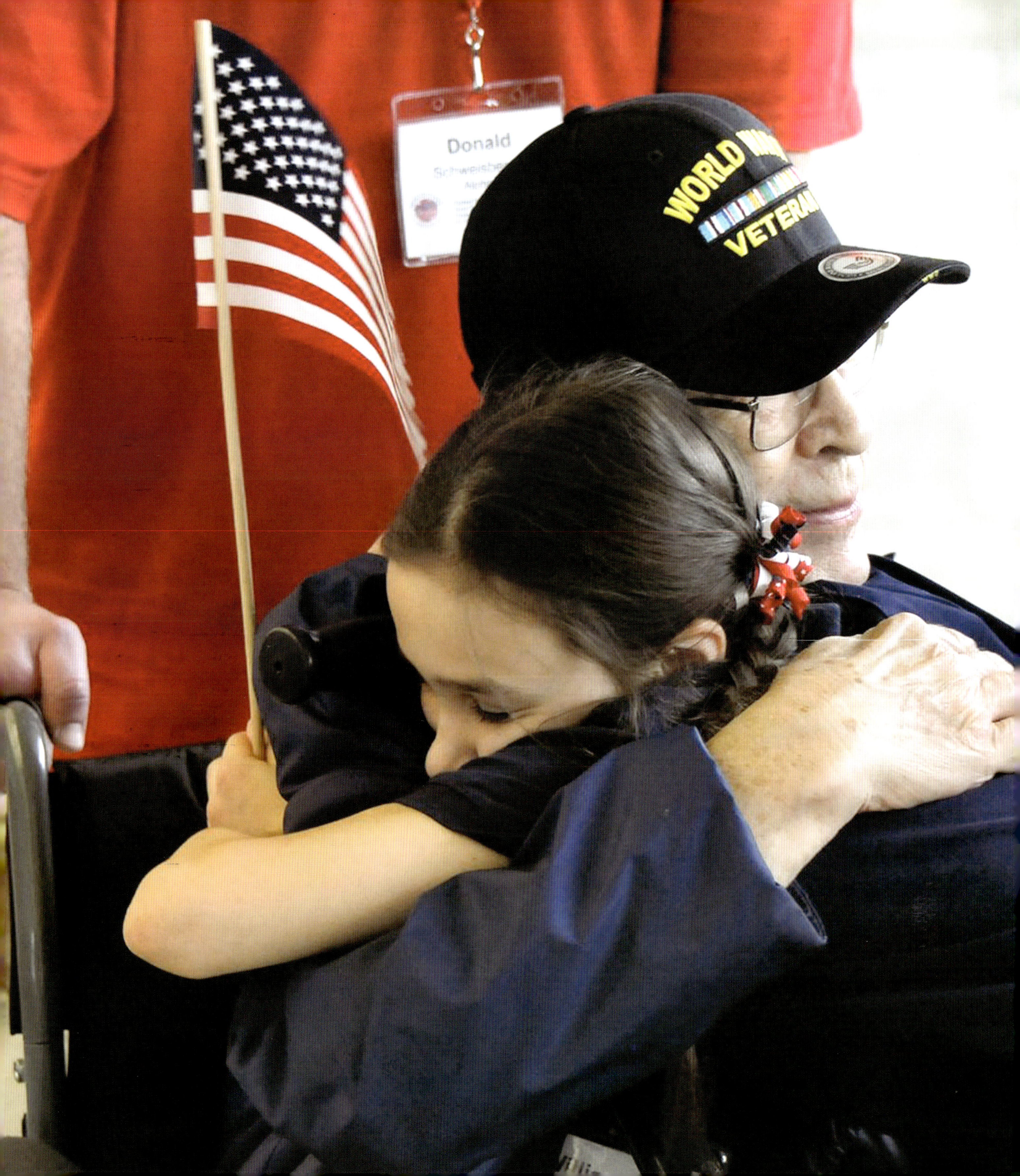
Donald
WORLD

115

The day-long escort from D.C. law enforcement and the Washington-area American Legion Riders help our veterans keep on a tight schedule that includes visits to the World War II Memorial, the Marine Corps Memorial (often called the Iwo Jima Memorial) and Arlington National Cemetery. Saluting the bus as it leaves is retired Air Force Lt. Col. Stephen Waller who has greeted countless Honor Flights.

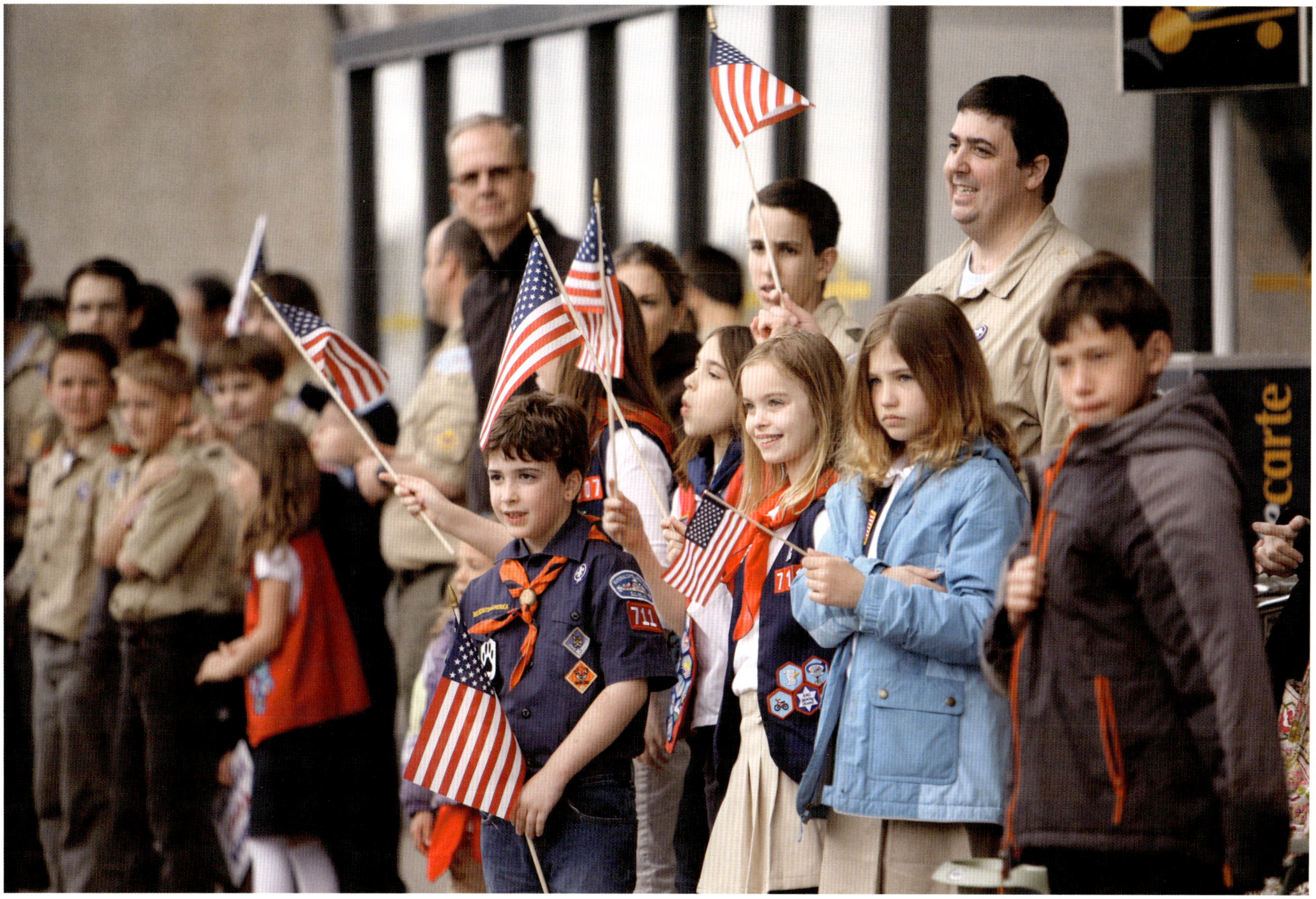
carte
711

Three-year-old Jackson Brandt has been greeting our veterans in Washington, D.C., since he was five months old. This is his mom's way of honoring her own grandfather, who did not live to see the completion of the National World War II Memorial.

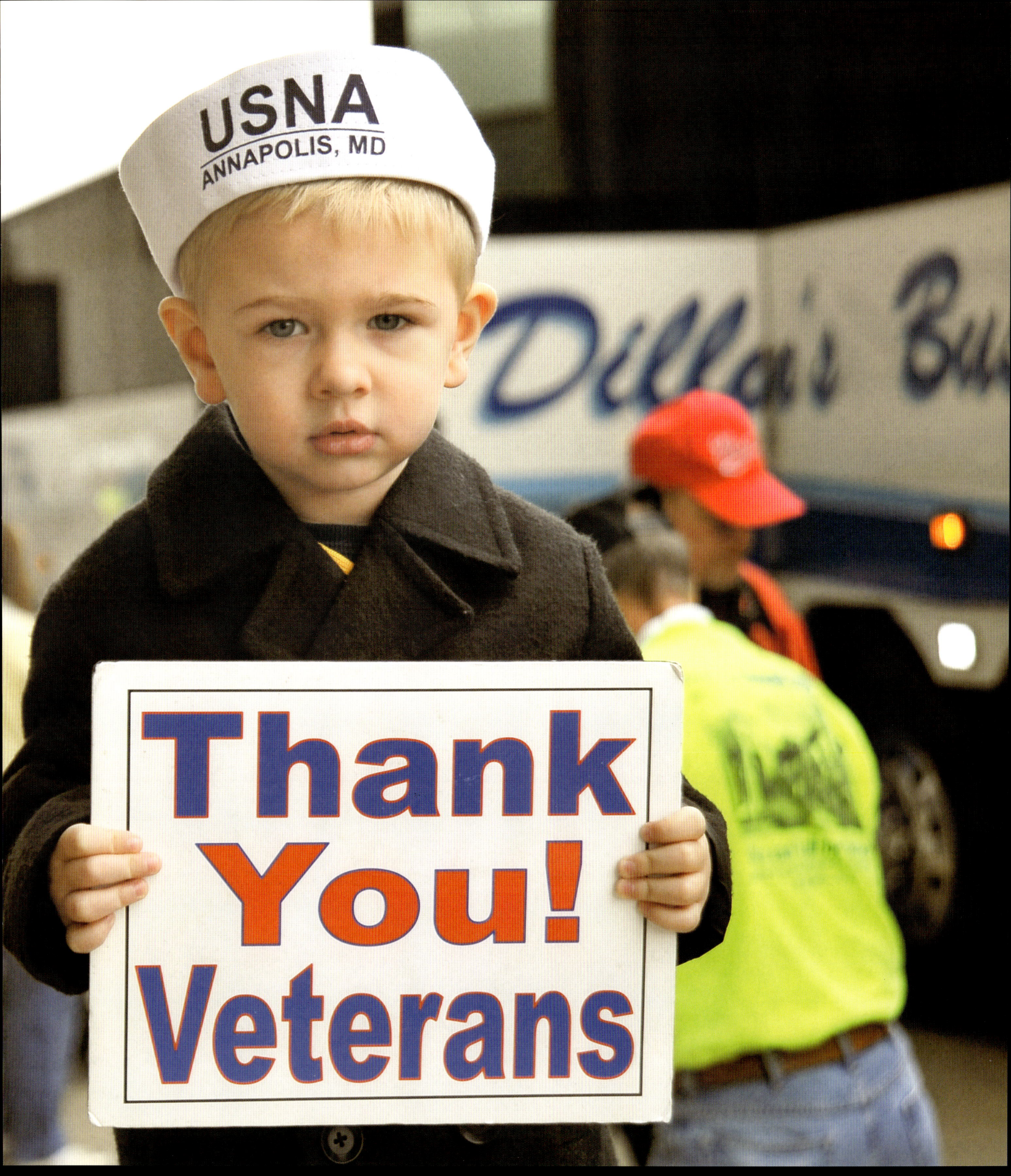
USNA
ANNAPOLIS, MD
Thank
You!
Veterans

The Memorials

★ ★ ★

1200 HOURS

NATIONAL WORLD WAR II MEMORIAL

Dedicated May 29, 2004

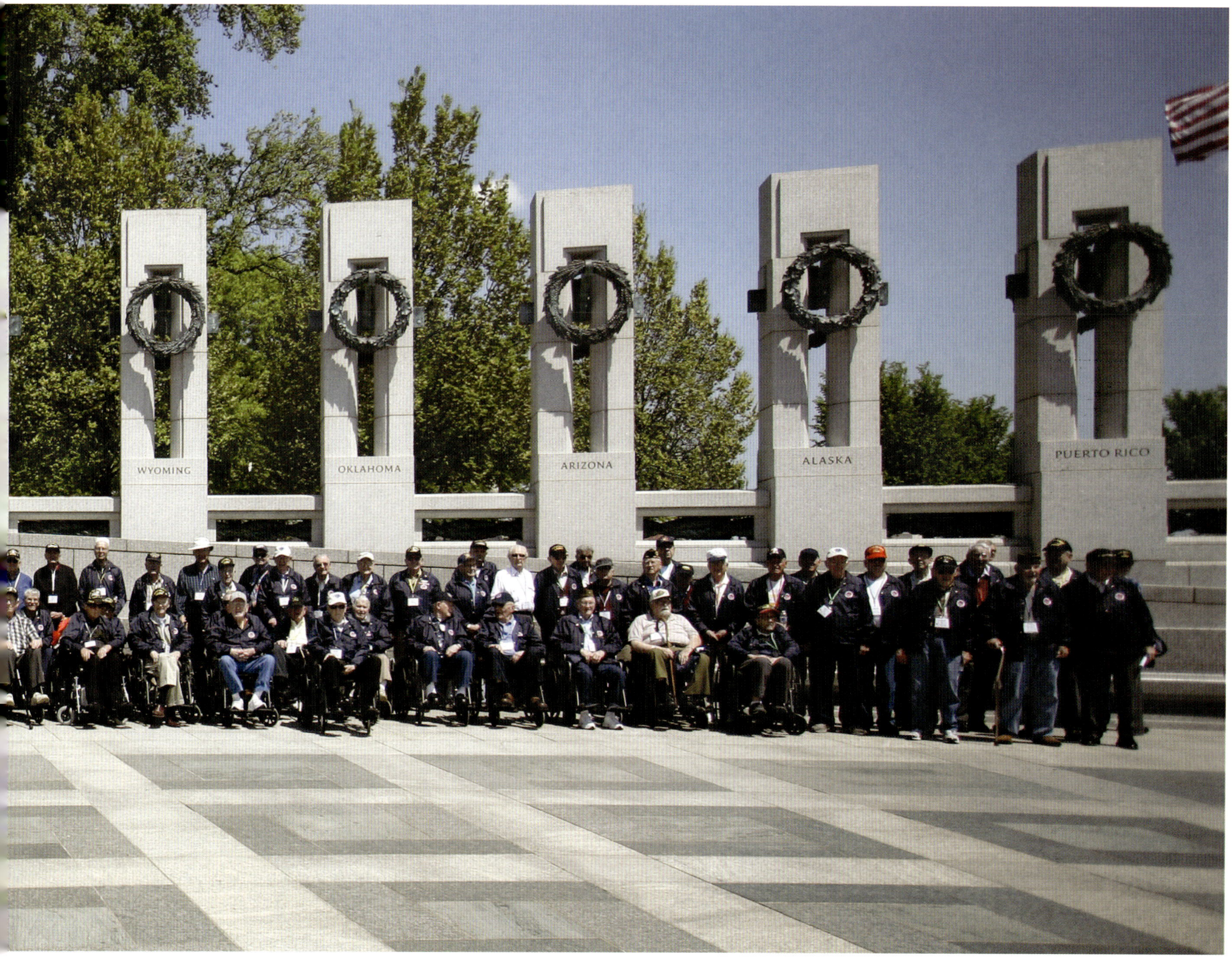
WYOMING
OKLAHOMA
ARIZONA
ALASKA
PUERTO RICO

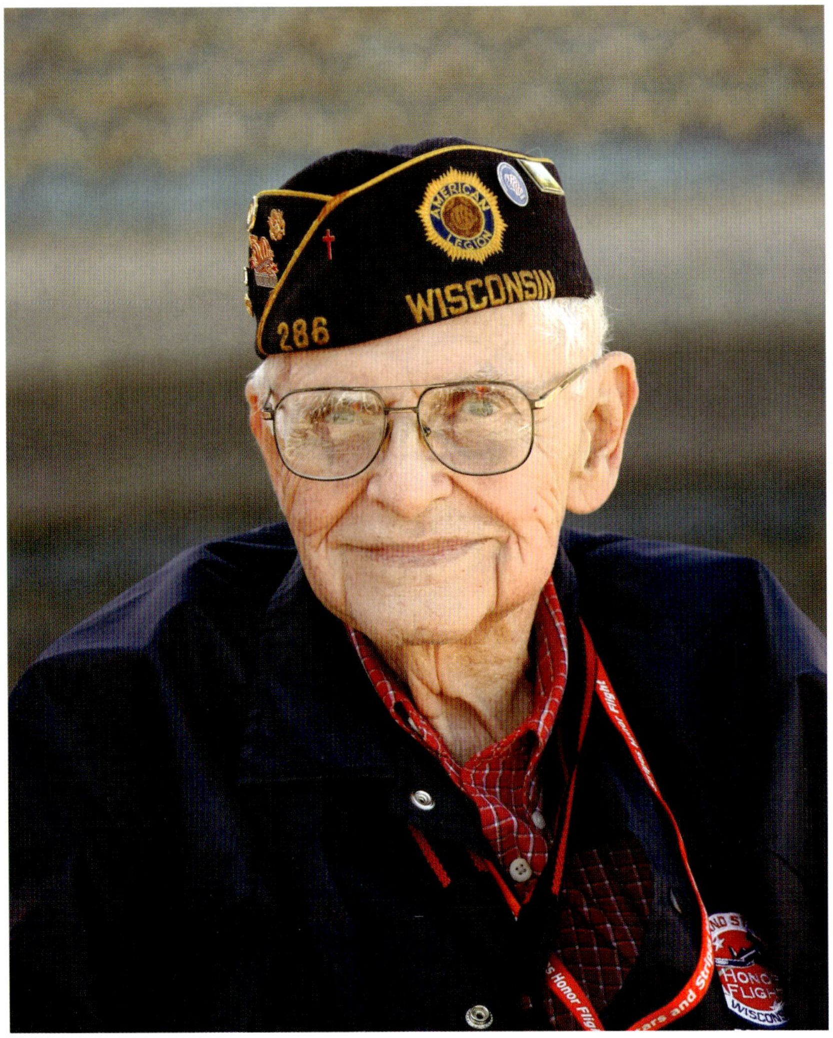
WISCONSIN
286

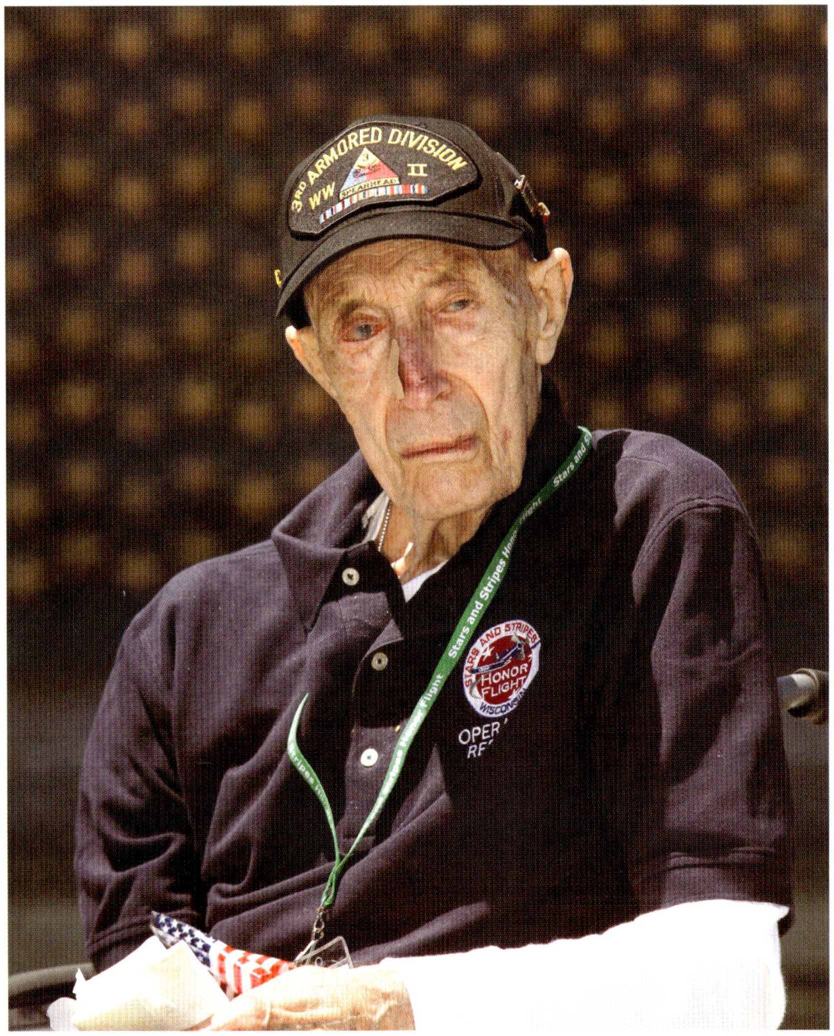
3RD ARMORED DIVISION
WW II

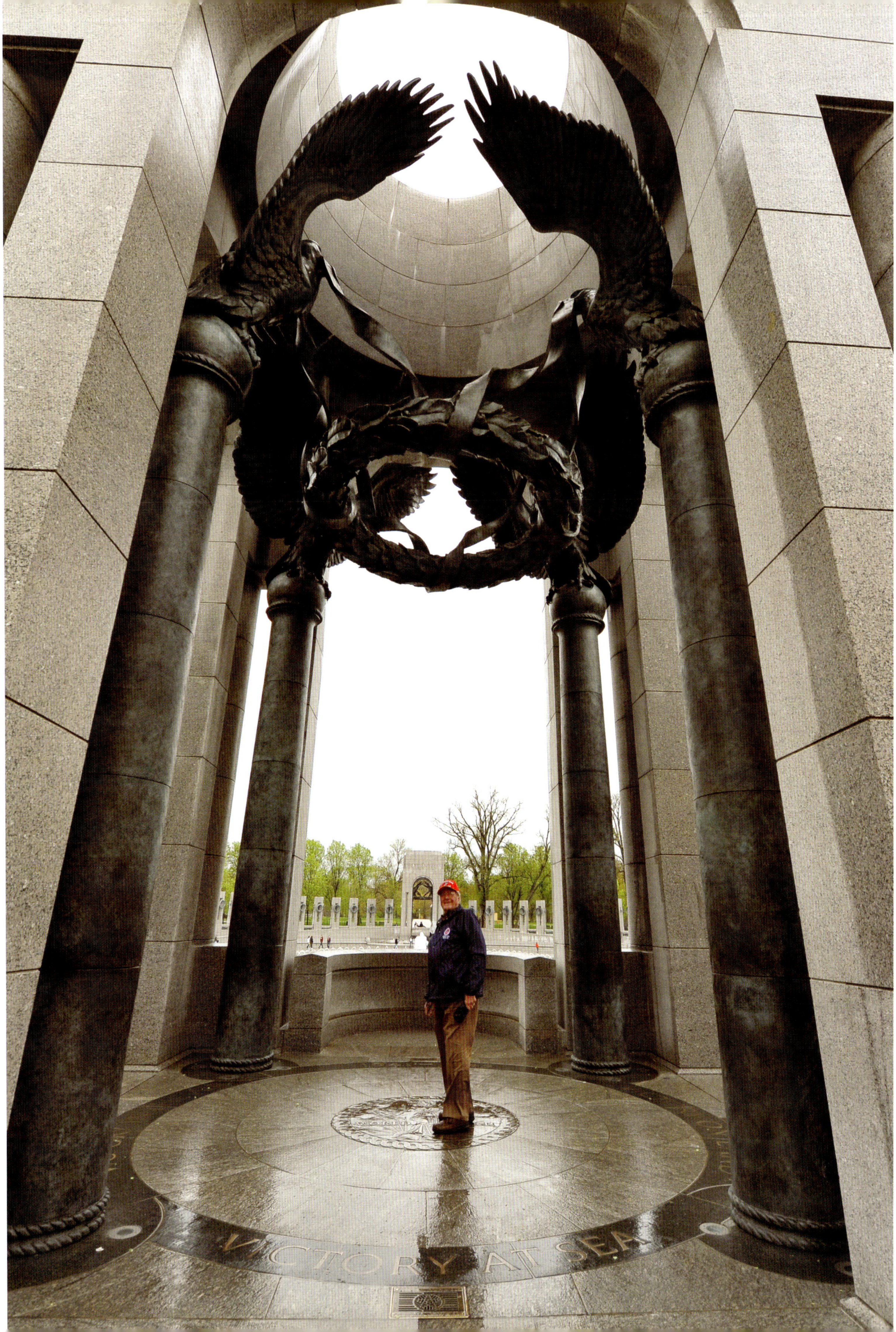
VICTORY AT SEA

Our WWII veterans are often overwhelmed when they first see their national memorial, which honors the 16,000,000 Americans who served, the more than 400,000 who died, and all those who supported the war effort at home. WWII veteran Julian Plaster recalls this from his Stars and Stripes Honor Flight: "When I first walked into the memorial I felt very small. Then I looked at the pillars surrounding me and felt like they were embracing me and welcoming me home."

PACIFIC
BATTLE OF MIDWAY JUNE 4-7 1942
THE WAR'S END
GUADALCANAL • NEW GUINEA • BUNA • TARAWA • KWAJALEIN • ATTU • SAIPAN TINIAN GUAM • PHILIPPINE SEA

U.S. COAST GUARD
VETERAN
HONOR FLIGHT
WISCONSIN
OPERATION
RESOLVE
Francis

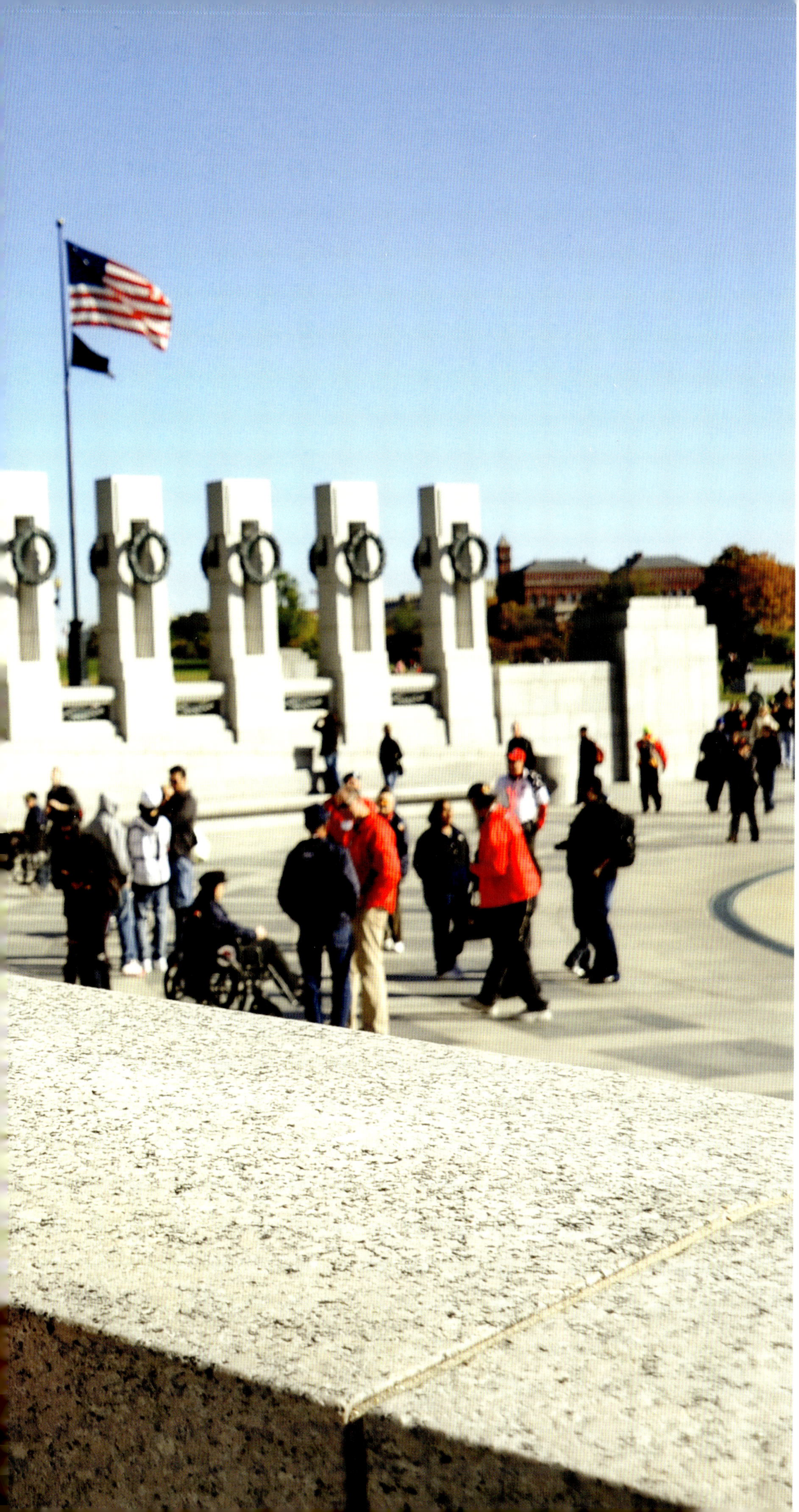

Former Senator Bob Dole (above, in white shirt) and his wife, former Senator Elizabeth Dole (opposite, orange shirt), have greeted thousands of Honor Flight veterans from across the country at the entrance to the WWII National Memorial. Senator Dole, himself a WWII veteran, was the driving force behind the memorial's funding and construction.

131

Sometimes our veterans are surprised by family and friends who have traveled to Washington, D.C., to greet them at the memorial. Often, our veterans are approached by strangers who simply want to shake their hands and thank them for their service.

132

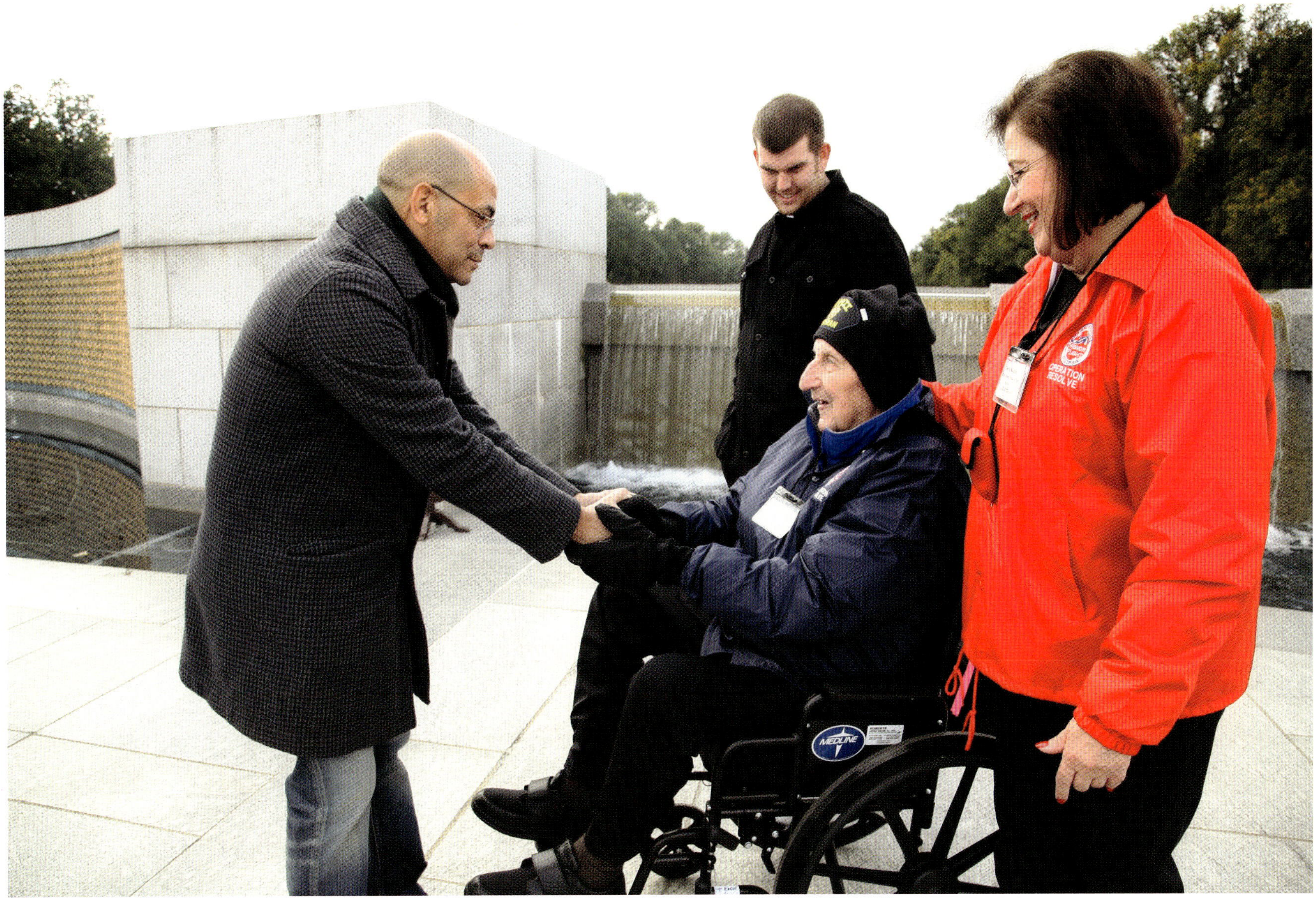
OPERATION
RESOLVE
MEDLINE

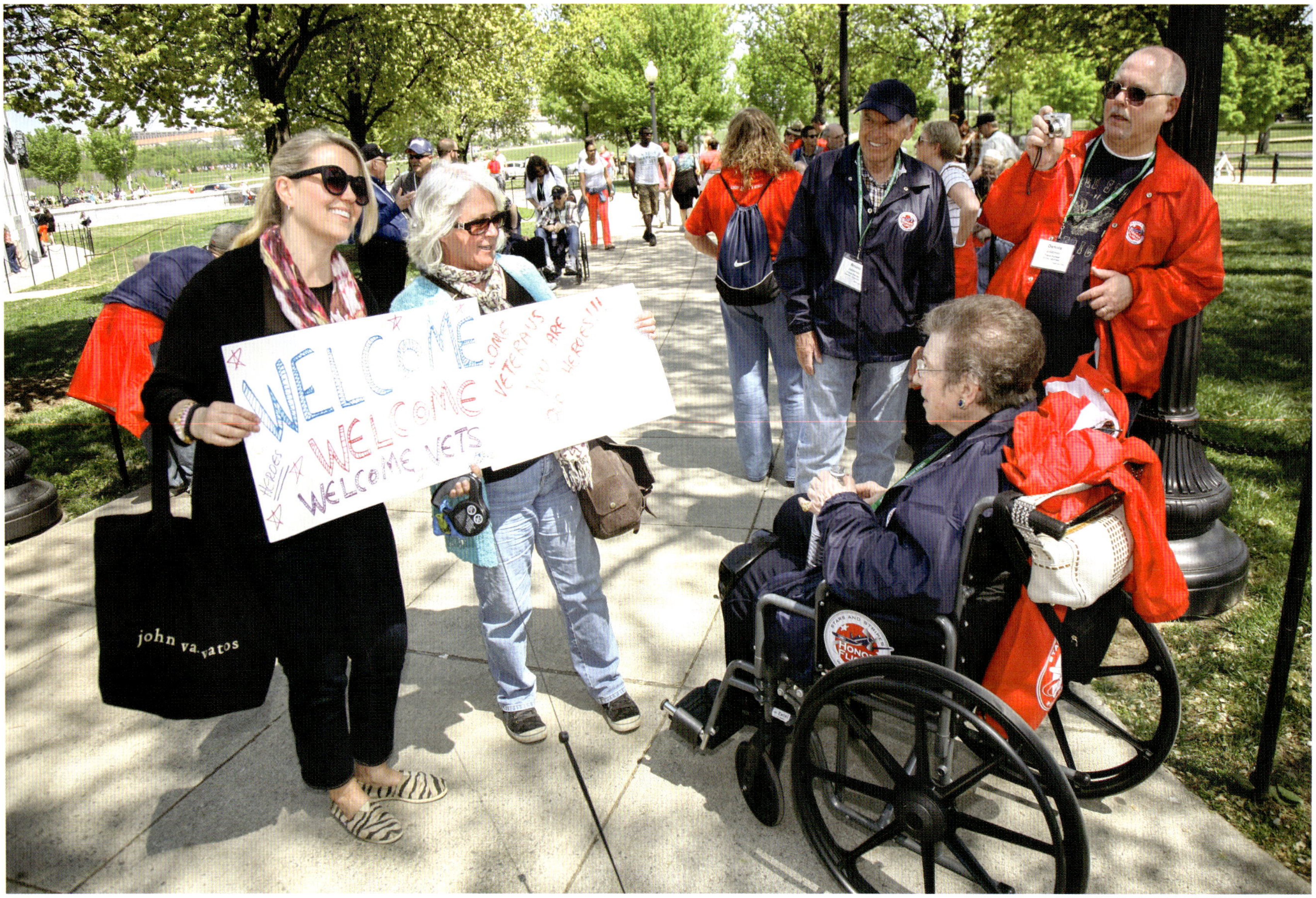
WELCOME
WELCOME
WELCOME VETS

HONOR FLIGHT
WISCONSIN
OPERATION RESOLVE
Stars and Stripes Honor Flight
Gustave
Heinecke
Ann Moore

Stars and Stripes Honor Flight founder Joe Dean (foreground, red shirt) and Retired U.S. Navy Vice Admiral and former Chief of the Navy Reserve Dirk Debbink address a SSHF group at the memorial.

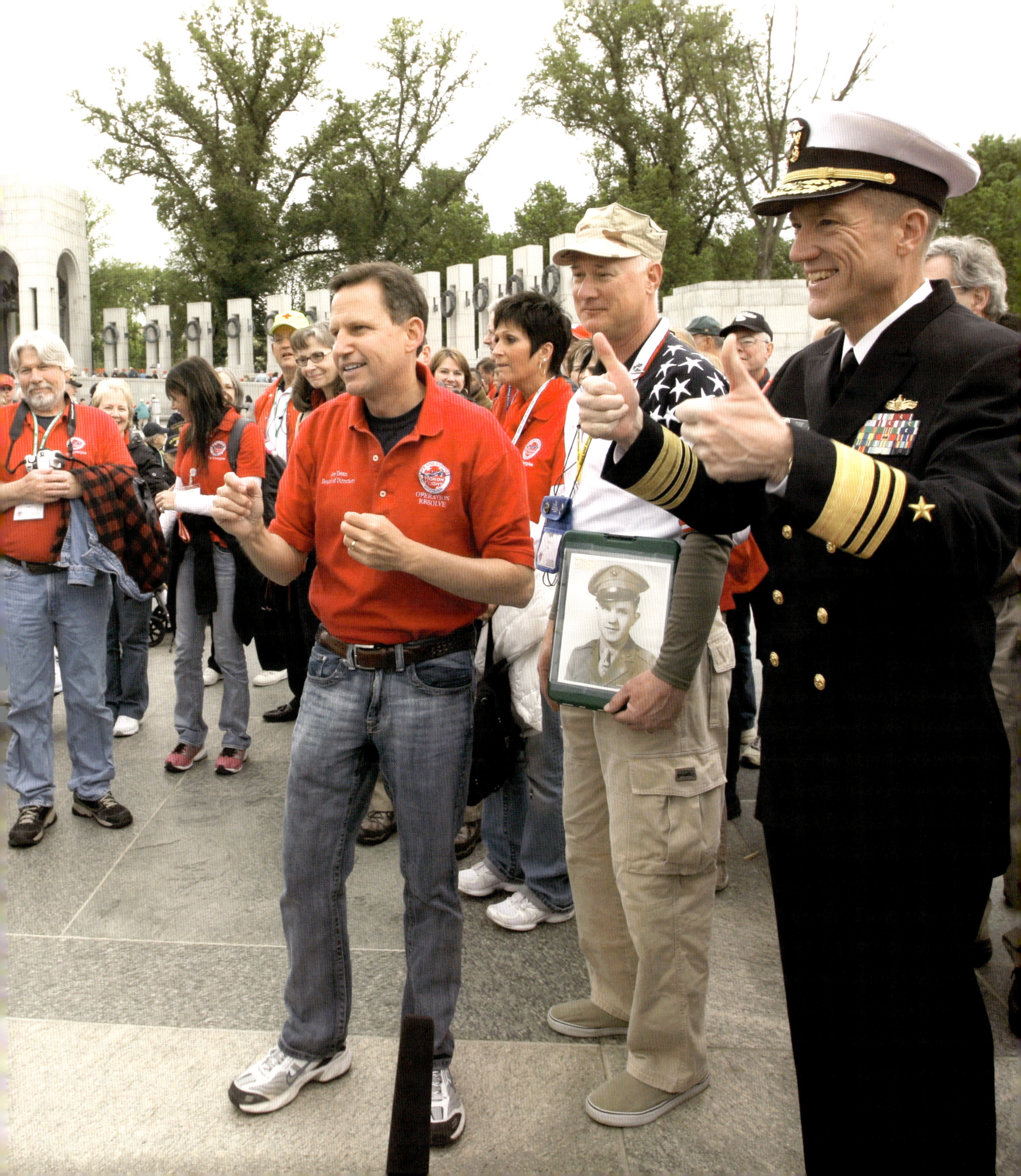
OPERATION
RESOLVE

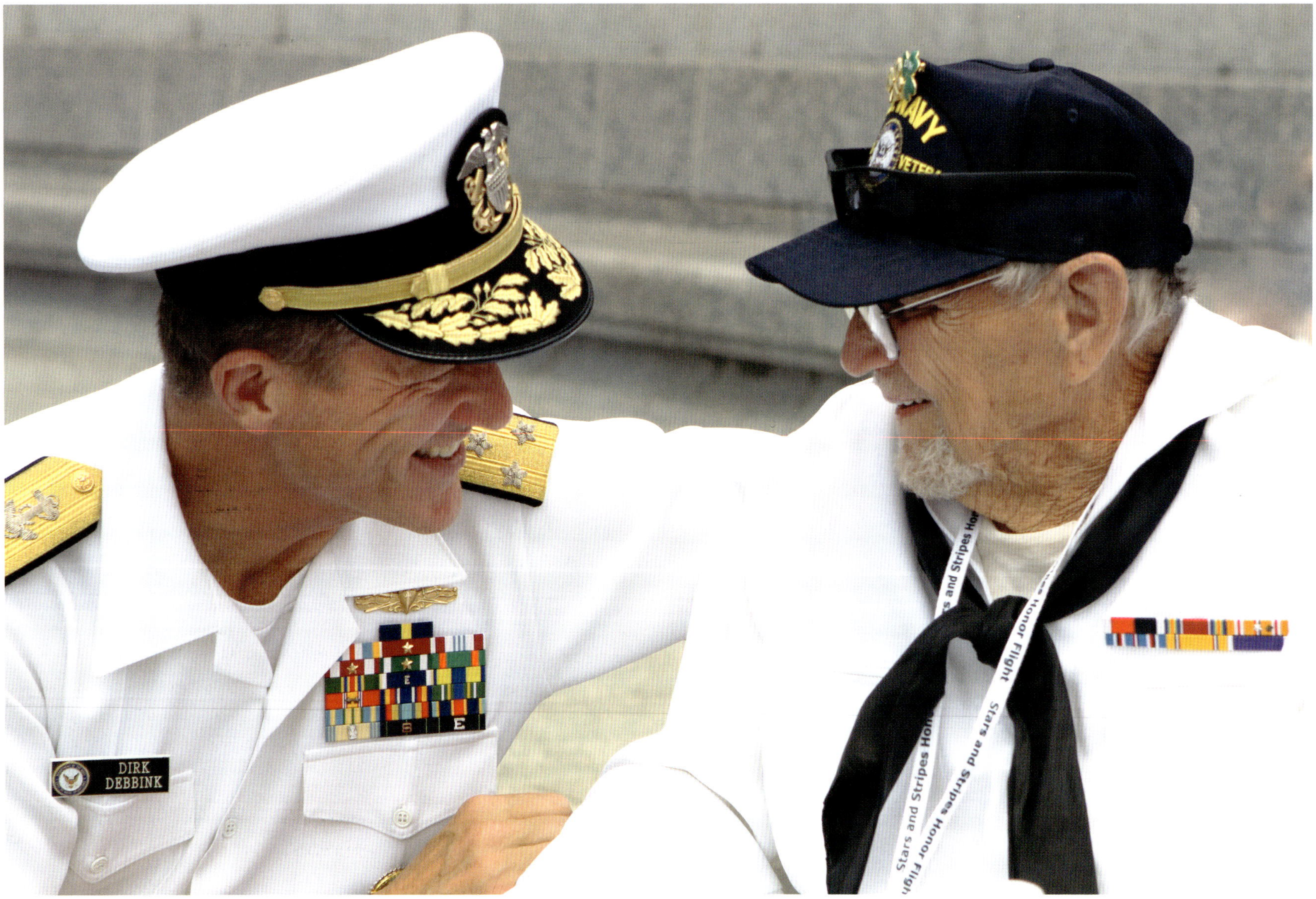
DIRK
DEBBINK
NAVY
Stars and Stripes Honor Flight

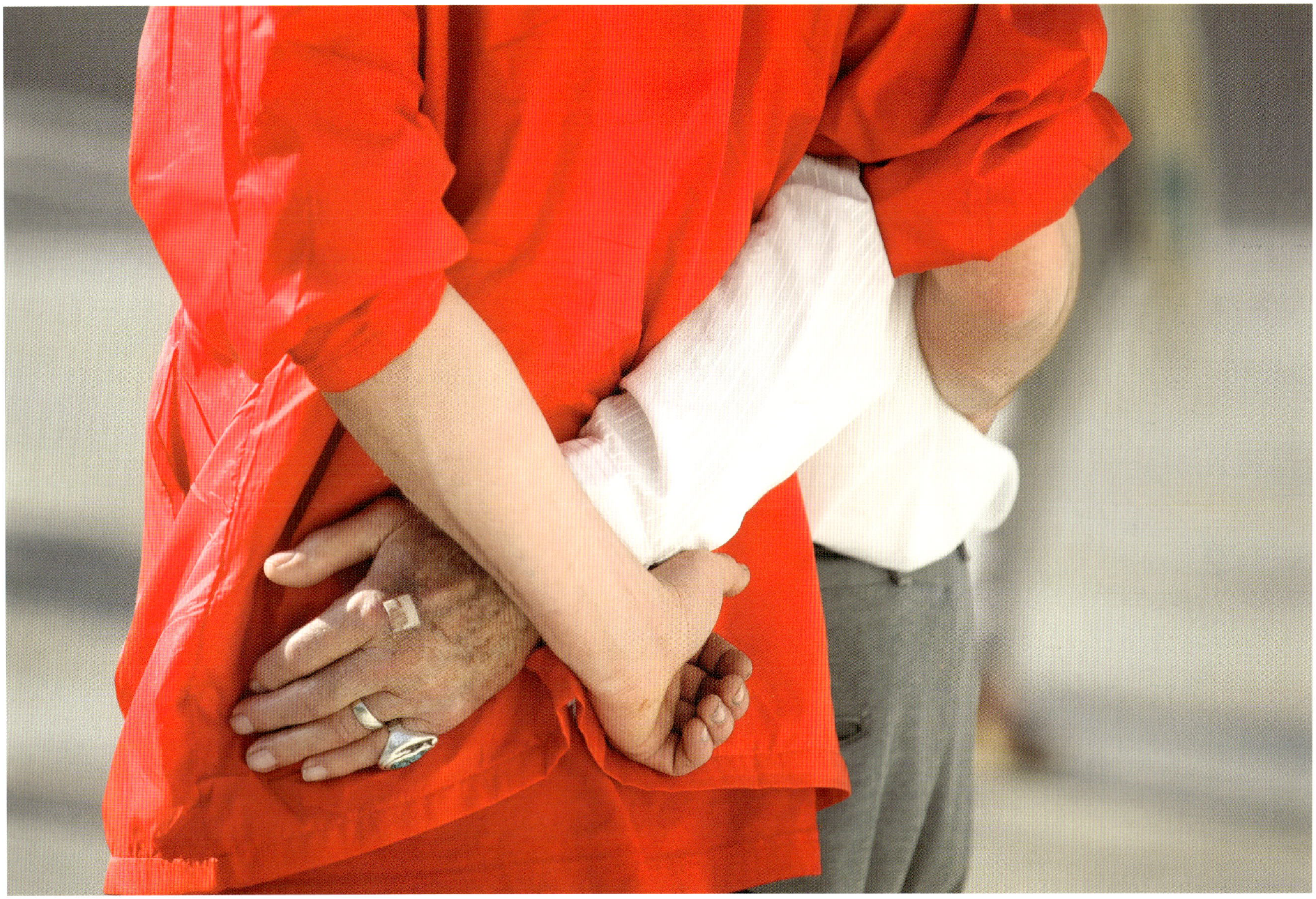

By the time the National WWII Memorial opened in 2004, only a quarter of the Americans who served were still alive. For those veterans who did not have a chance to see their memorial, their families find a different way to honor them.

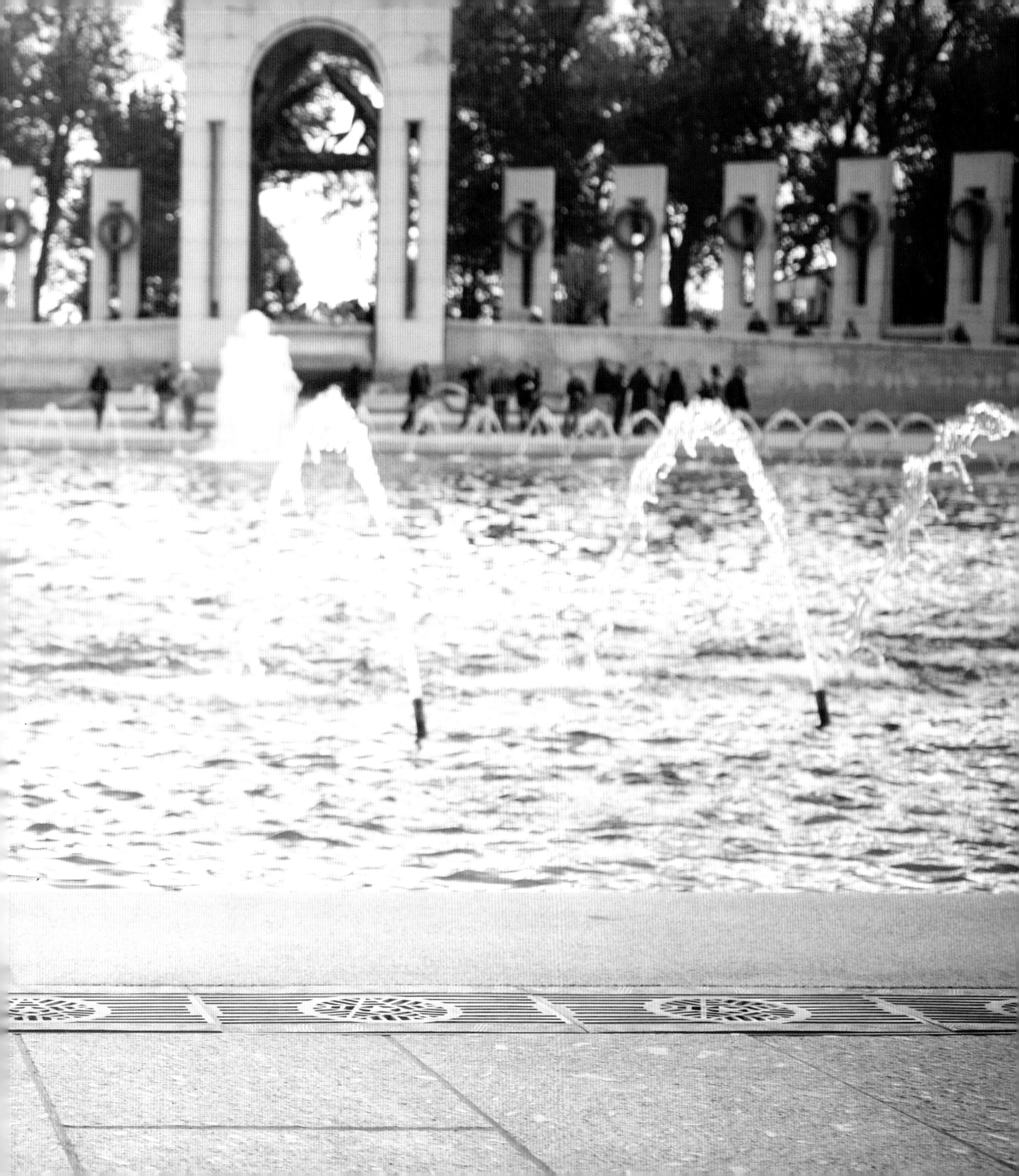

Since the beginning of the Honor Flight Network, the common sentiment expressed by so many of our WWII veterans is that they are undeserving of such an experience. They made it out alive, they reason; the real heroes are the ones who didn't come back. This notion weighs heavy on the hearts of our veterans when they visit the memorial, and many of them are moved to honor their fallen brothers and sisters. Here, a veteran participates in a flag ceremony at the Wisconsin pillar representing all the men and women from our state who gave their last full measure of devotion.

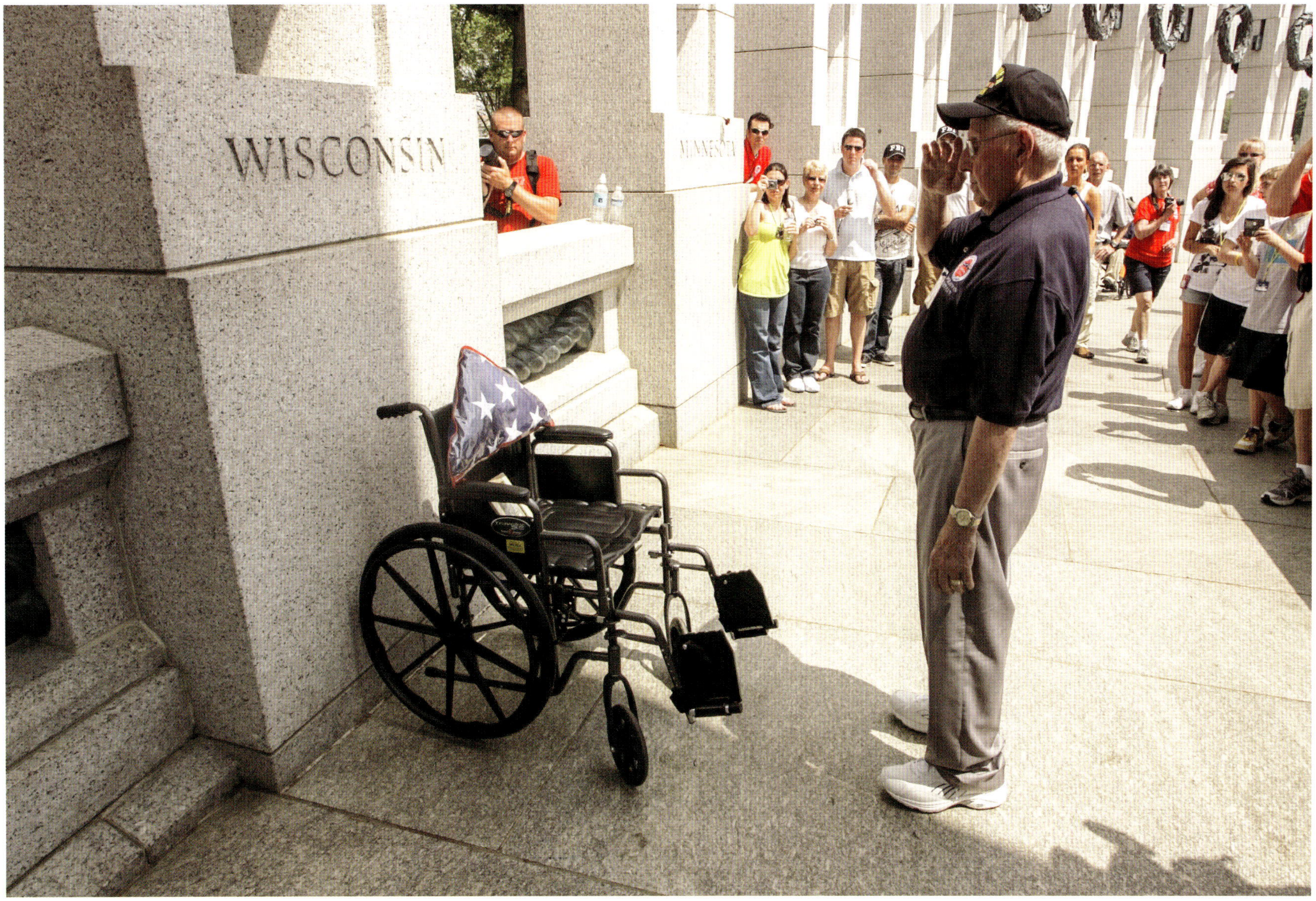
WISCONSIN
MINNESOTA

KILROY
WAS
HERE

IN MEMORY OF
JAMES M.
Schachner
U.S. ARMY
WWII

WISCONSIN

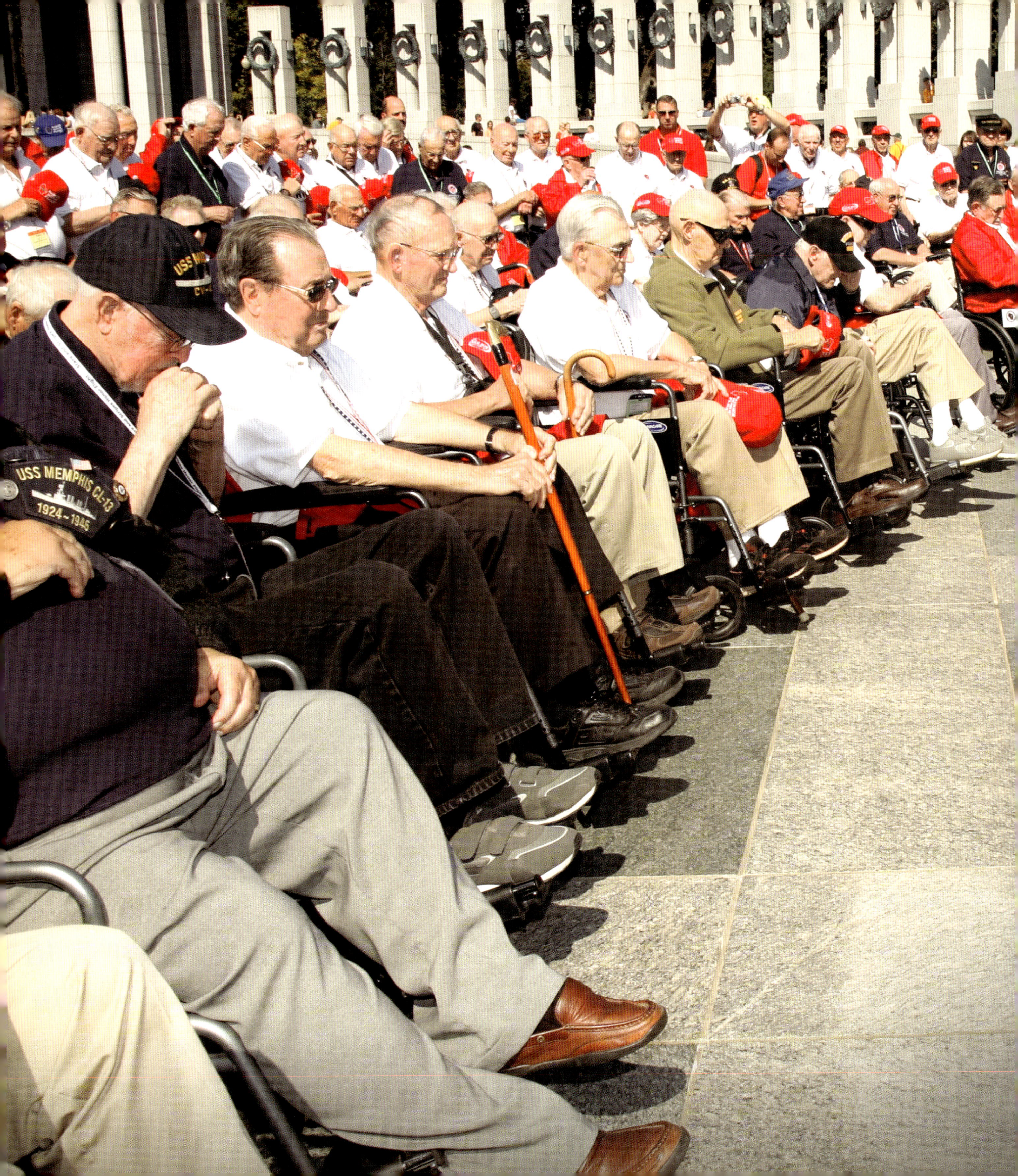
USS MEMPHIS CL-13
1924~1946

Stars and Stripes Honor Flight founder Joe Dean often leads the group of veterans in prayer on the site of the National WWII Memorial. Joe reminds the veterans that they are in the shadow of the Lincoln Memorial and will reflect on what our 16th president said of a different time, "The world will little note nor long remember what we say here, but it can never forget what you have done."

Alvin Kind
Stars and Stripes Honor Flight
Alpha 4
STARS AND STRIPES
HONOR FLIGHT
WISCONSIN
OPERATION RESOLVE

149

434
OAK
Gary Masnak
STARS AND STRIPES
HONOR FLIGHT
WISCONSIN
OPERATION
RESOLVE

434
STARS AND STRIPES
HONOR FLIGHT
WISCONSIN
OPERATION
RESOLVE
Henry Masnak
Stars and Stripes Honor Flight

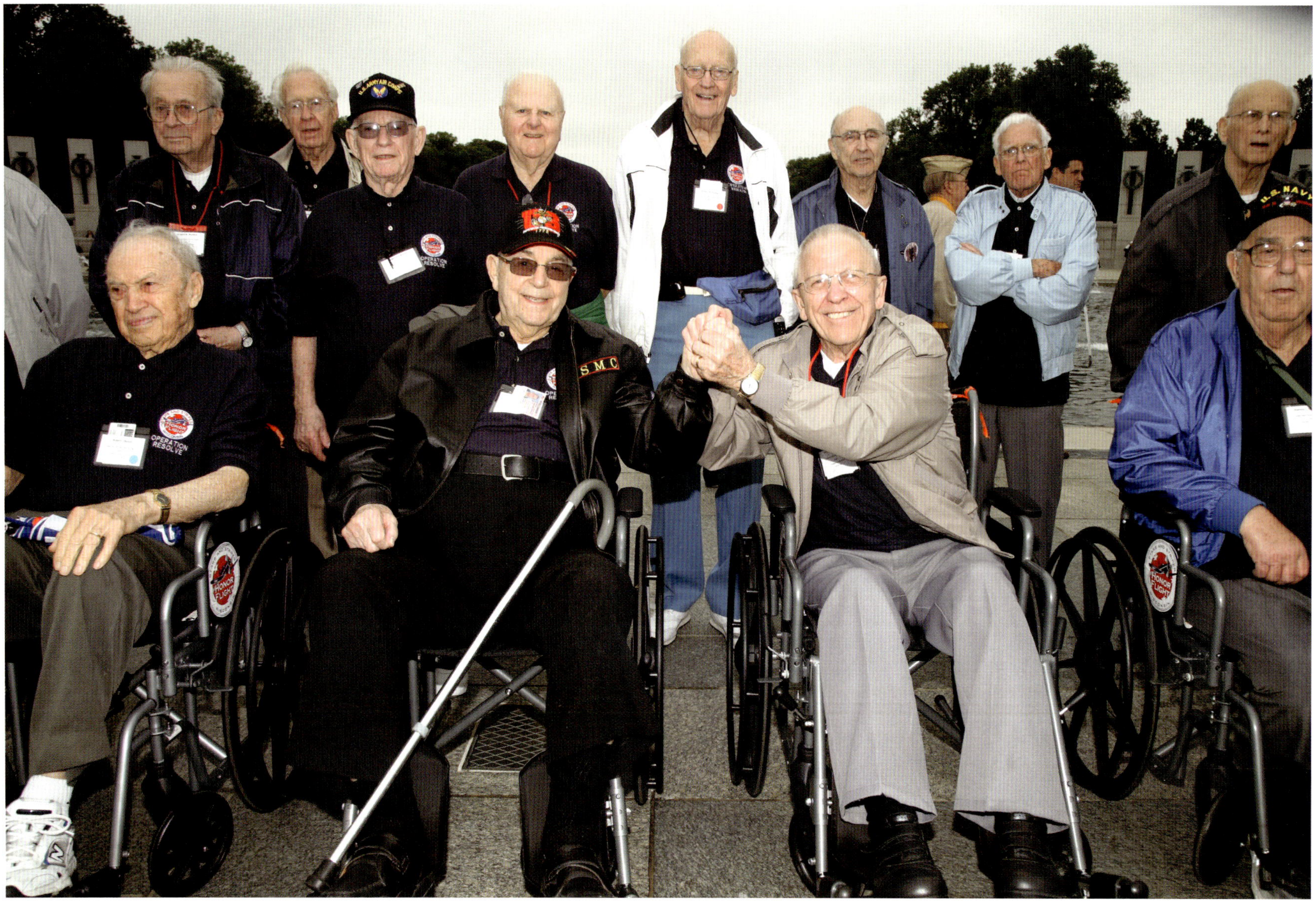
OPERATION RESOLVE
S.M.C
U.S. NAVY

HONOR FLIGHT
WISCONSIN
OPERATION
RESOLVE
George J. Collura

154

U.S. MARINE CORPS
VETERAN
NAVY
Canon
OPERATION RESOLVE
MISS USO

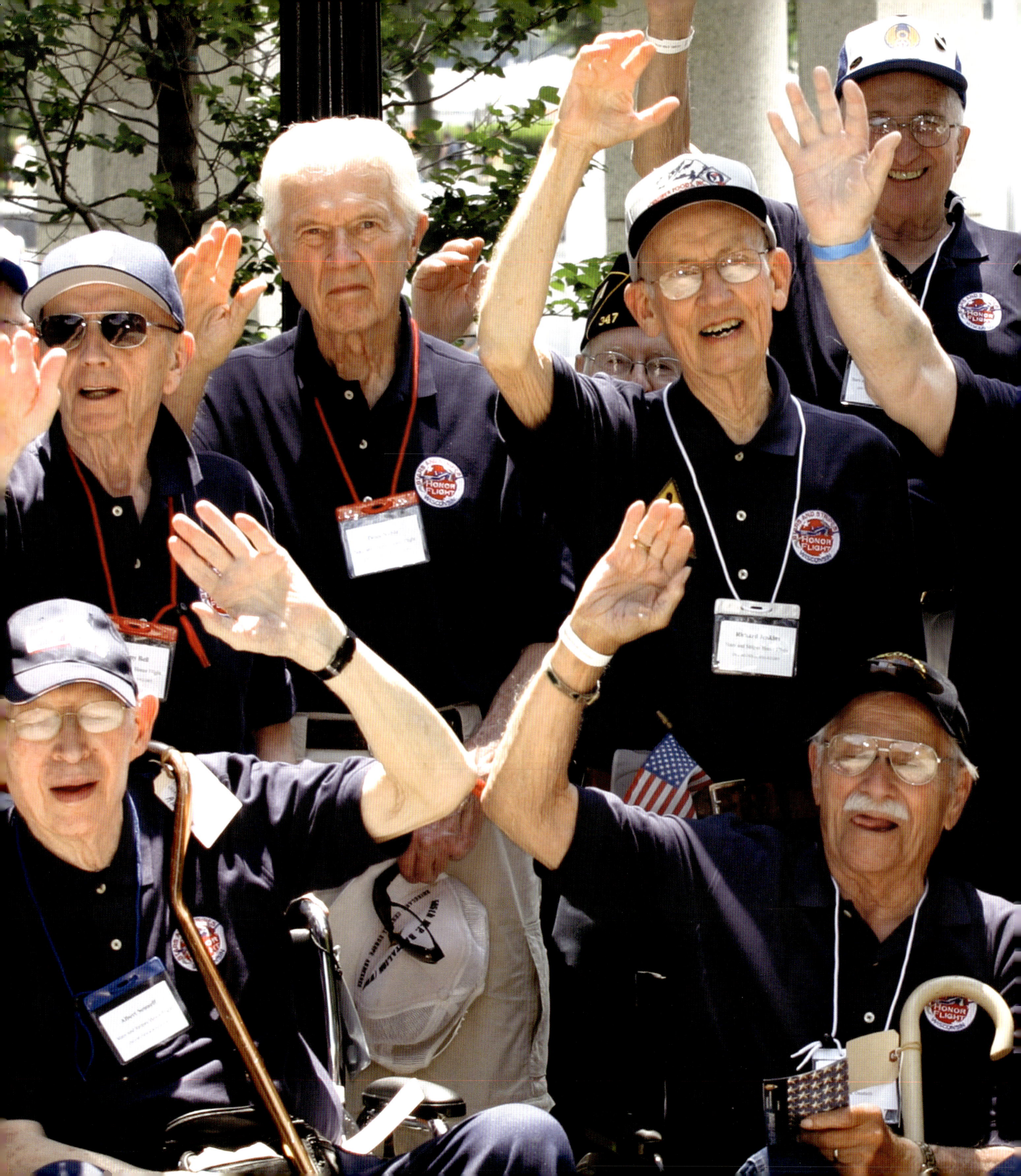
HONOR FLIGHT
347

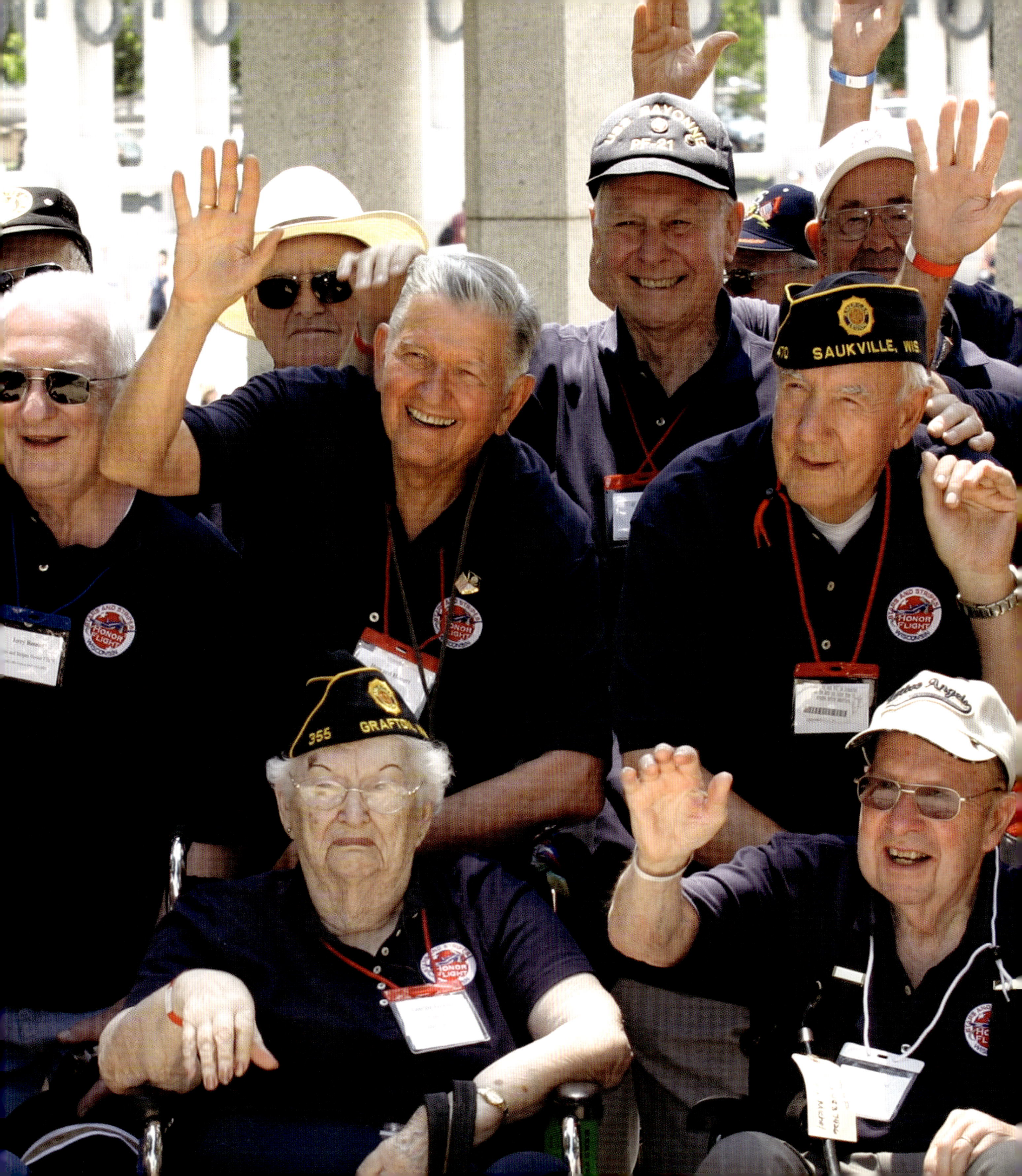
470 SAUKVILLE, WIS.
355 GRAFTON
HONOR FLIGHT

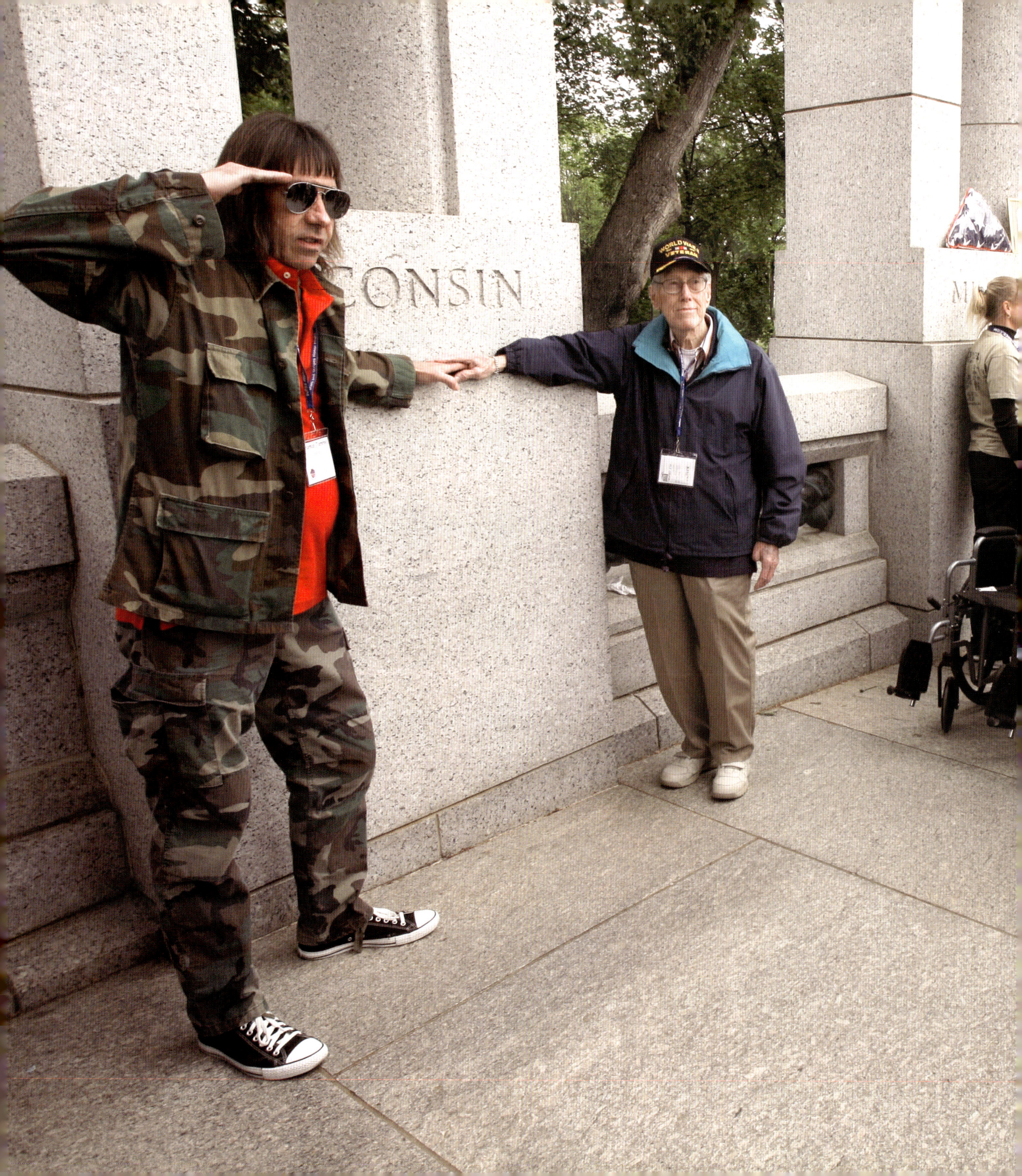
CONSIN

The home-state pillar of each Honor Flight hub is a popular place to take photographs. The 56 granite columns of the WWII Memorial represent the wartime unity of the 48 states, seven federal territories and the District of Columbia.

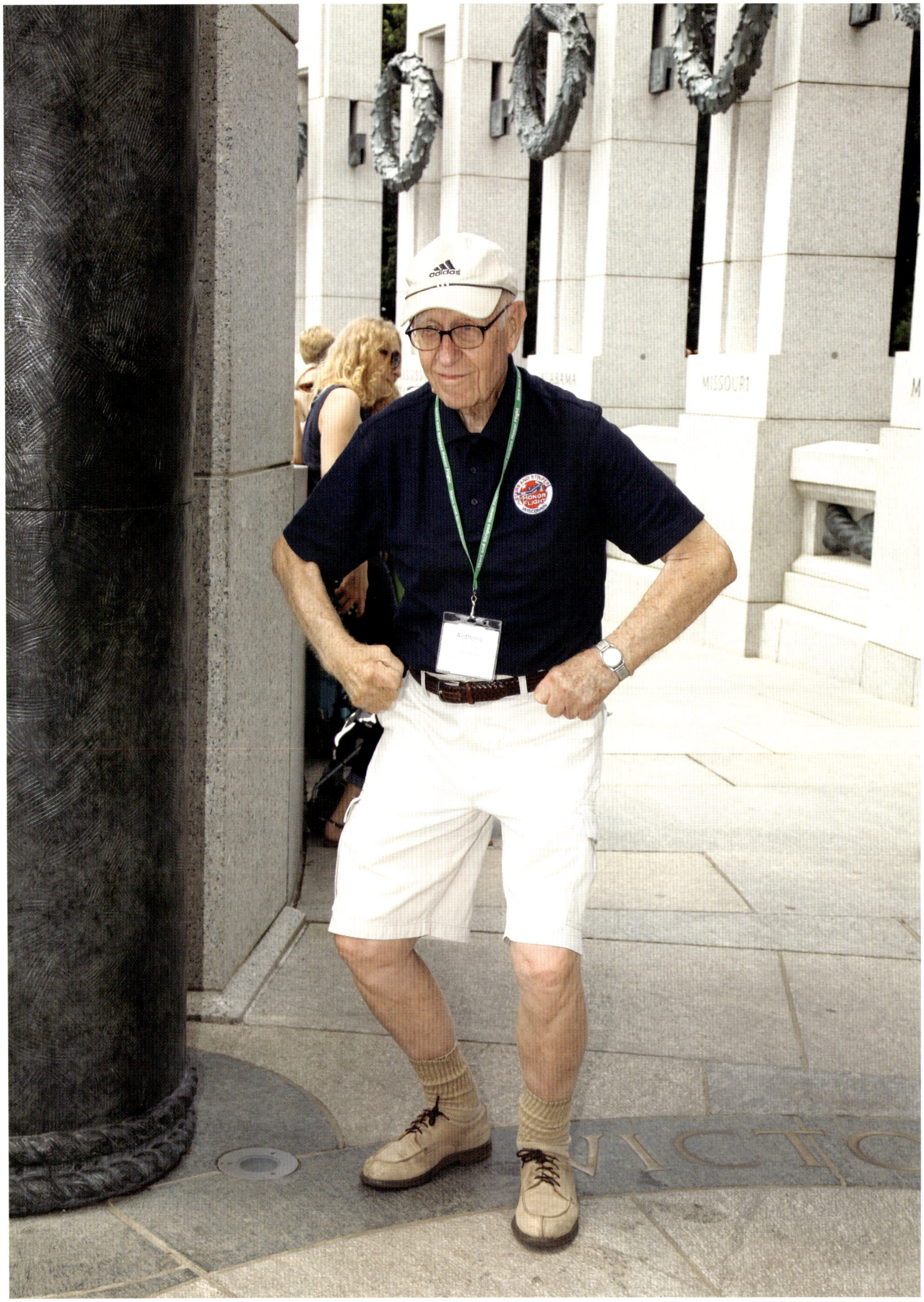
adidas
MISSOURI
VICTO

We often say an Honor Flight is like a "fountain of youth" for our veterans. Veterans in their 80s and 90s will tell us that visiting this memorial makes them feel 18 again – the age they were when they went off to war to protect their country.

DEVOTION

BATTLE OF T

DUTY AND SKILL IN BATTLE.

ENERAL DWIGHT D. EISENHOWER

GERMANY

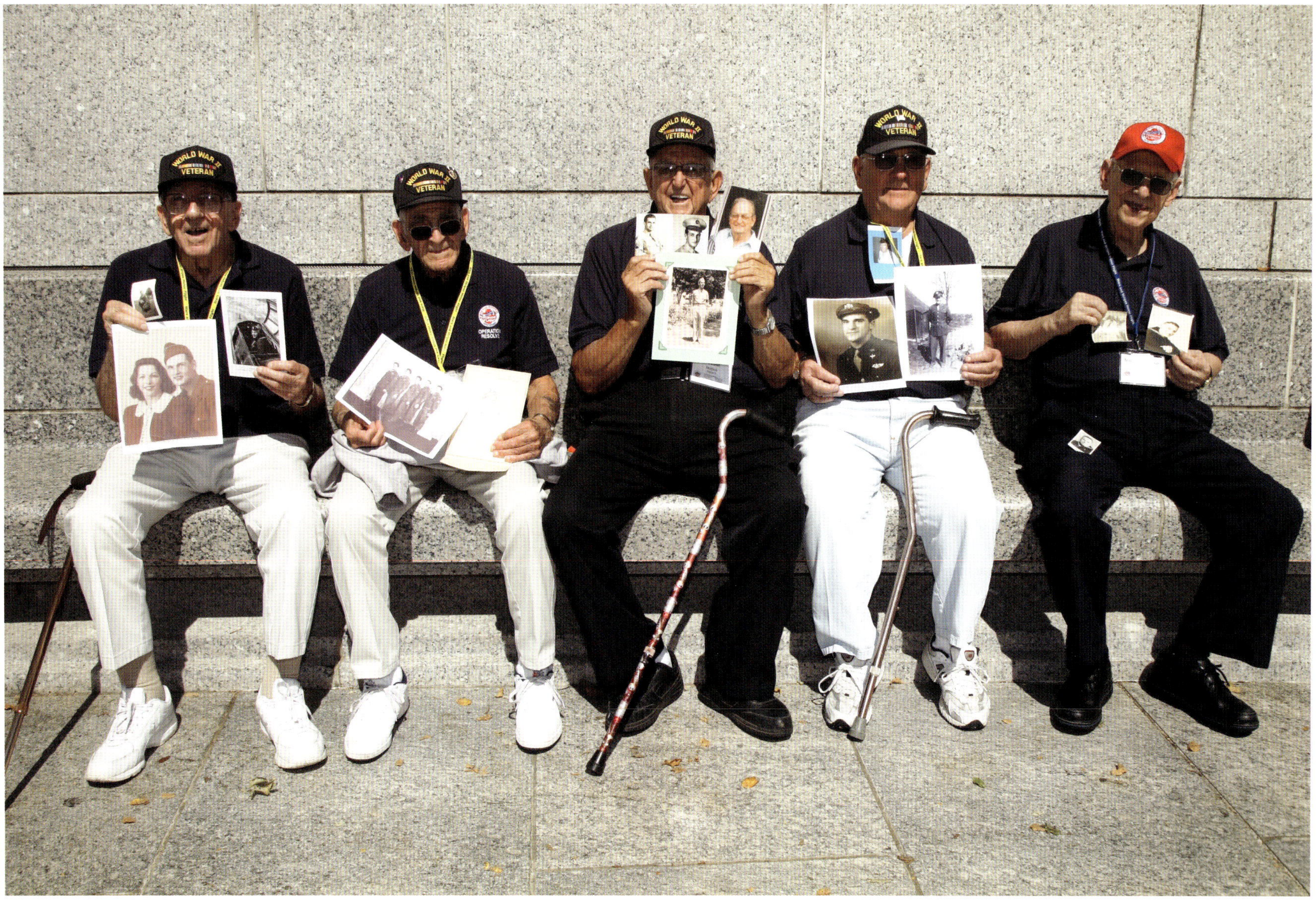
WORLD WAR II
VETERAN

> WOMEN WHO STEPPED UP
> WERE MEASURED AS CITIZENS
> OF THE NATION, NOT AS WOMEN...
> THIS WAS A PEOPLE'S WAR,
> AND EVERYONE WAS IN IT.
>
> — COLONEL OVETA CULP

The field of 4,048 gold stars on the Freedom Wall is a place for somber reflection for Honor Flight veterans. Each star represents 100 American service personnel who died or remain missing. Yet for our veterans each star is more than a number; it represents their friends who never came home. When a family lost a loved one during WWII, a gold star was hung in the front window of the family home as a memorial.

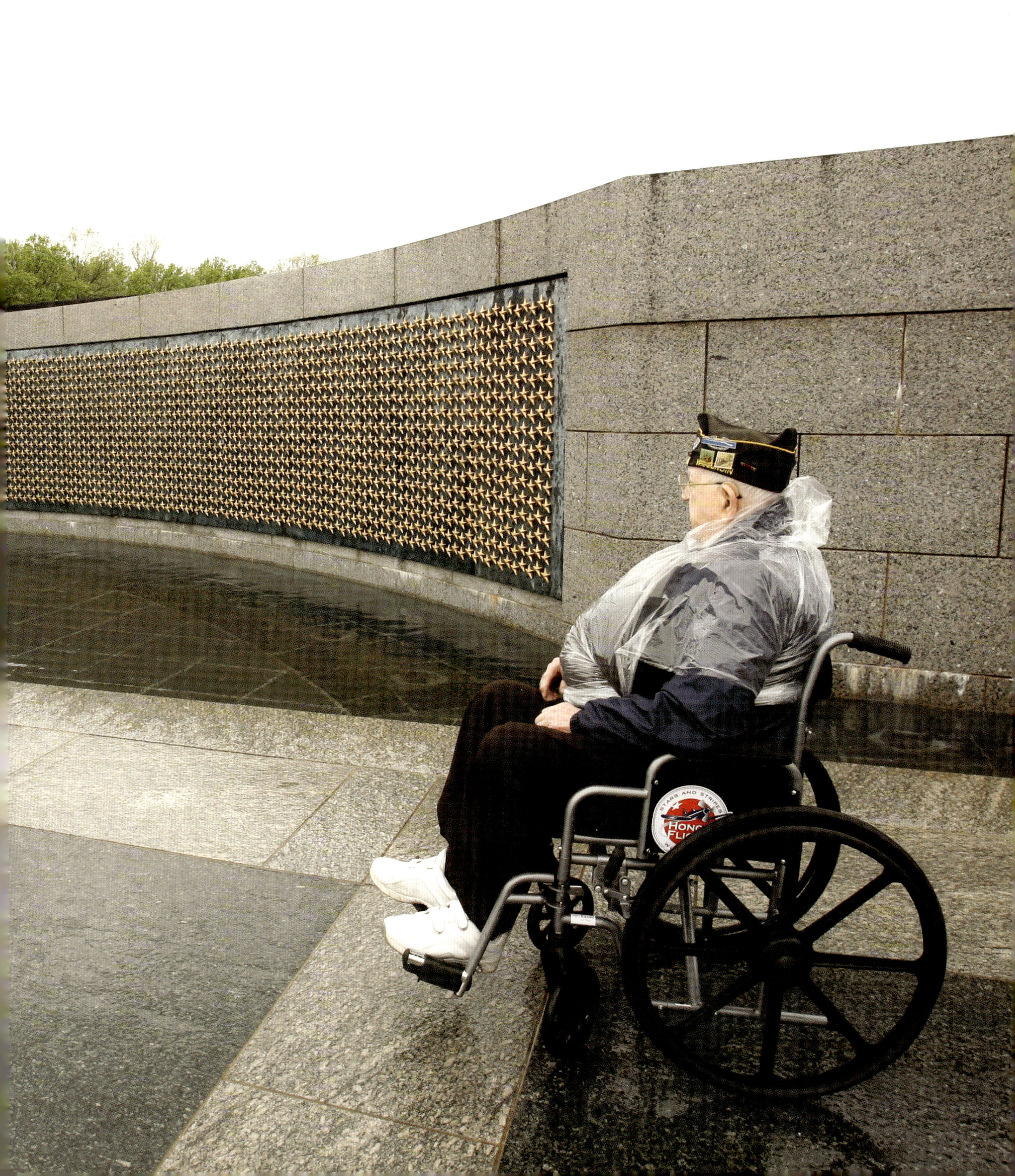
STARS AND STRIPES

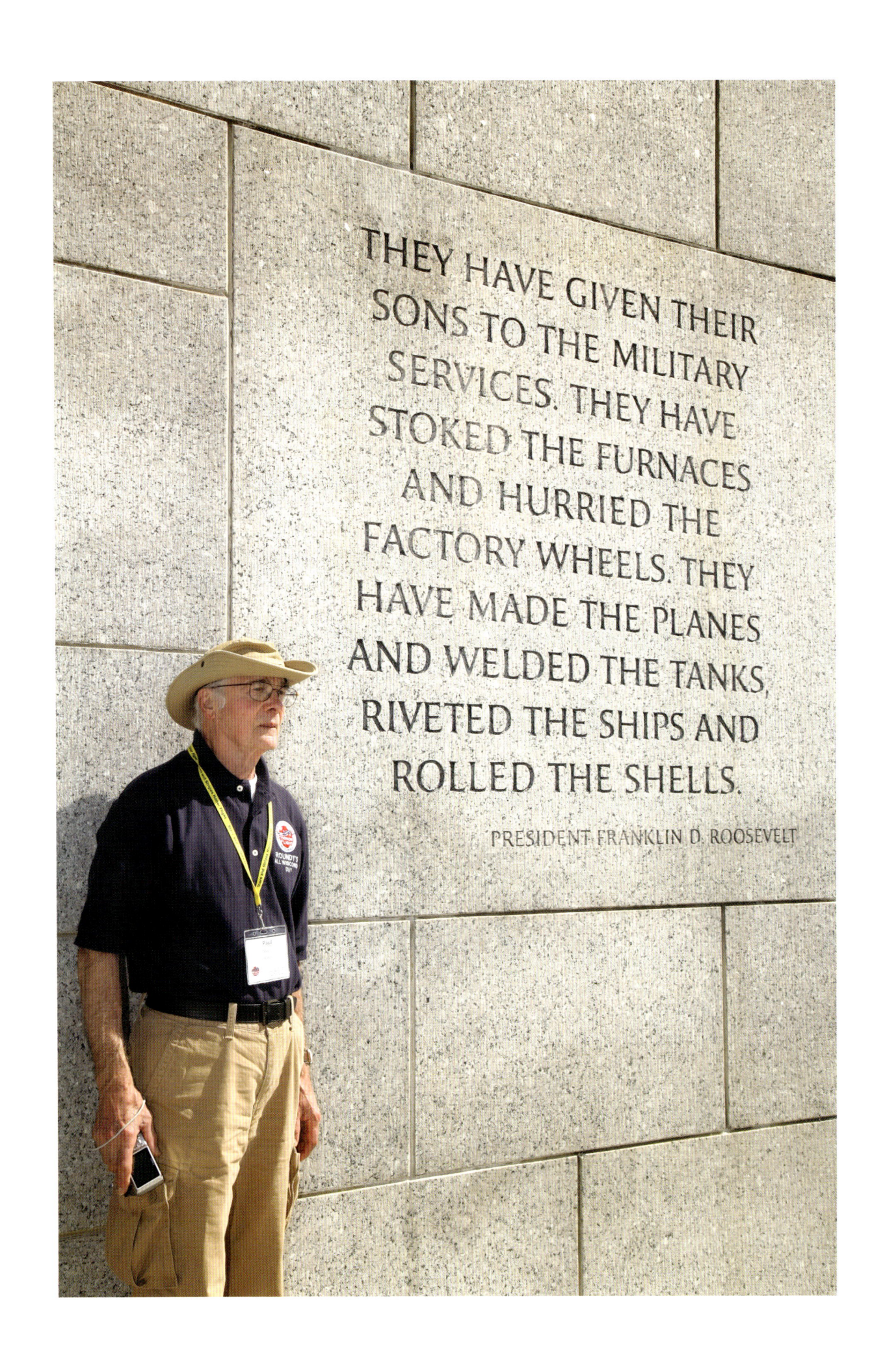

THEY HAVE GIVEN THEIR SONS TO THE MILITARY SERVICES. THEY HAVE STOKED THE FURNACES AND HURRIED THE FACTORY WHEELS. THEY HAVE MADE THE PLANES AND WELDED THE TANKS, RIVETED THE SHIPS AND ROLLED THE SHELLS.

PRESIDENT FRANKLIN D. ROOSEVELT

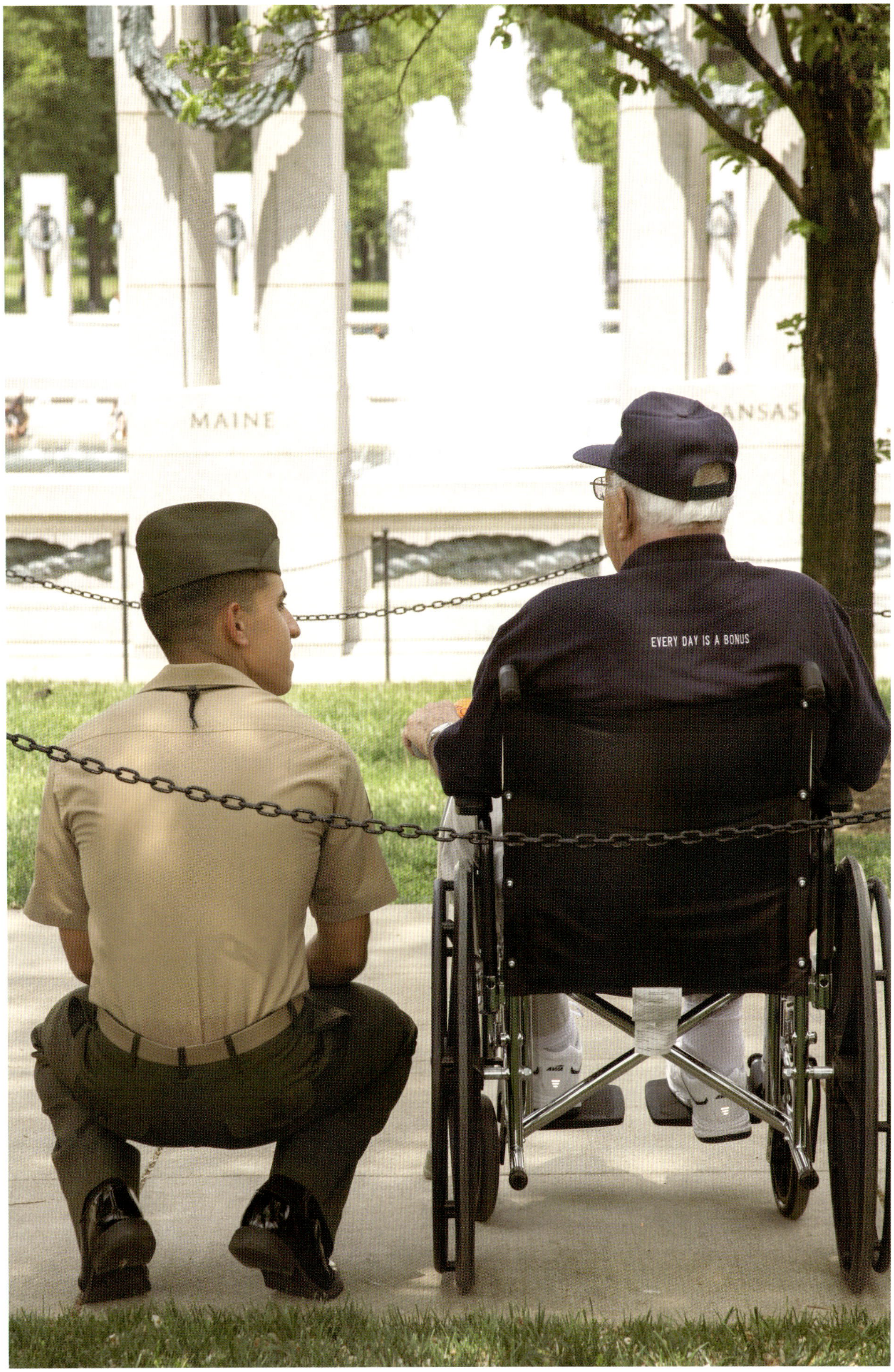
MAINE
EVERY DAY IS A BONUS

170

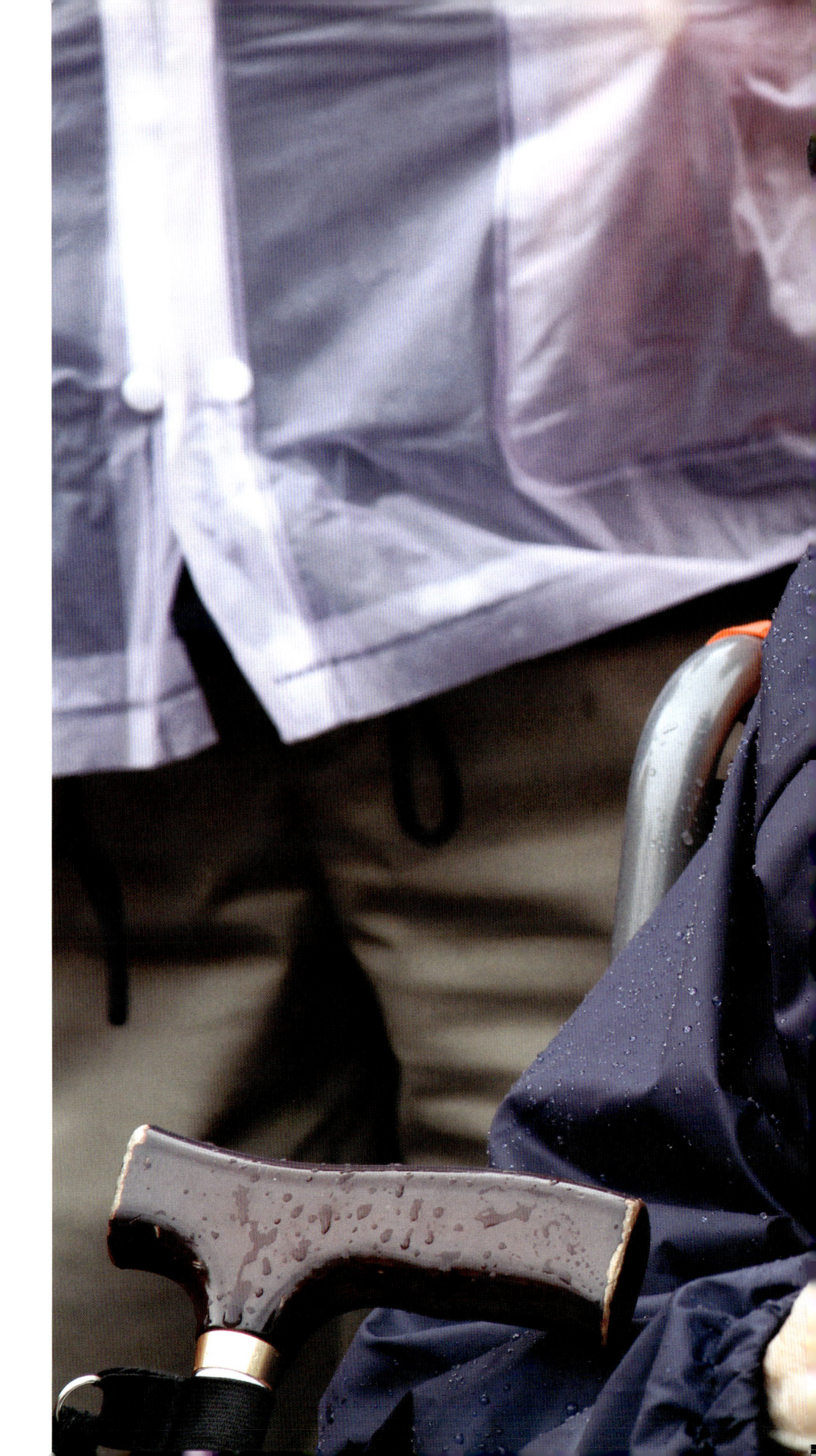

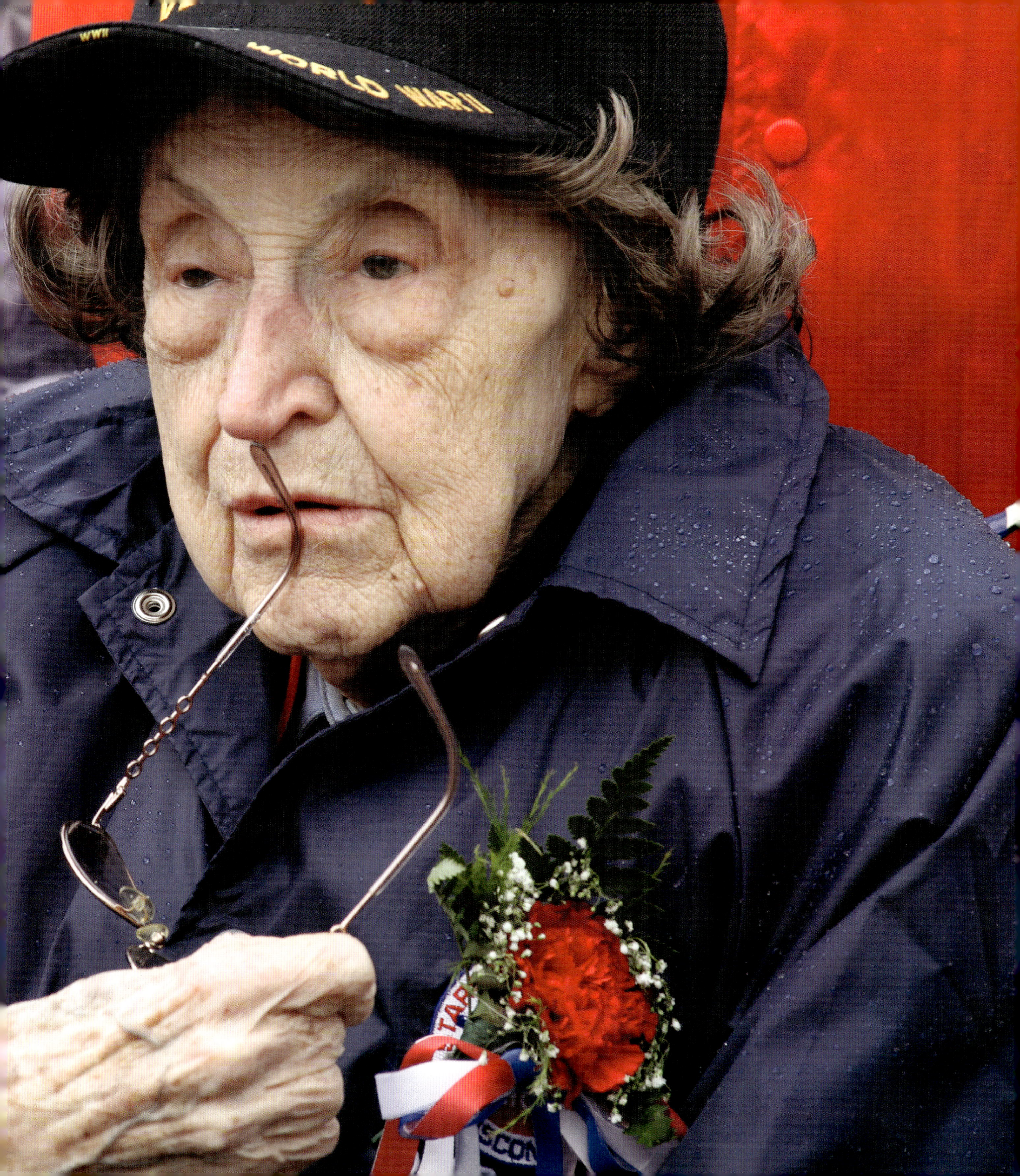
WWII
WORLD WAR II

Many WWII veterans are moved to see the special nod to the doodle that made its way around the world during the war. Veterans and visitors try to find the two hidden "Kilroy was Here" etchings at the memorial.

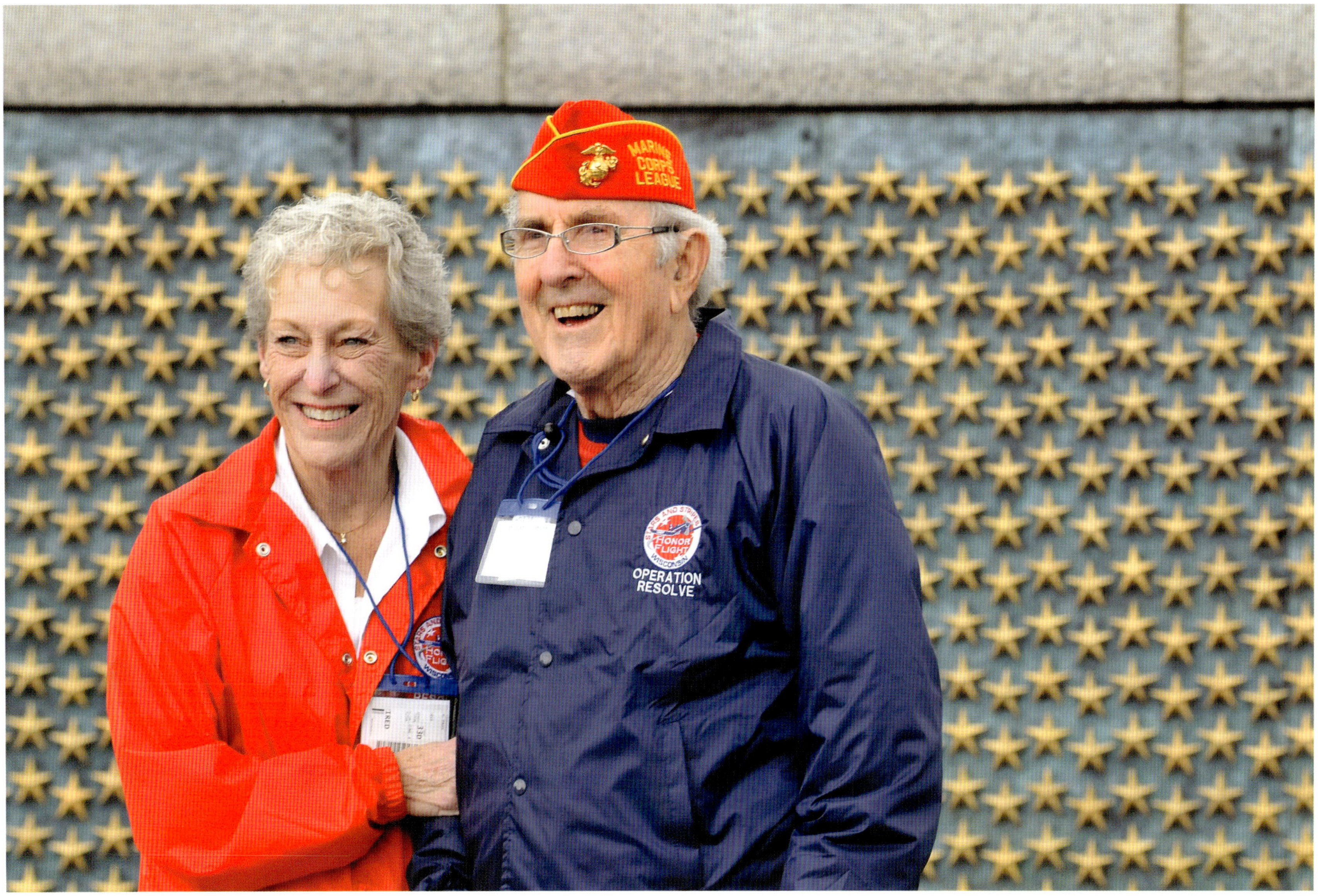
HONOR FLIGHT
OPERATION
RESOLVE

IWO JIMA
SURVIVOR
TODAY THE
HAS ENDED. A C
NO LONGER RAIN
MEN EVERYW
THE EN
Stars and Stripes Honor Flight
OPERATIO
RESOLVE

THE WAR'S END

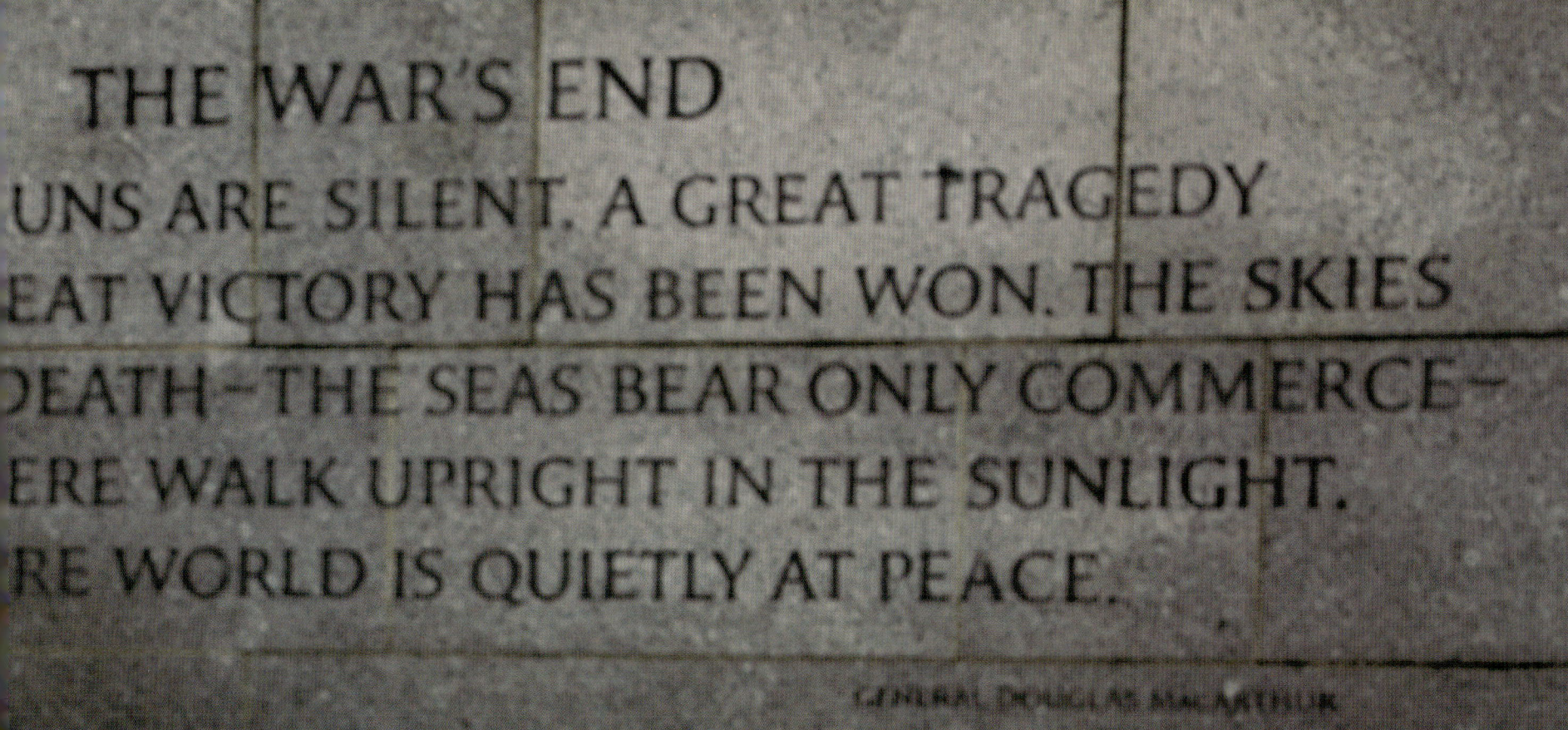

...UNS ARE SILENT. A GREAT TRAGEDY
...EAT VICTORY HAS BEEN WON. THE SKIES
...DEATH – THE SEAS BEAR ONLY COMMERCE –
...ERE WALK UPRIGHT IN THE SUNLIGHT.
...RE WORLD IS QUIETLY AT PEACE.

GENERAL DOUGLAS MACARTHUR

STARS AND STRIPES
HONOR FLIGHT
WISCONSIN
OPERATION
RESOLVE

The Old Man Remembers

The old man is no more, the temple is crumbling.
The old man looks back at his walk through the battle field of life.
The old man never dodged the opportunity to serve his country.
The old man remembers stepping onto the battle field of war.
The old man remembers the bombs of anxiety, fear of losing a friend.
The old man remembers coming home to face more challenges of taking on a partner, being a parent, a neighbor.
The old man dodges the bombs of deceit, hatefulness, discrimination, unemployment, again the bombs of losing a friend, a loved one.
The old man can't dodge the bomb of his temple.
The old man is no more in his temple, the temple is crumbling to dust from which it came.
The old man's temple is no more, but wait the spirit of the old man springs forth as a flower from the dust.
The spirit of the old man will flourish because it is being cared for in his Gods garden.
The spirit of the old man will now find peace and contentment
The temple of the old man is gone, but the spirit of the old man lives on because of the loving care in his God's garden. Amen   Julian R Plaster

HANDWRITTEN BY JULIAN PLASTER, APRIL 2013

Julian traveled with Stars and Stripes Honor Flight in April 2011 and is featured in the film *Honor Flight*

KOREAN WAR VETERANS MEMORIAL
Dedicated July 1995

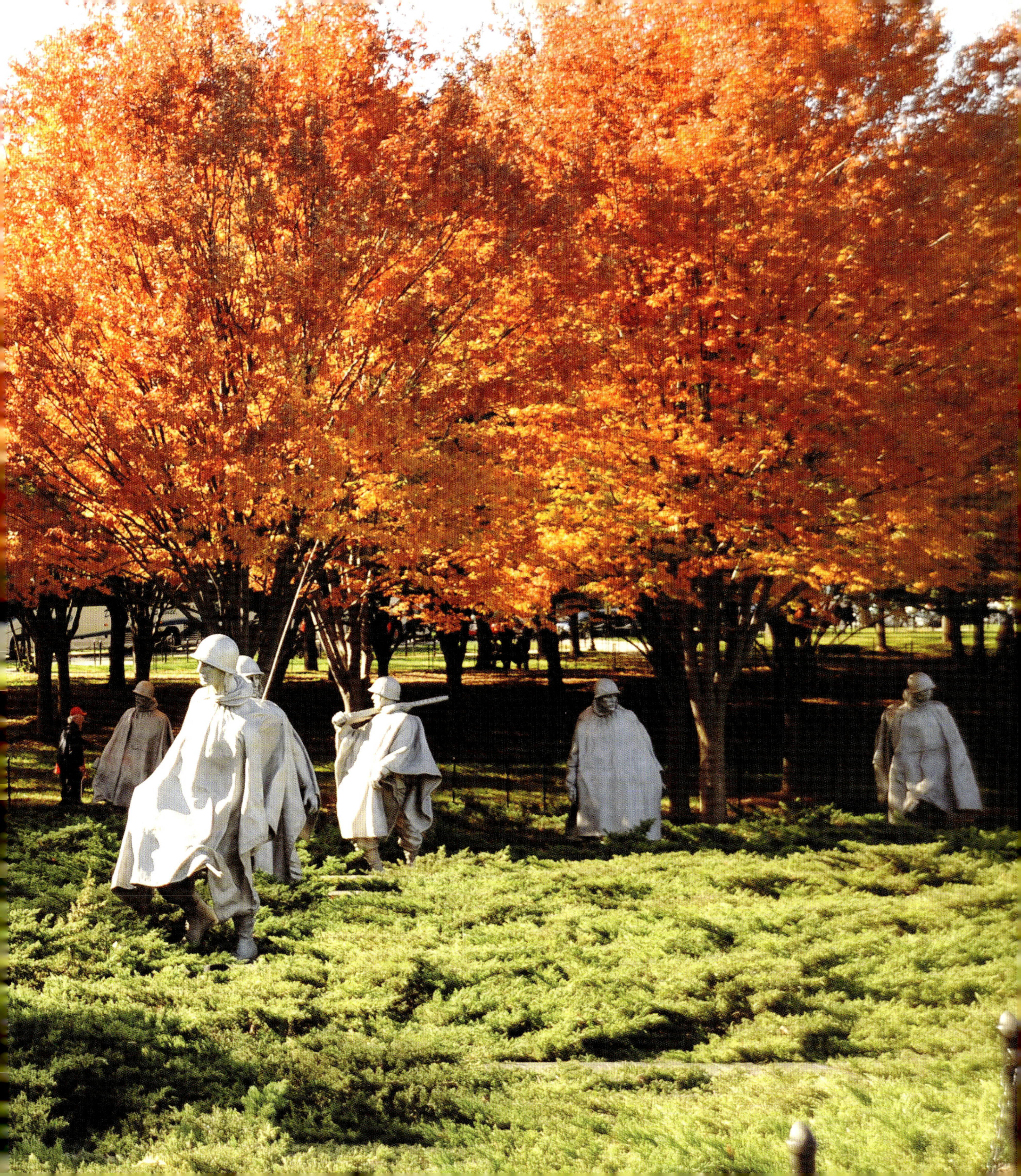

Best known for its 19 stainless-steel "Ghost Patrol" statues, the Korean War Memorial also commemorates its veterans with 2,500 archival images that have been sandblasted onto a 164-foot-long granite wall.

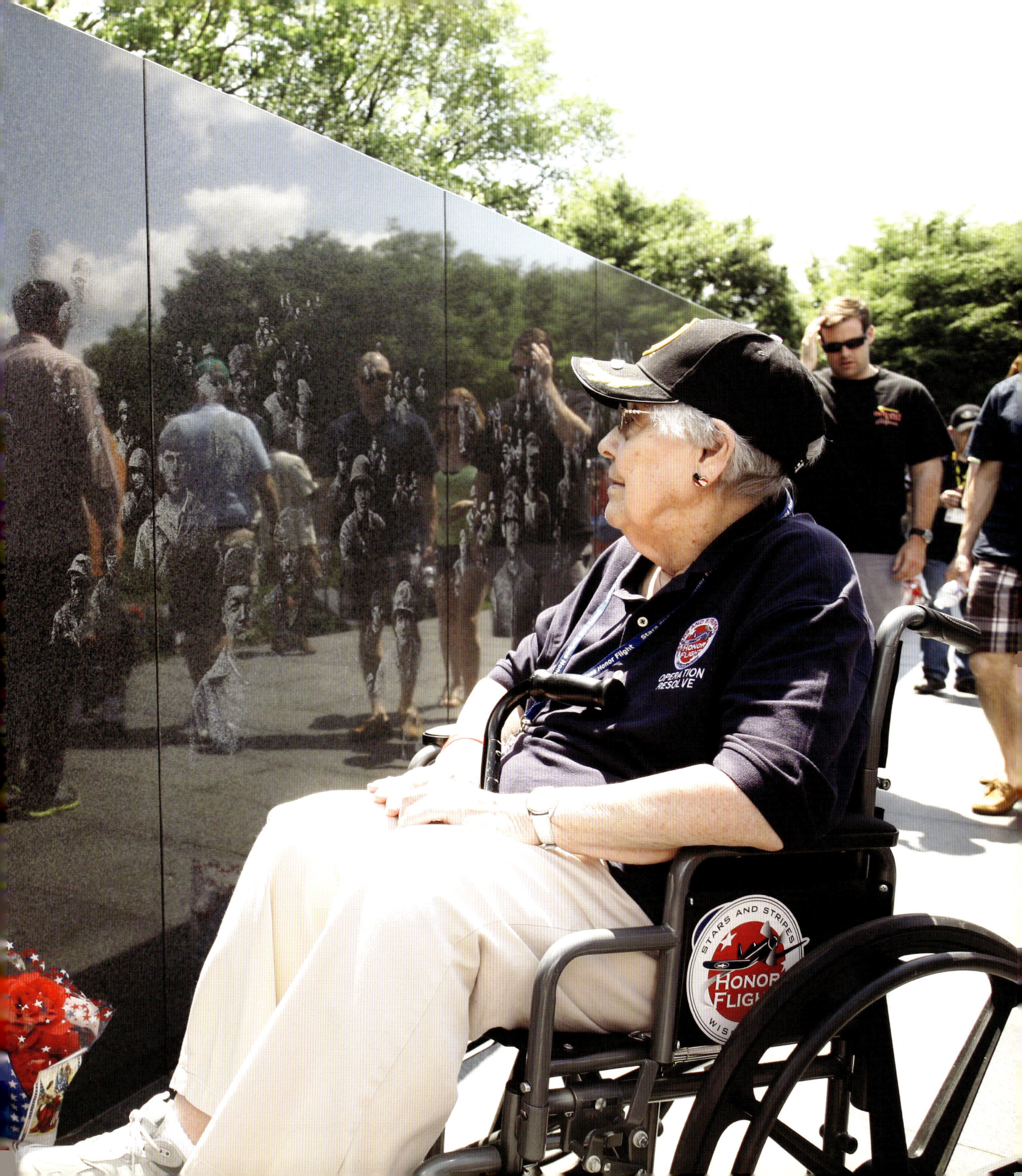
OPERATION
RESOLVE
STARS AND STRIPES

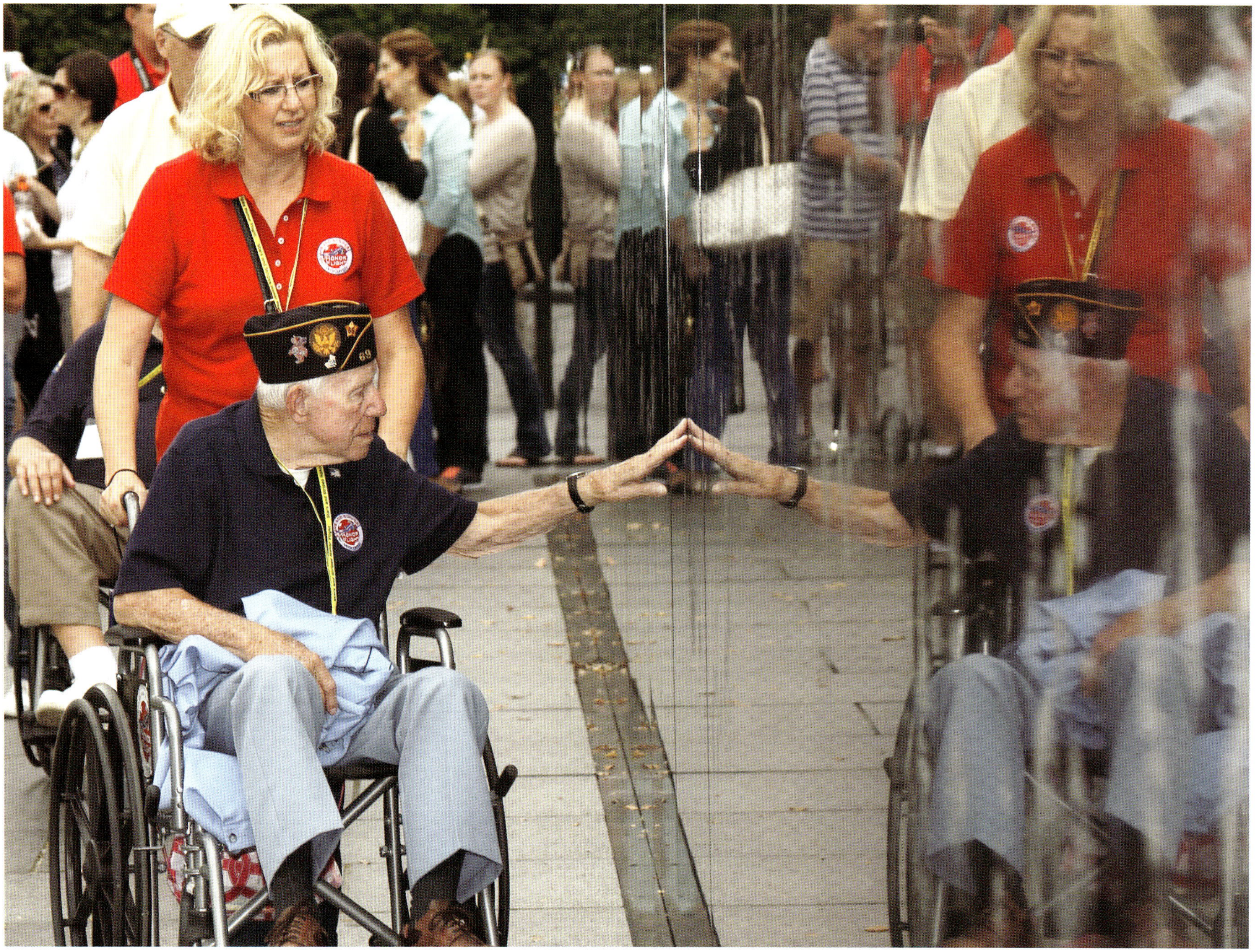

JOHN PALESE —
Thanks for your service!!
TWO WAR VETERAN
WWII
KOREA
Stars and Stripes Honor Flight
STARS AND STRIPES HONOR FLIGHT WISCONSIN

STARS AND STRIPES
HONOR FLIGHT
WISCONSIN
OPERATION
RESOLVE

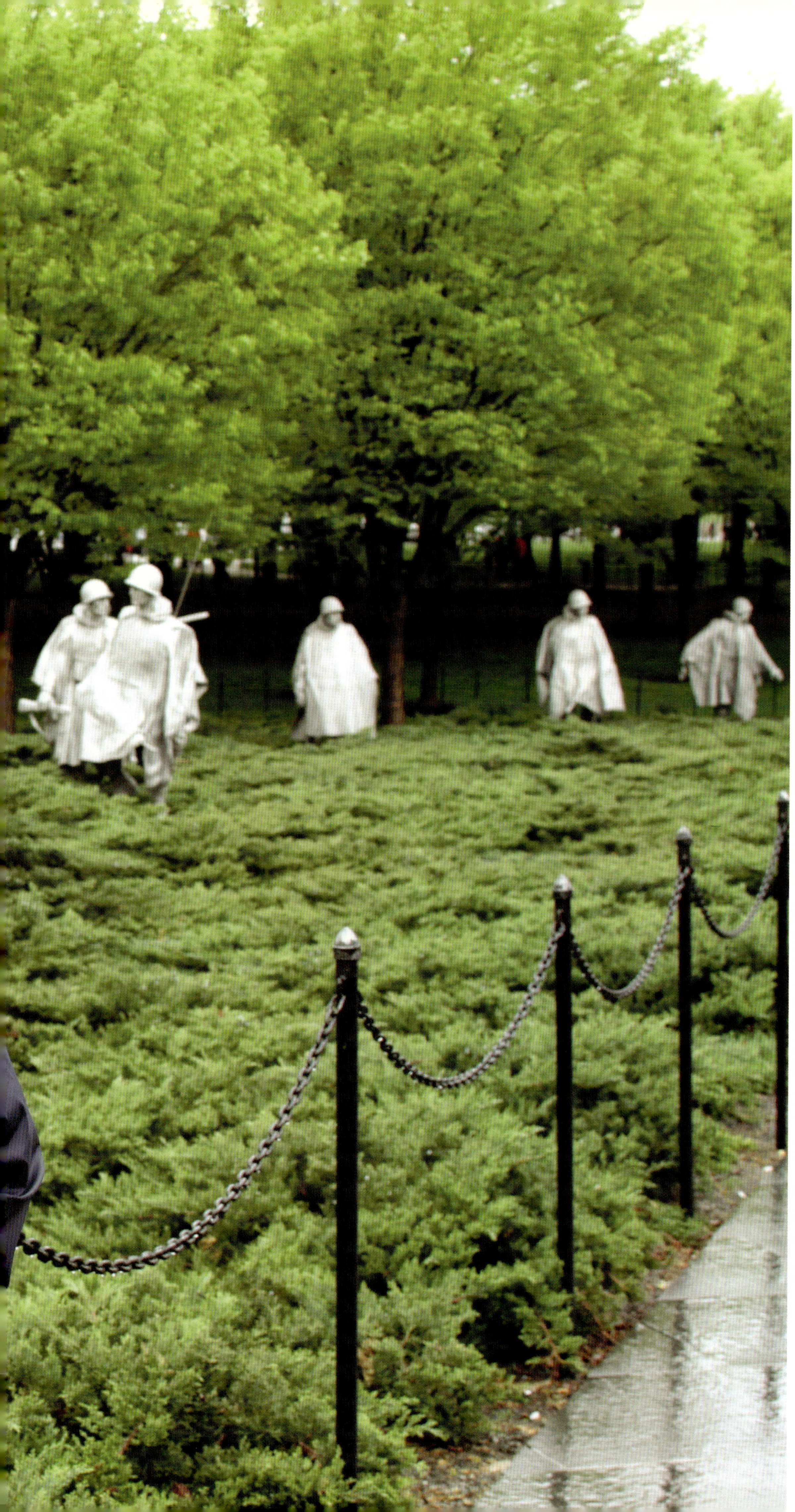

A special part of every Honor Flight is the chance for veterans to connect with their WWII compatriots. On the April 2011 Honor Flight, Milwaukee WWII veteran Daniel Marchewka (left) wore a hat that marked his place of service – the 38th Army Field Hospital. The hat caught the eye of fellow veteran Kenneth Smith from Brown Deer, Wisconsin, who also served in a U.S. Army field hospital. As they swapped stories, they discovered they had both completed basic training in Texas within weeks of each other in the spring of 1943 and had both served in the South Pacific.

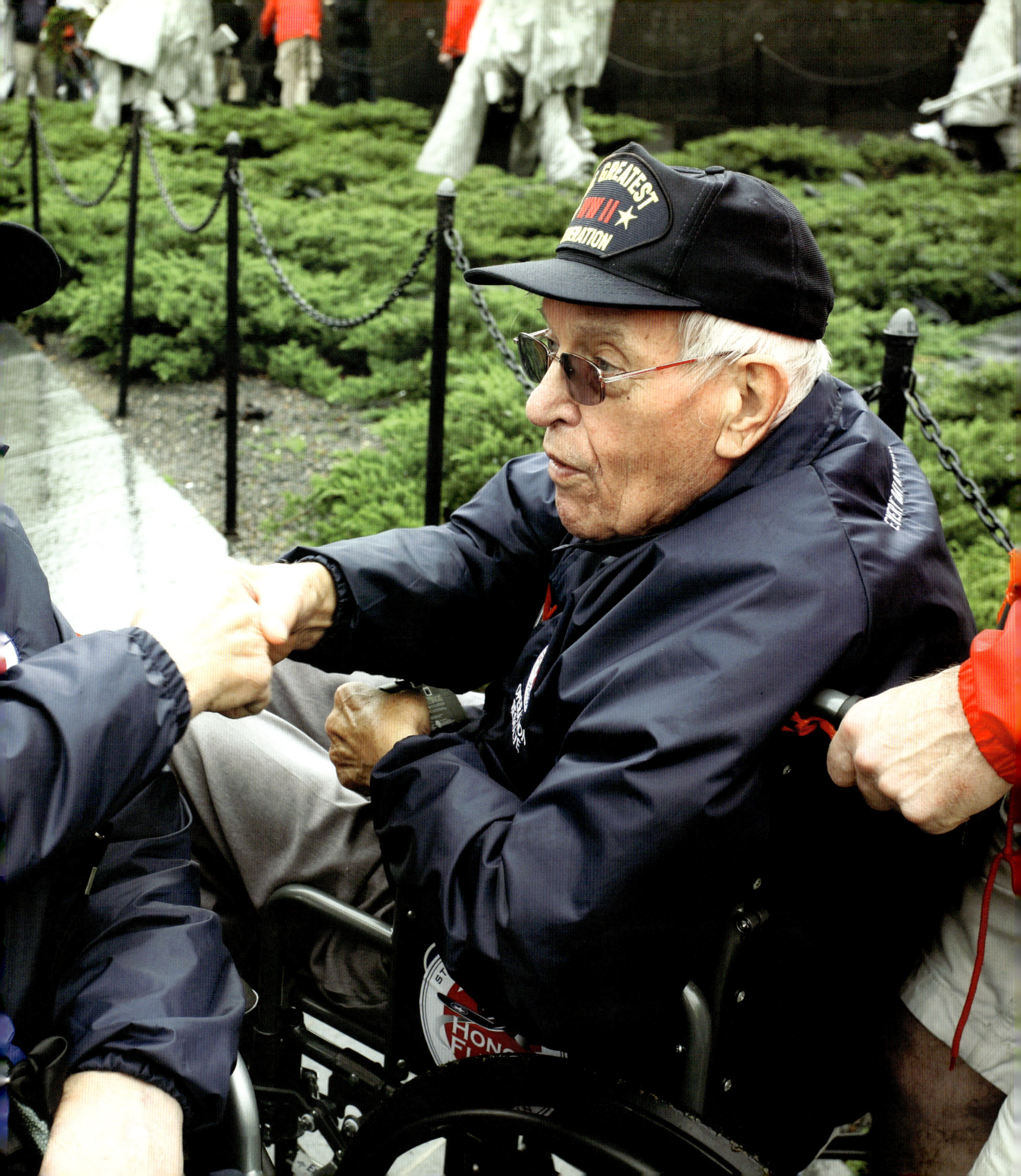
GREATEST
WW II

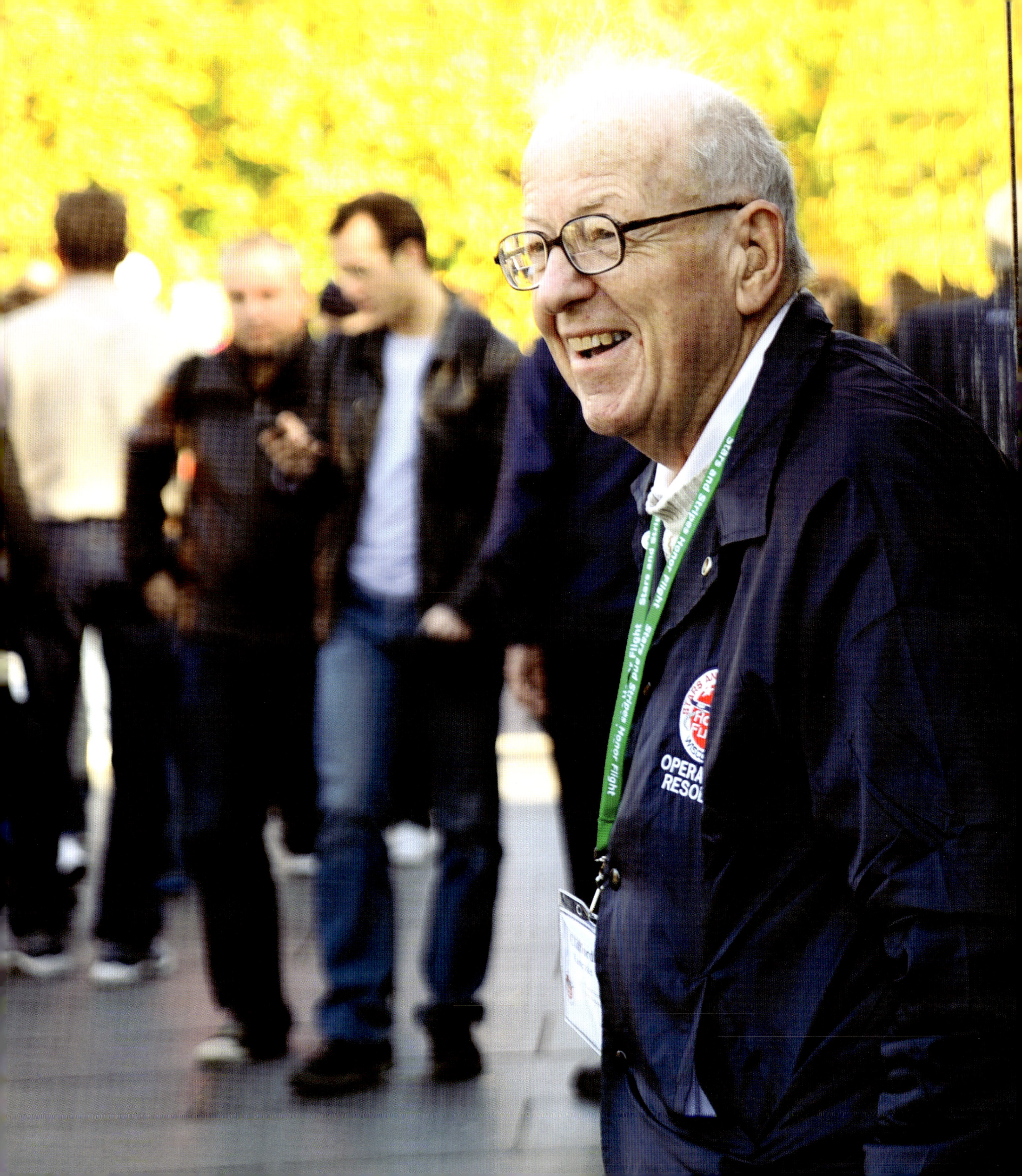
Stars and Stripes Honor Flight

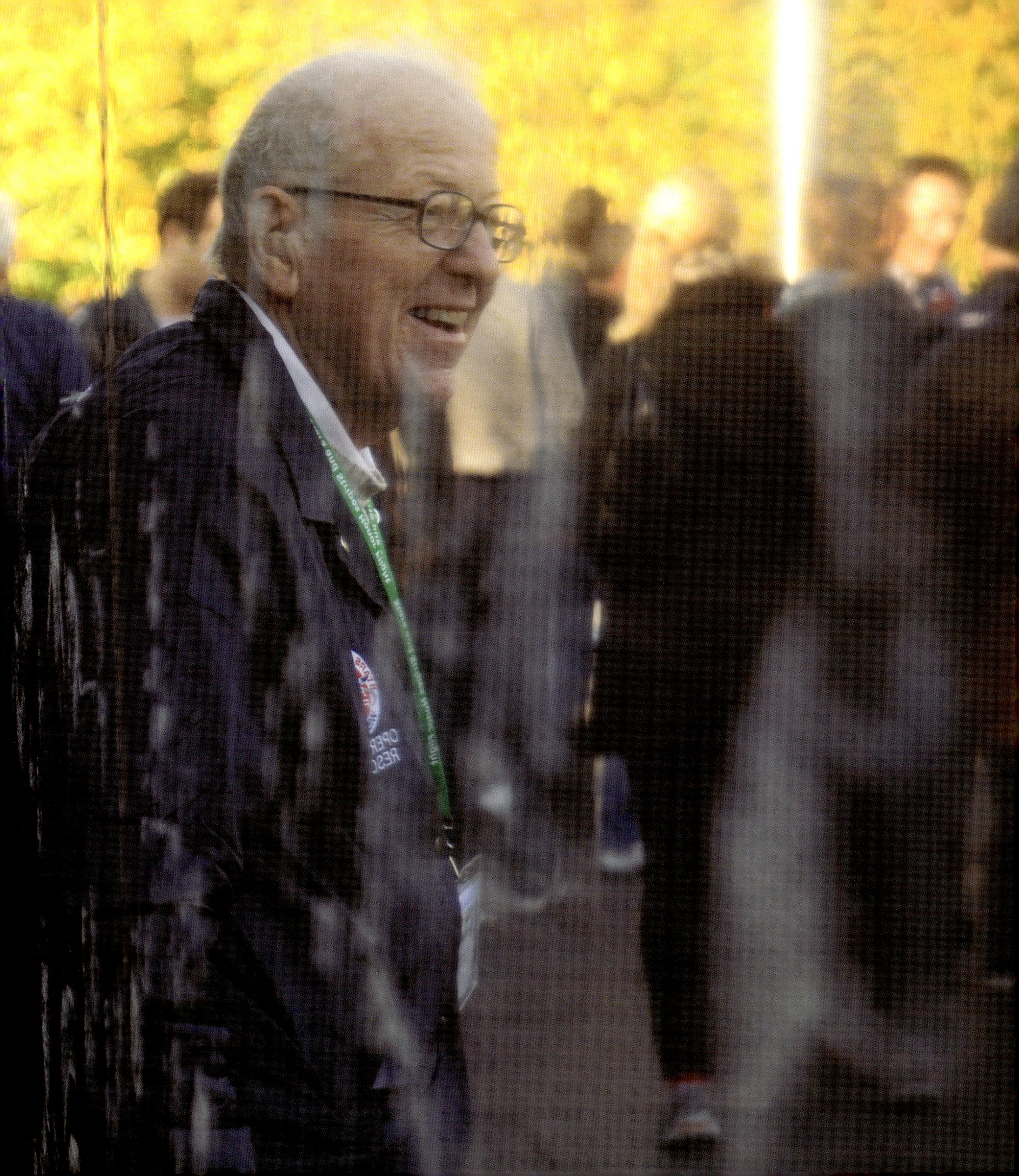

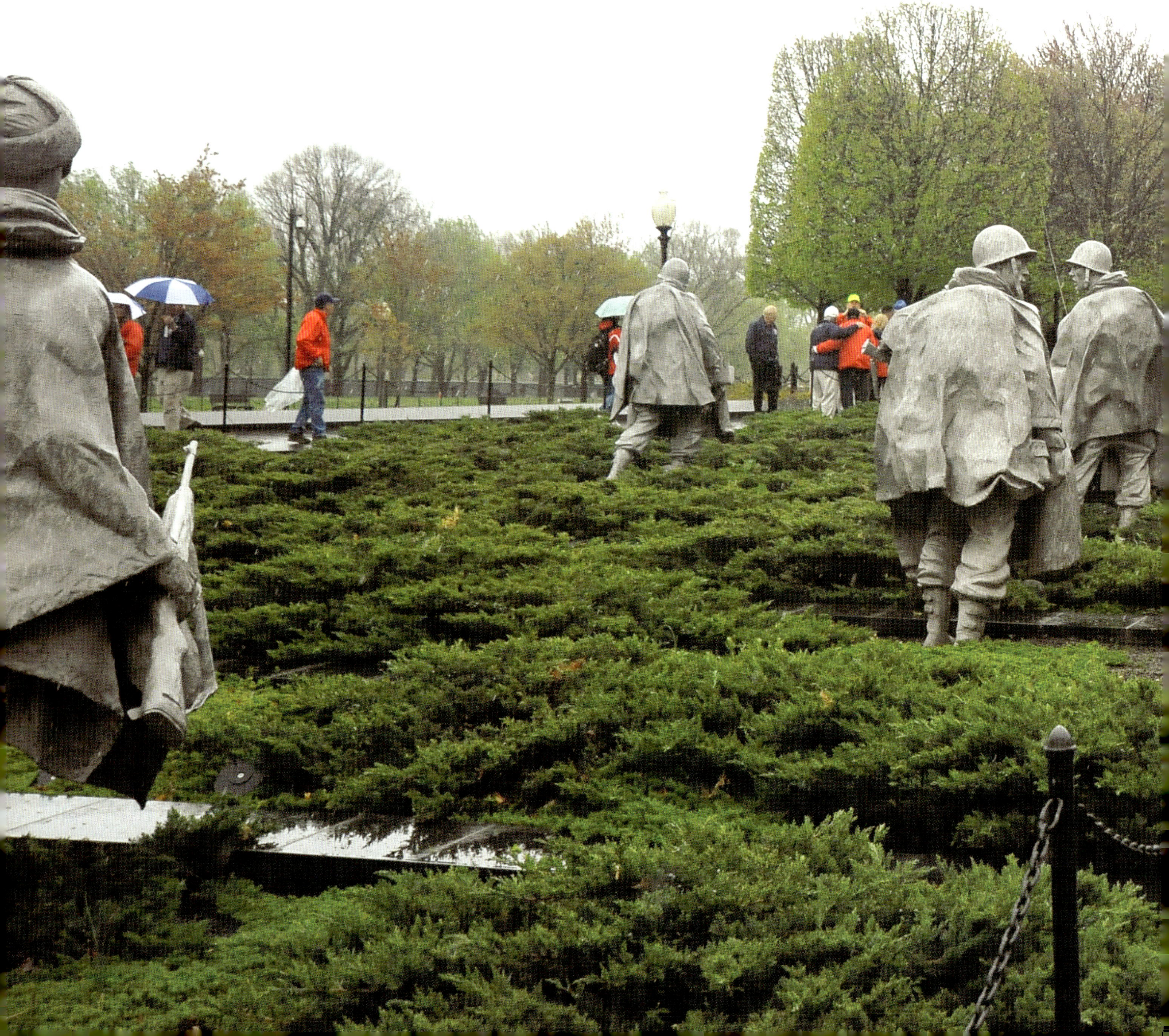

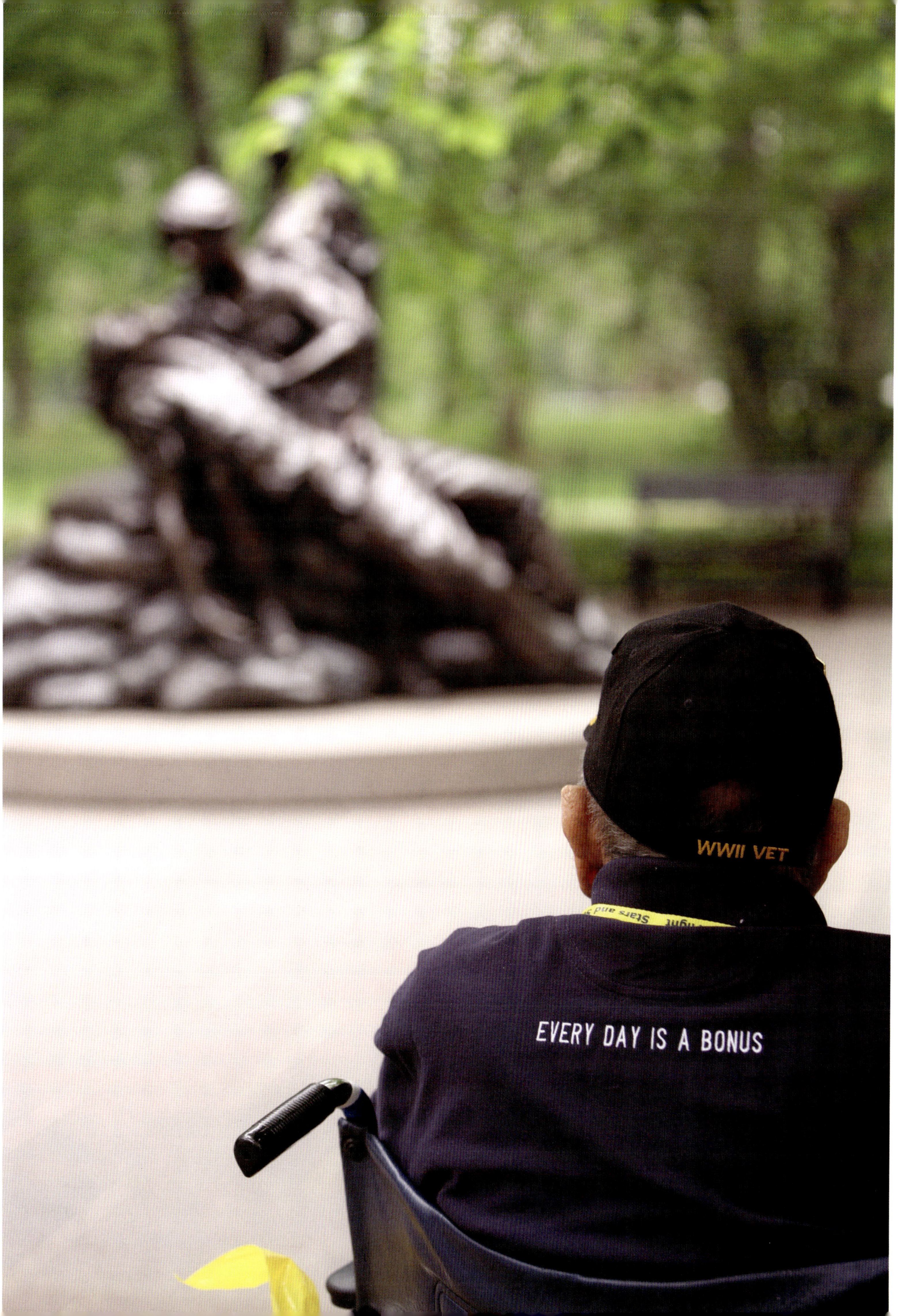
WWII VET
EVERY DAY IS A BONUS

VIETNAM MEMORIAL

Dedicated November 1982

The Vietnam Veterans Memorial was added to our itinerary when on an early flight, a WWII veteran asked if we could make an unscheduled stop at the Wall. When he was told that stop was not on our agenda, the Greatest Generation hero said, "Oh that's a shame. My son's name is on that wall." Team SSHF called an immediate audible and since then, every trip to Washington, D.C., includes this memorial.

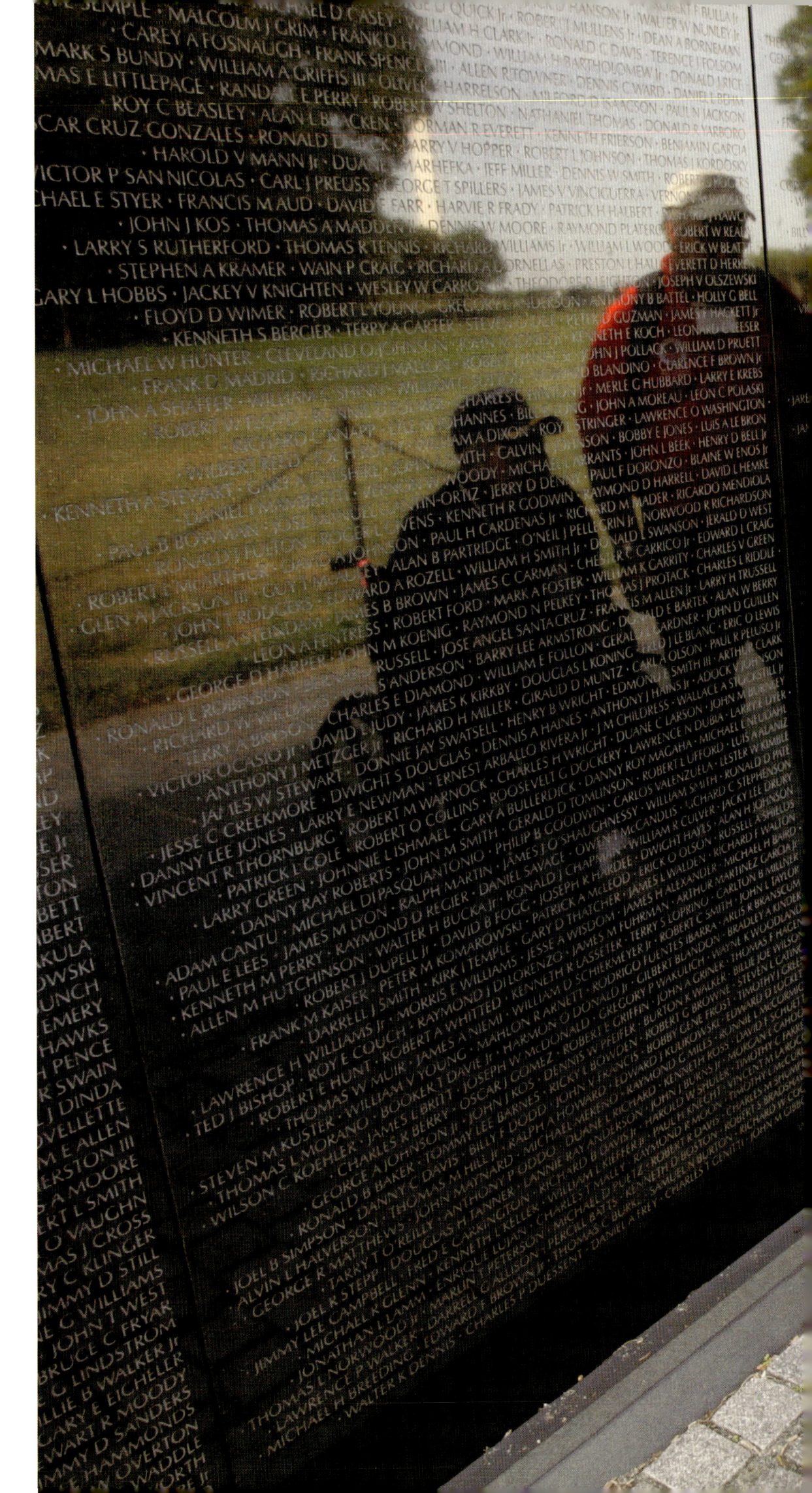

196

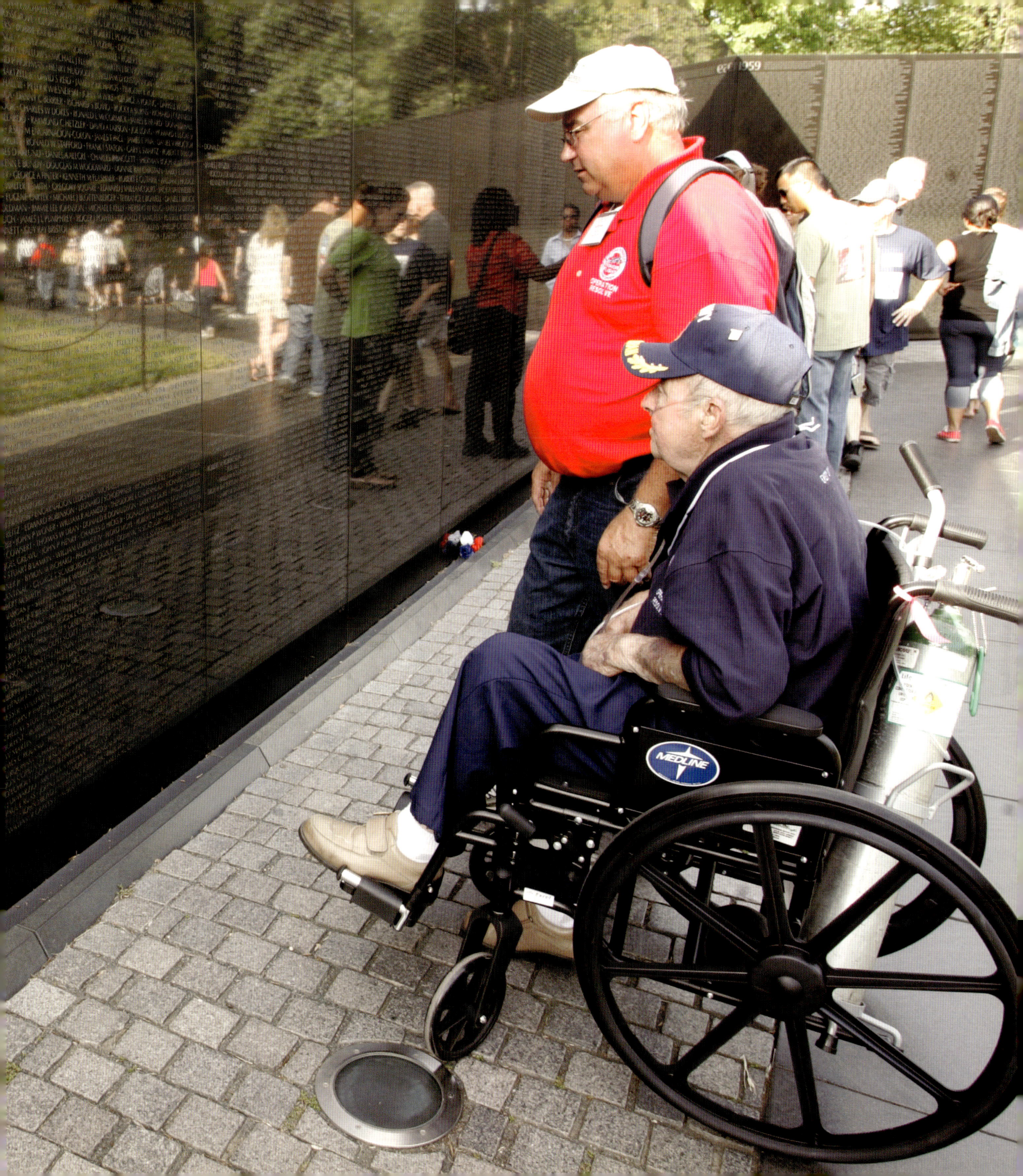
MEDLINE

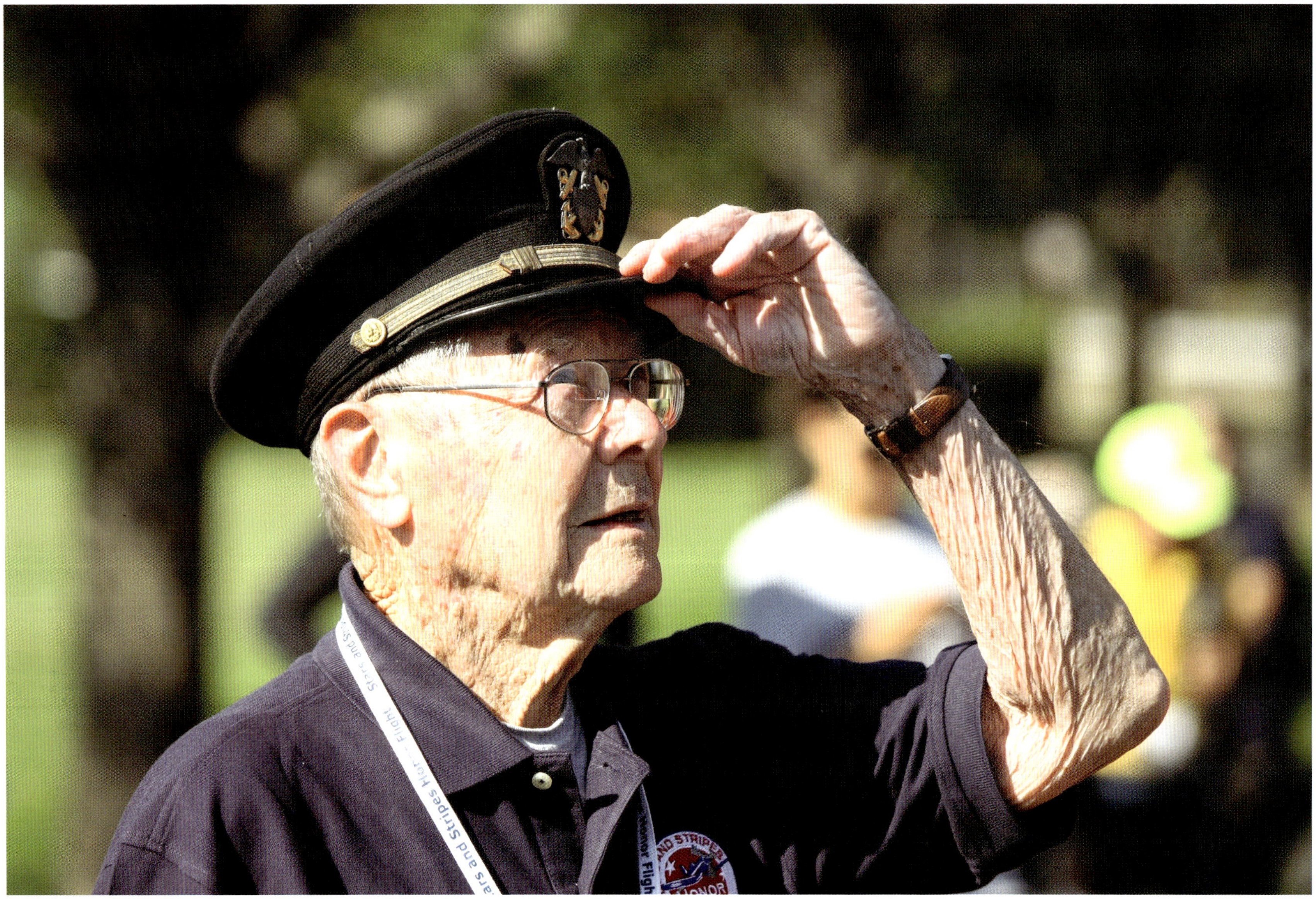

NT SMITH ·
HAROLD R STAFFORD ·
HEN W STARK ·
RNARD D THOMPSON Jr ·
RON · JAMES M VIELBAUM ·
OHN D WARD Jr ·
TERRY JOE WILLIAMS ·
R WOODALL ·
STEVEN W ZIEGLER ·
THOMAS G D'EUSTACHIO ·
RGE A CAMPBELL ·
RT L CONLEY ·
NBUTZ · JOHN E GAGNON ·
AMES L GRIFFIS ·
JOHN R SHELL

AIR FORCE MEMORIAL
Dedicated October 2006

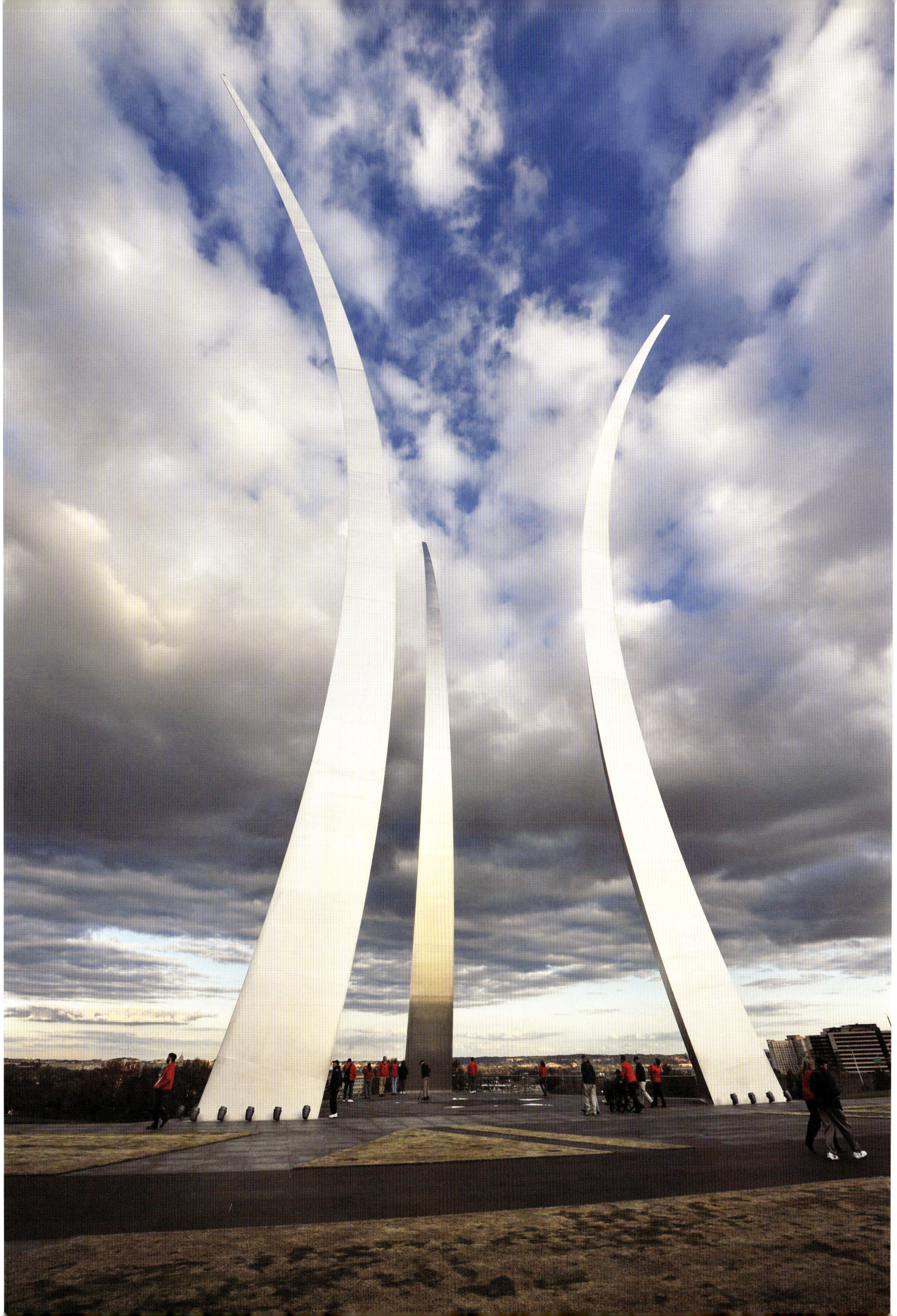

202

AMERICAN LEGION
LA VALLE, WIS.
Stars and Stripes Honor Flight
STARS AND STRIPES
HONOR FLIGHT
WISCONSIN
OPERATION
RESOLVE

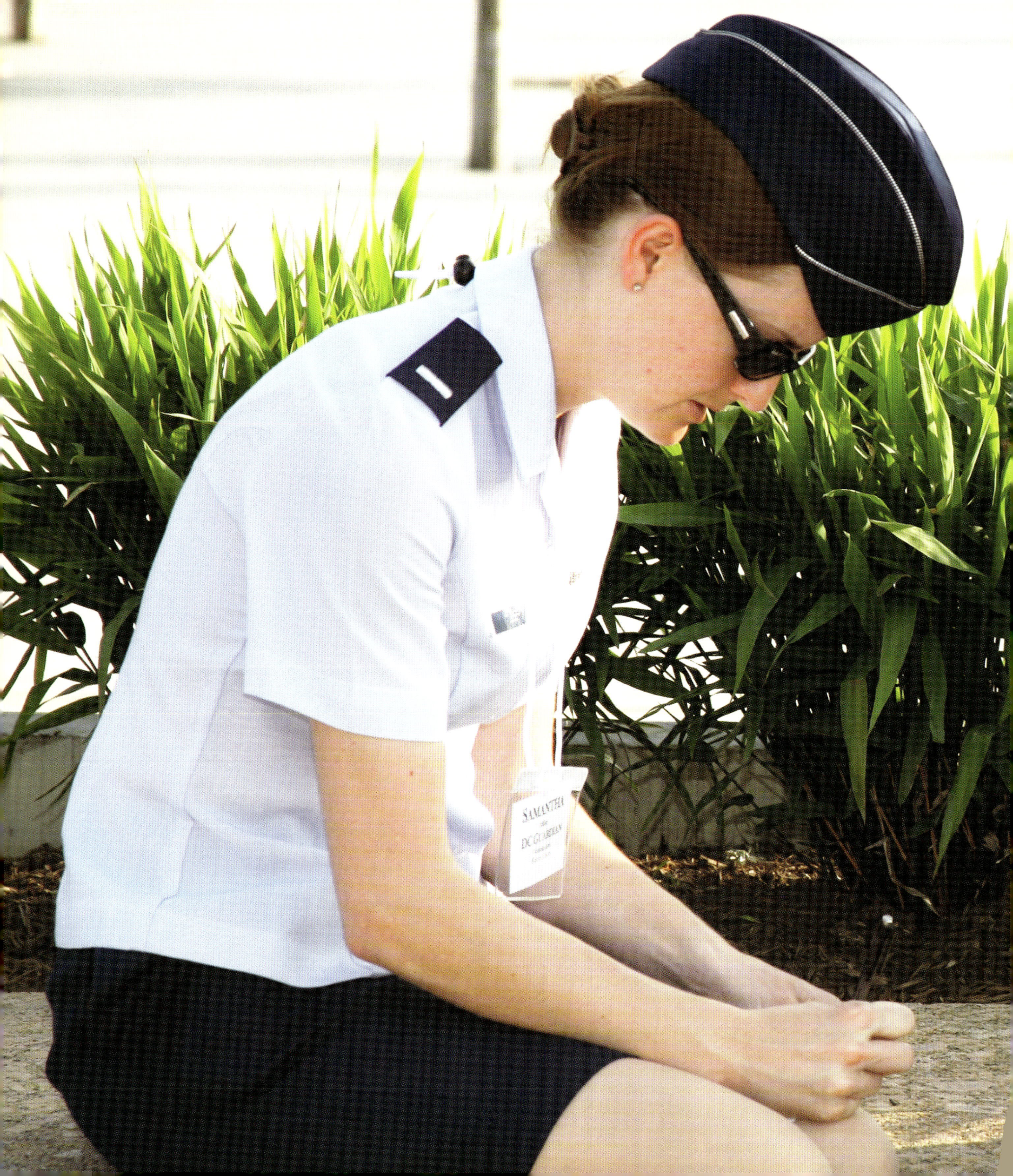
SAMANTHA
DC GUARDIAN

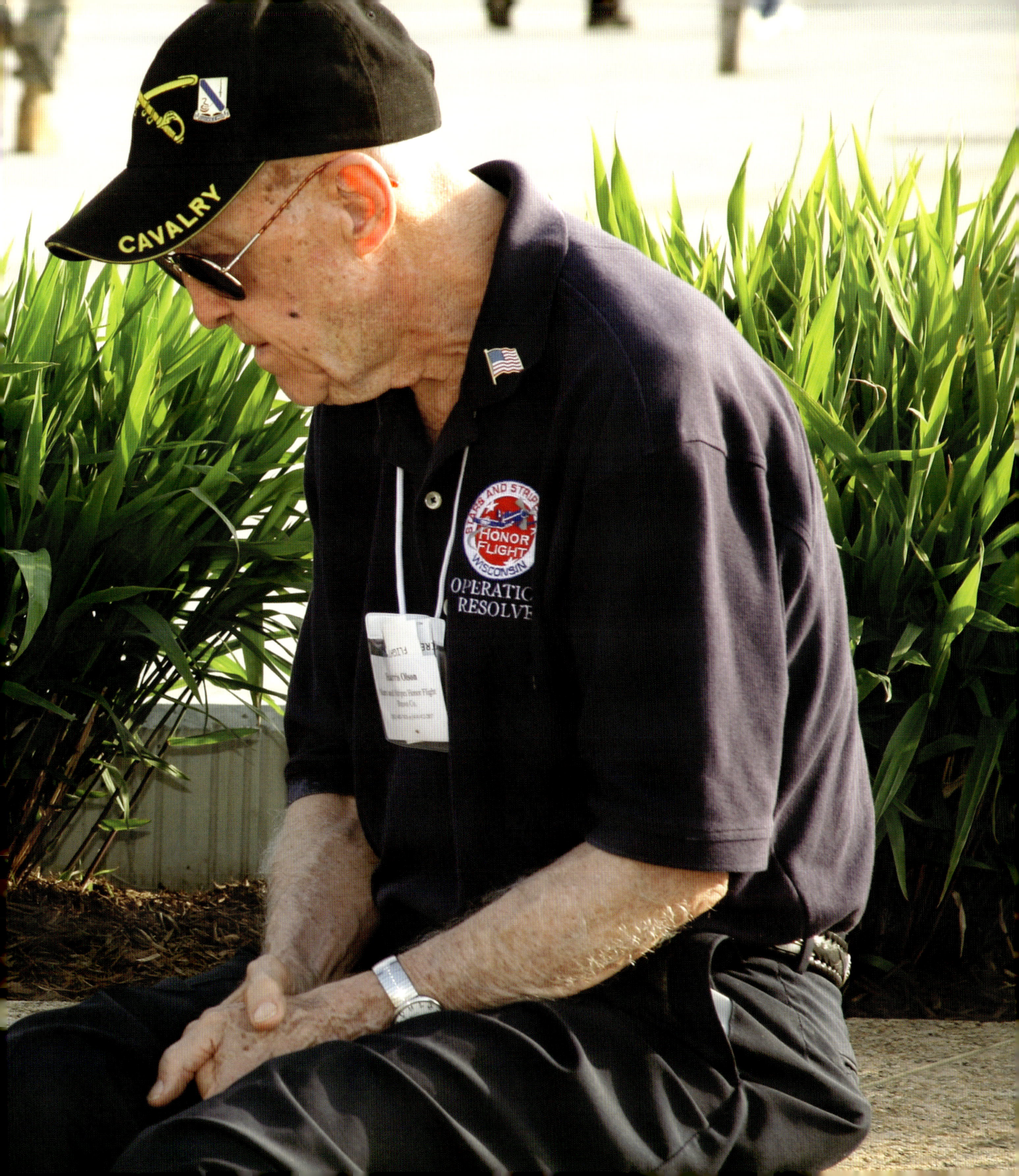
CAVALRY
HONOR
FLIGHT
WISCONSIN
RESOLVE

U.S. MARINE CORPS WAR MEMORIAL
Dedicated November 1954

EVOLUTIONARY·WAR·1775-1783 × FRENCH·NAVAL·WAR·1798-1801 × TRIPOLI 1801-1805 × WAR OF 1812-1815 × FLORIDA INDIAN WARS
FIDELIS

FRIENDS IN FREEDOM

When Navy veteran Harvey Kurz (opposite, right) visited the Iwo Jima Memorial as part of his Honor Flight experience, he wondered aloud at the immense human suffering and cost of taking "this tiny island." Harvey had wrestled with this question for seven decades.

Just before this photo was taken, an aging pilot introduced himself to Harvey and said, "You saved my life!" The pilot told Harvey that during one mission in 1945, he thought he would be forced to ditch his embattled plane into the Pacific Ocean, some 650 miles south of the Japanese mainland. "Surely, I was going to die," he said.

But when he saw the American flag on Iwo Jima, the pilot made a split-second decision to try to land there. After telling Harvey his story, the pilot's eyes welled with tears as he showed Harvey pictures of his grandchildren.

Never before had so much healing come so quickly to such a deserving man. Our hero, Harvey Kurz.

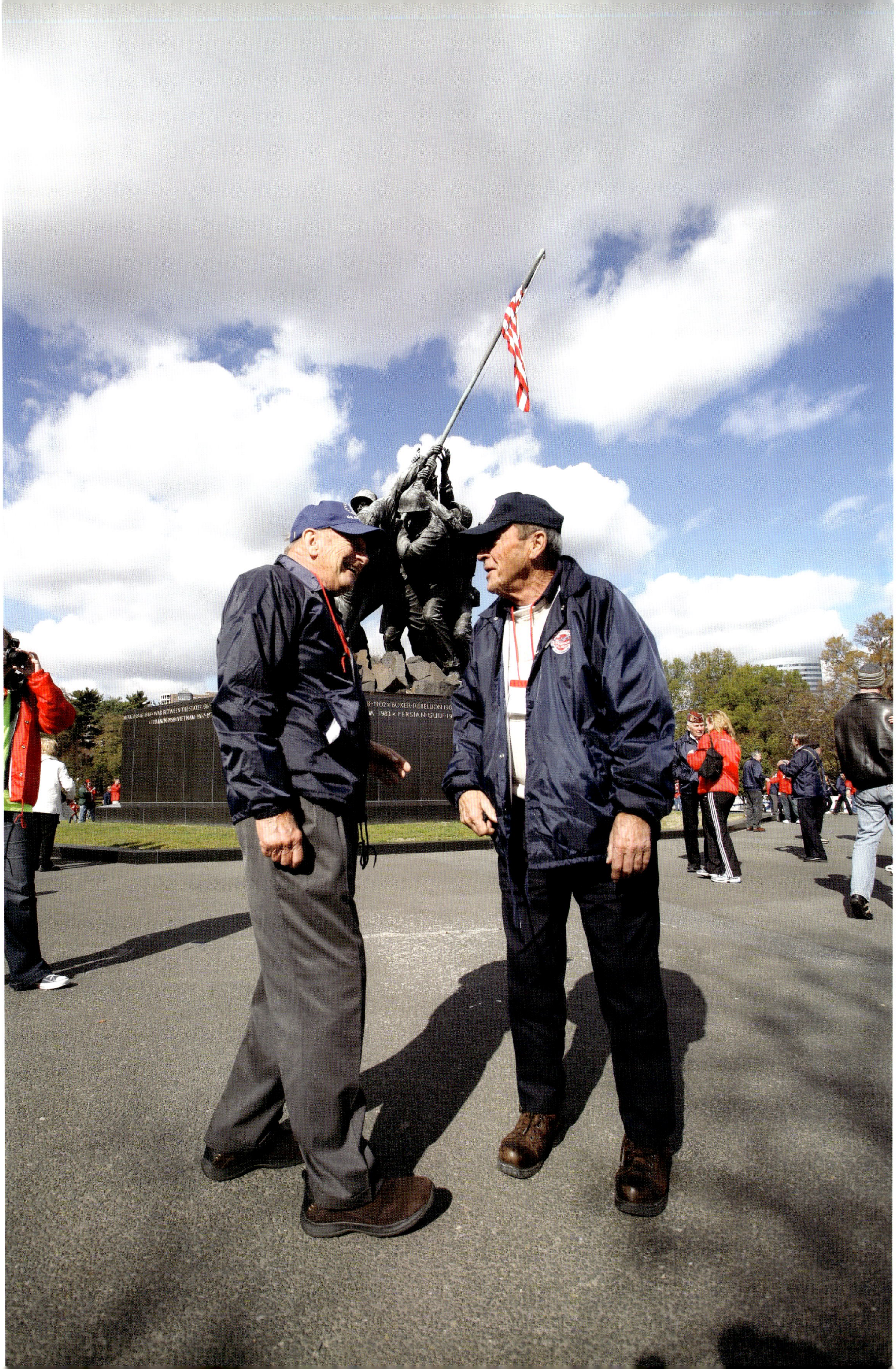

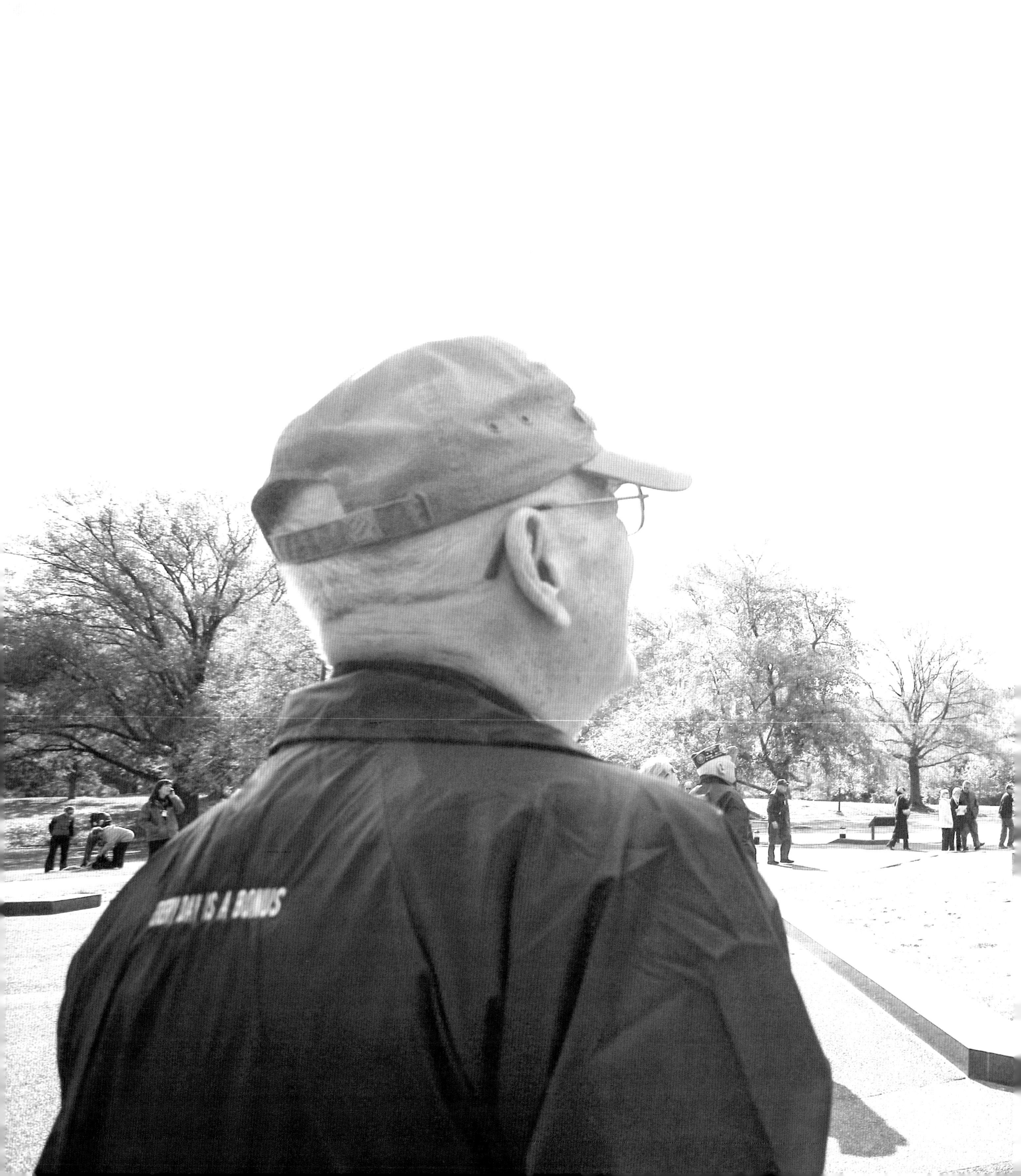
IS A BONUS

IN HONOR AND MEMORY
OF THE MEN OF THE
UNITED STATES MARINE CORPS
WHO HAVE GIVEN
THEIR LIVES TO THEIR COUNTRY
SINCE 10 NOVEMBER 1775

...SANTO DOMINGO 1916-1924 ★ WORLD WAR I 1917-1918 ★ BELLEAU WOOD・SOISSONS・ST MIHIEL・BLANC MONT・MEUSE-ARGONNE ★ NICARAGUA 1926-1933 ★

★ SOMALIA・1992-1994 ★

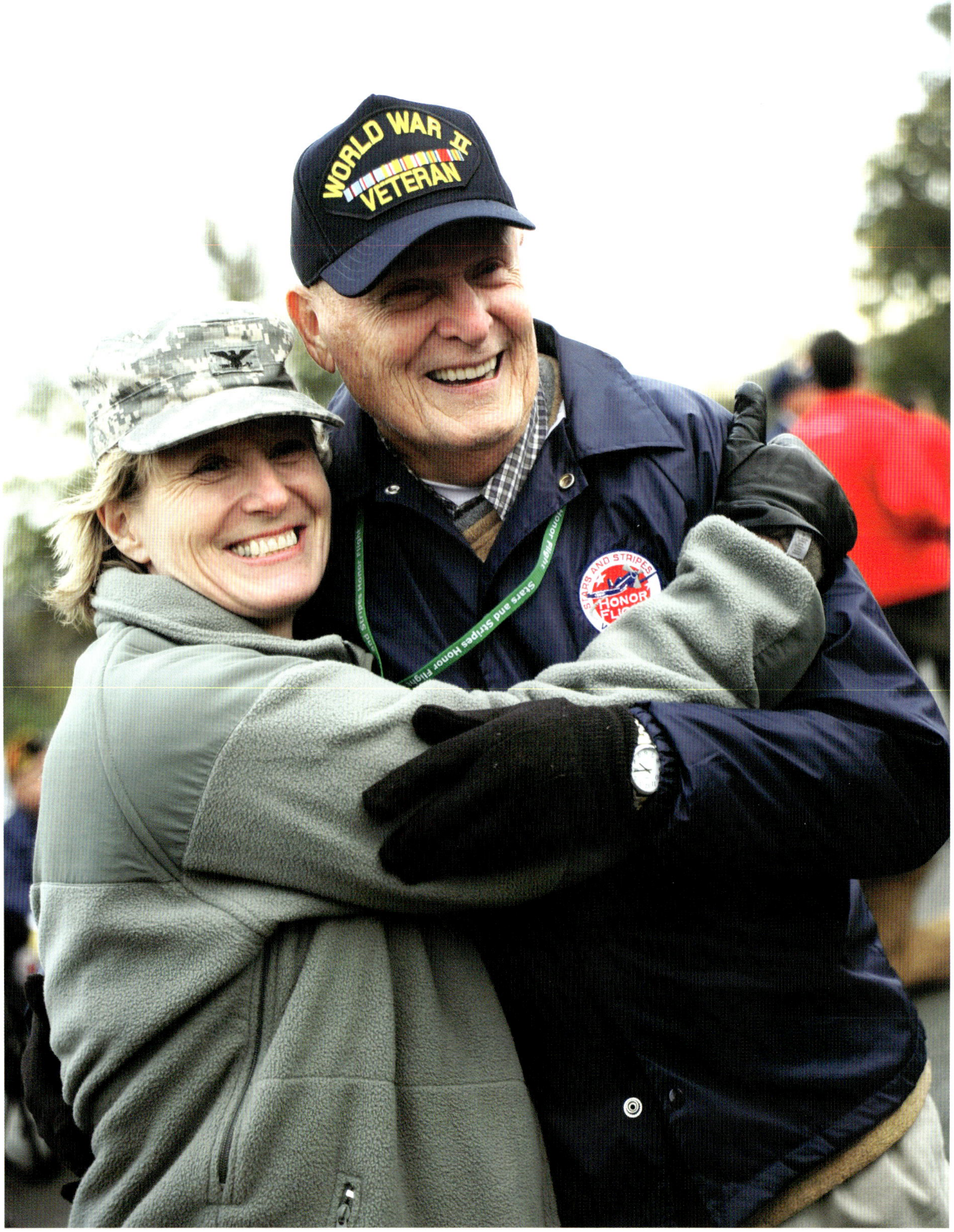
WORLD WAR II
VETERAN
STARS AND STRIPES
HONOR

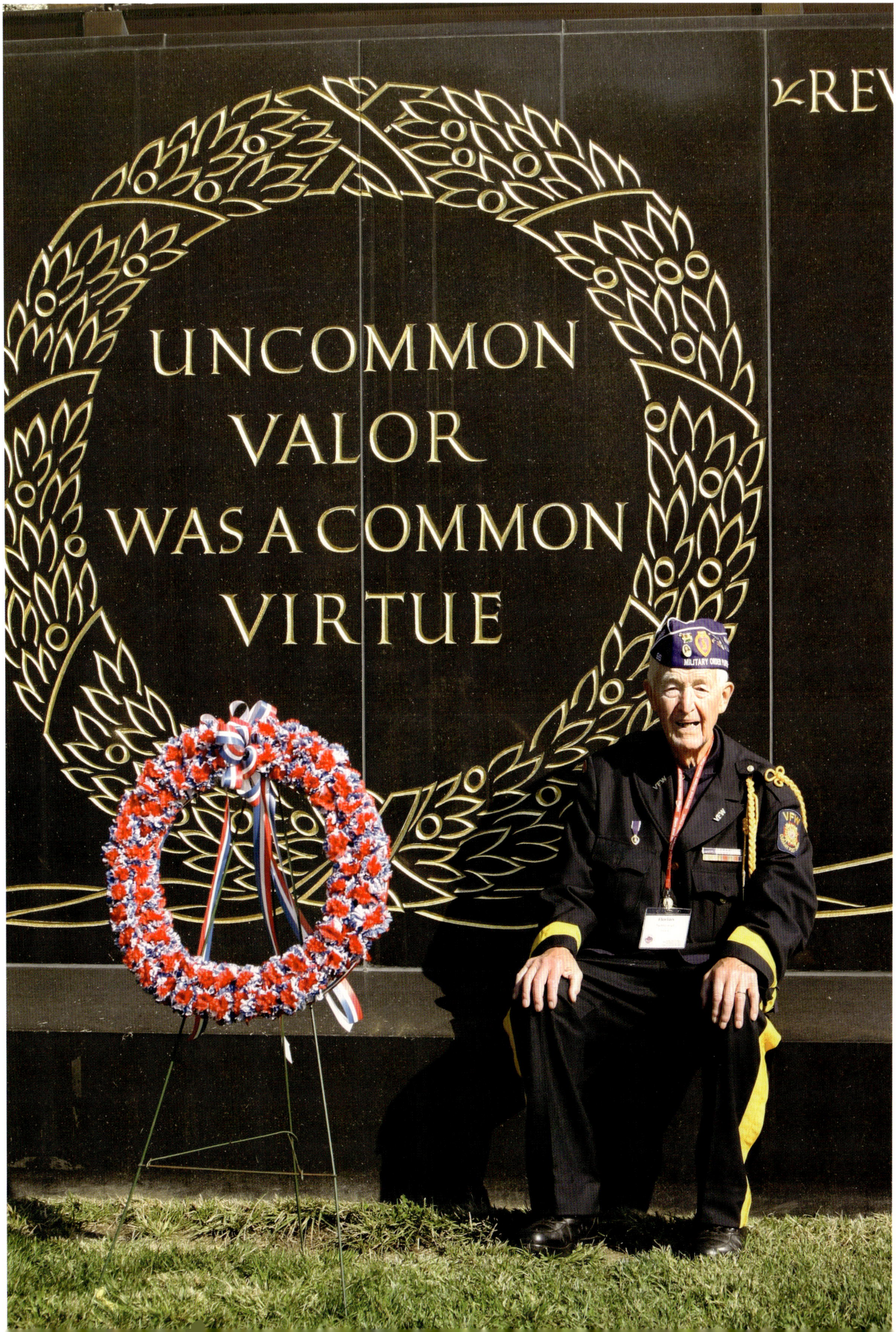

REV
UNCOMMON VALOR WAS A COMMON VIRTUE

ITI·1915-1934 SANTO·DOMINGO·1916-1924 WORLD·WAR·I·1917-1918·BELLEAU·WOOD·SOISSONS·ST·M
IN·HONOR·AND·MEMORY
OF·THE·MEN·OF·THE
UNITED·S MARINE·CORPS
W AVE·GIVEN
THEIR IR·COUNTRY
SI MBER·1775

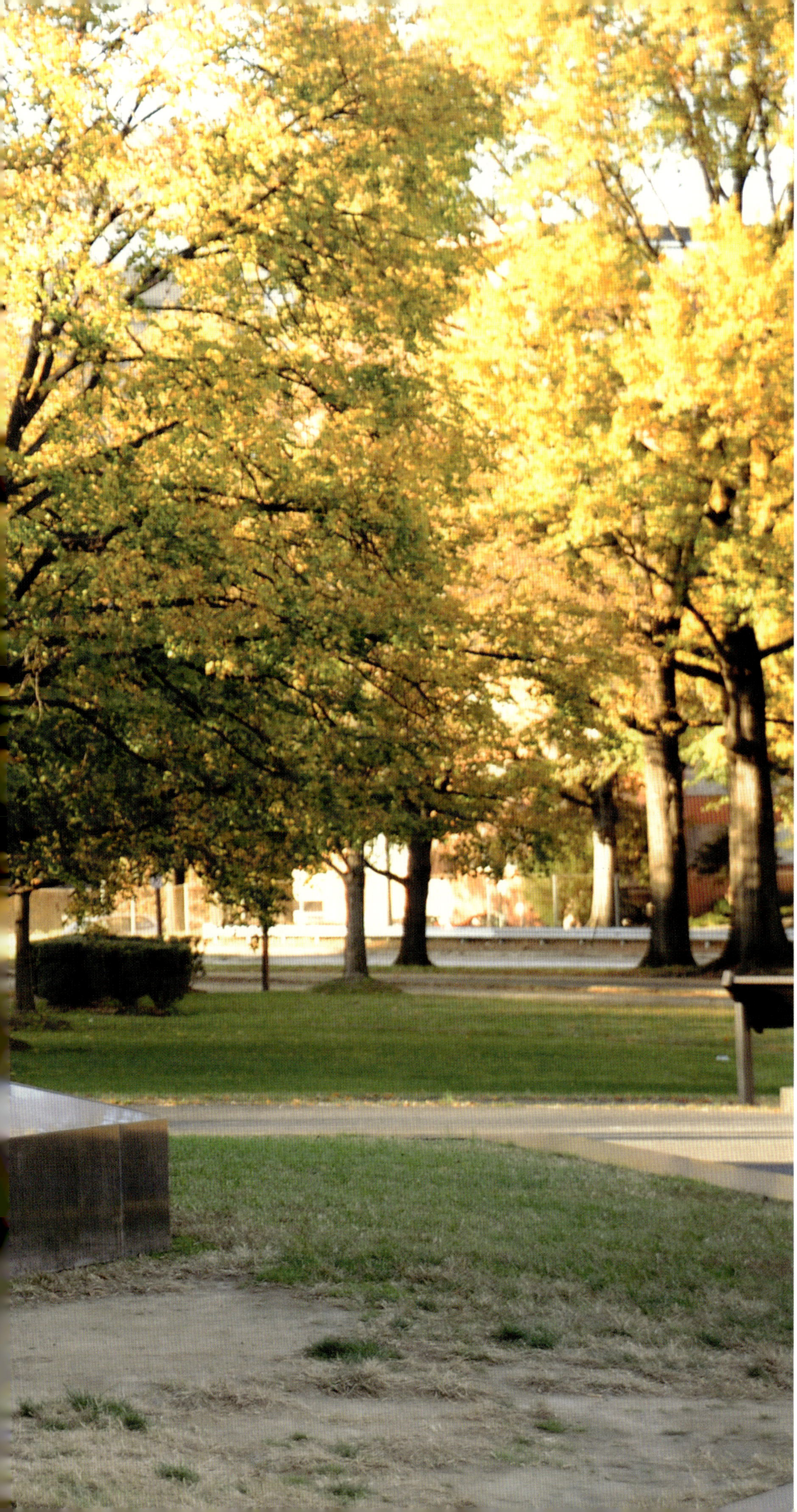

NEW GEORGIA BOUGAINVILLE TARAWA NEW BRITAIN 1944 MARSHALL ISLANDS MARIANAS ISLANDS PELELIU 1945 IWO JIMA OKI

1945·IWO JIMA·OKINAWA·KOREA·1950· ★REVOLUTIONARY·WAR·1775–1783 ★ FRENCH·NAVAL·WAR·1798–

UNCOMMON
VALOR
WAS A COMMON
VIRTUE

SEMPER FIDELIS

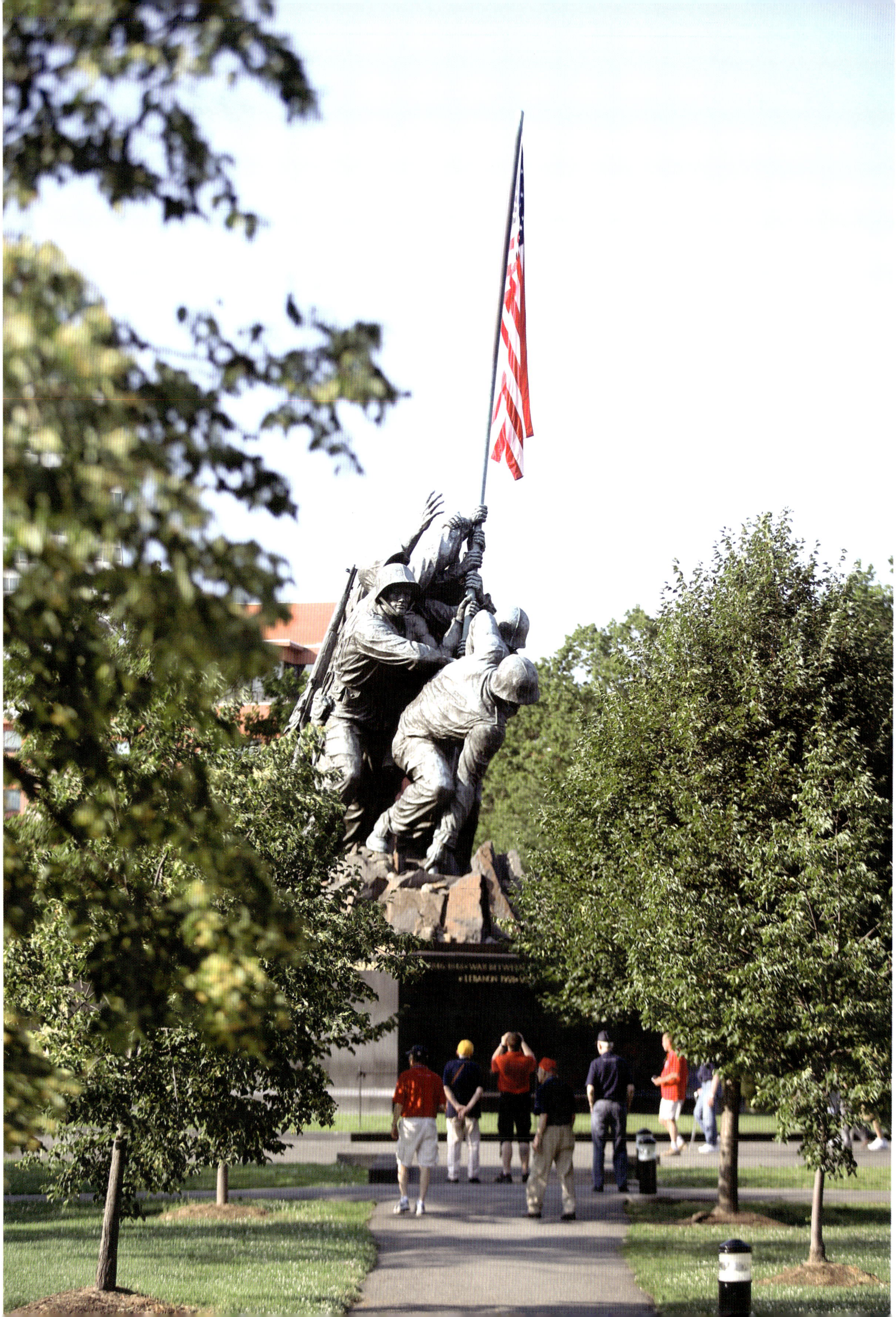

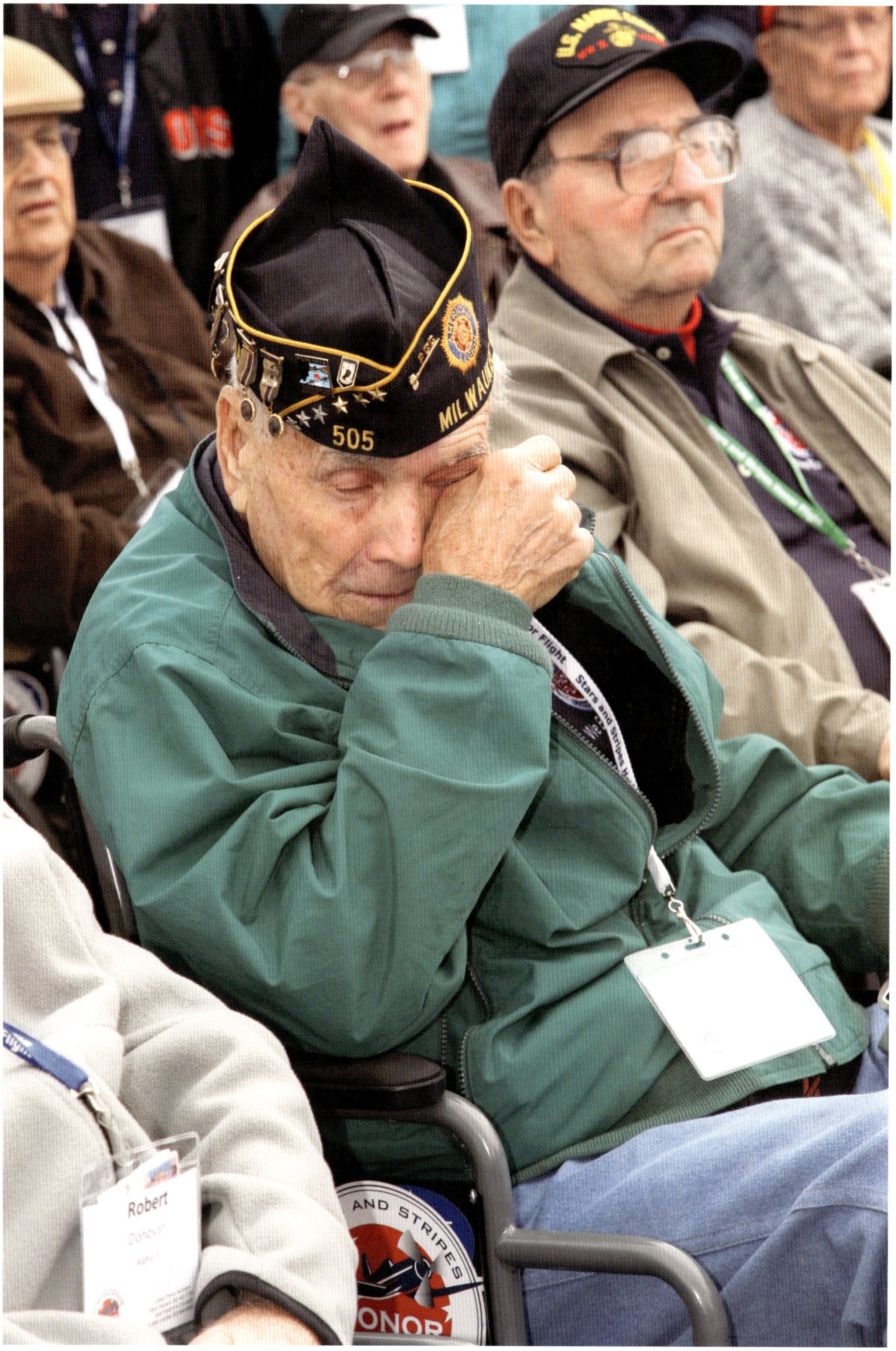
505
Robert
AND STRIPES

KOREA·1950·
REVOLUTIONARY·WAR·1775–1783
FRENCH·NAVAL·WAR·1798–1801
USAA

IPOLI·1801-1805 ✕ WAR·OF·1812-1815 ✕ FLORIDA·INDIAN·WARS·1835-1842 ✕

Arlington

★ ★ ★

1630 HOURS

ARLINGTON NATIONAL CEMETERY
Founded 1882

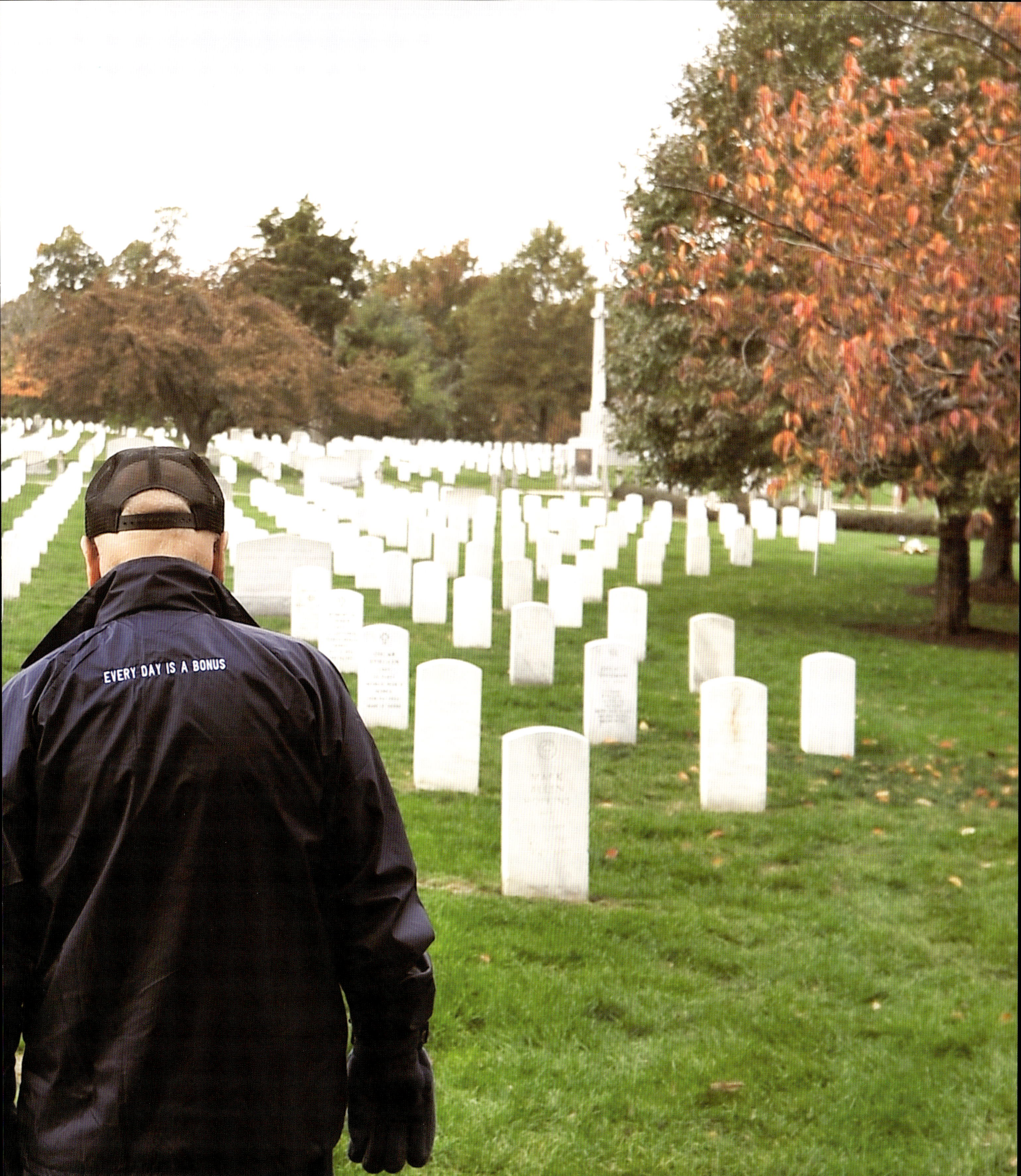
EVERY DAY IS A BONUS

EVERY DAY IS A BONUS

EVERY DAY IS A BONUS

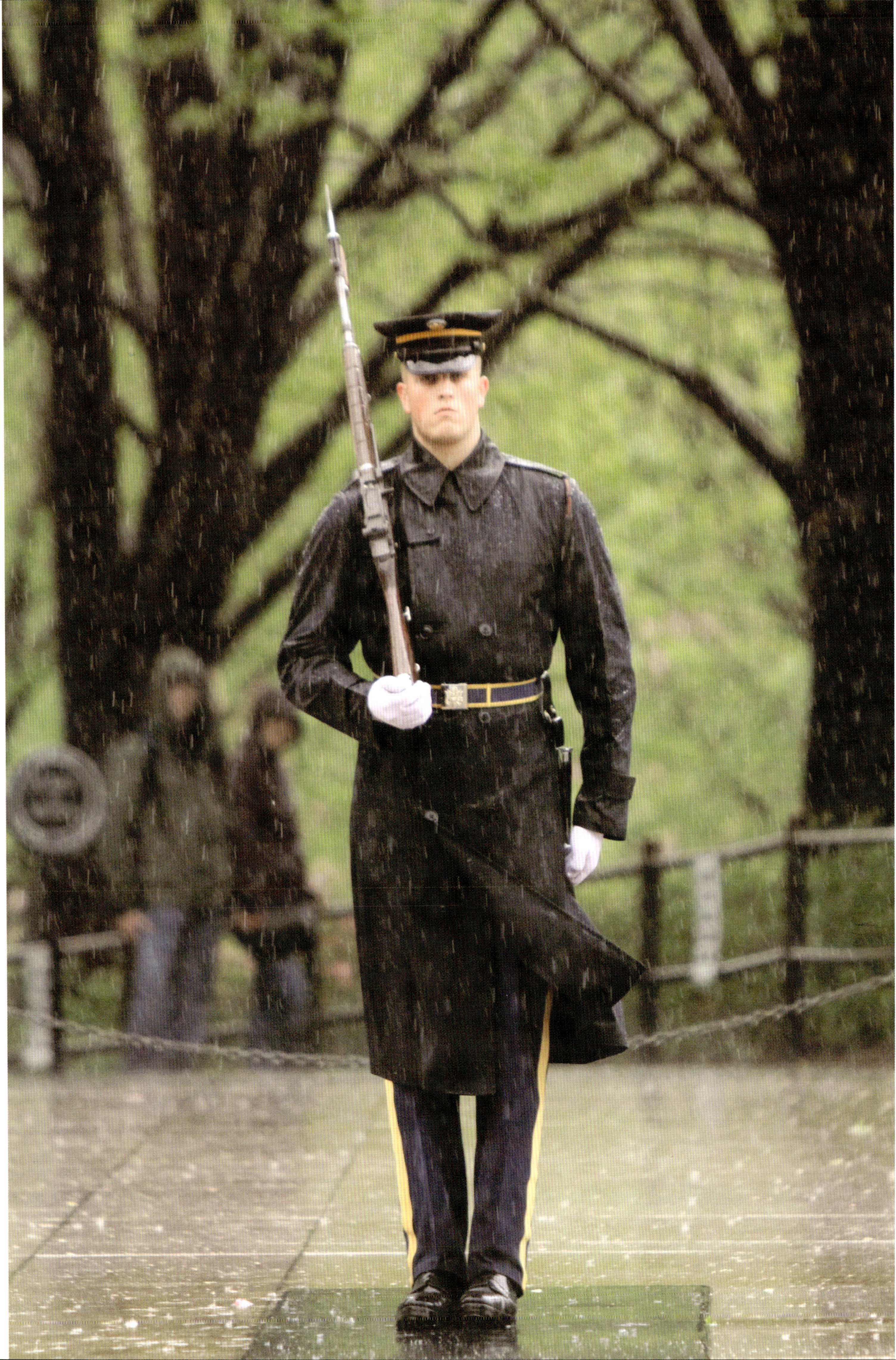

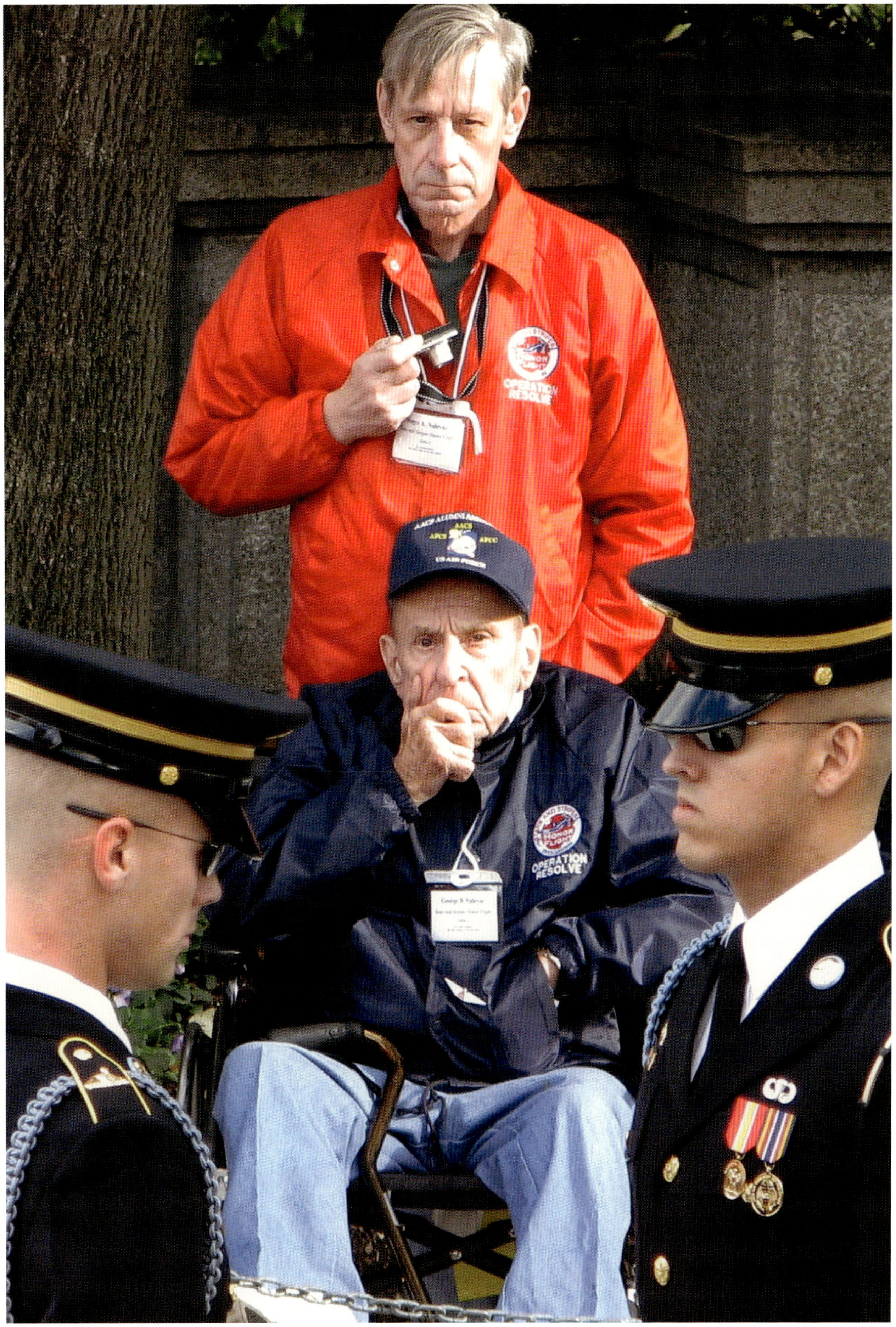
OPERATION RESOLVE
OPERATION RESOLVE

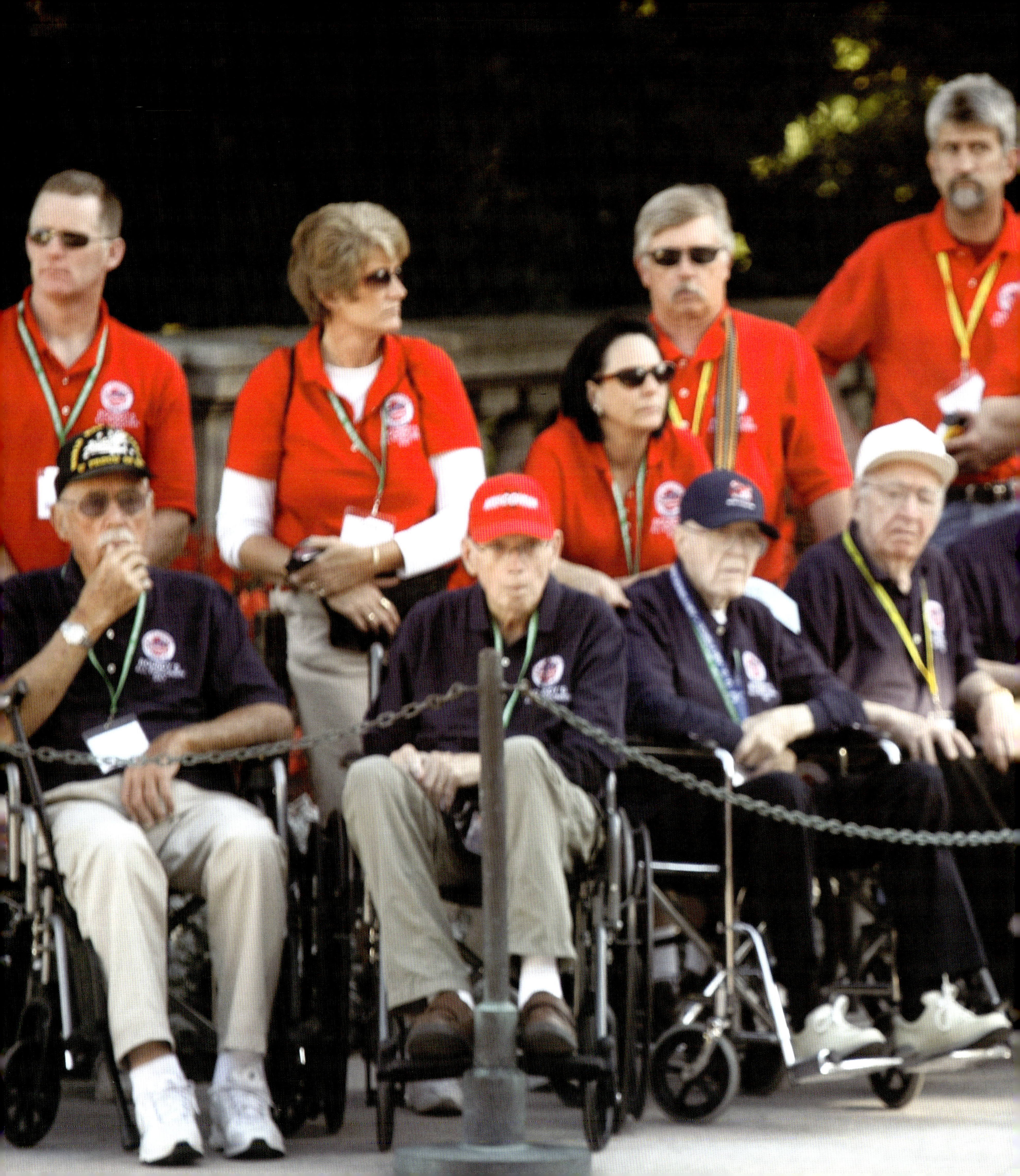

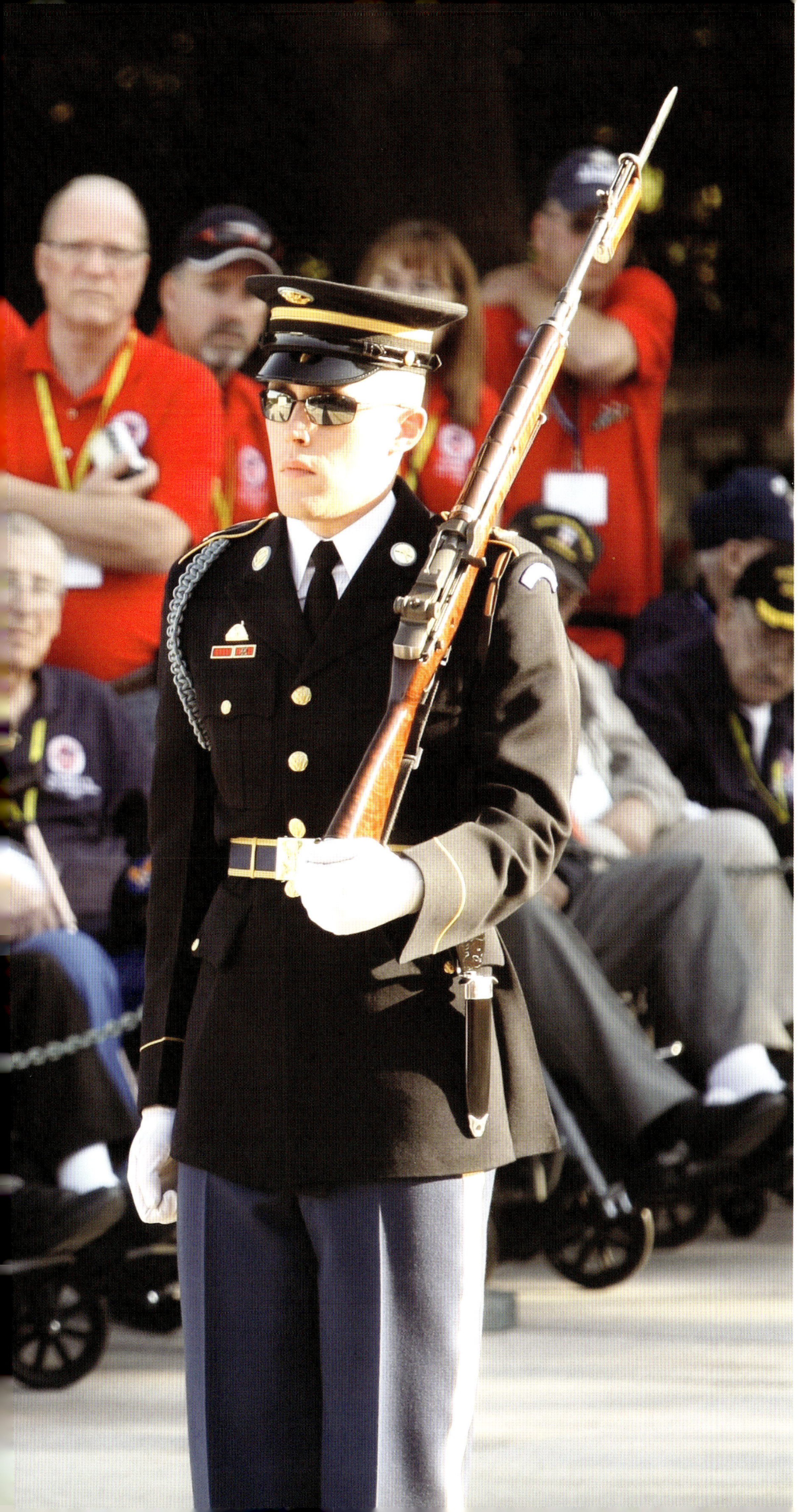

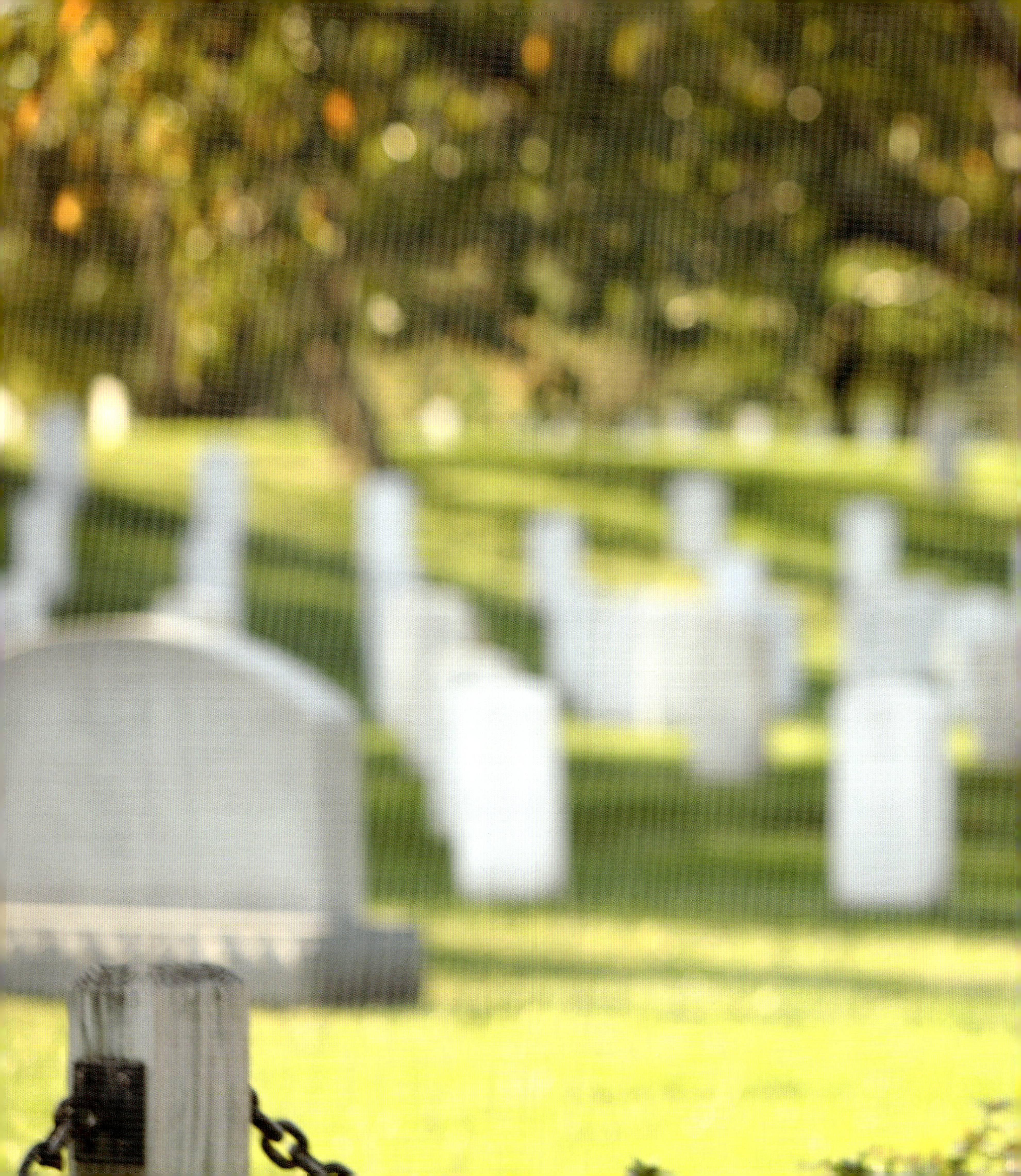

ROUNDY'S
ALL WISCONSIN
DAY
HONOR FLIGHT
Stars and Stripes Honor Flight

WWII Army nurse Lucy Cohn told us she had dressed up for her Honor Flight because she had a date with her husband. Married to Lt. Col. Norman Cohn for 54 years, Lucy had not been back to Arlington National Cemetery since his burial there ten years earlier. Lucy found her Norman's gravestone and shared this quiet moment with him.

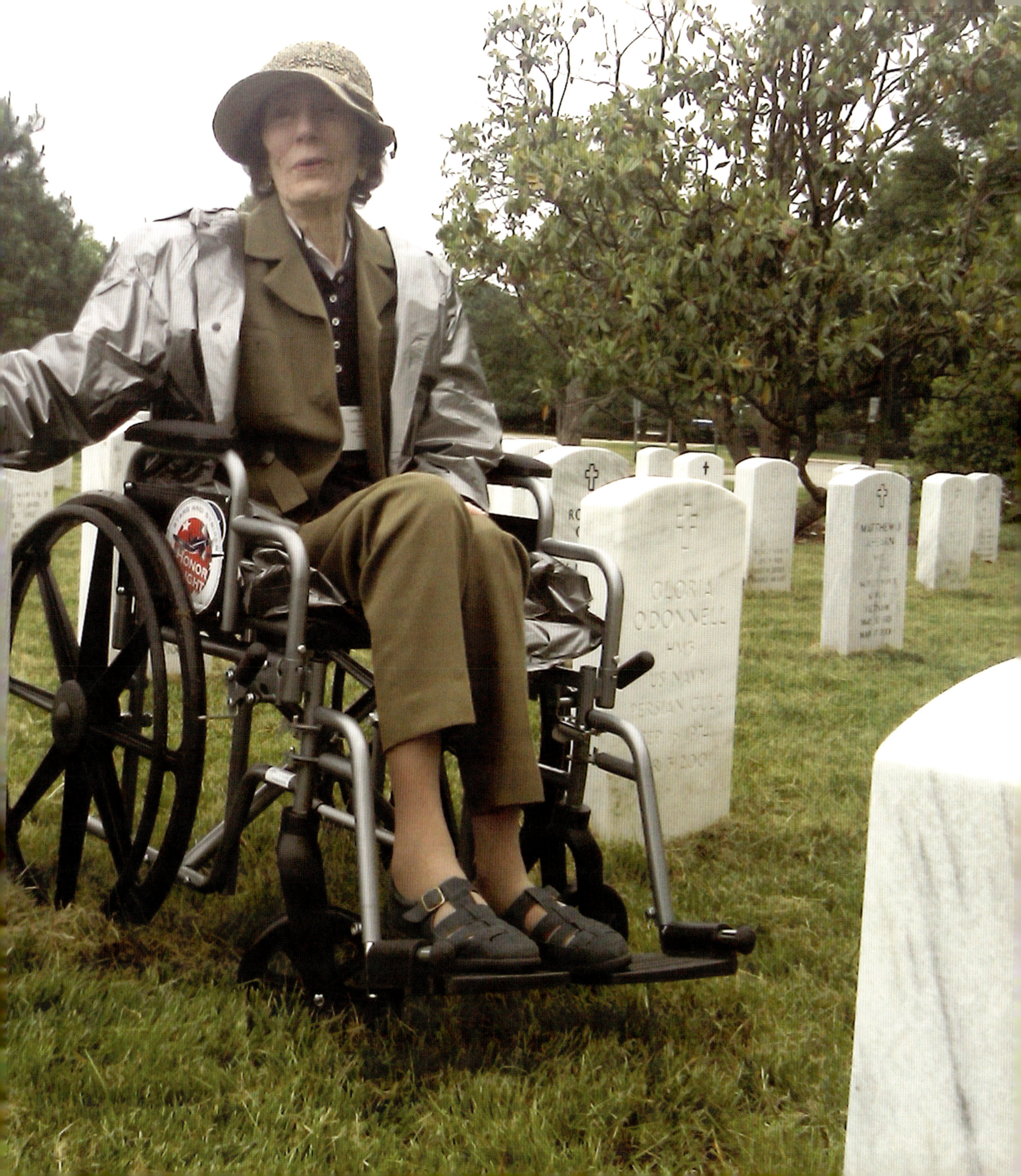
ODONNELL

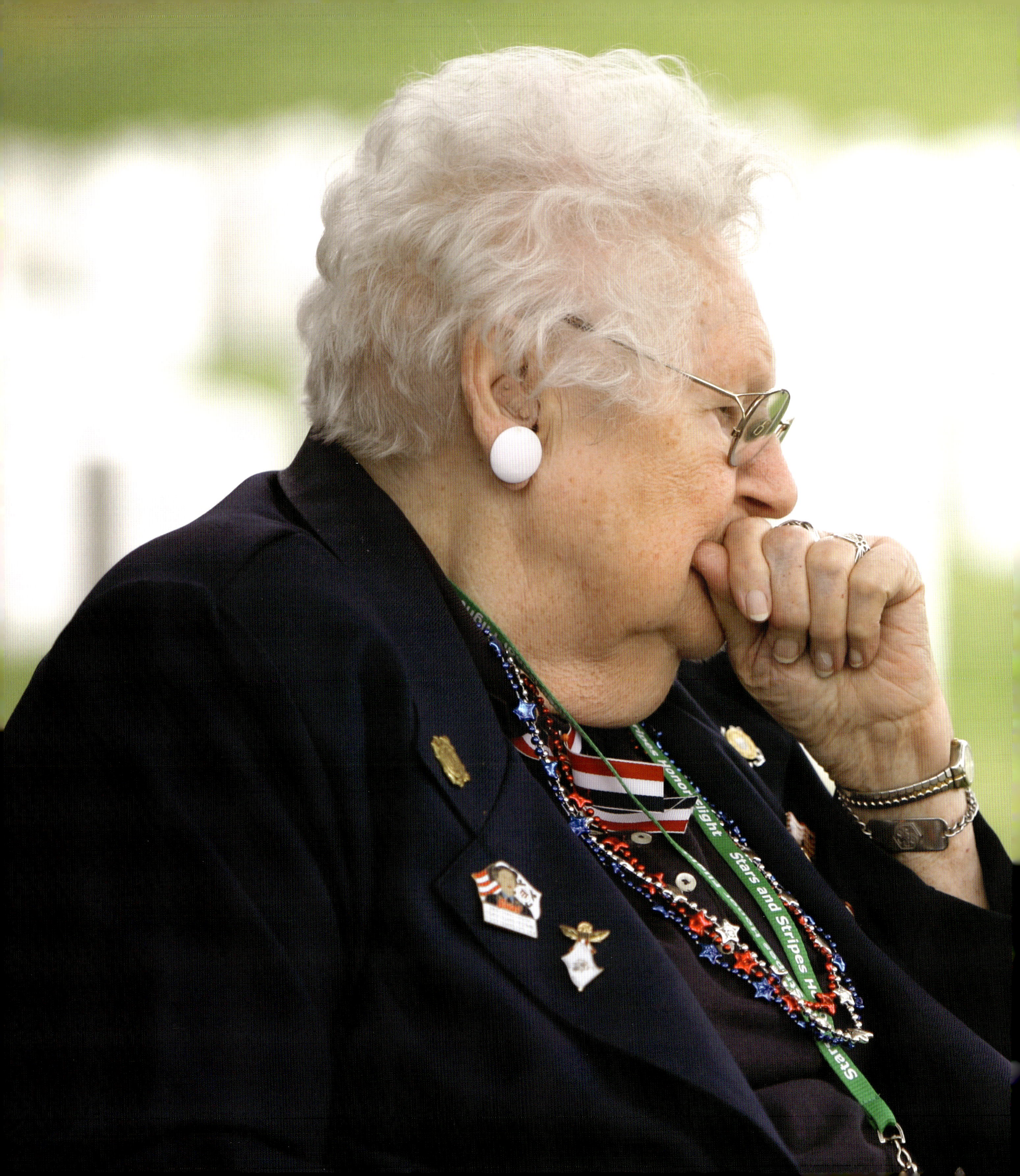
Honor Flight
Stars and Stripes

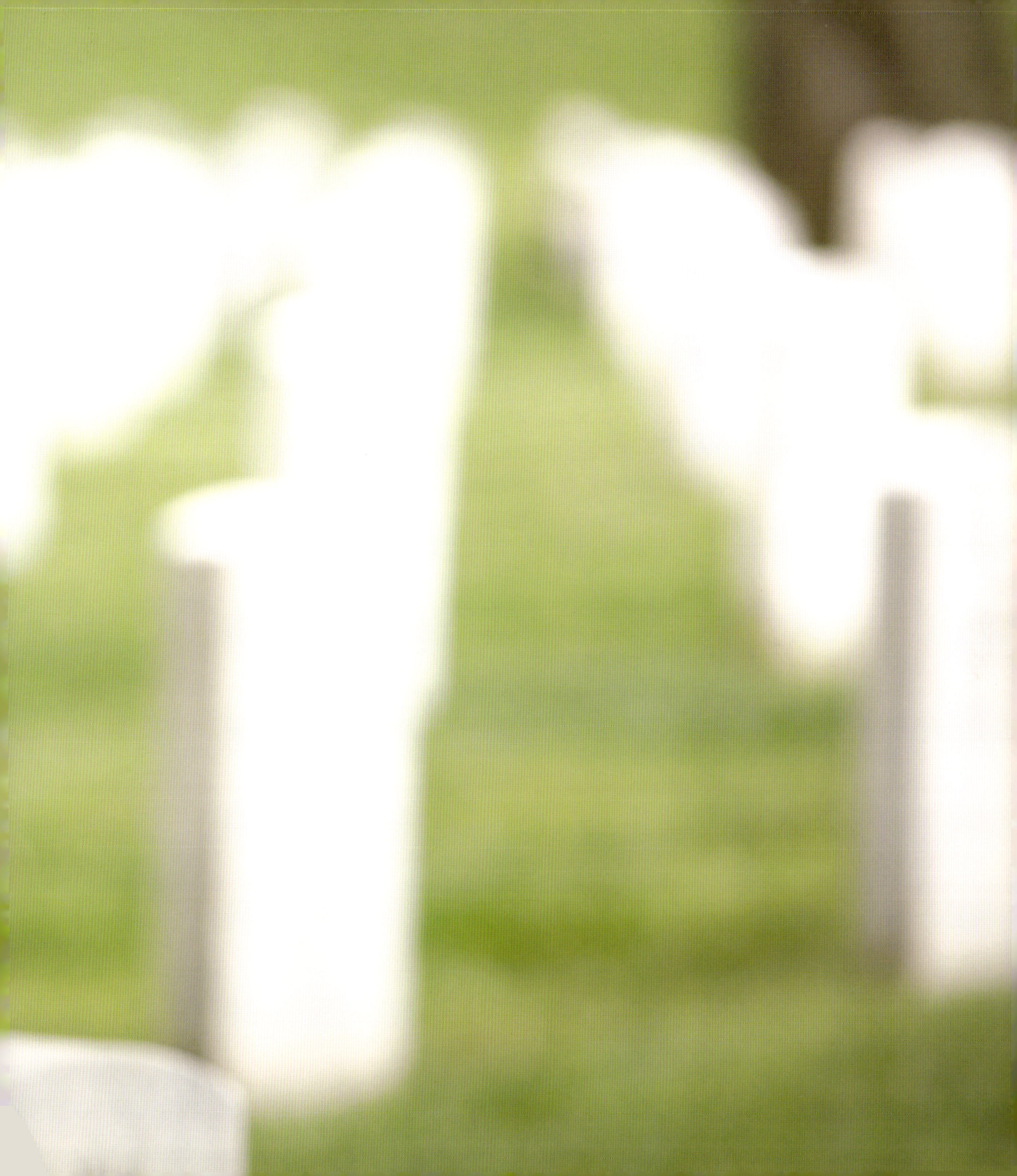

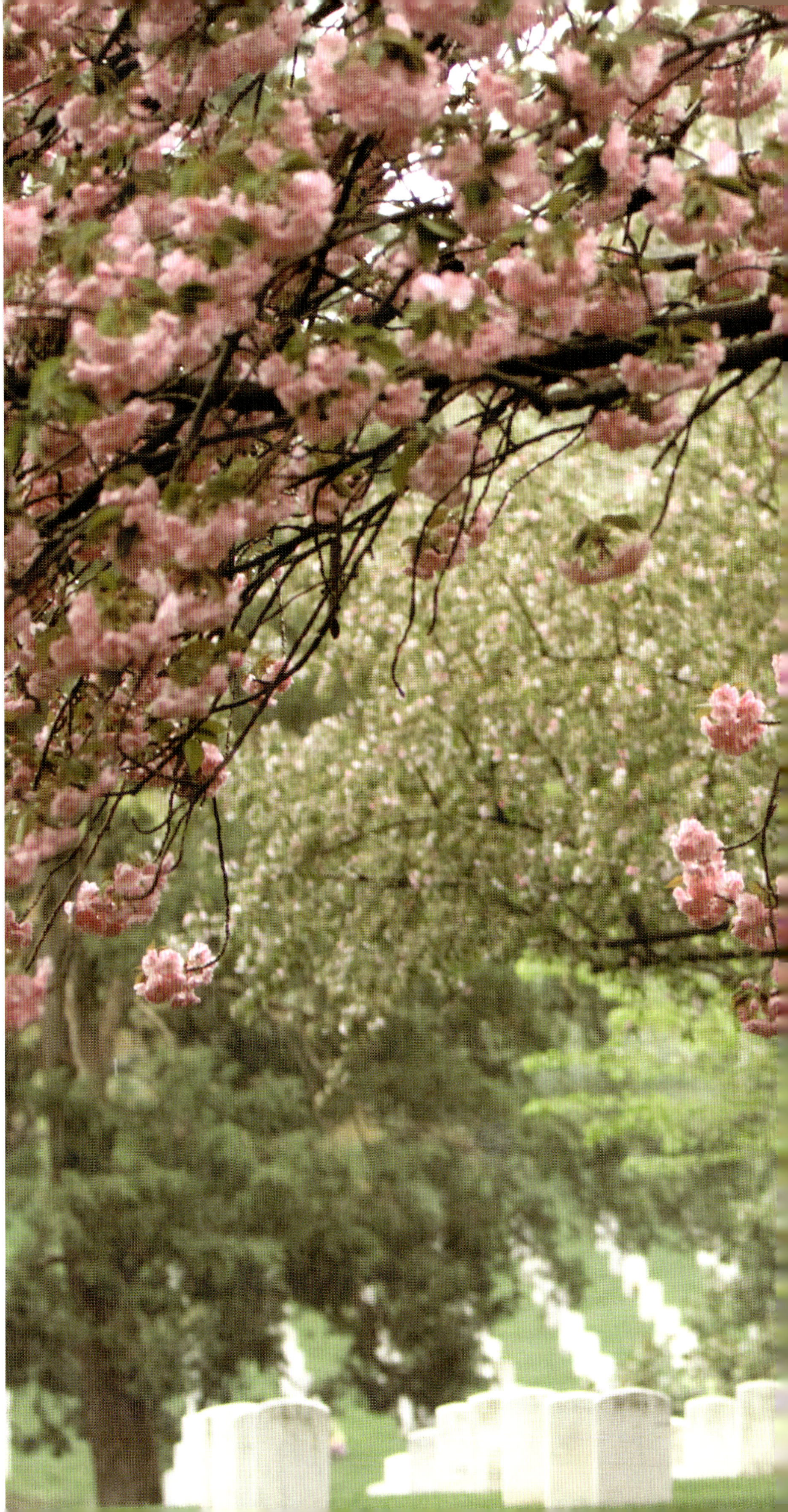

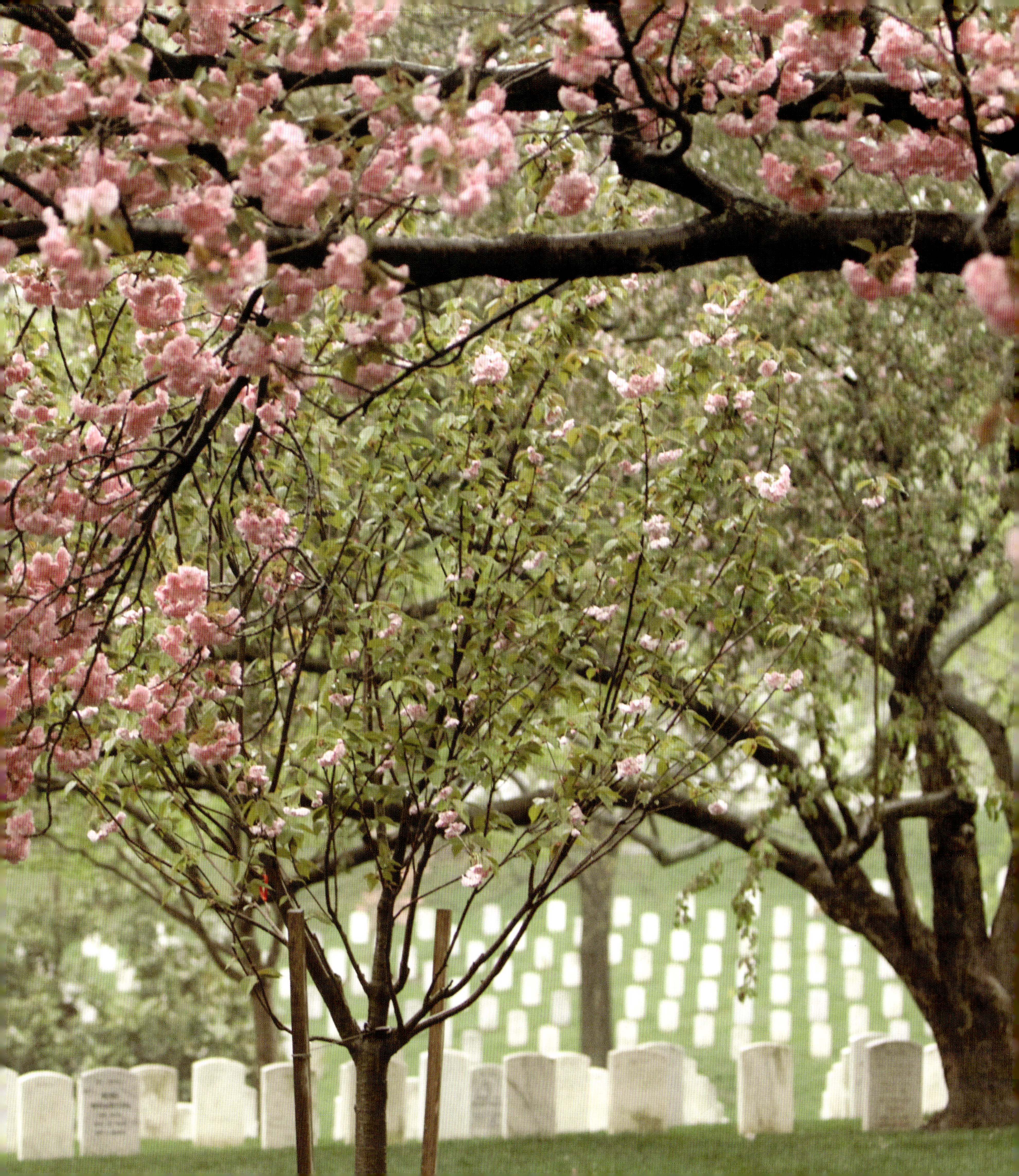

Mail Call

★ ★ ★

1900 HOURS

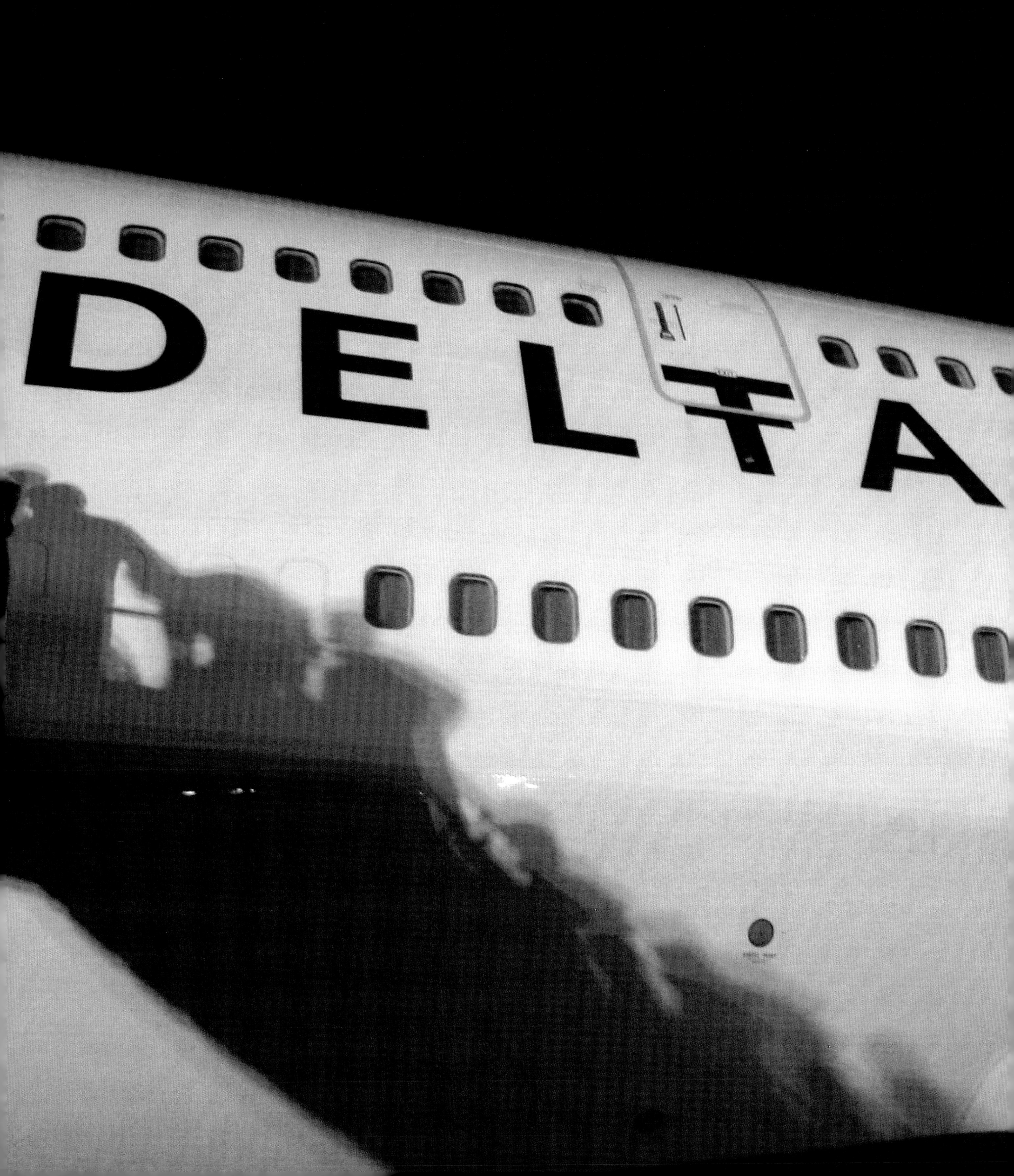
DELTA

After a whirlwind day in Washington, the weary veterans board the plane for the flight to Milwaukee.

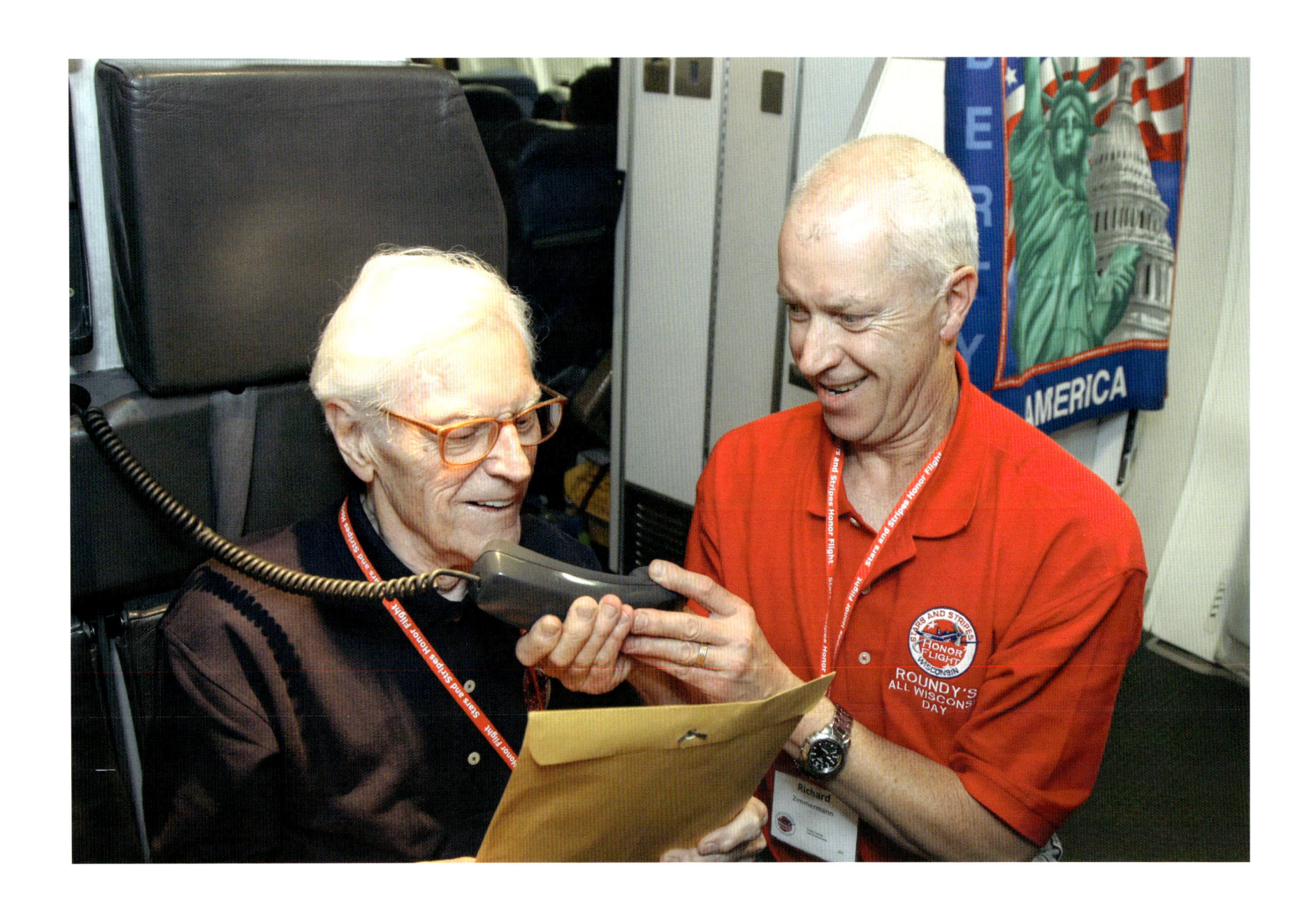

WWII veteran Carl Zimmermann, announces Mail Call, an emotion-packed experience as veterans receive packets of letters, drawings and photos from their family, friends and even strangers who want to thank them for their service. An award-winning radio and television broadcaster, Carl began his 50-year career as a combat reporter with the U.S. Army during World War II. During the Korean War, he created and narrated the Army's syndicated program, *The Big Picture*.

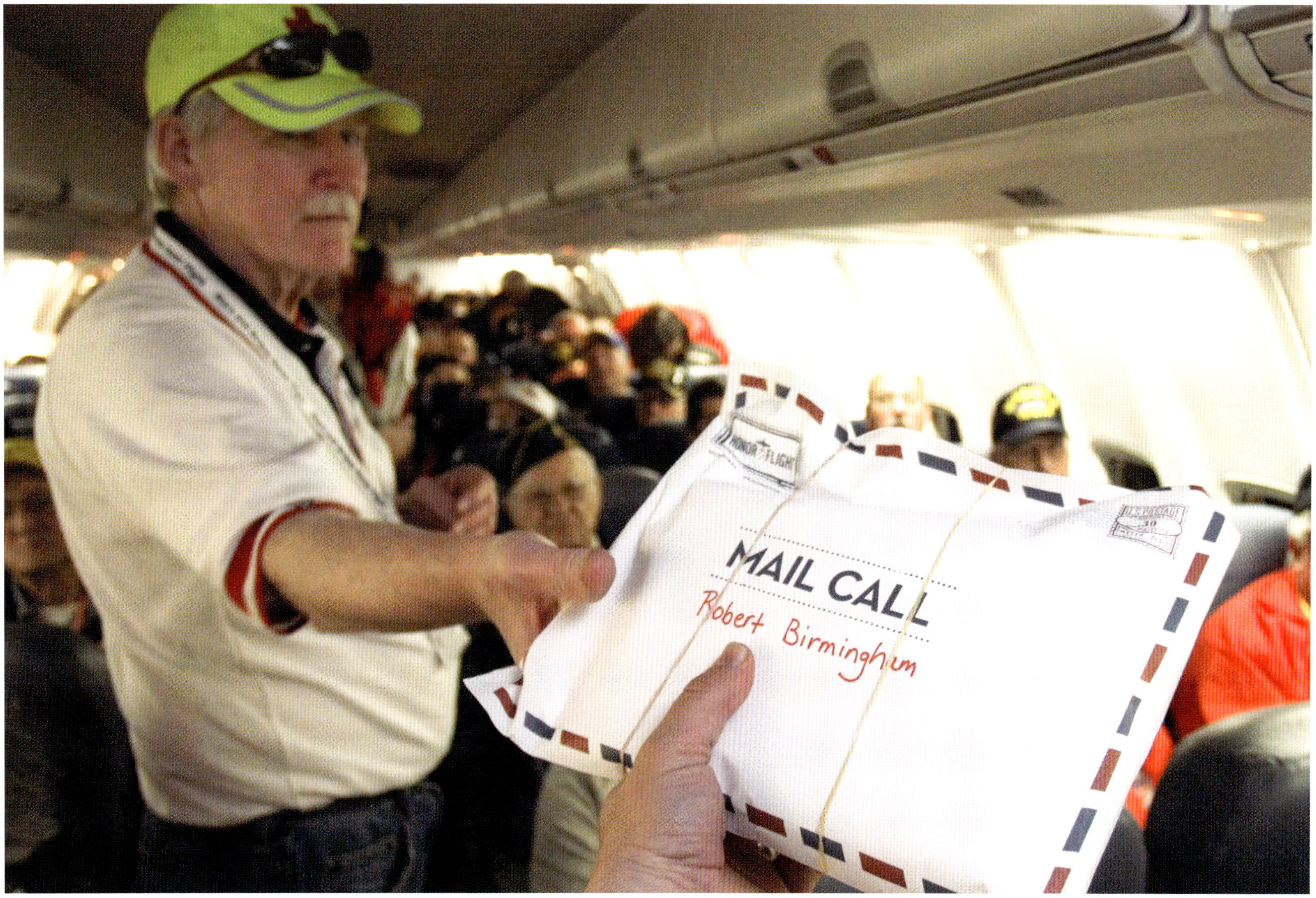
MAIL CALL
Robert Birmingham

Robert Budjac
Stars and Stripes Honor Flight
Bravo 2
RIFLE
BAYONET

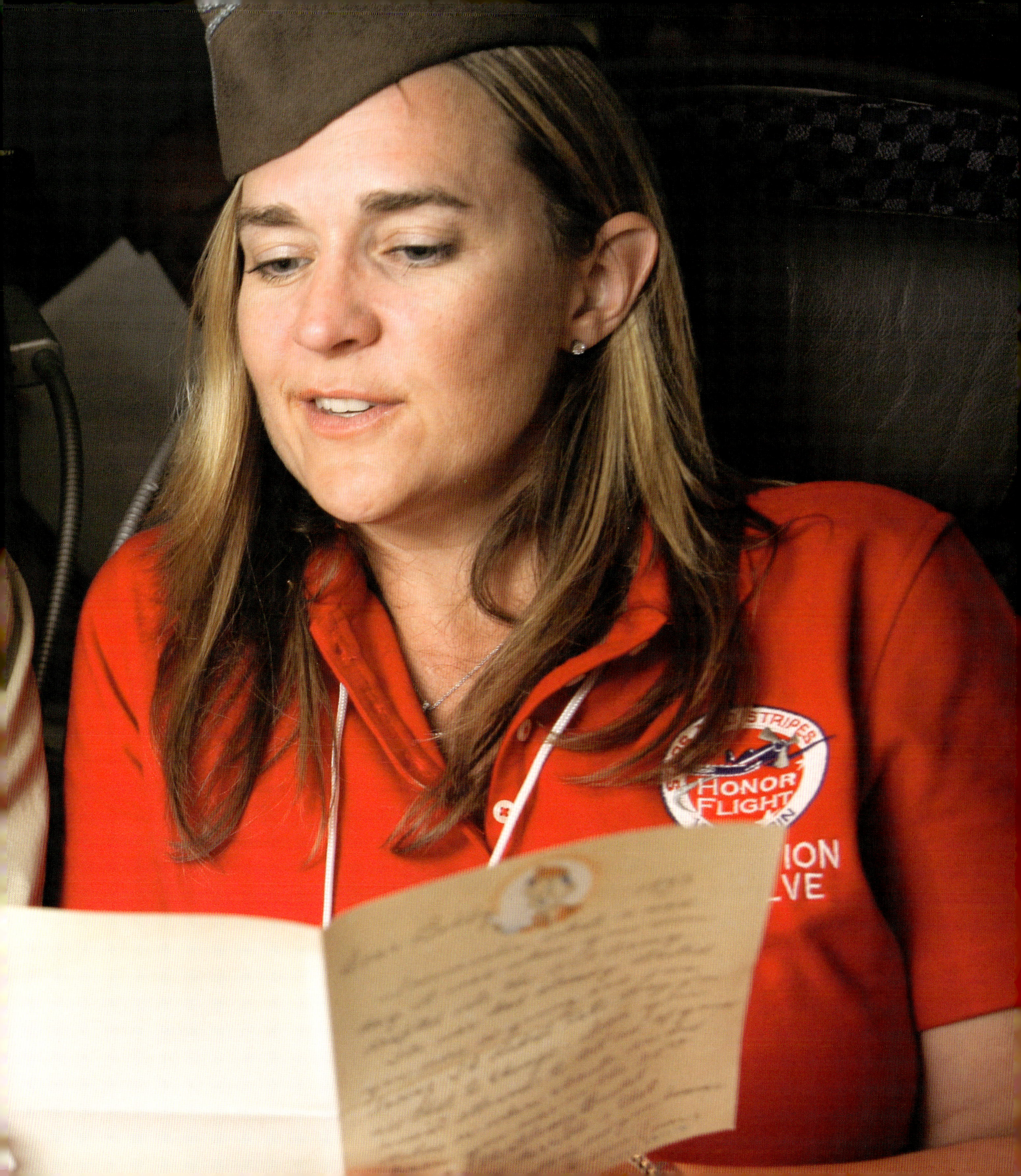
HONOR
FLIGHT

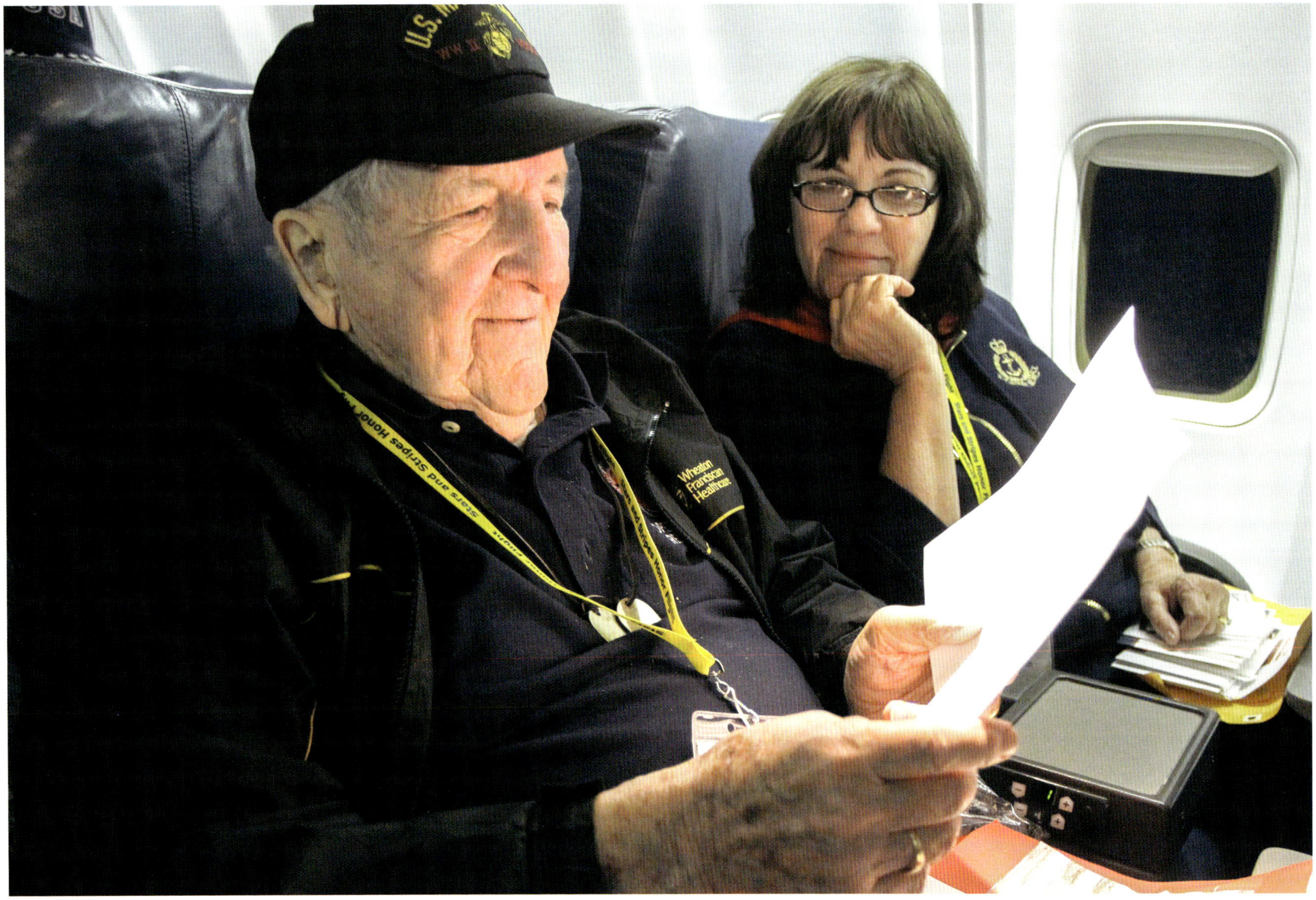
Wheaton
Franciscan
Healthcare

Dad —
Just wanted to let you know
how proud we are of you and of
your service to the country.
Not many kids nowadays understa[nd]
what it meant to be drafted at a t[ime]
when your adult life was just begi[nning].
Thank you for serving your coun[try]
and your family so well.
You have done a great job r[aising]
a fine family and we all lov[e you]
for it.
Besides, if it hadn't been [for]
[you] and a wonderful "pen p[al"]
[thr]ough the mail — w[e]
[m]ight not be here toda[y].
Luck for us, you and M[om]
[got] to write! You had a wonde[rful]
[life, you] had a honor[able life]
[to ser]ve the
Lov[e]

HONOR
OPERATION RESOLVE
Shelly Schnitzer
Veteran is
Joseph Liberto
GRANDPA

Joseph Liberto
Stars and Stripes Honor Flight
Bravo 3
STARS AND STRIPES
HONOR FLIGHT
WISCONSIN
OPERATION
RESOLVE

252

Orville Lemke (above) was featured in the award-winning film *Honor Flight*. He passed away six weeks after this photo was taken. His widow Marion attends every Stars and Stripes Honor Flight Homecoming in memory of Orville.

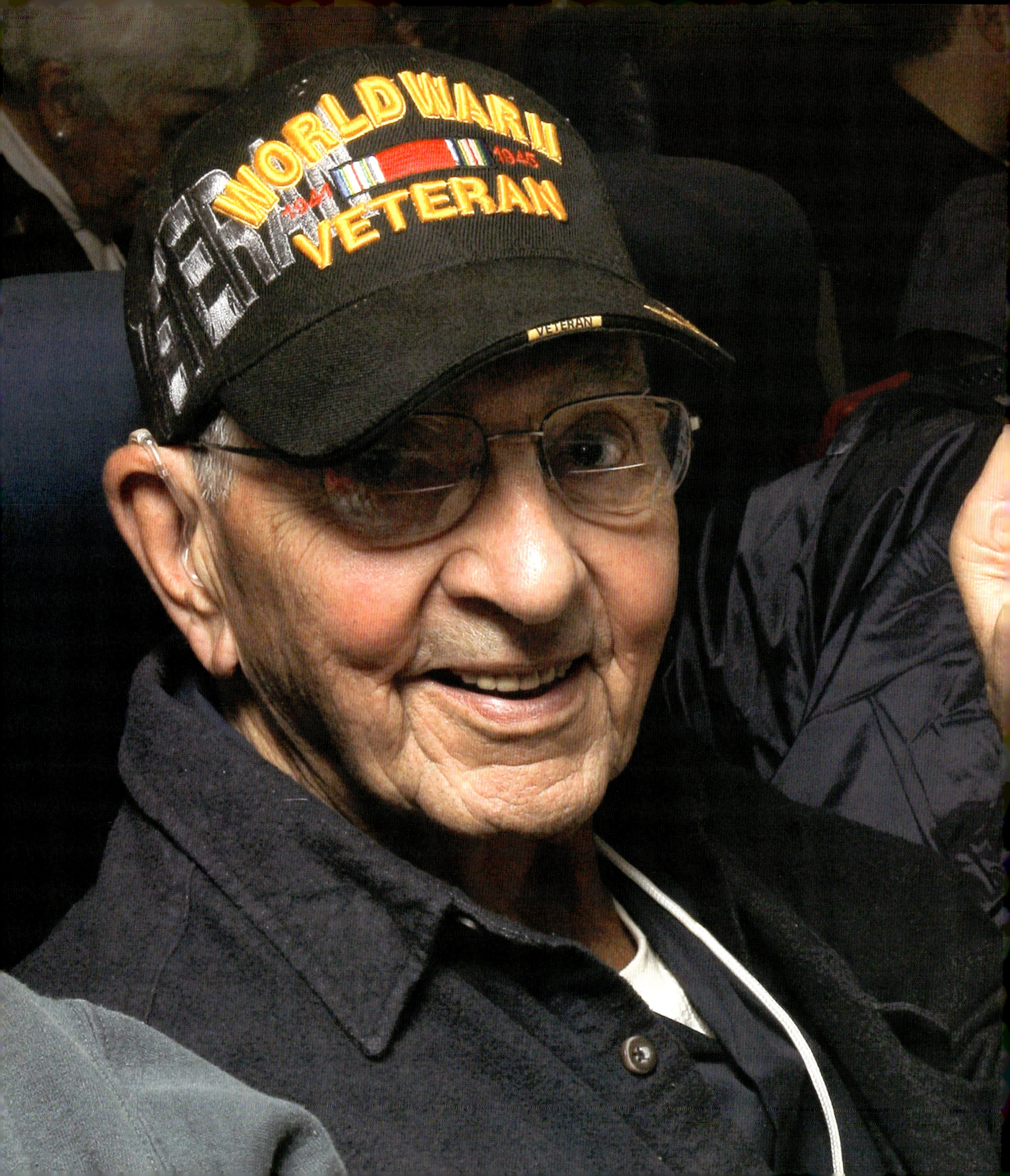
WORLD WAR II
1941 1945
VETERAN
VETERAN

THANK YOU for FIGHTING for our freedom!!!

XXOOXXOO

Lauren

Field of Honor Observer
SATURDAY, AUGUST 11th, 2012
MILLER PARK
PEACE!
WAR ENDS. V-DAY PROCLAIMED!
The Story Behind "Every Day is a Bonus"
How The National Honor Flight Movement Began
STARS AND STRIPES
and Stripes Honor Flight

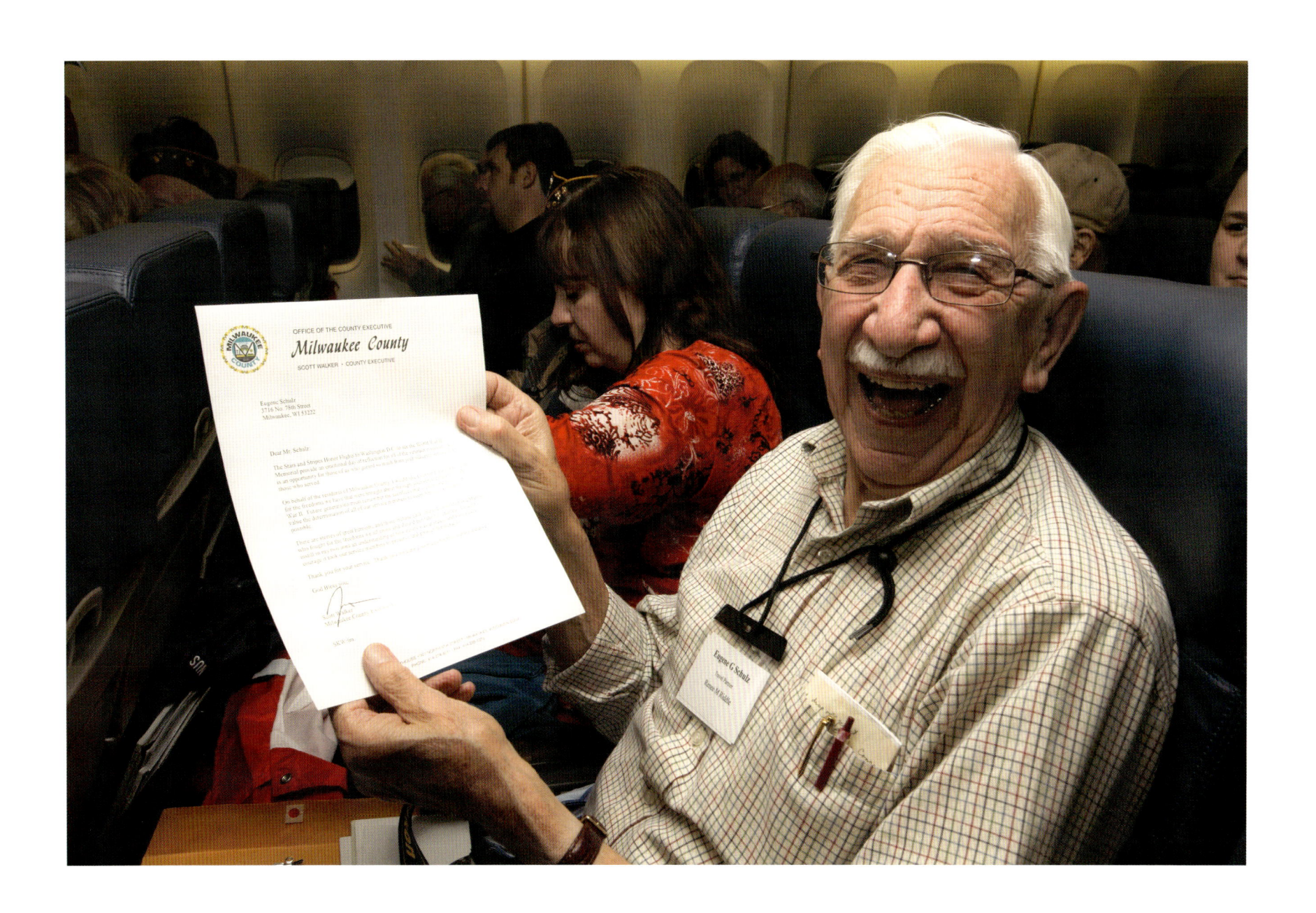

NAVY
STARS AND STRIPES
HONOR FLIGHT
WISCONSIN
ROUNDY'S
ALL WISCONSIN
DAY
Leonard

U.S. COAST GUARD
STARS AND STRIPES
HONOR FLIGHT
WISCONSIN
ROUNDY'S
ALL WISCONSIN
DAY
Stars and Stripes Honor Flight
Roman

November 2011 . Stars & Stripes Honor Flight
i love you
grandpa
what an amazing gift you are to our family
and to the world!
thank YOU
for your WWII service
I hope this day and your travels have been refreshing
rewarding and re-energizing to you more
You deserve this, and so much
for the selfless gift of service that you have given
to the whole country without expecting anything
in return. WOW
I am so proud of you, your stature, your patience,
your strength, your endless amount of love for us.
your granddaughter, Allison

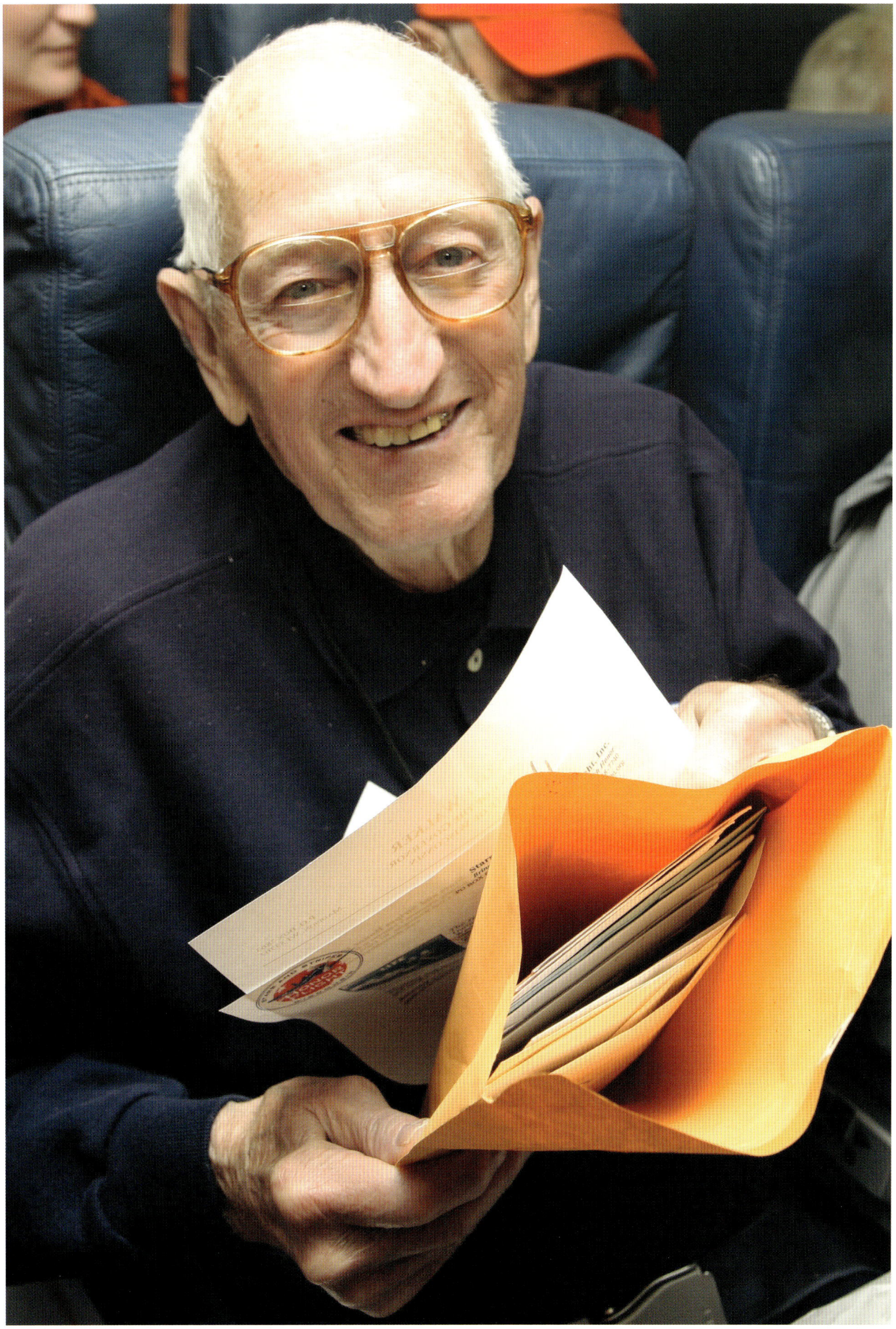

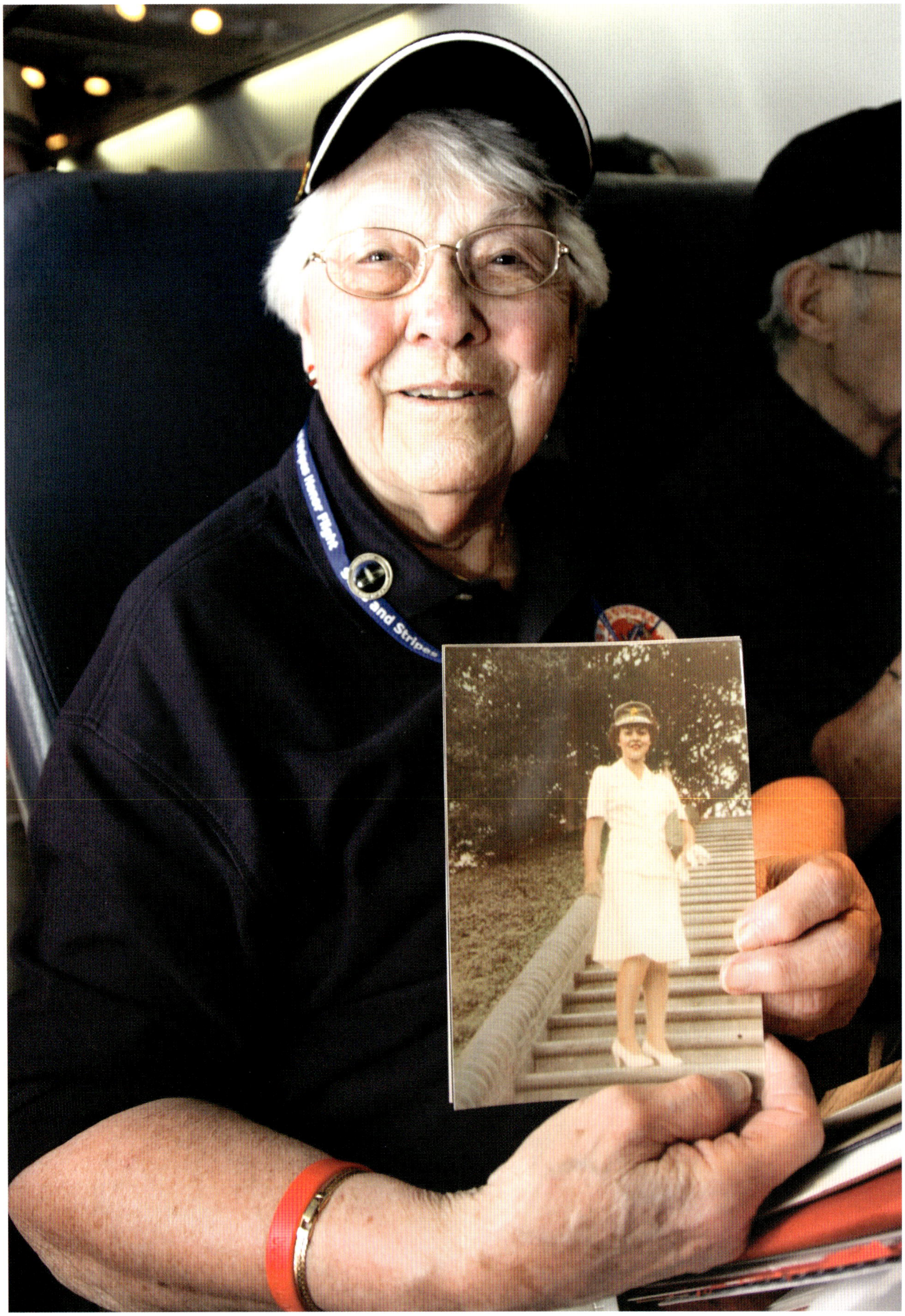
and Stripes

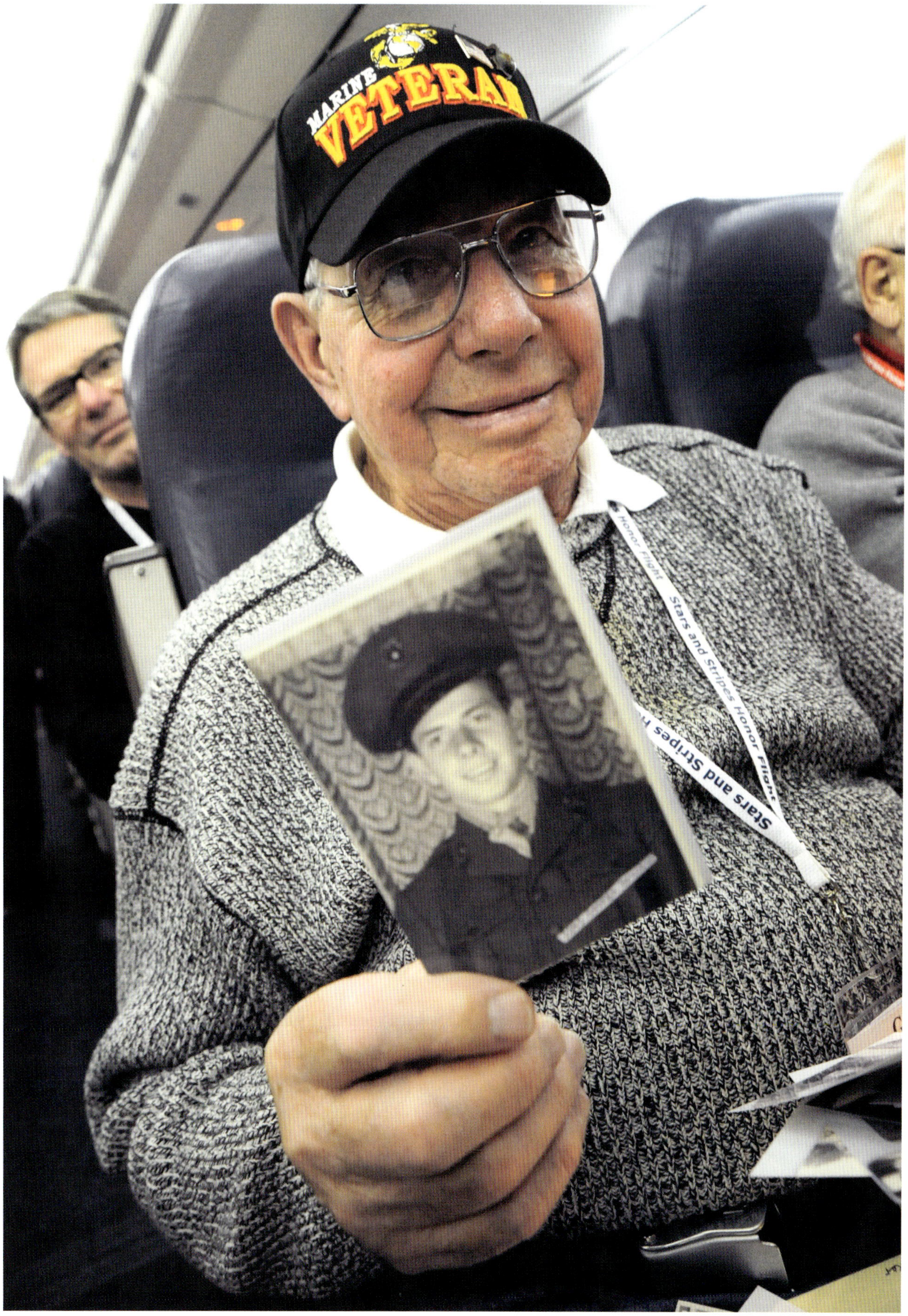
MARINE
VETERAN
Stars and Stripes Honor Flight

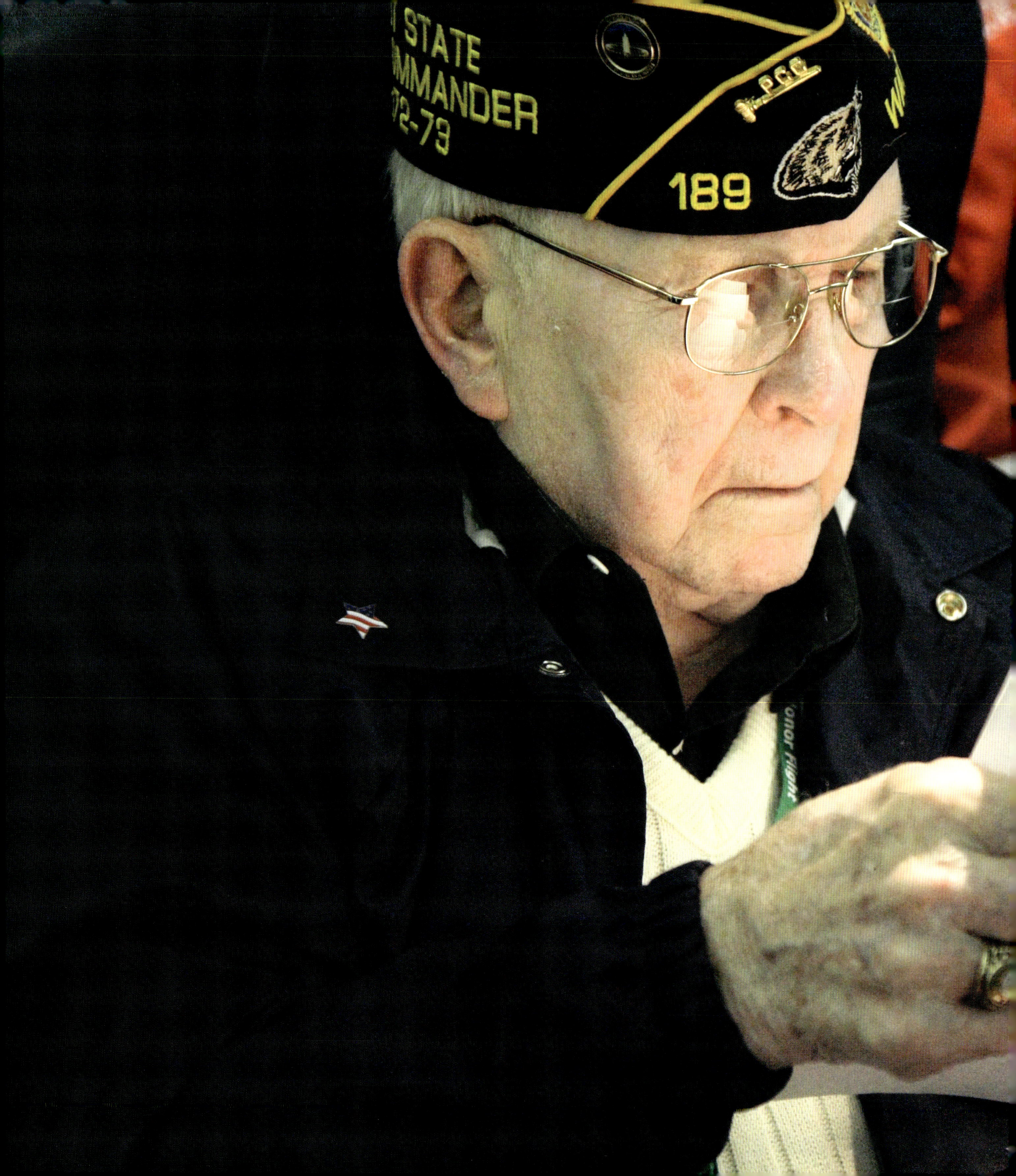
STATE
PCC
189

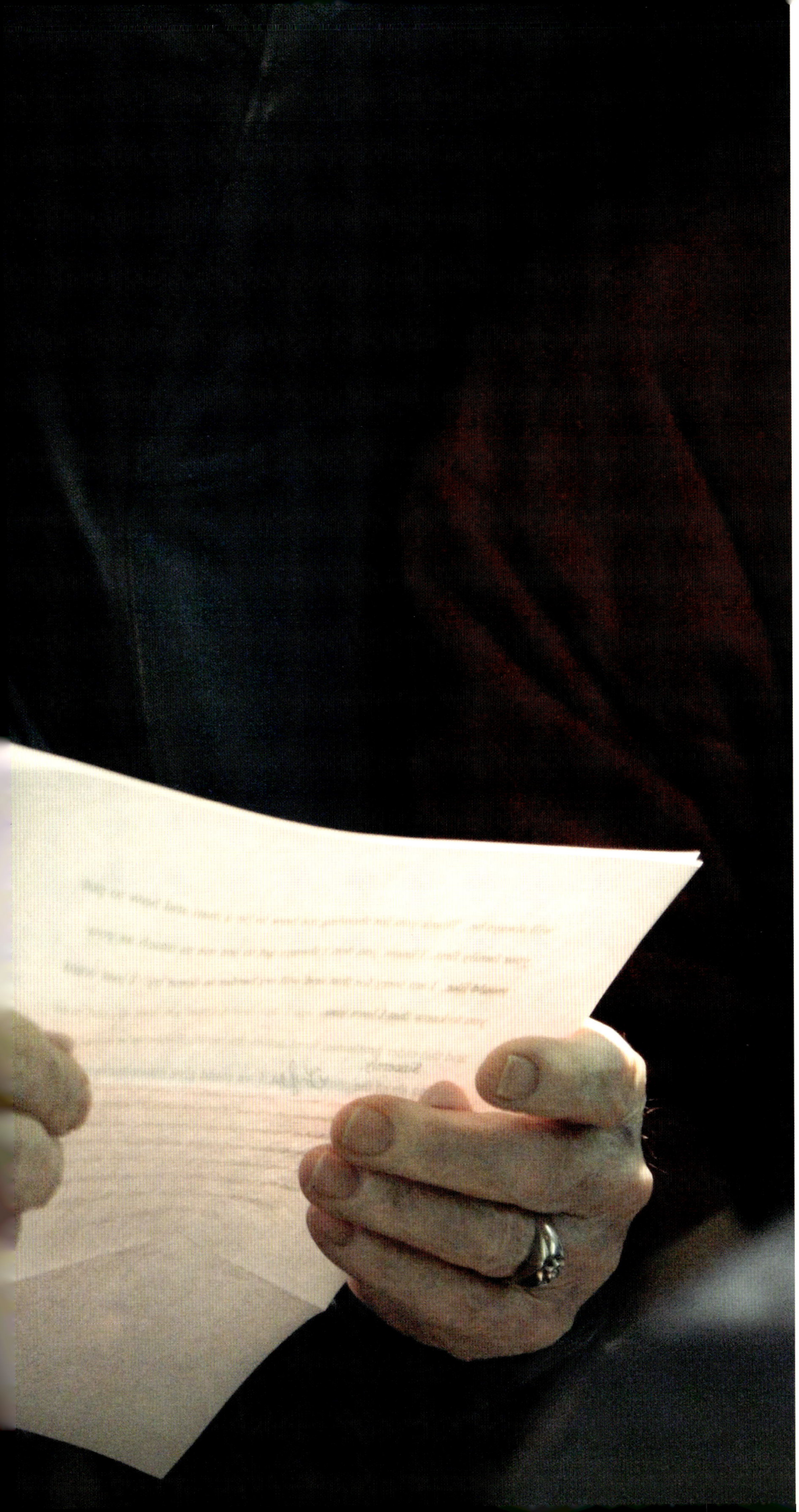

Homecoming

★ ★ ★

2100 HOURS

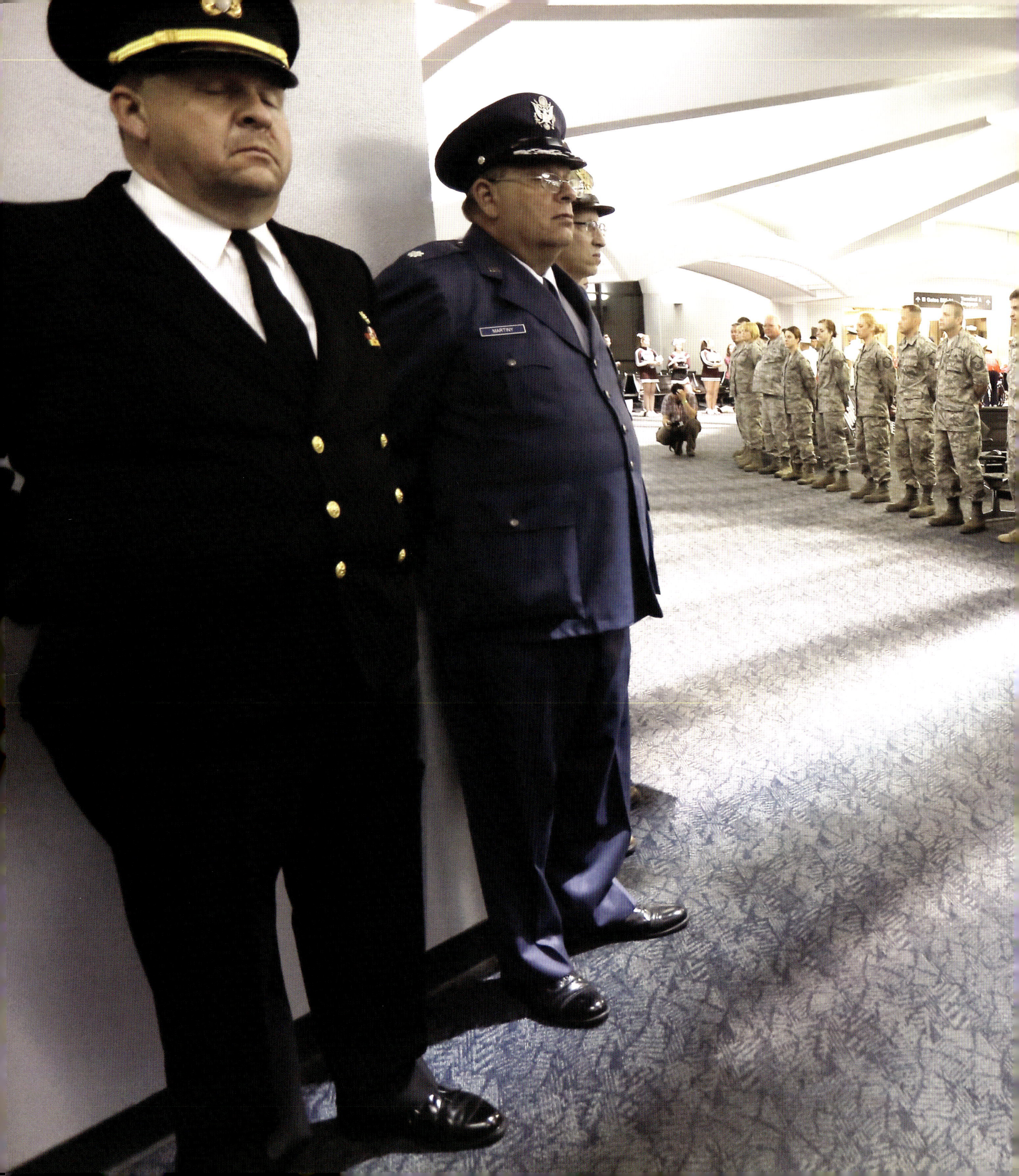
MARTINY

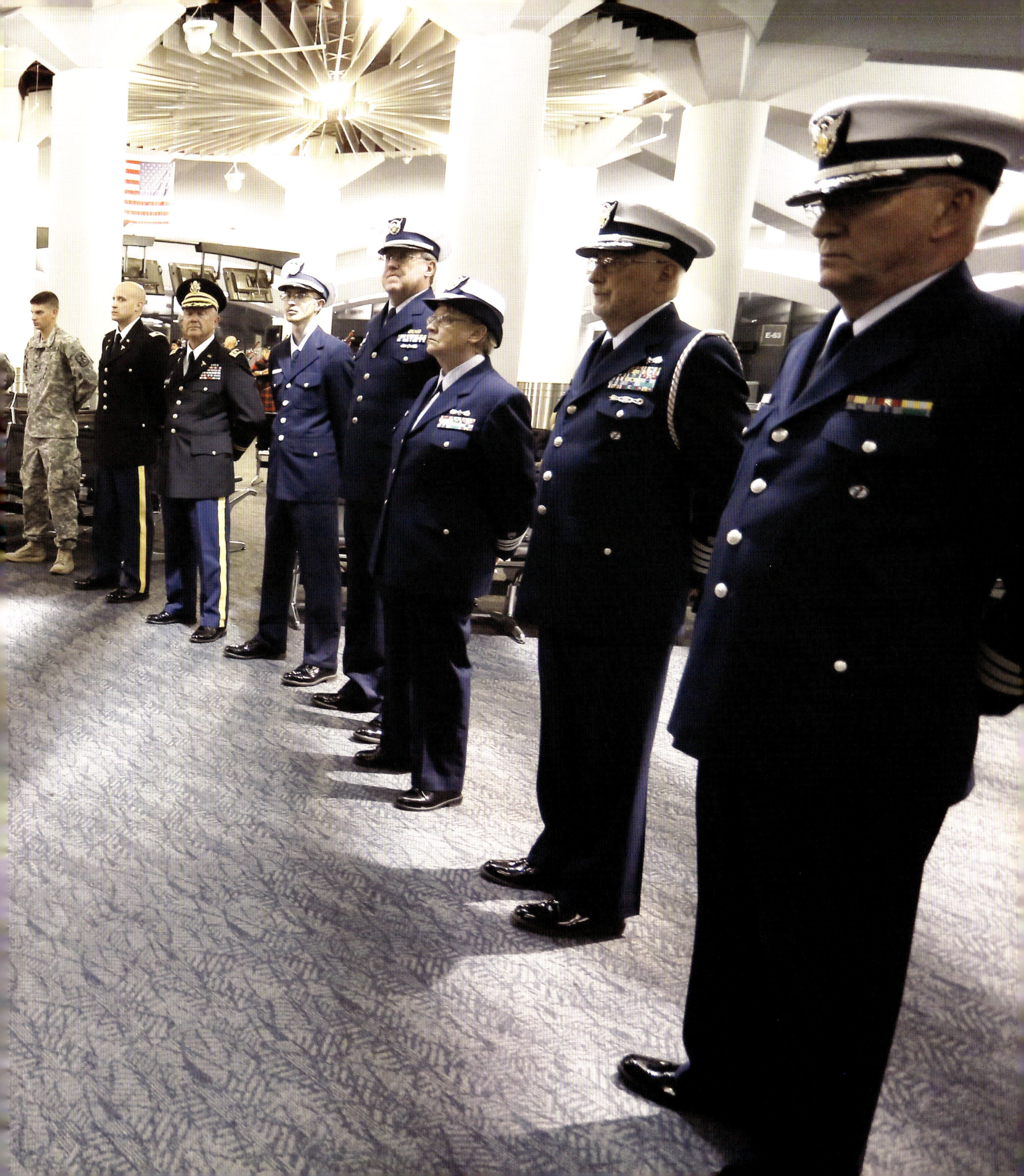

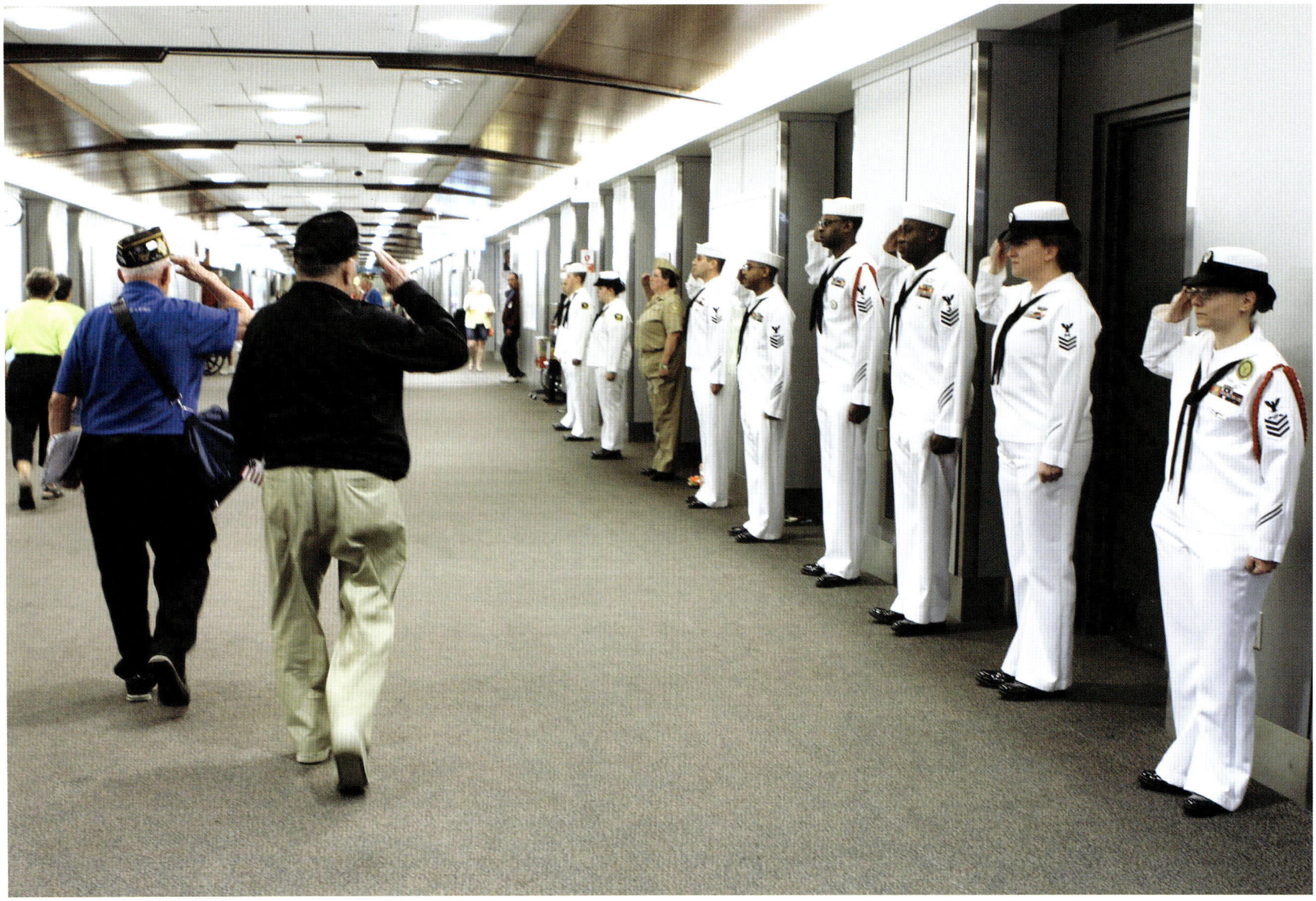

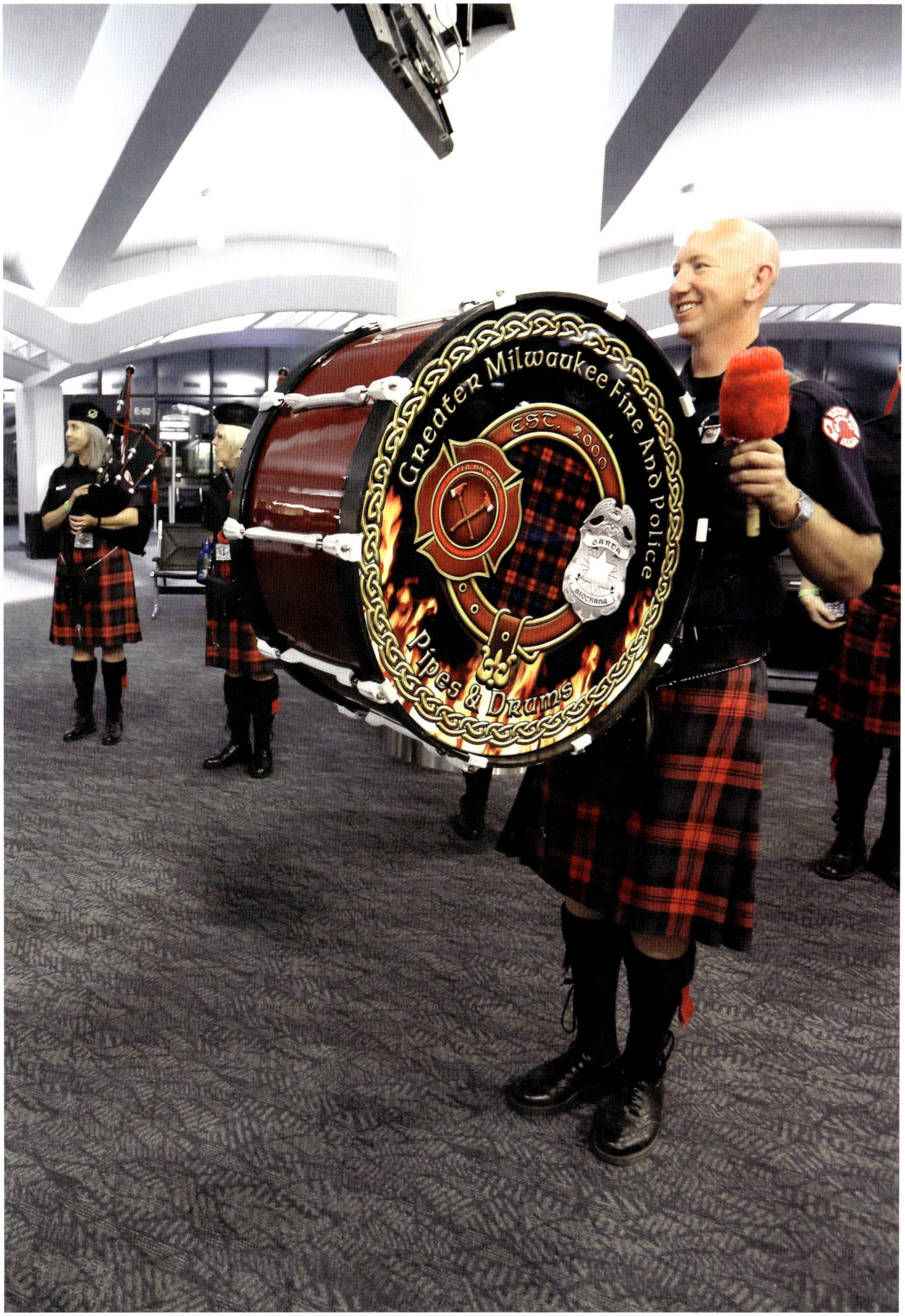
Greater Milwaukee Fire And Police
EST. 2000
Pipes & Drums

Sailors from Naval Station Great Lakes, the Navy's largest training station and only boot camp, volunteer to attend these Homecoming celebrations. The silent, solemn display of respect from a younger active-duty generation often inspires a return salute from the aging veterans.

FAMILY
E 60
Welcome
Välkommen
Zoosab Togtxais
MILWAUKEE
स्वागत
DO NOT ENTER
Terminal and Baggage

"Hurry up and wait, just like the old days," we jokingly remind our tired heroes as they deplane in Milwaukee near the end of their long journey. Soon, they begin to sense that this time, this place, this community has something very special in store for them. Rounding the corner to the main concourse, eyes widen and the ear-to-ear smiles melt into joyful, cathartic tears as the bands play and a chorus of cheers resounds throughout General Mitchell International Airport. Welcome home, hero. Welcome home!

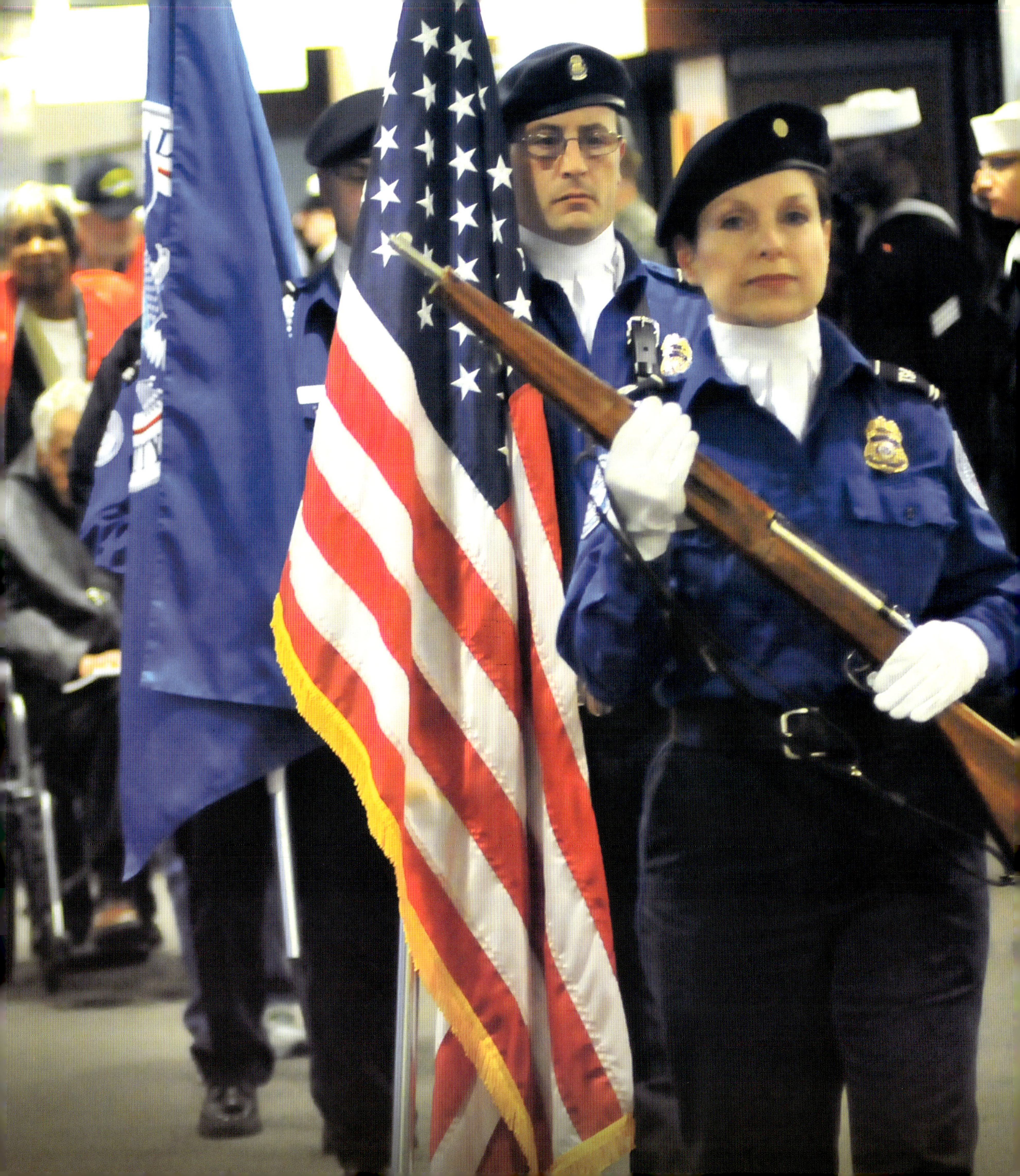

Welcome Home Vet's
WELCOME HOME
THANK YOU
Proud of You GrandPa
US
LY IS A BONUS

Welcome Home WWII VETS
Thank You!
COFFEE
WELCOME HOME HEROES!
Concourse C
Shops
WELCOME

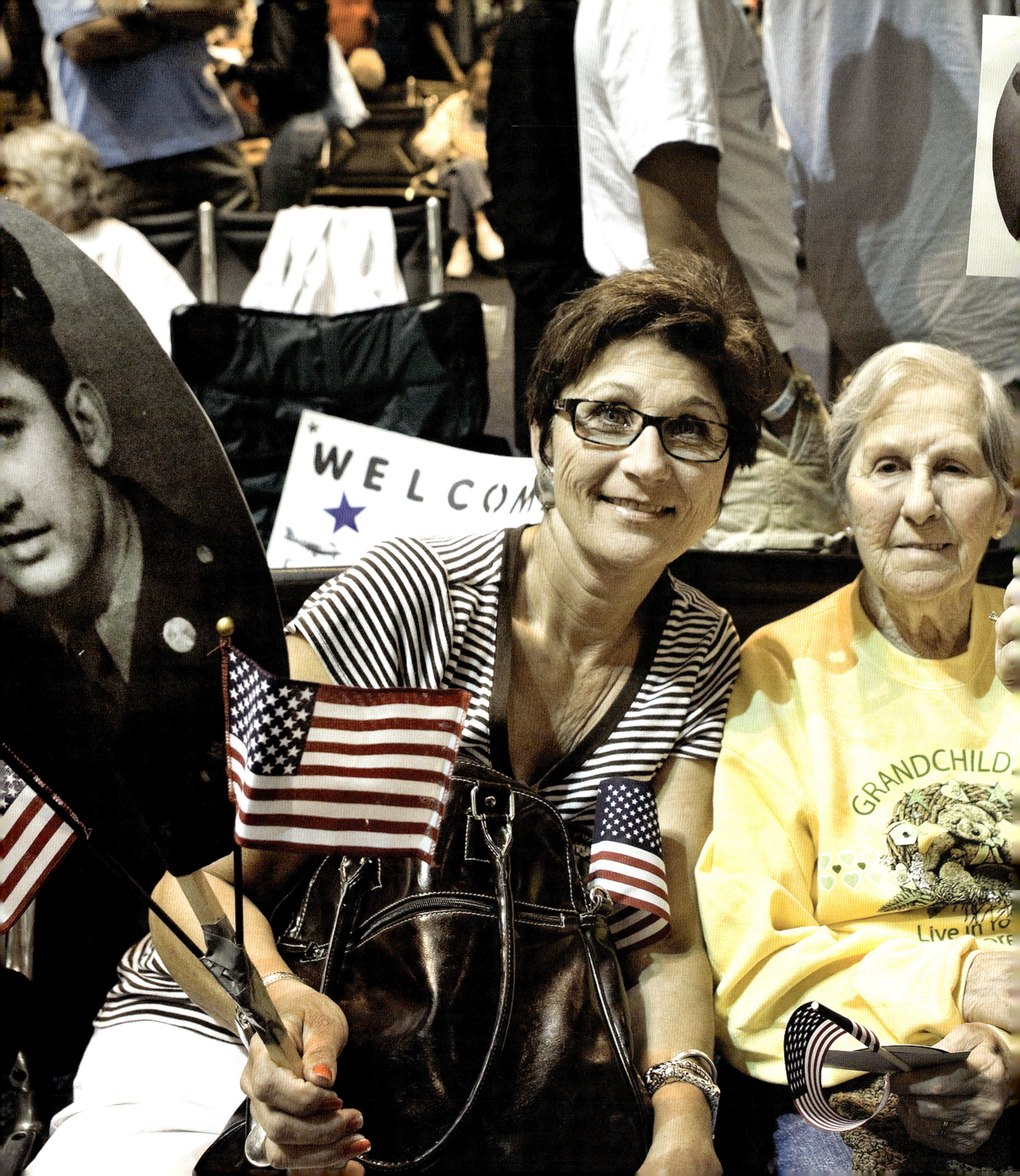
WELCOM
GRANDCHILD

The Homecoming crowd gathers hours beforehand just for the chance to shake hands with a WWII veteran and to be a part of this emotional ceremony.

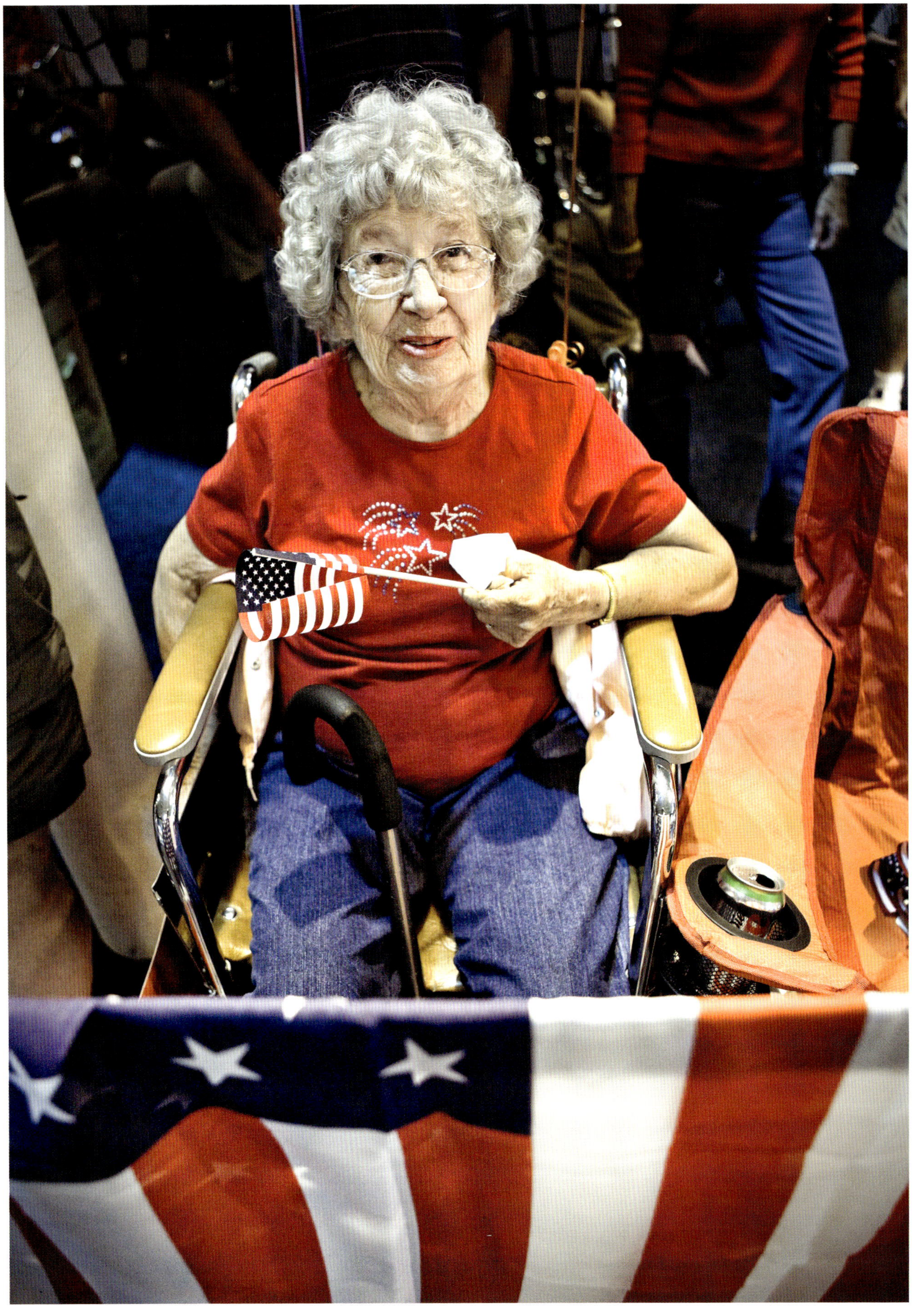

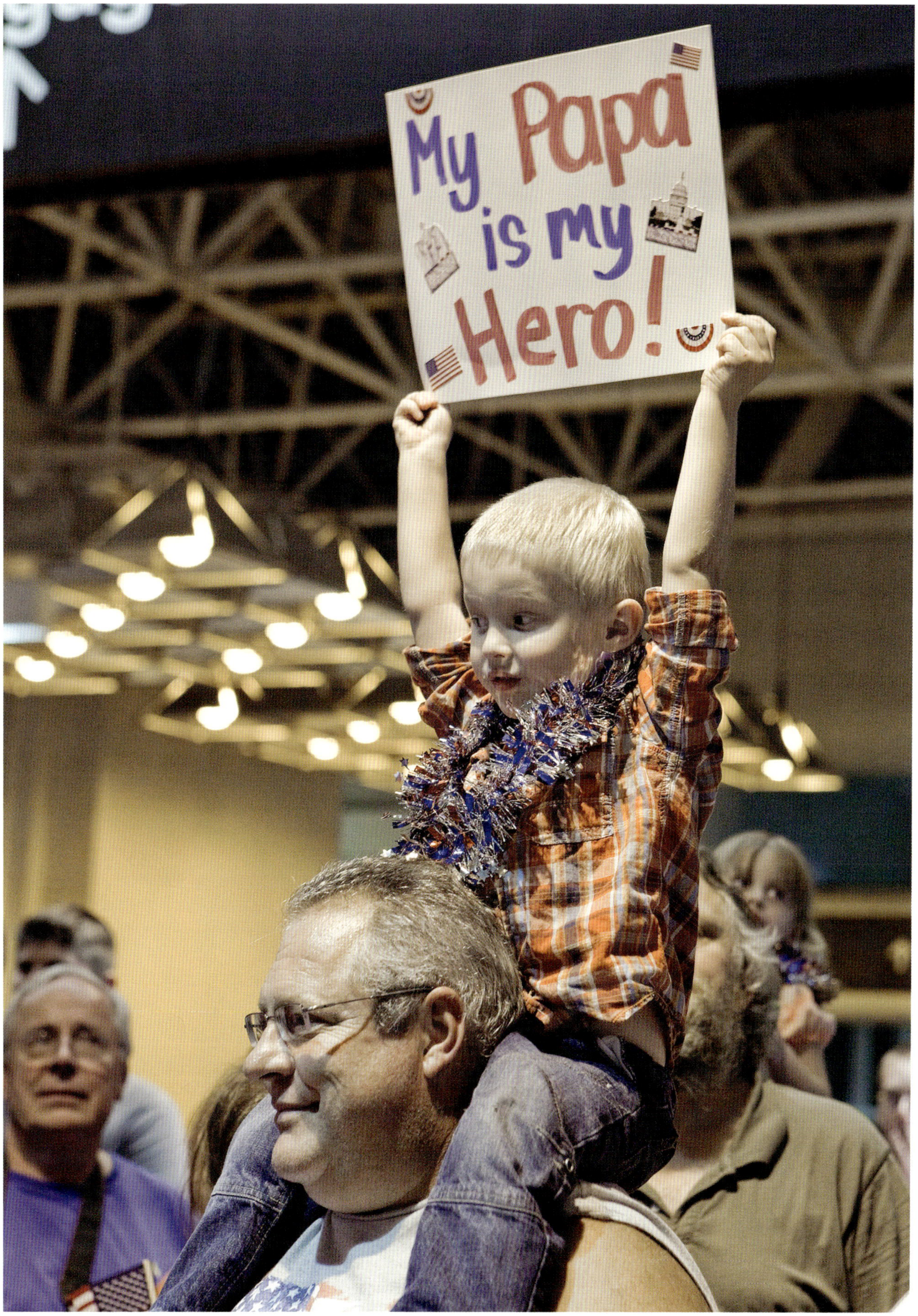
My Papa
is my
Hero!

282

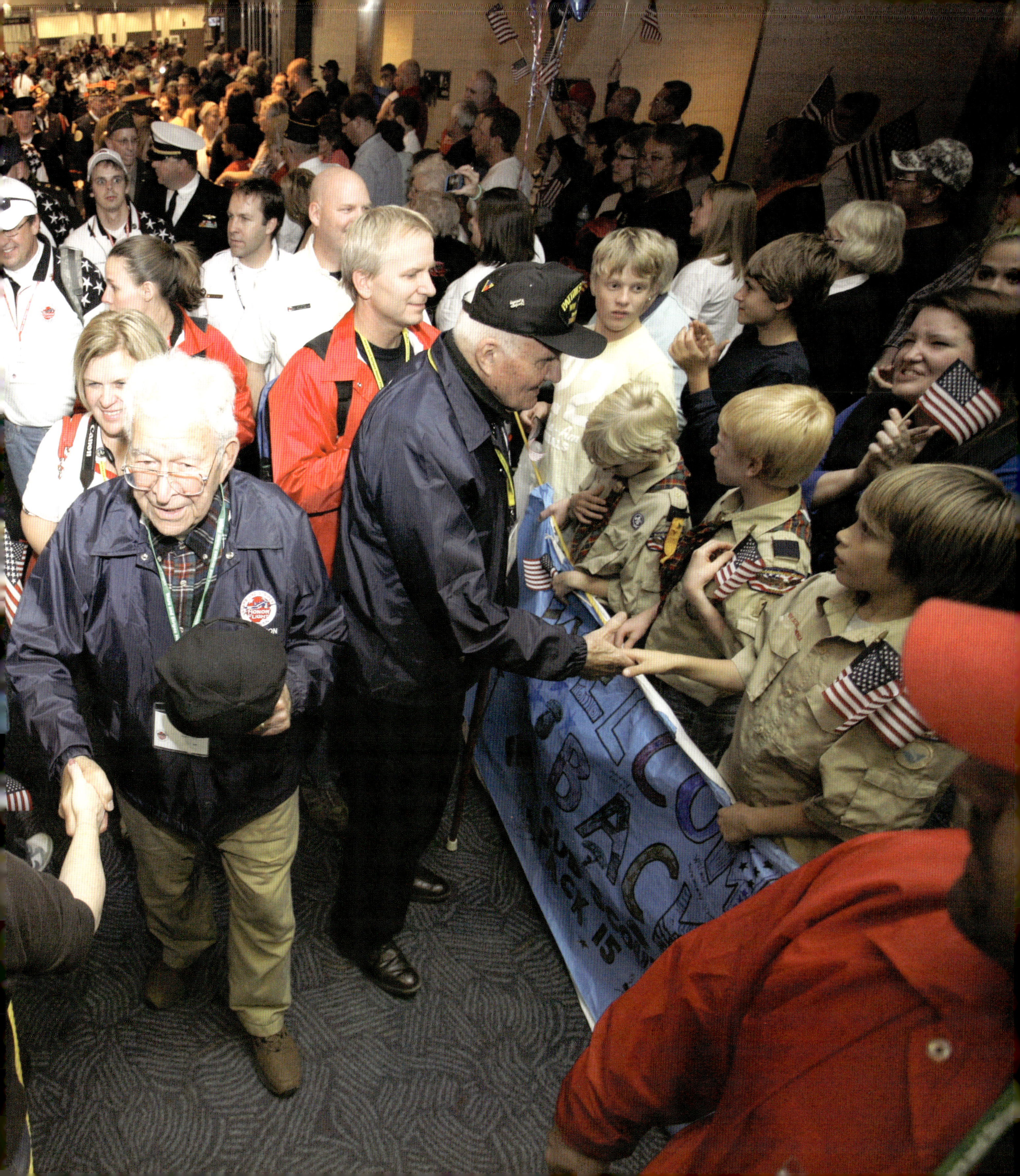

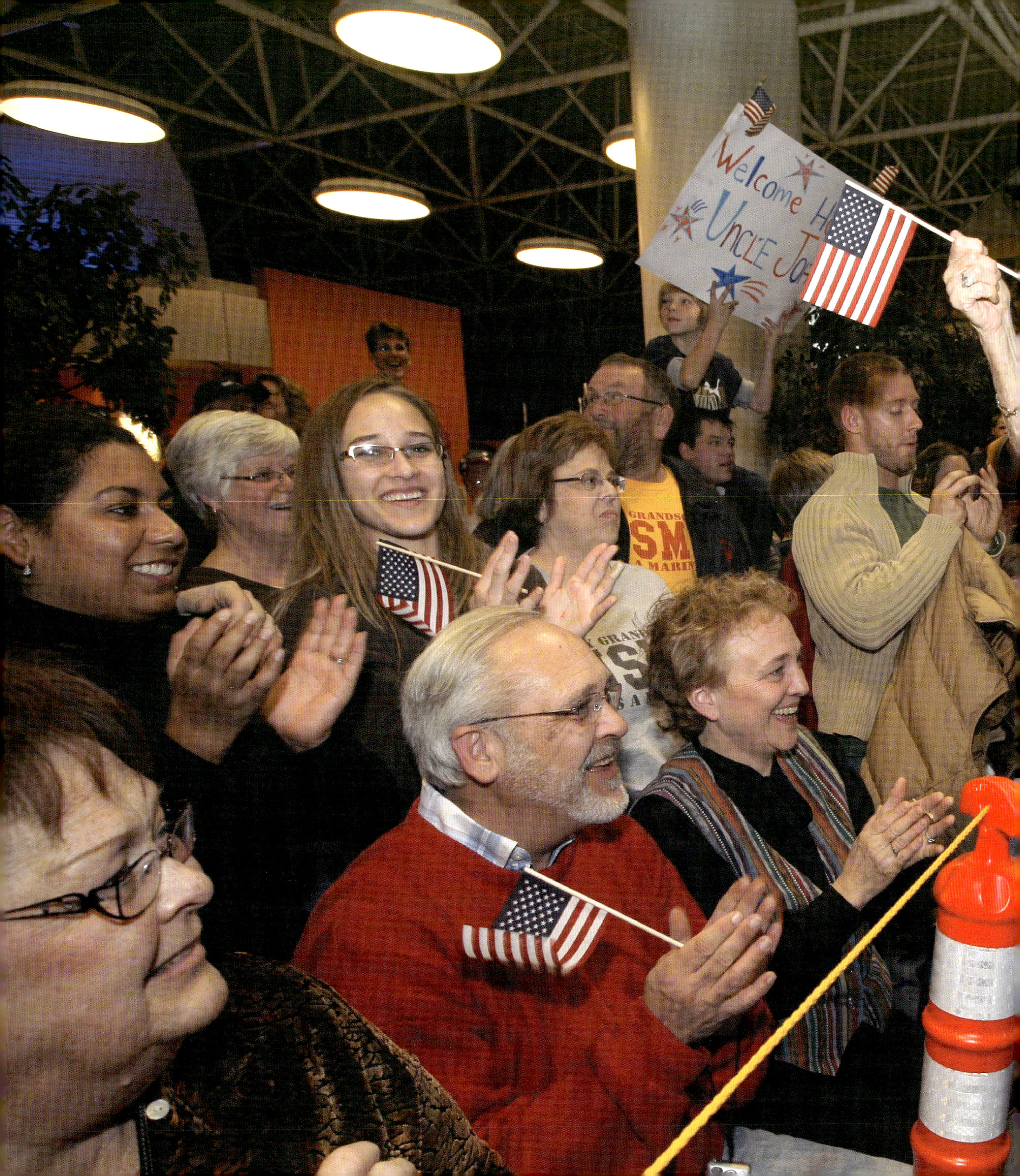
Welcome
Uncle

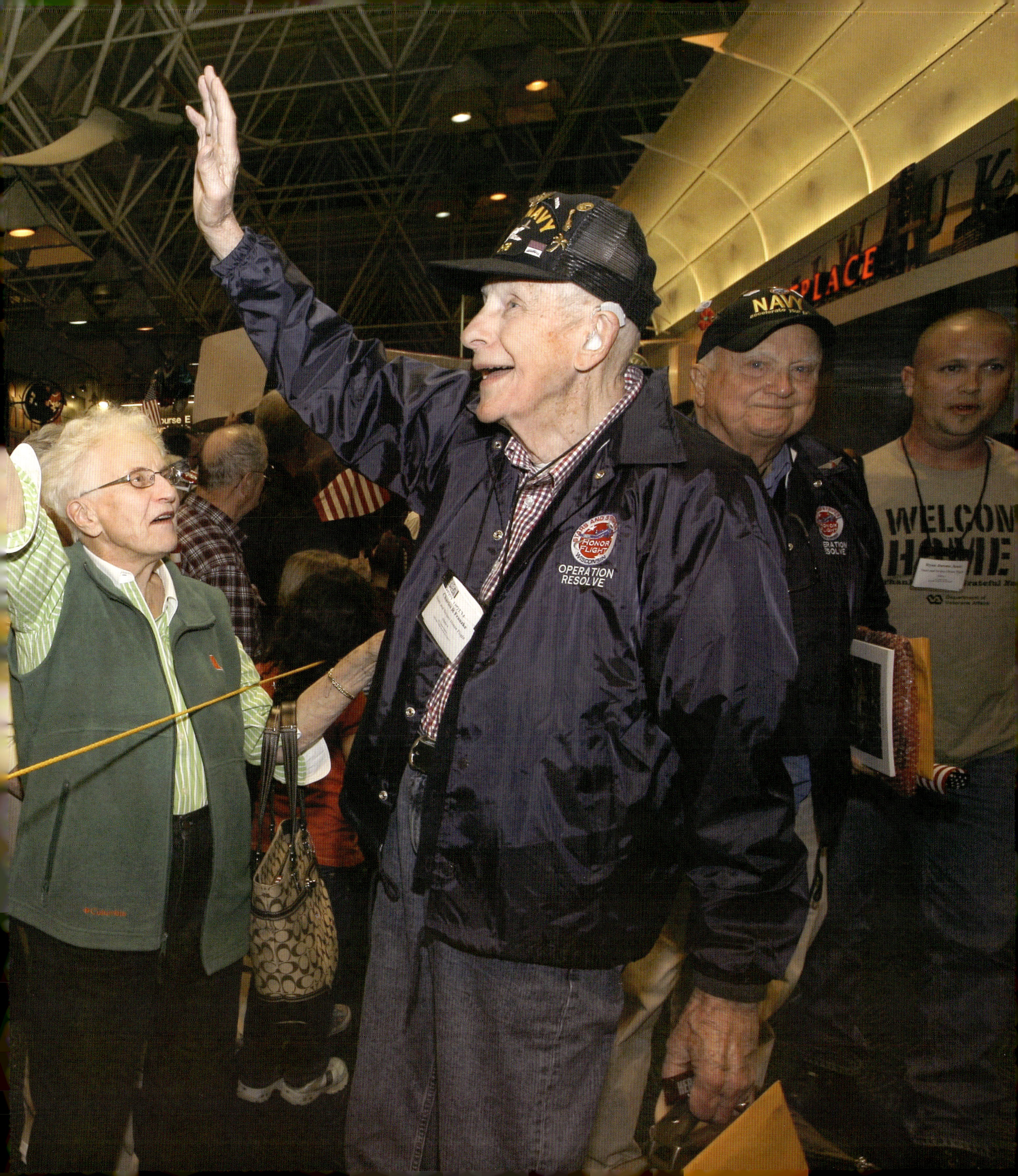
NAVY
PLACE
HONOR FLIGHT
OPERATION RESOLVE

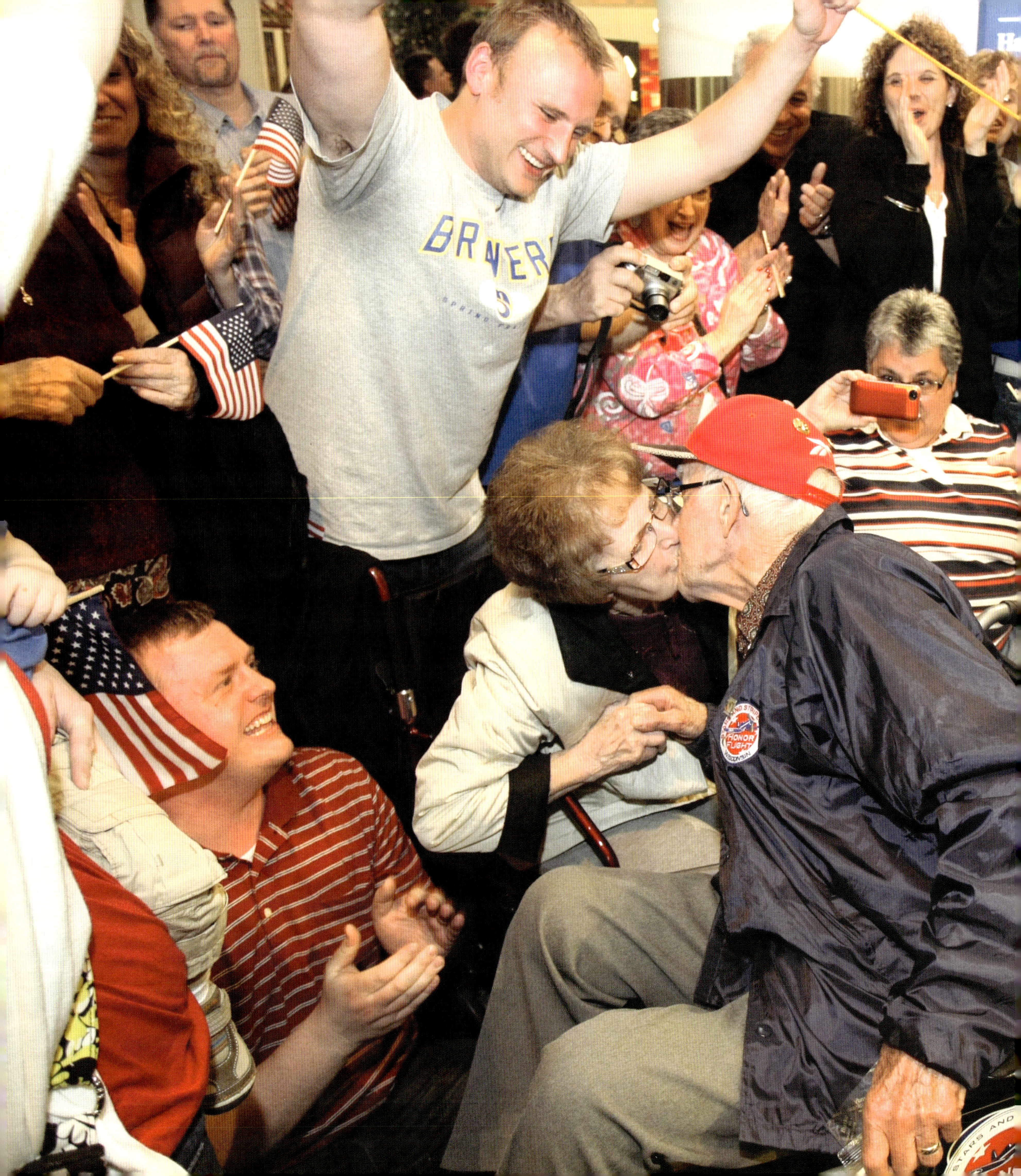
HONOR
FLIGHT

287

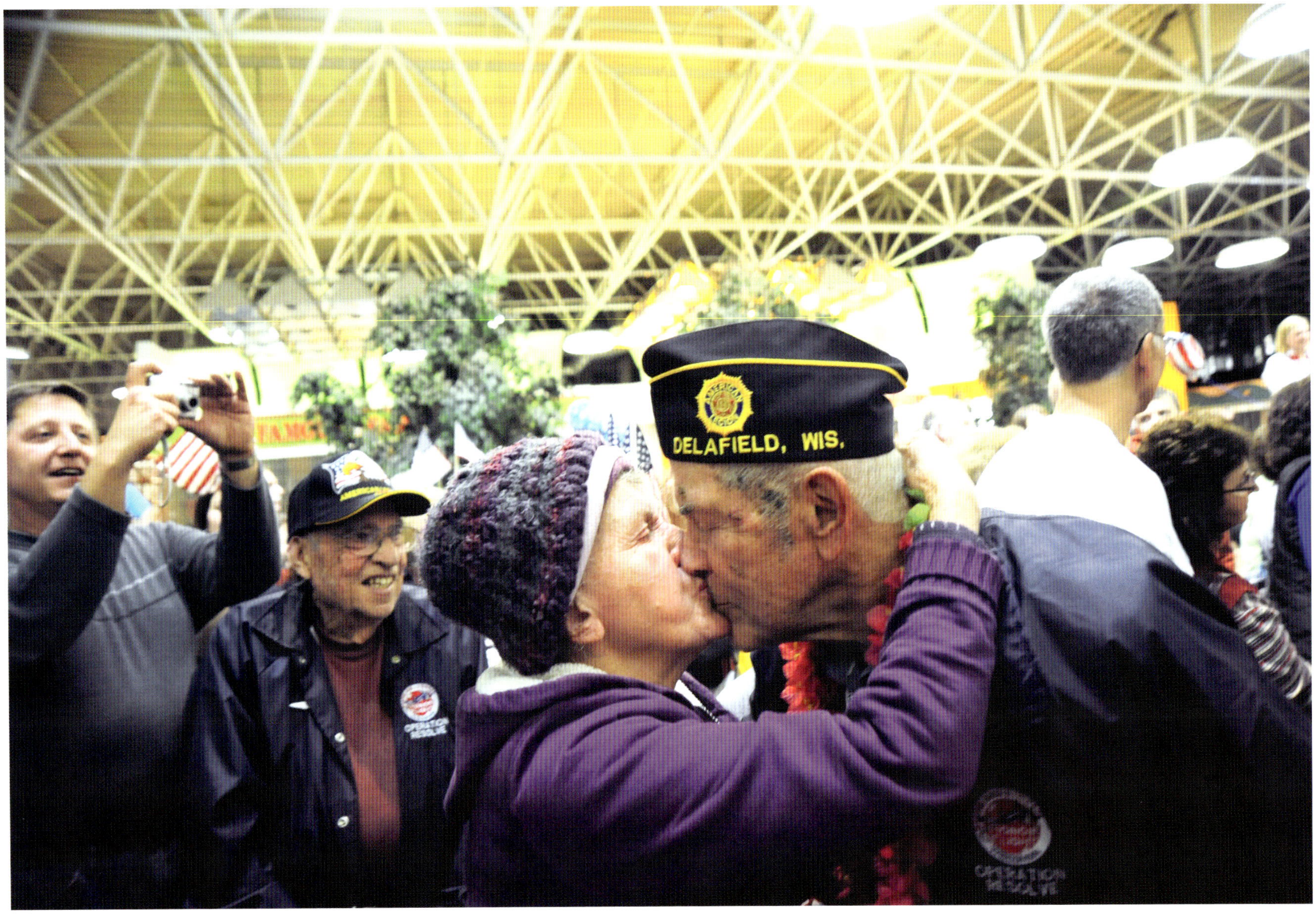
DELAFIELD, WIS.
OPERATION RESOLVE

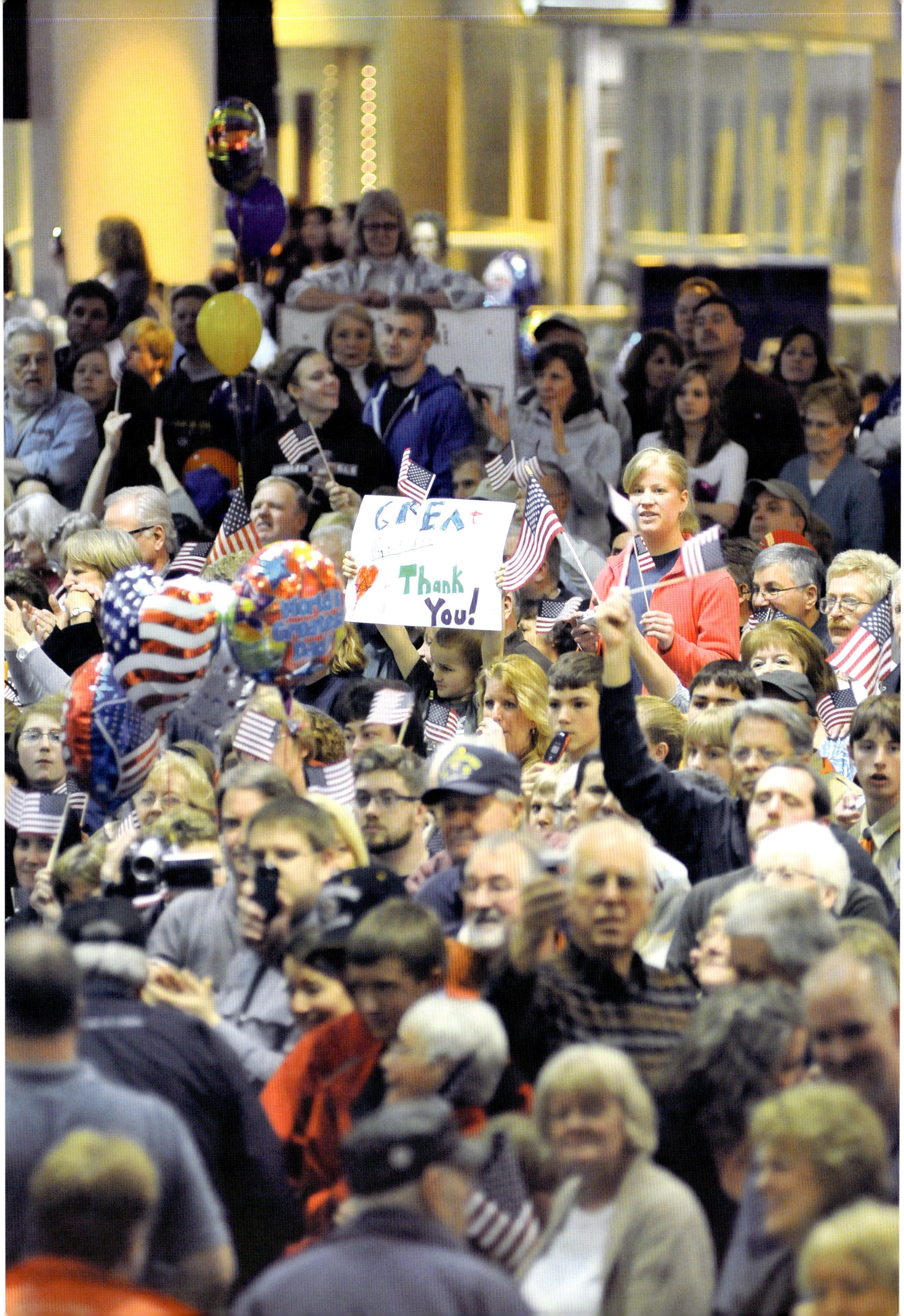
Thank
You!

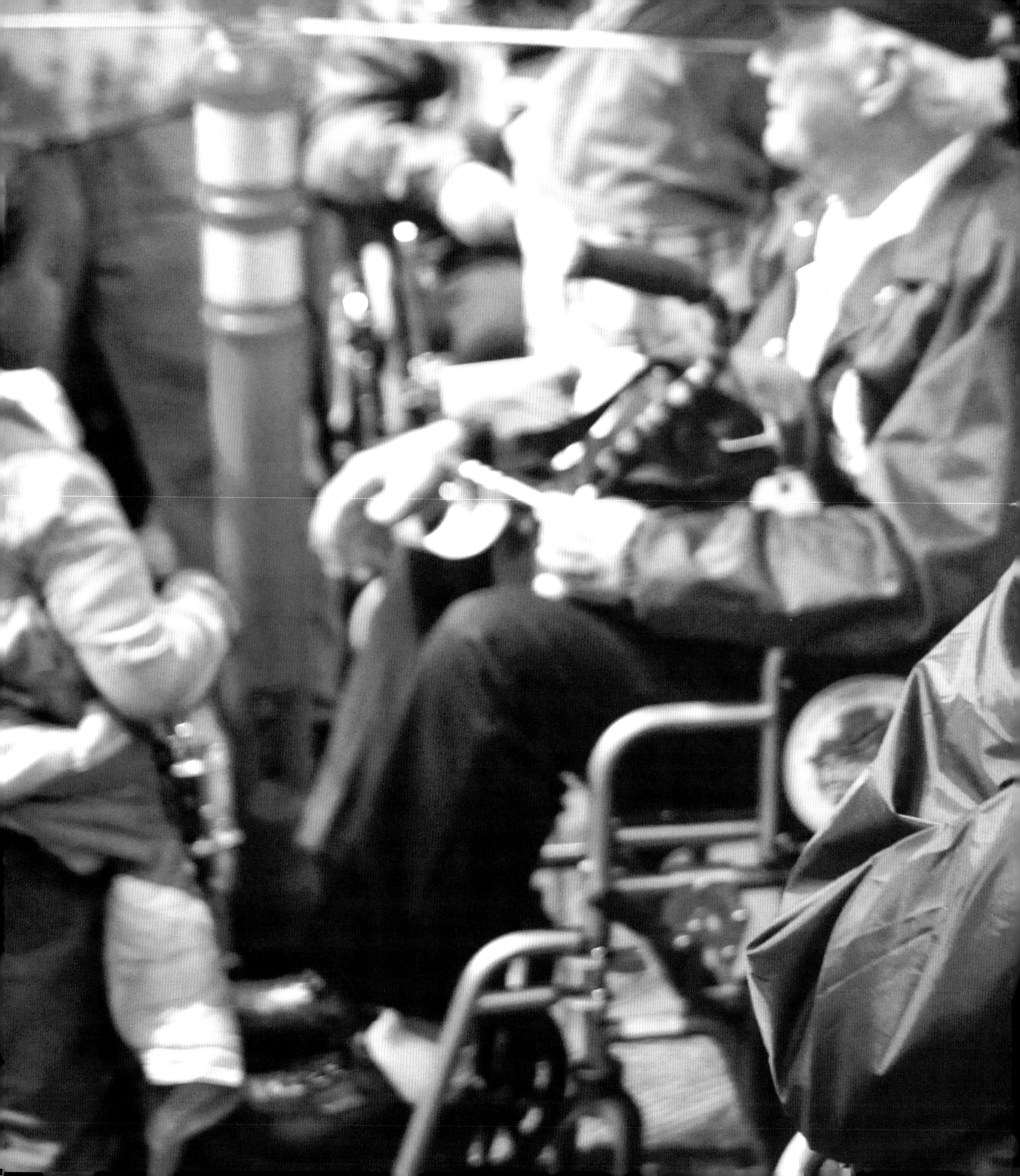

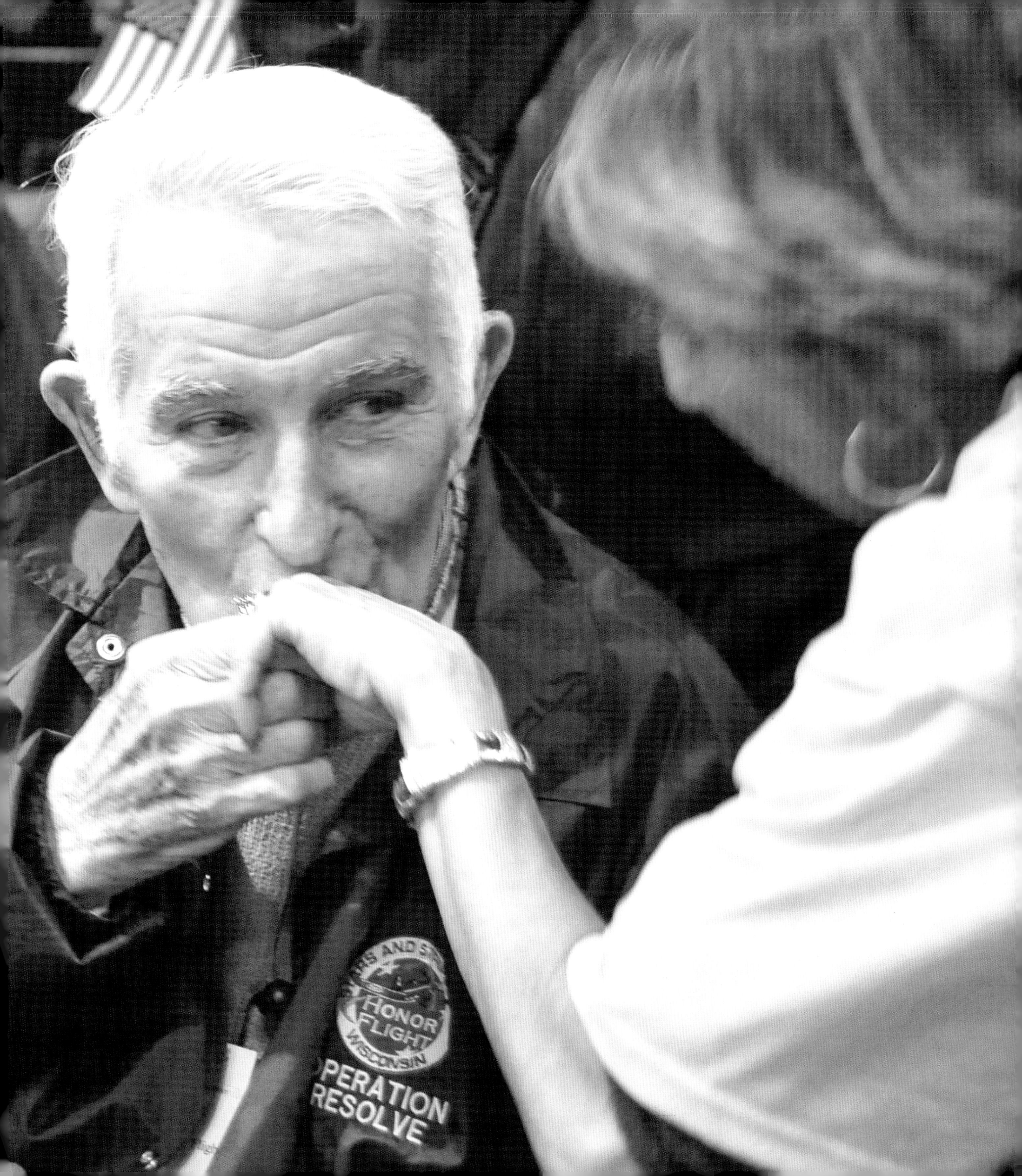
HONOR FLIGHT
WISCONSIN
OPERATION
RESOLVE

U.S. MARINES
HERO
GRANDPA
CHET
MY HERO
MARINES
DAD
THANK YOU FOR
OUR FREEDOM
GRANDPA
THANK YOU F
OUR FREEDOM

293

Max Zadra (opposite) waits for his grandpa, Battle of the Bulge veteran Joe Zadra. As a master sergeant in the war, Joe sewed intelligence maps into the lining of his jacket, which Max, 13, is wearing here.

295

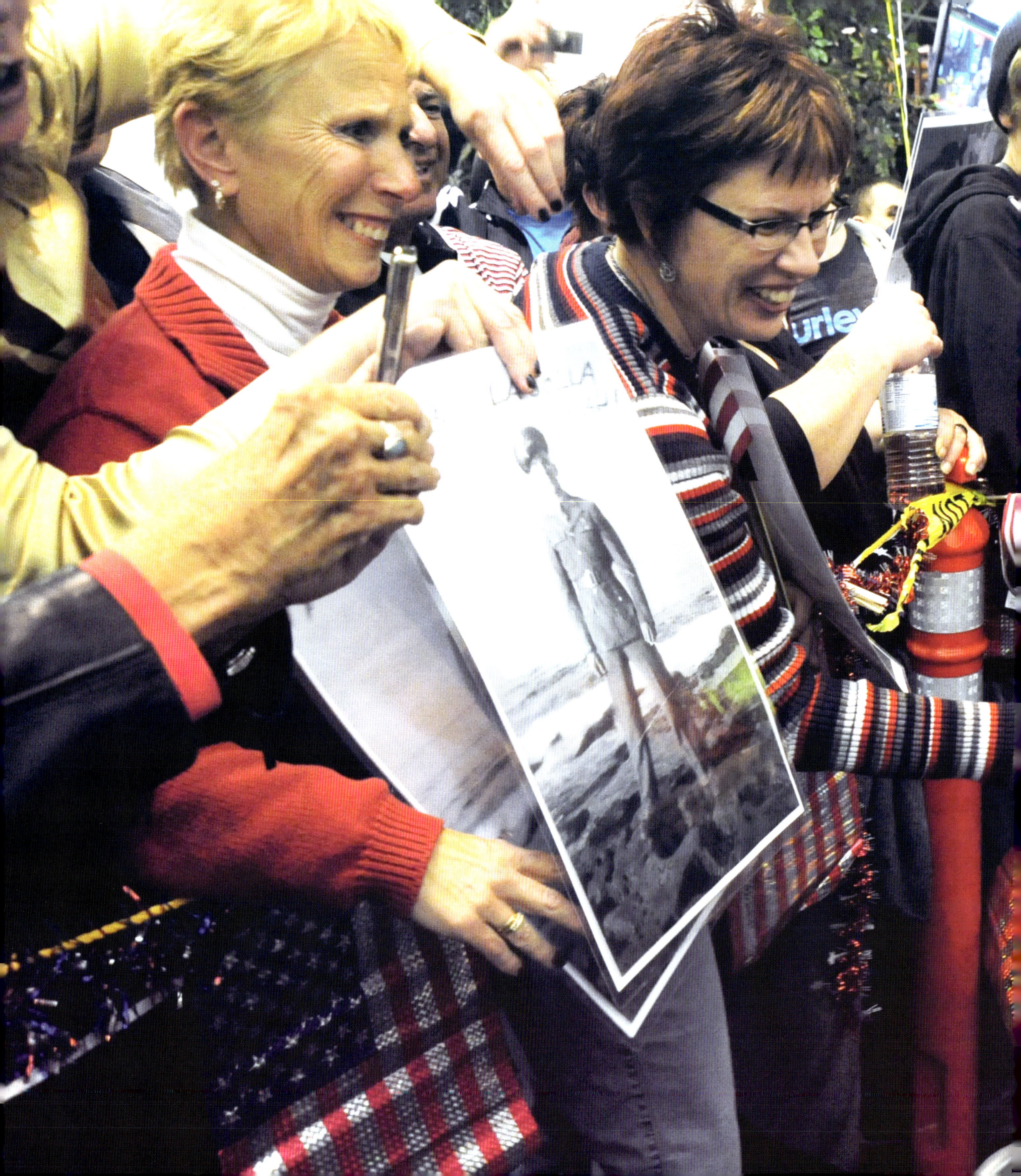

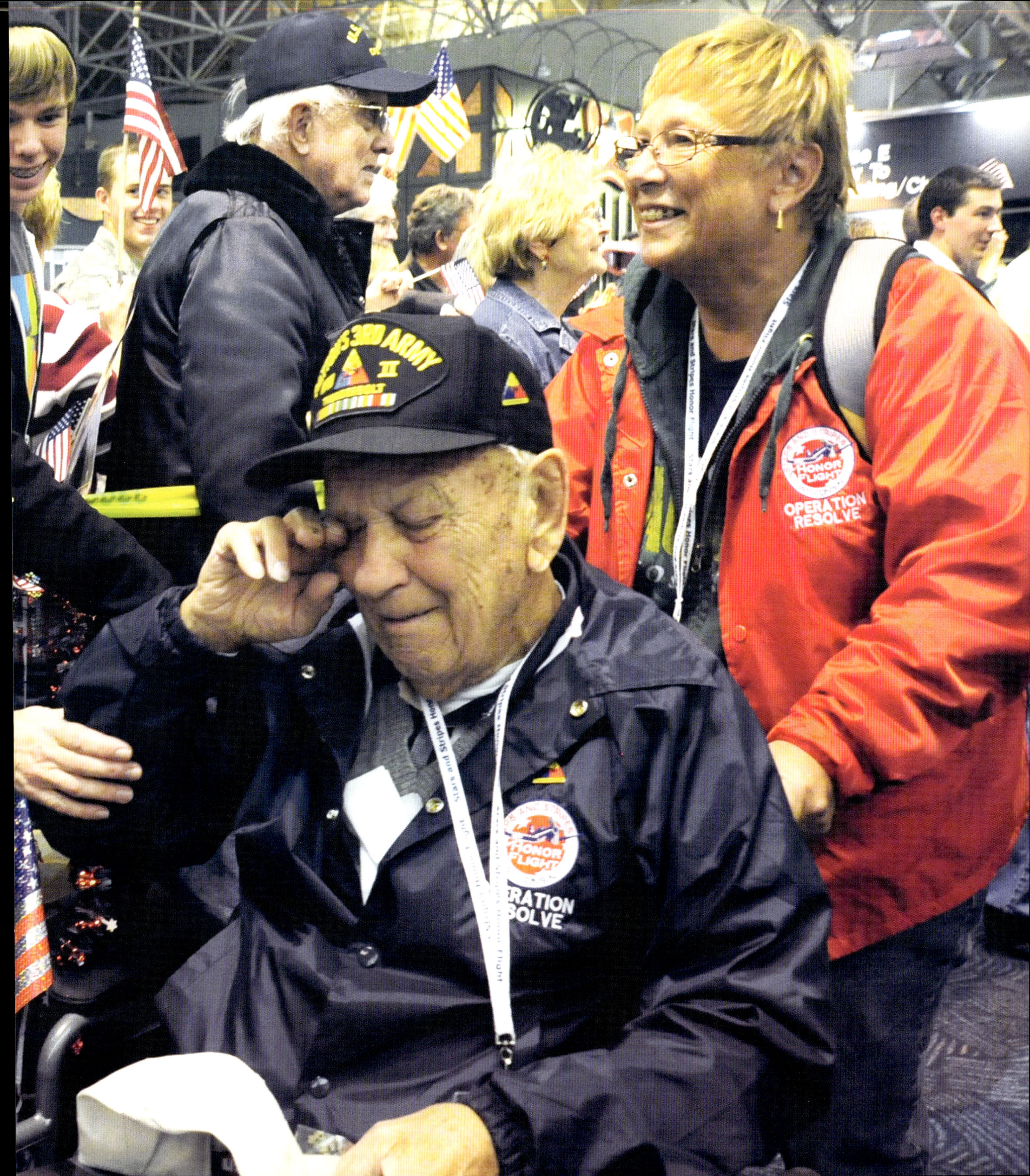
HONOR FLIGHT
OPERATION RESOLVE

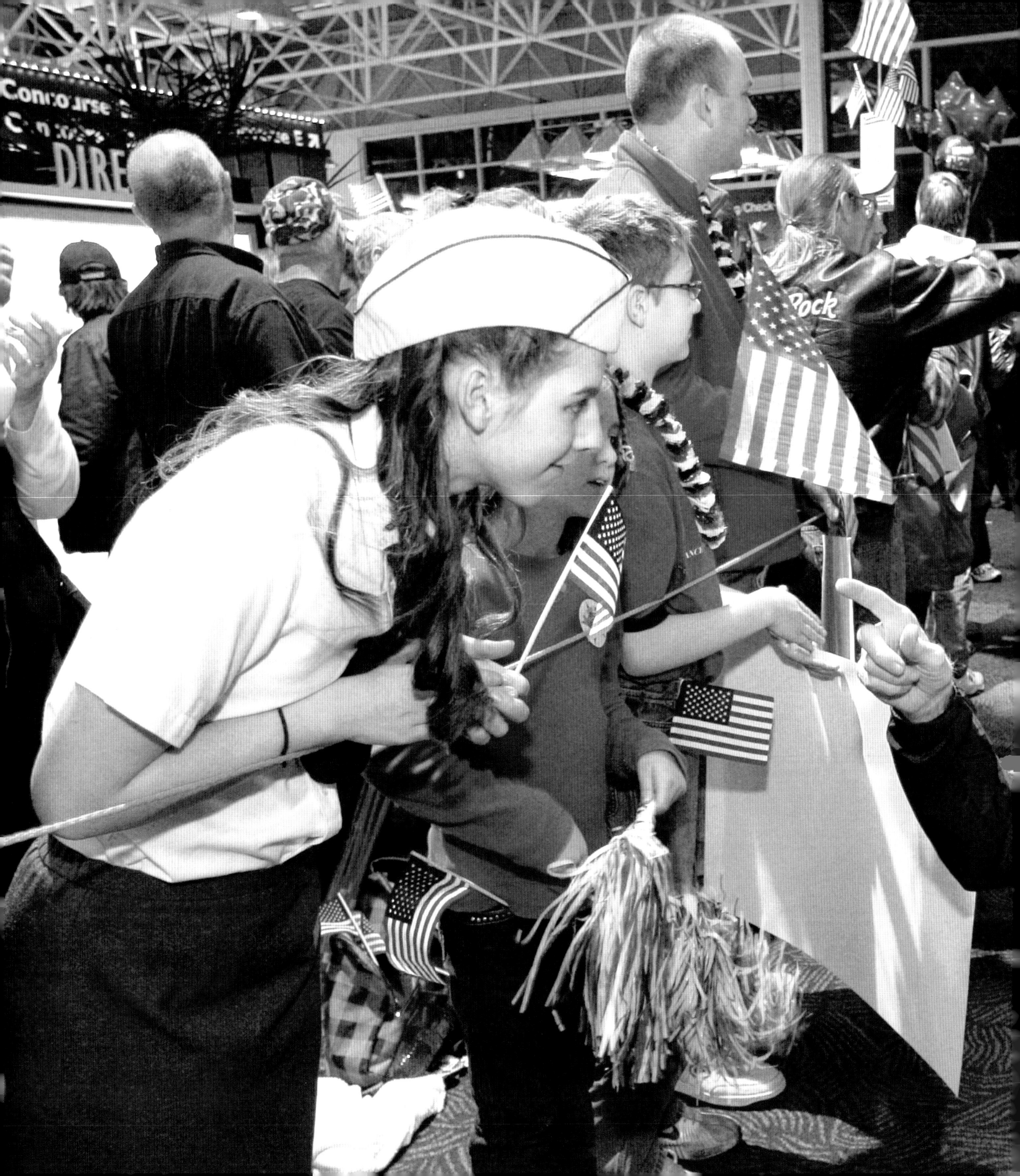
Concourse
DIRE
Rock

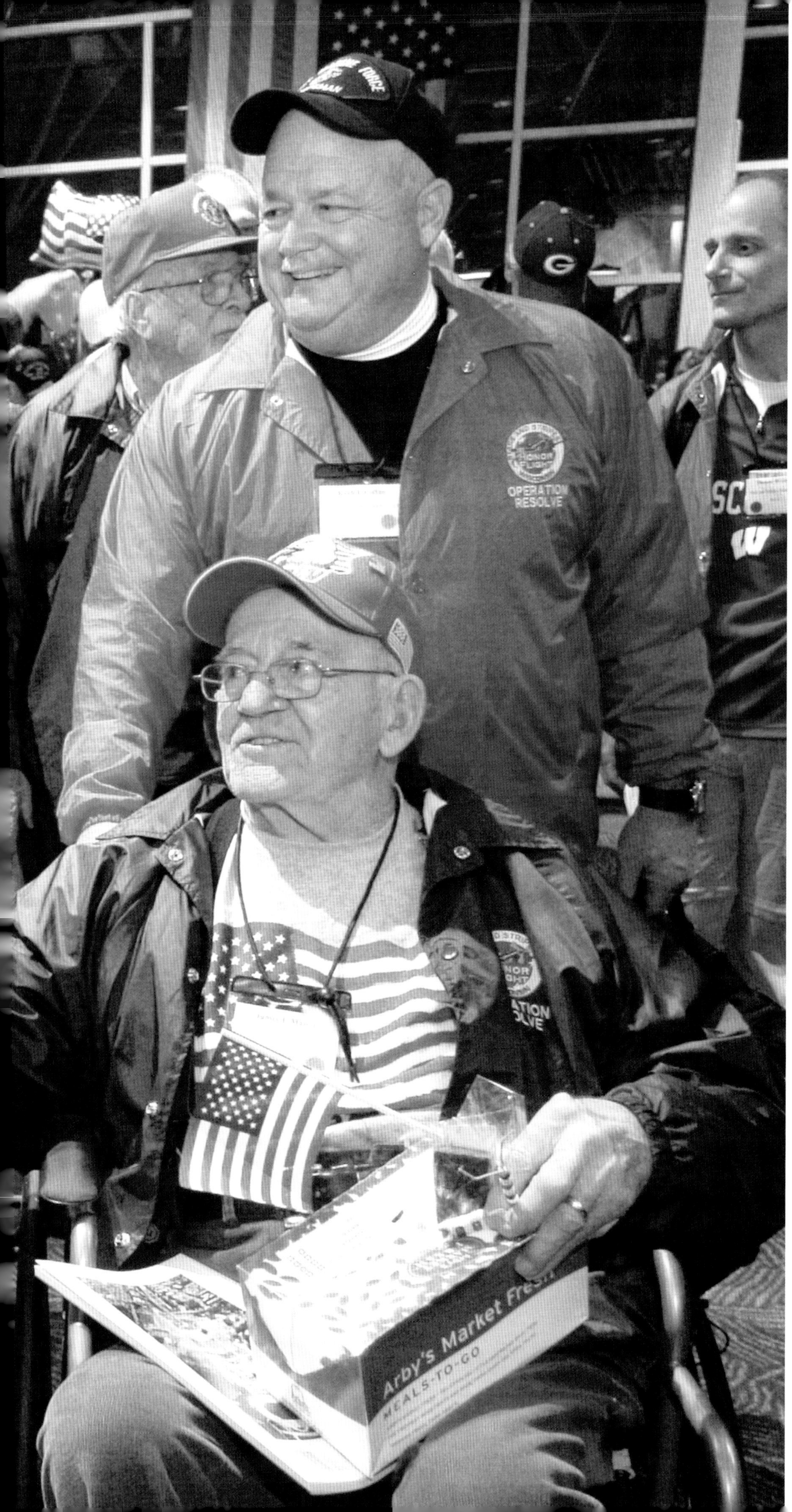
OPERATION
RESOLVE
Arby's Market Fresh
MEALS-TO-GO

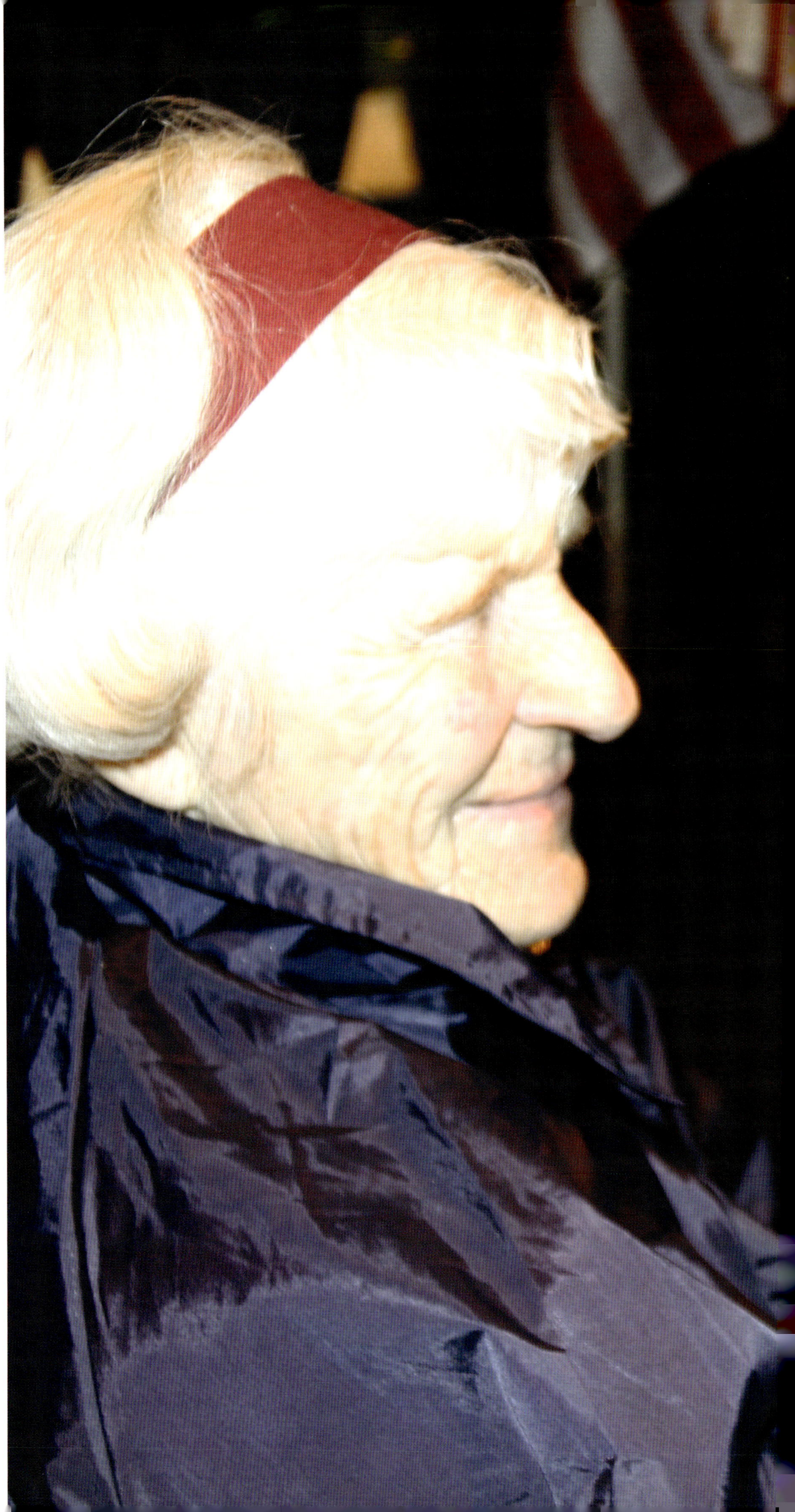

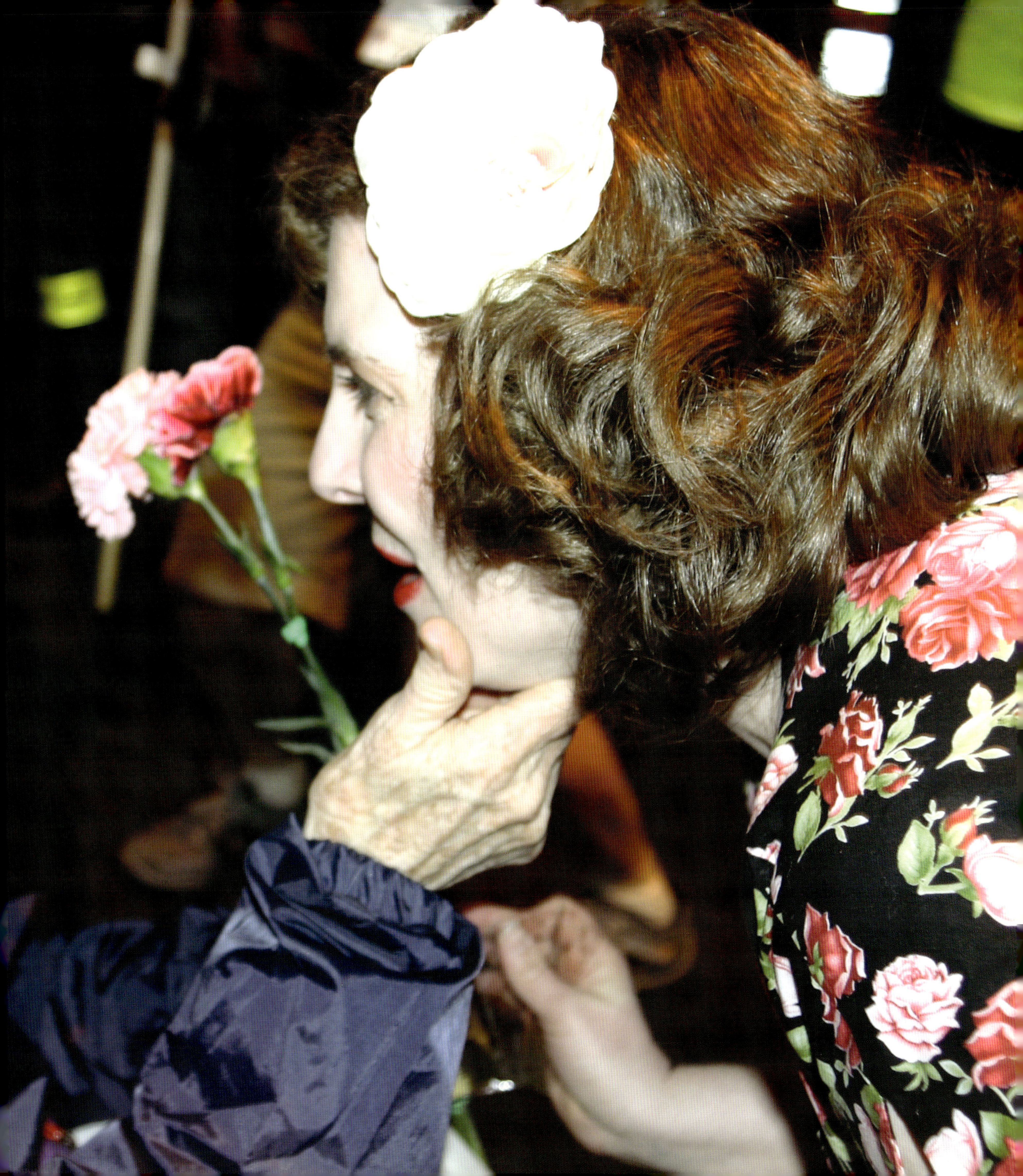

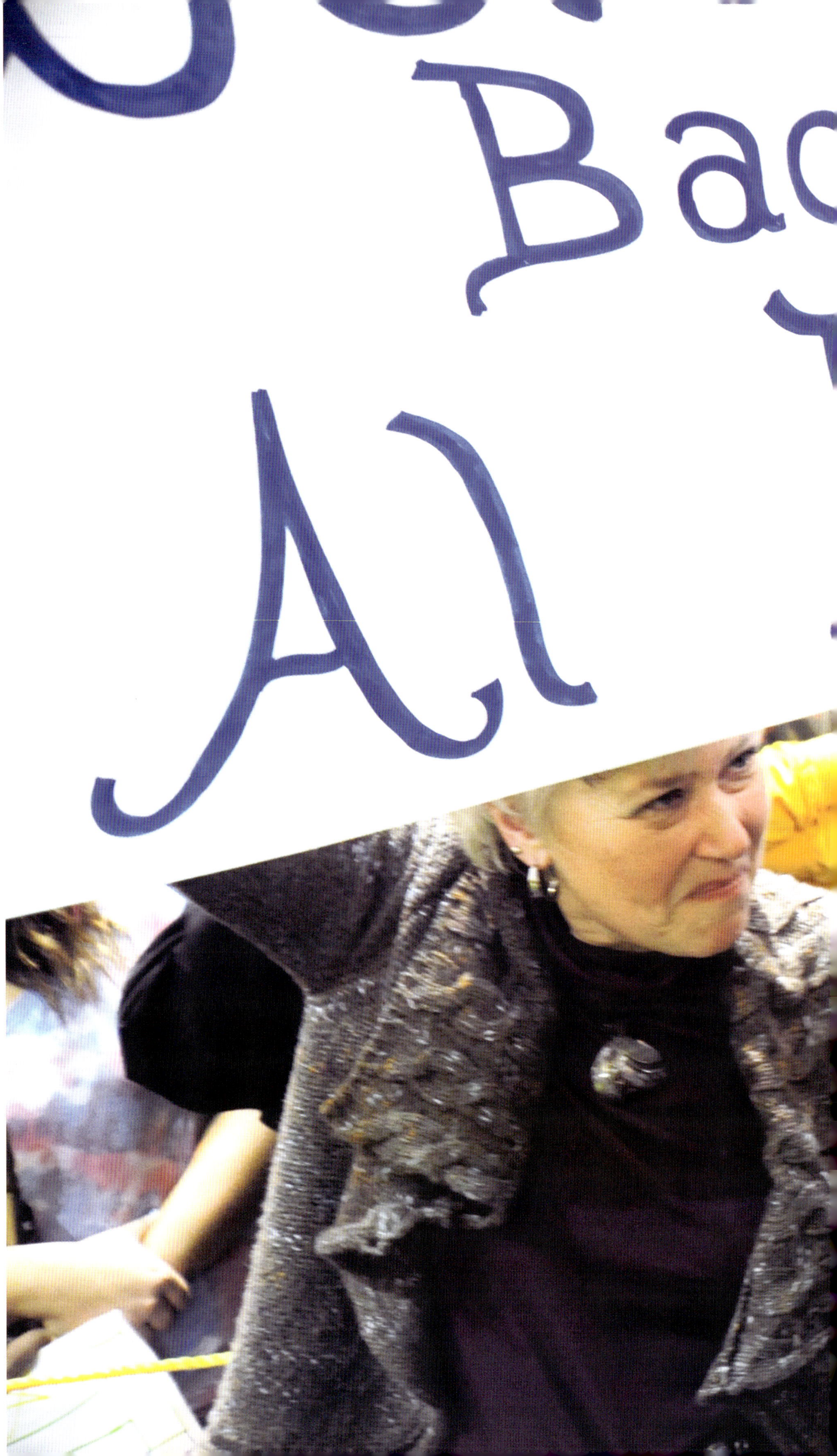

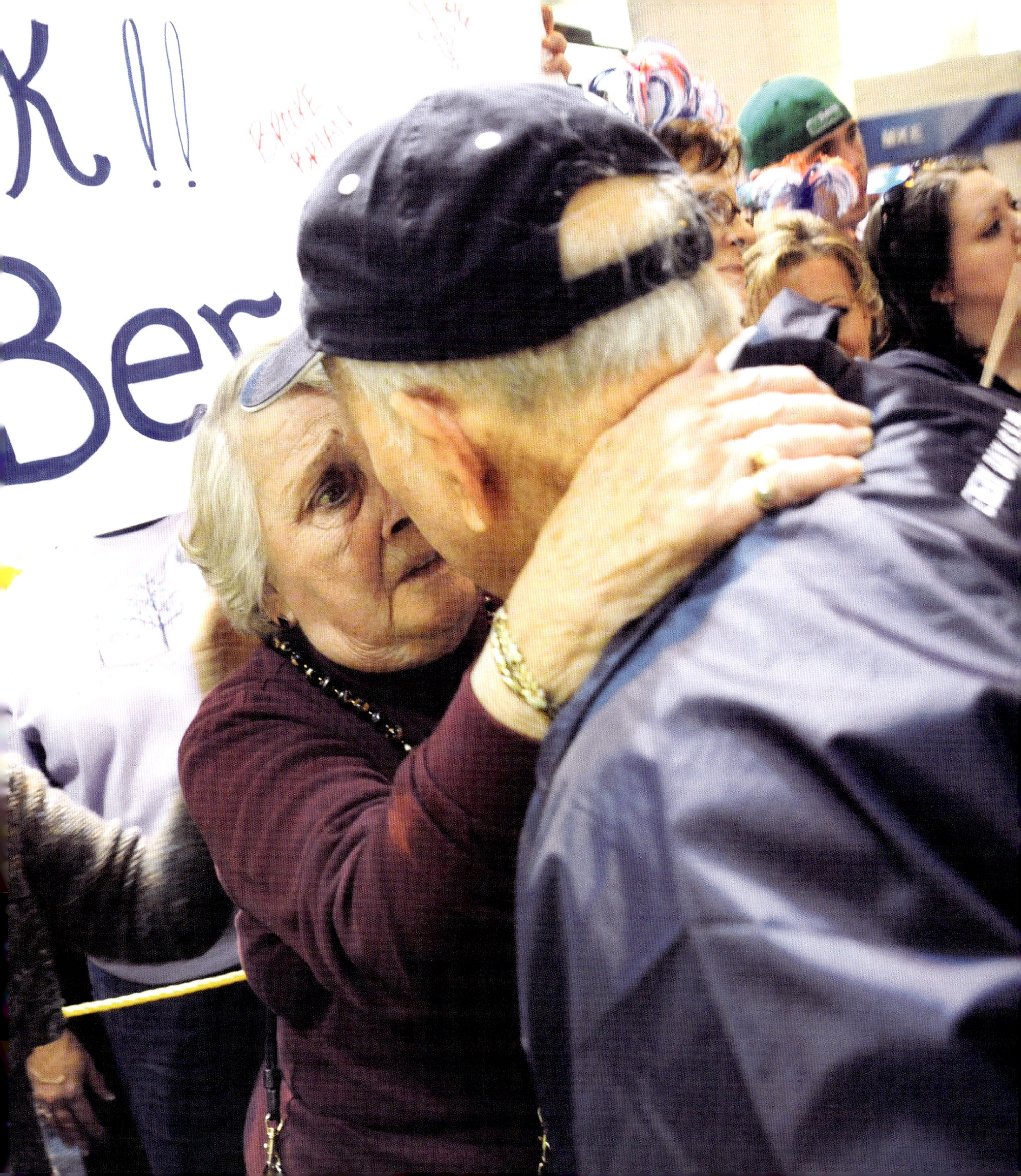
K!!
Ber

304

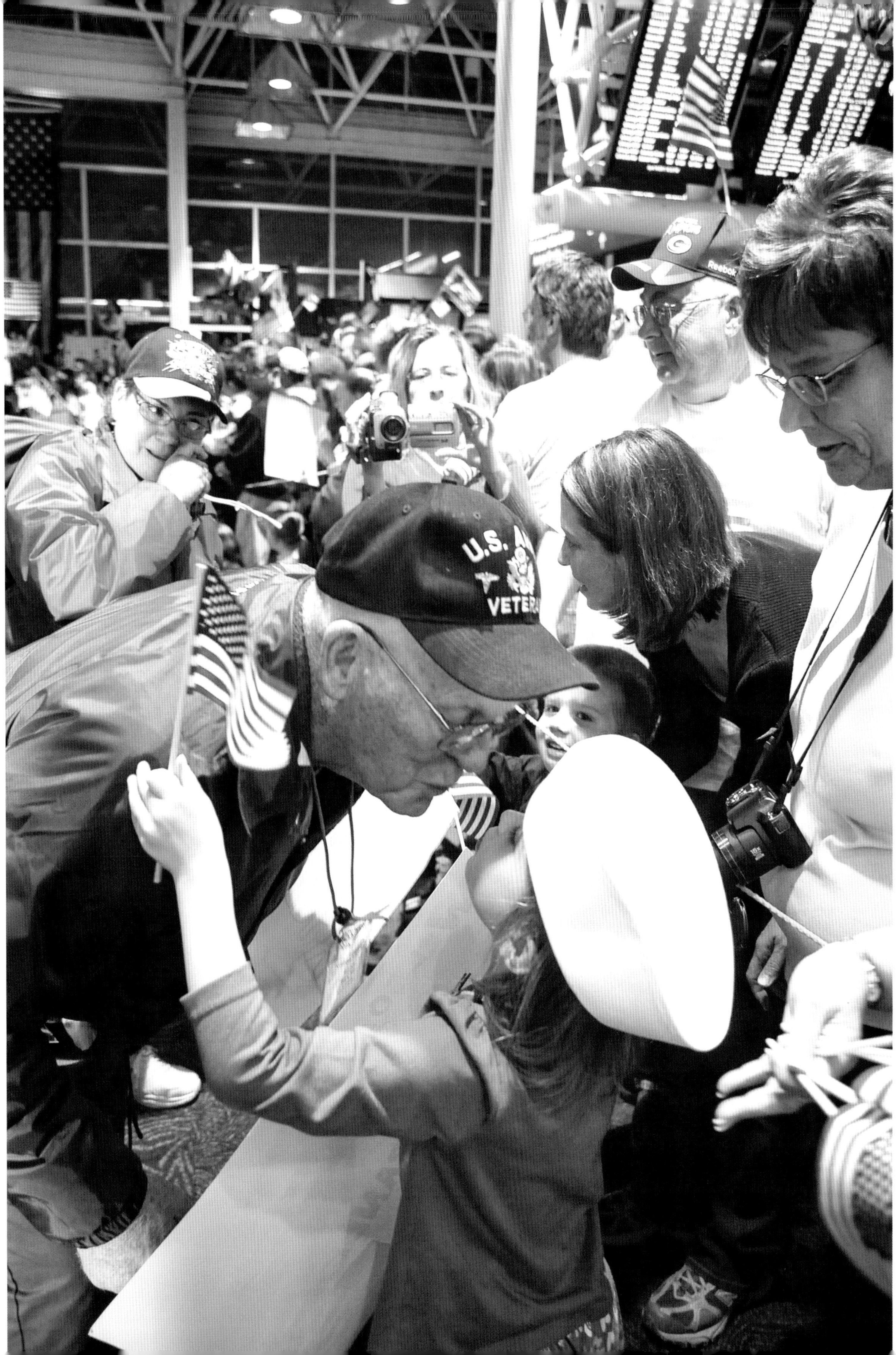
Reebok

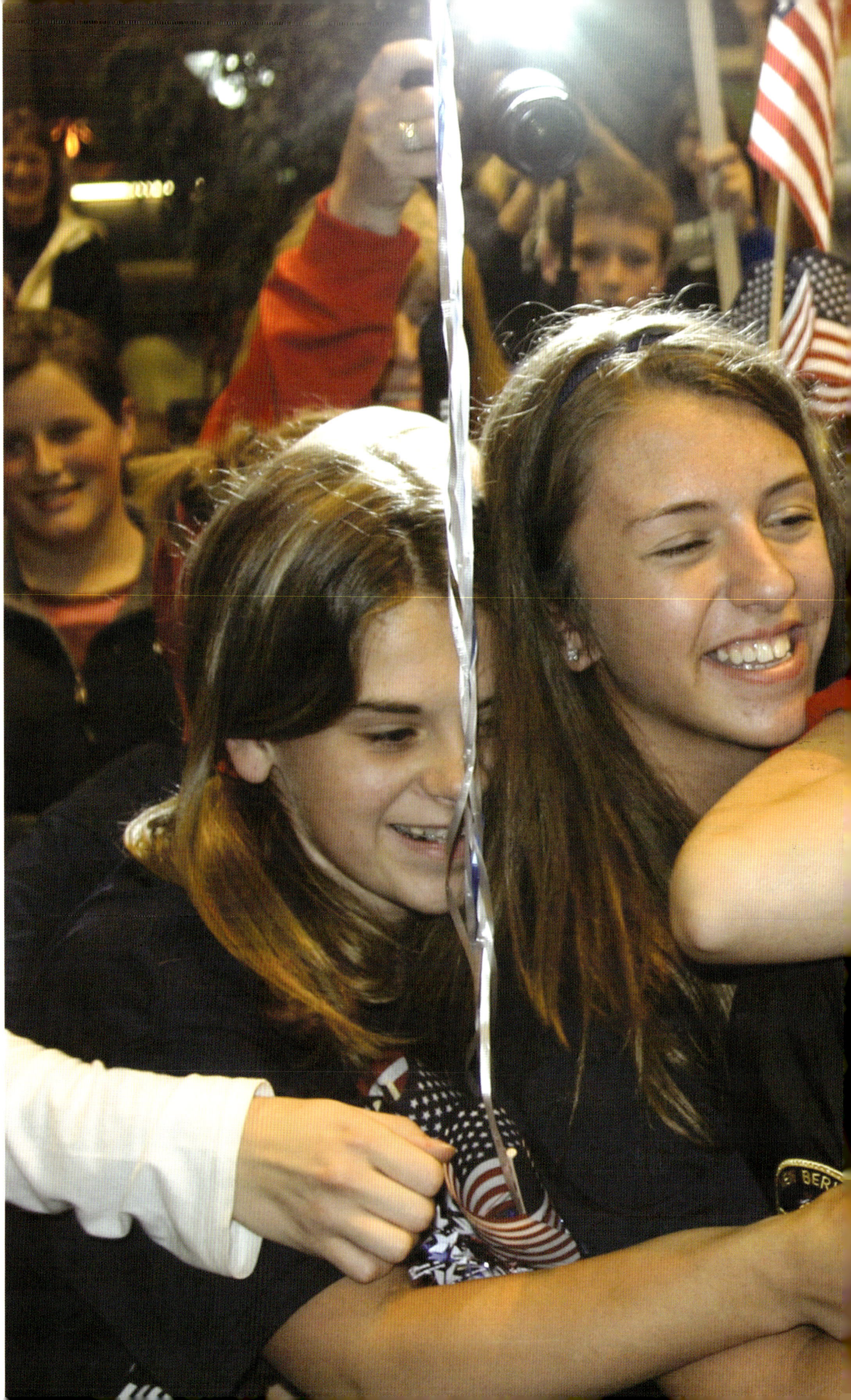

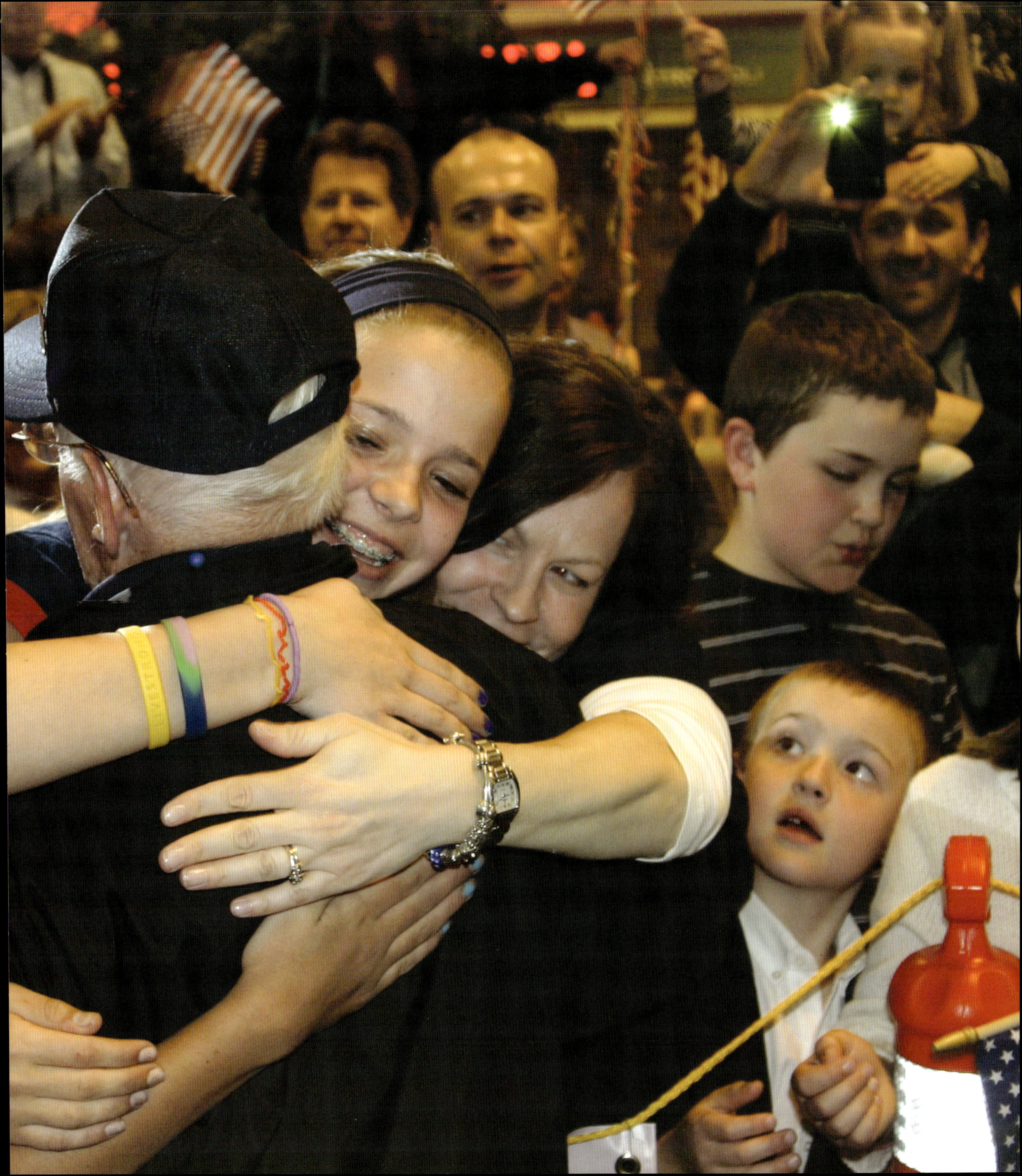

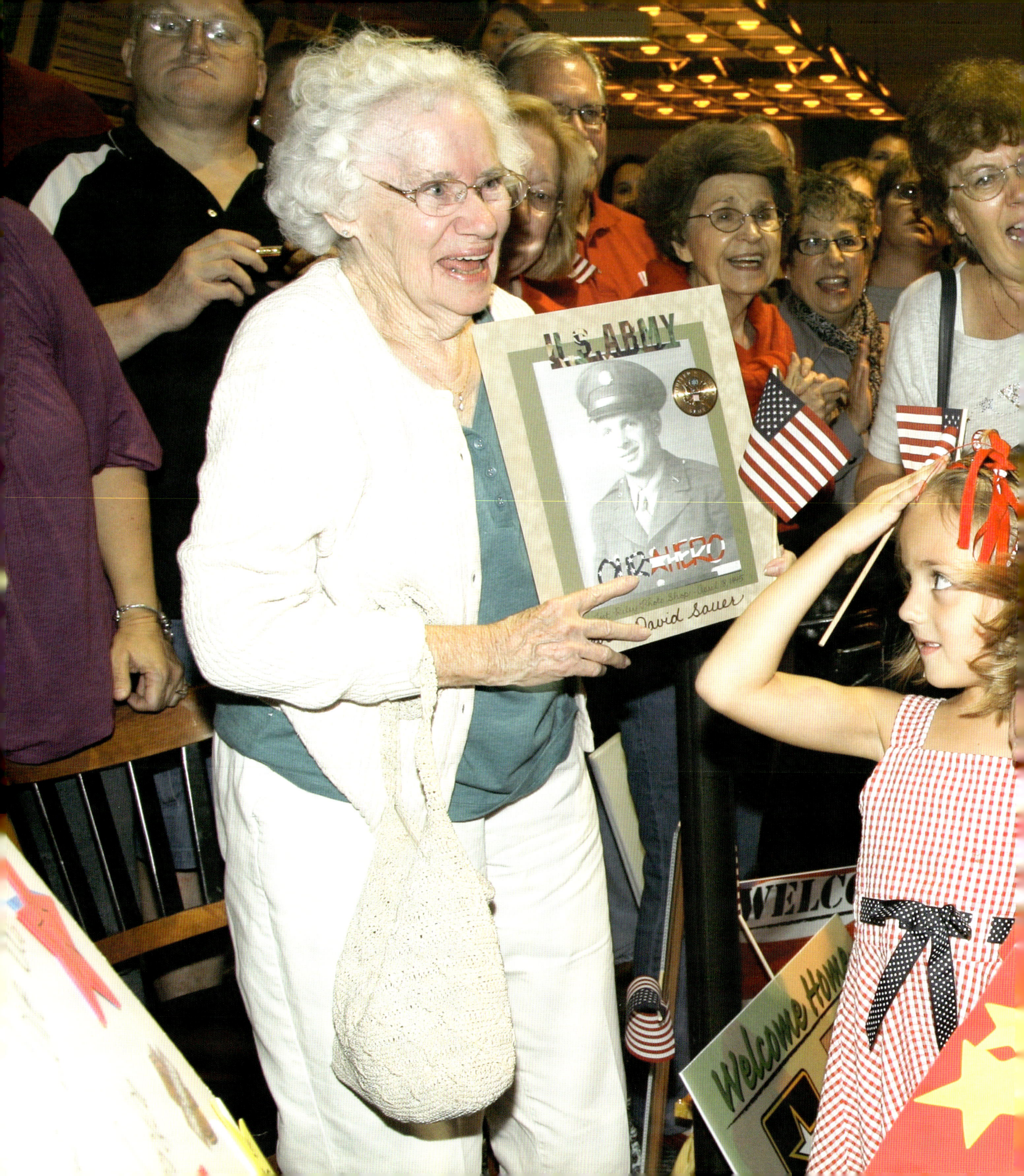
U.S. ARMY
OUR HERO
David Sauer
WELC
Welcome Home

STARS AND STRIPES
HONOR FLIGHT
WISCONSIN
ROUNDY'S
ALL WISCONSIN
DAY
Stars and Stripes Honor Flight
5TH CAVALRY
Julie Smith
Ryan

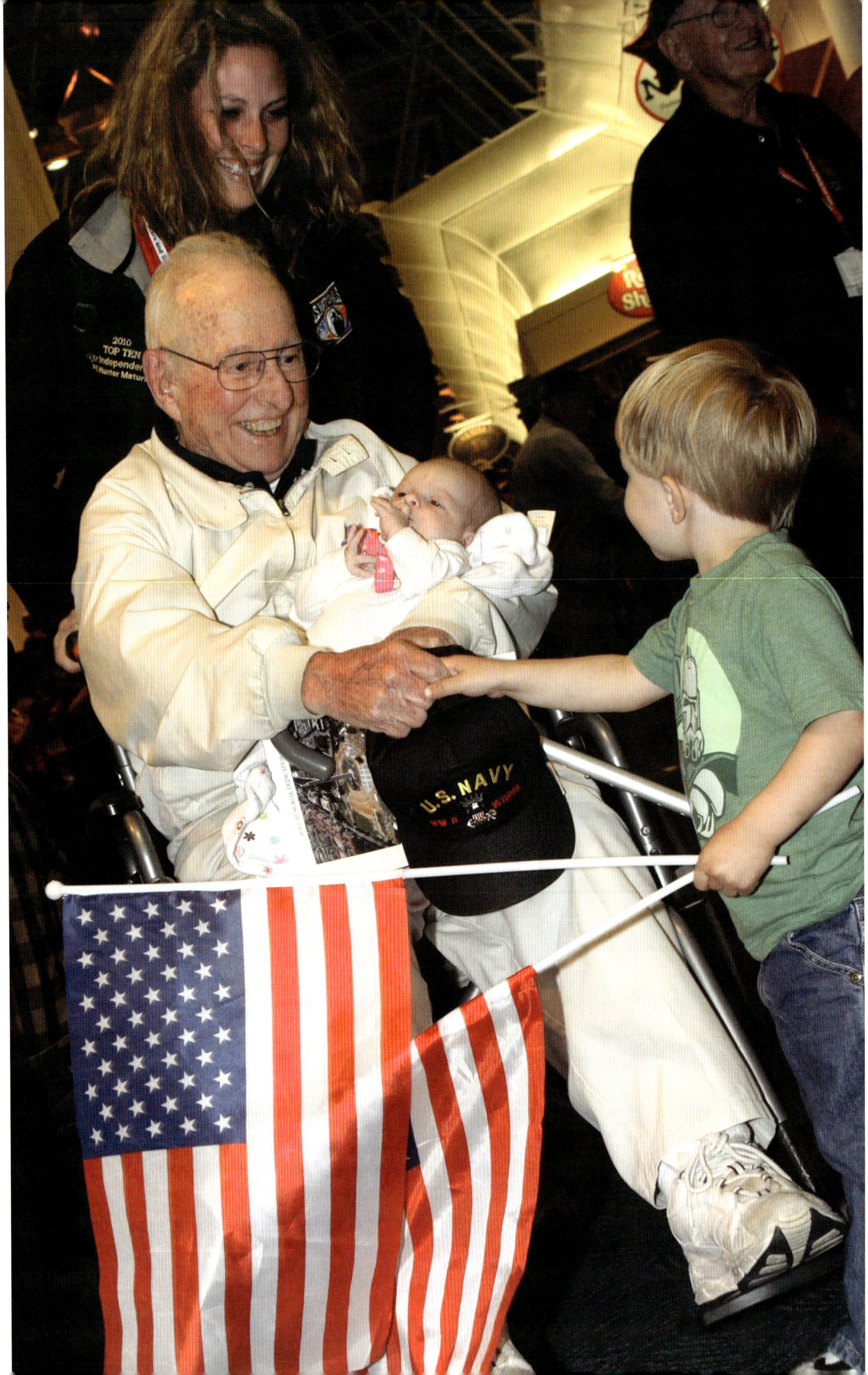
2010
TOP TEN
U.S. NAVY

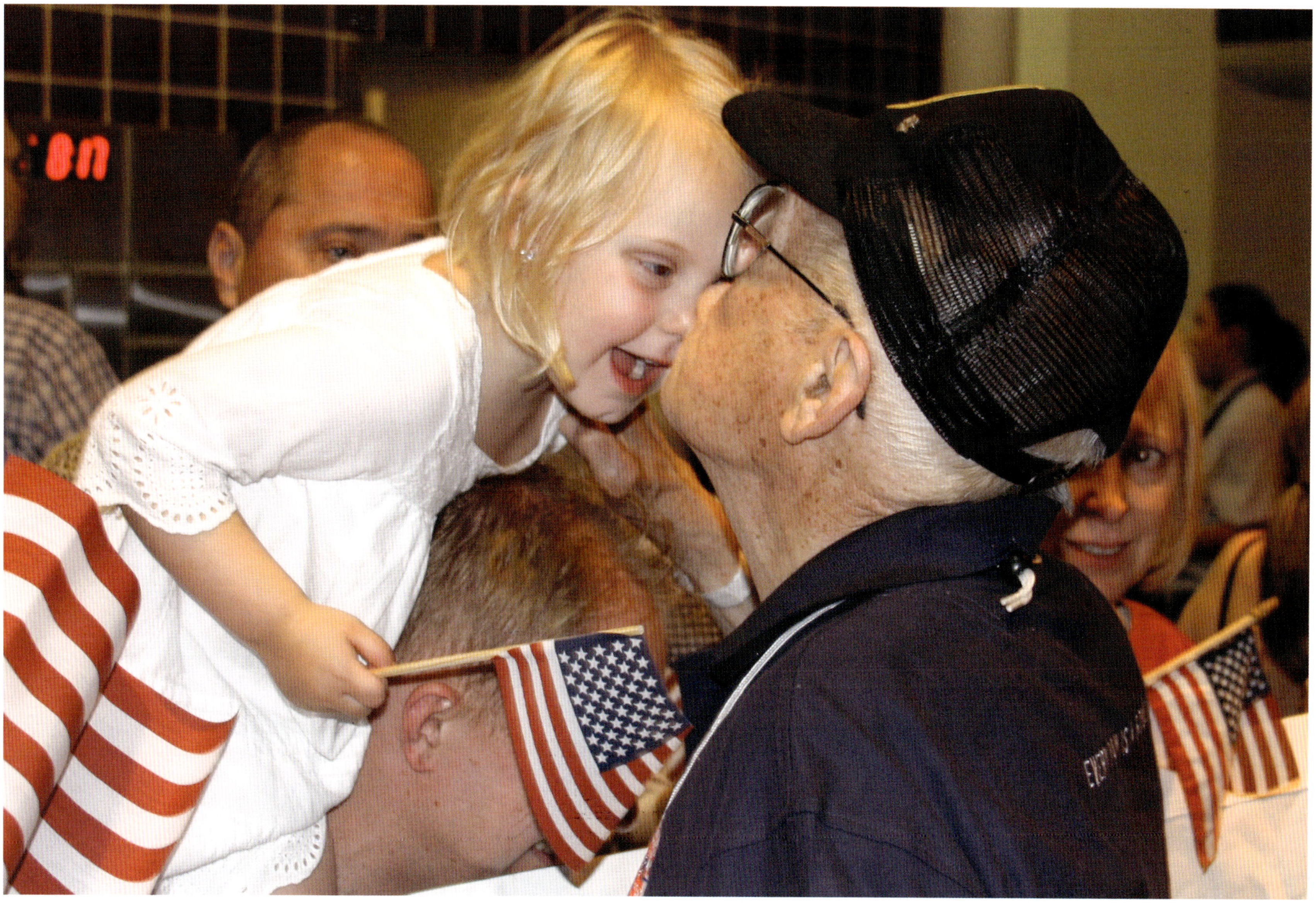

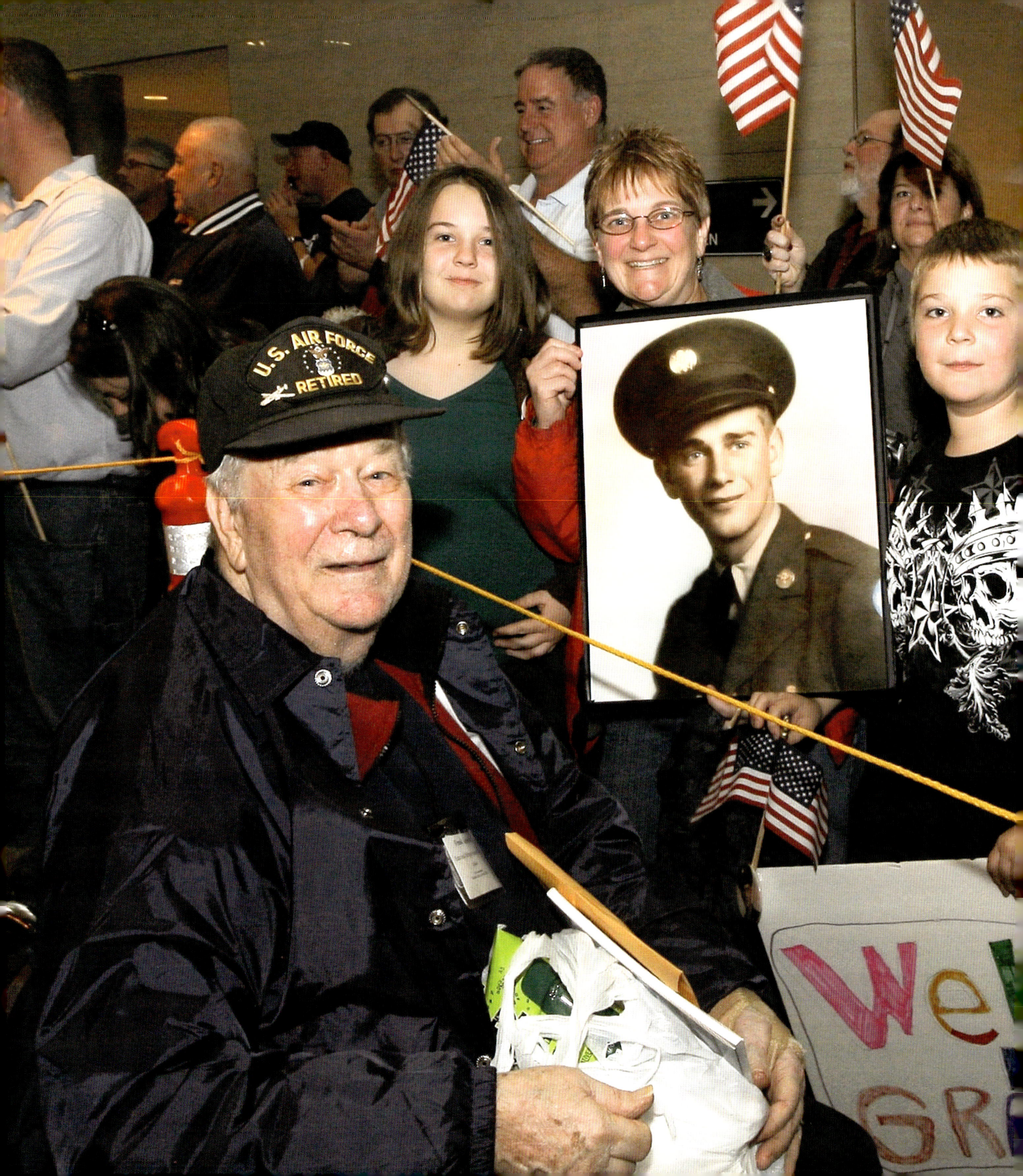
U.S. AIR FORCE
RETIRED

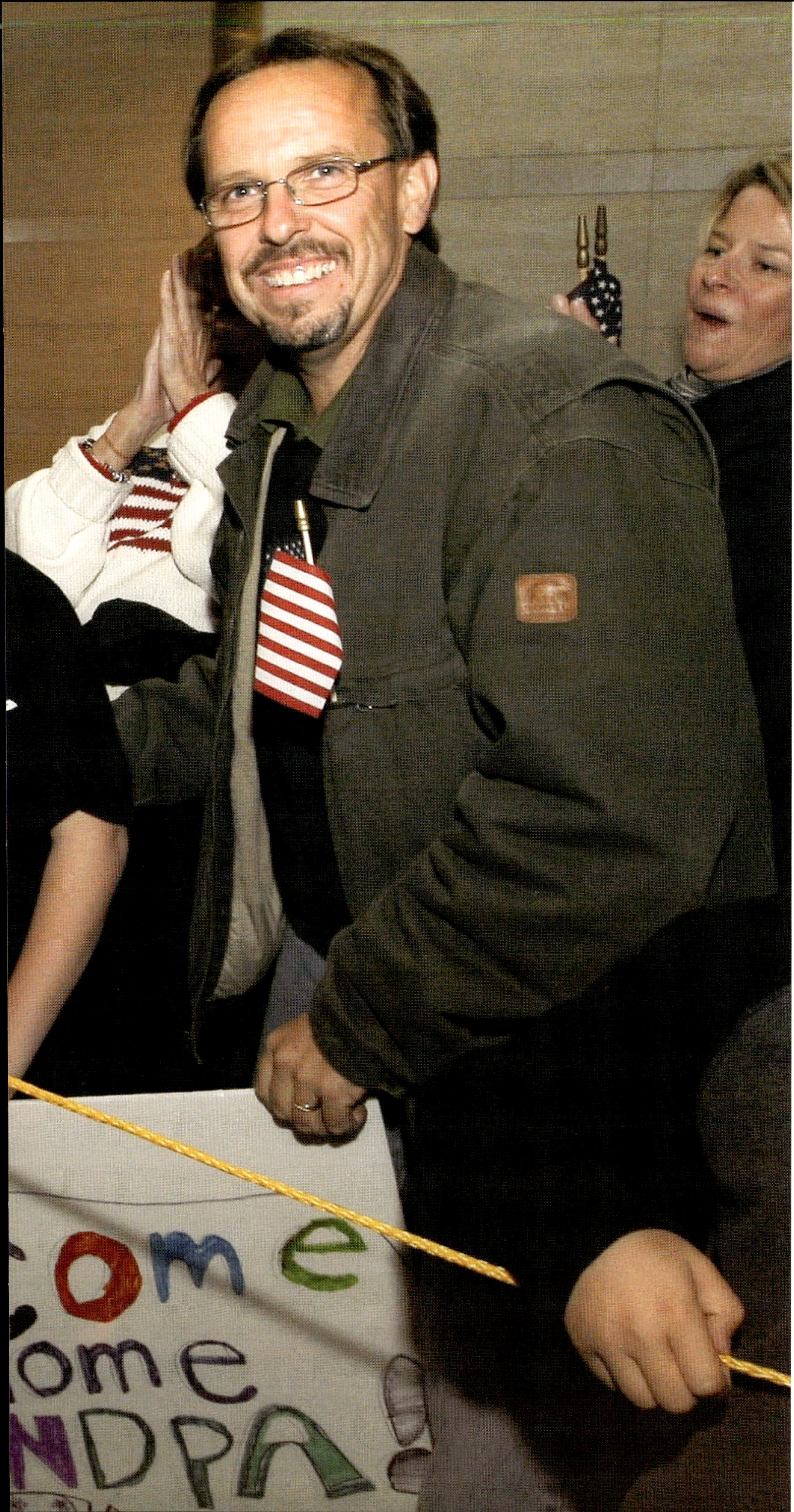
come
ome
NDPA

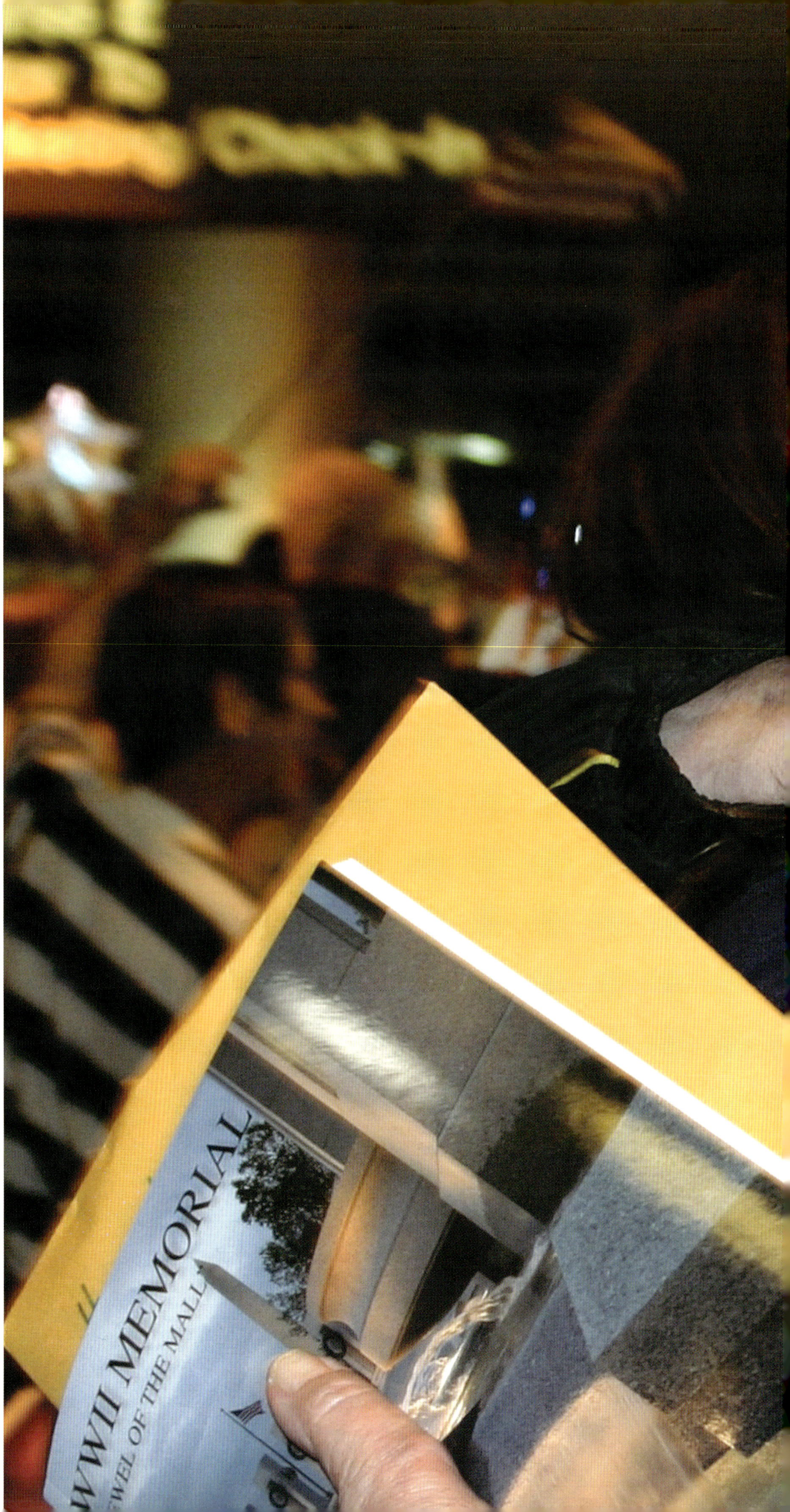
WWII MEMORIAL
JEWEL OF THE MALL

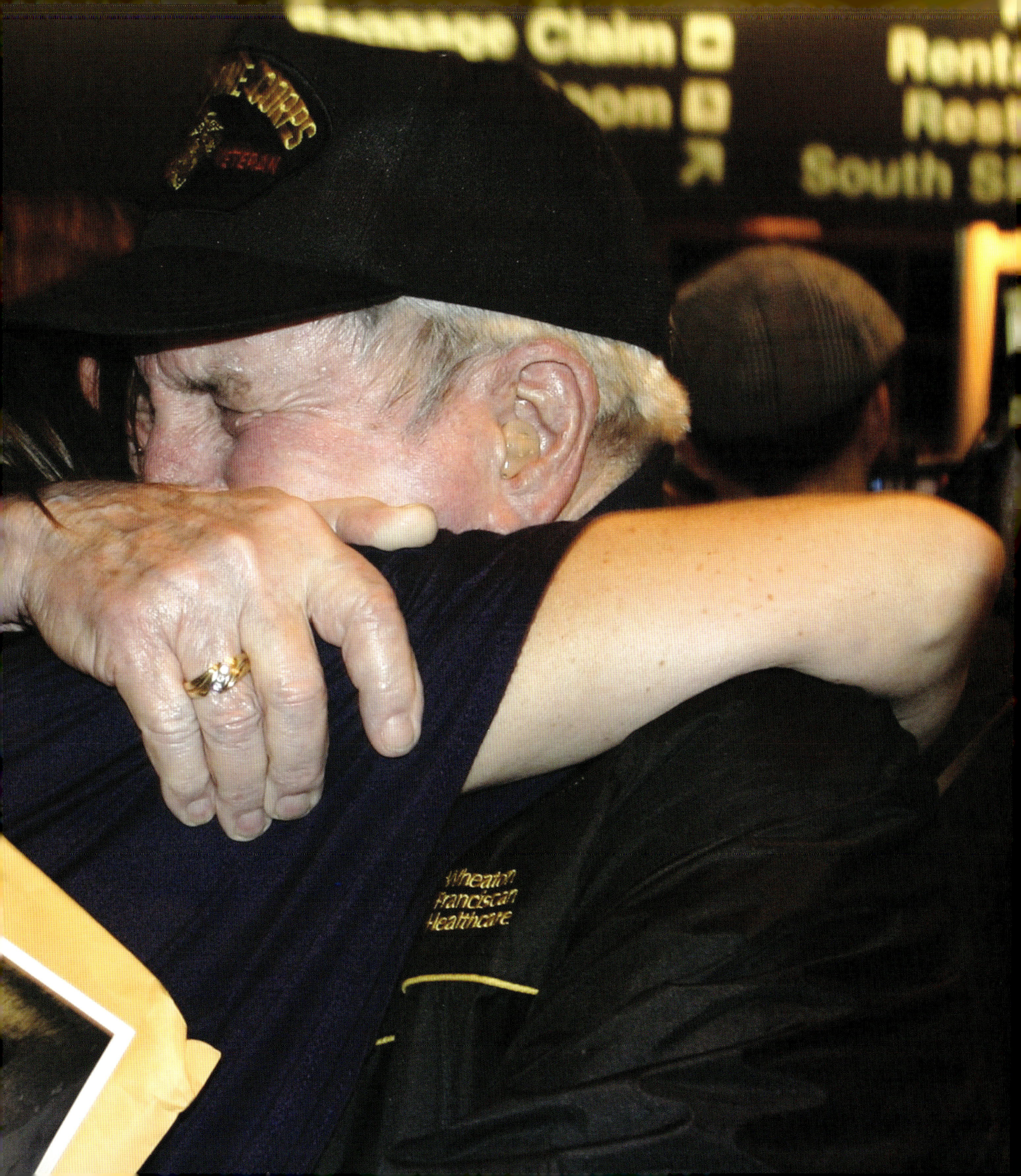
Claim
South
Wheaton
Franciscan
Healthcare

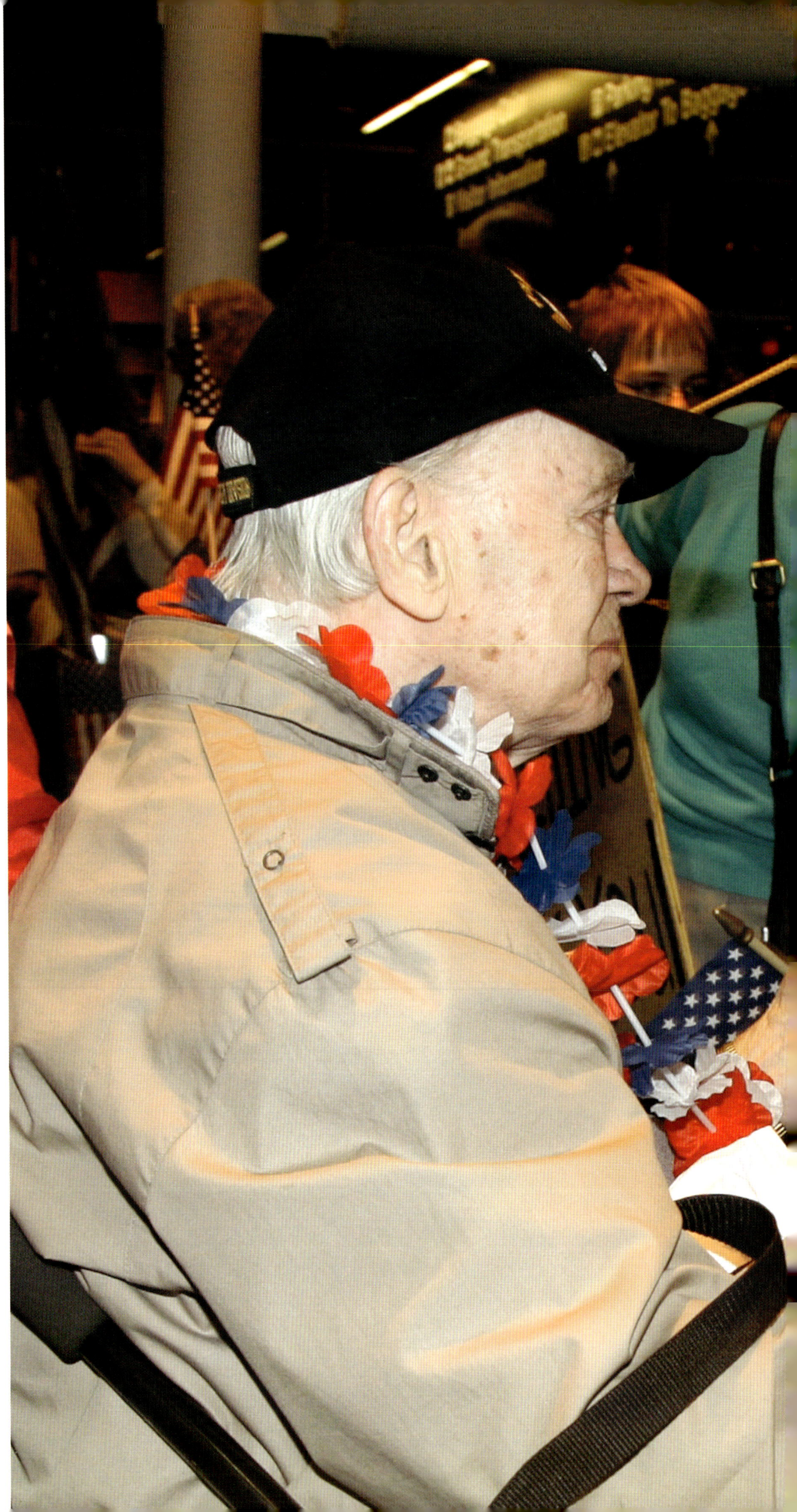

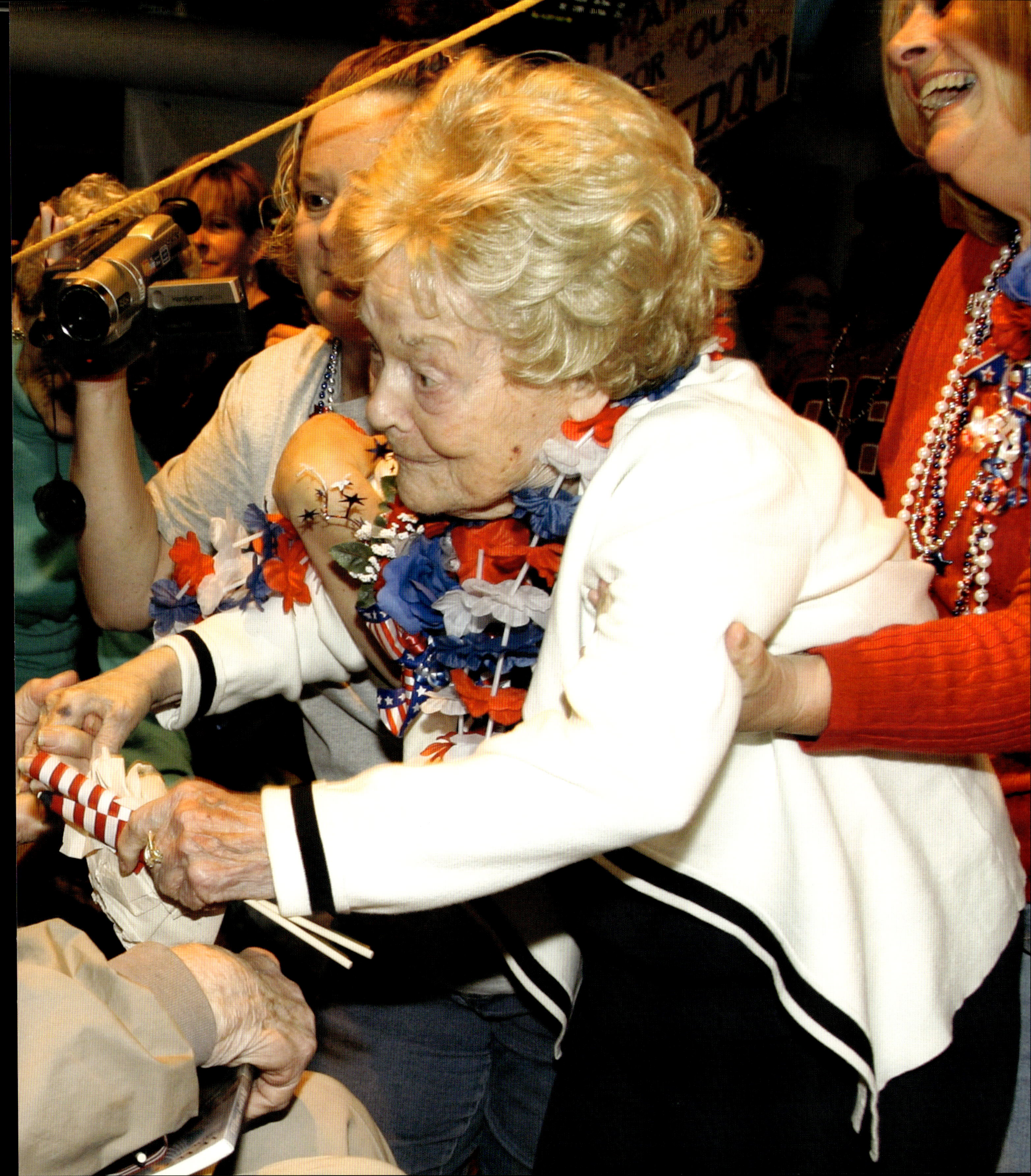

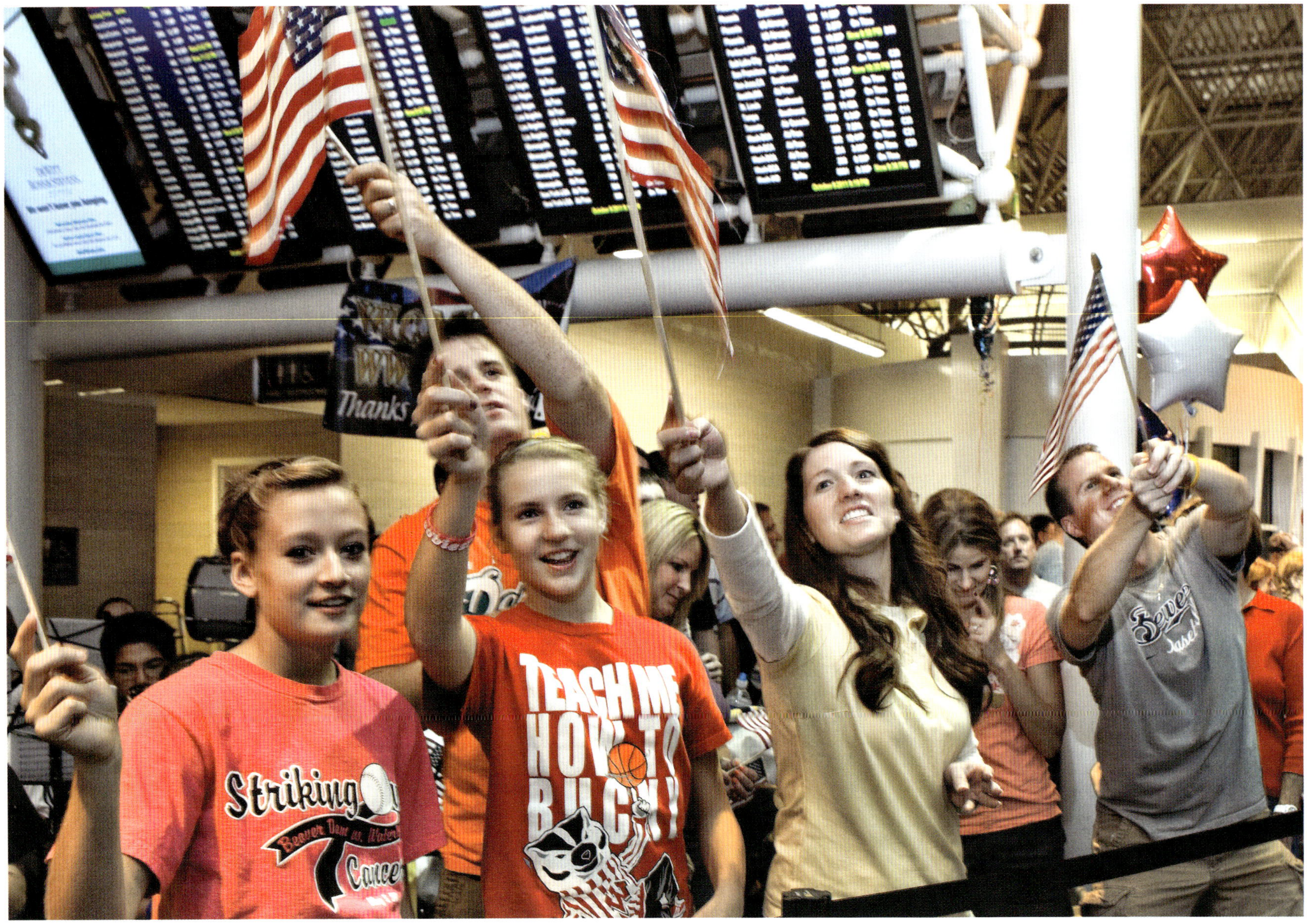
Thanks
TEACH ME
HOW TO
Striking

WISCONSIN
STARS AND STRIPES
HONOR FLIGHT
WISCONSIN
ROUNDY'S
ALL WISCONSIN
DAY
Stars and Stripes Honor Flight

We ♥ Grandpa BELL

PAST POST COMMANDER
MONROE, WIS.
STARS AND STRIPES
HONOR
We Energies
Stars and Stripes Honor

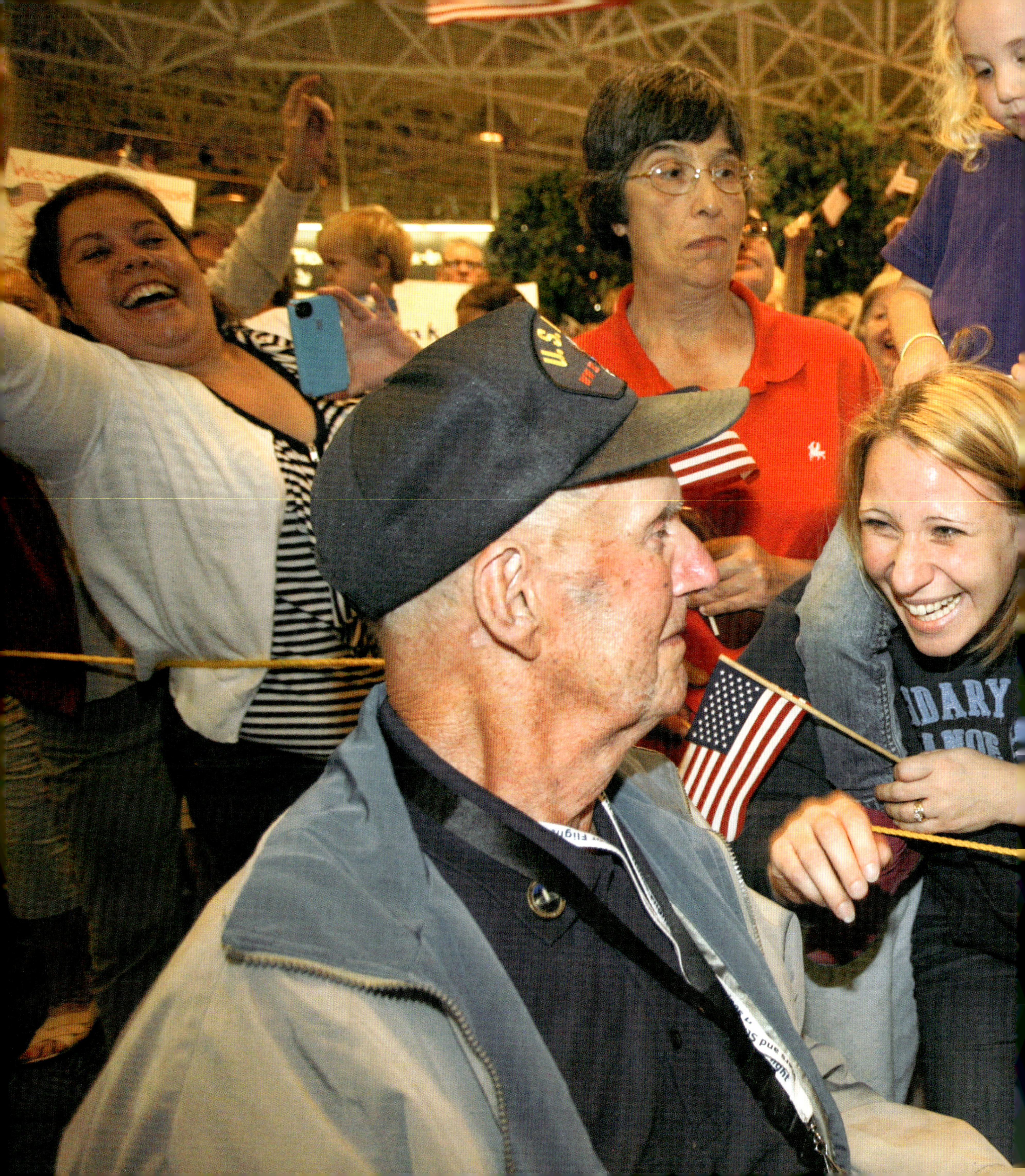

323

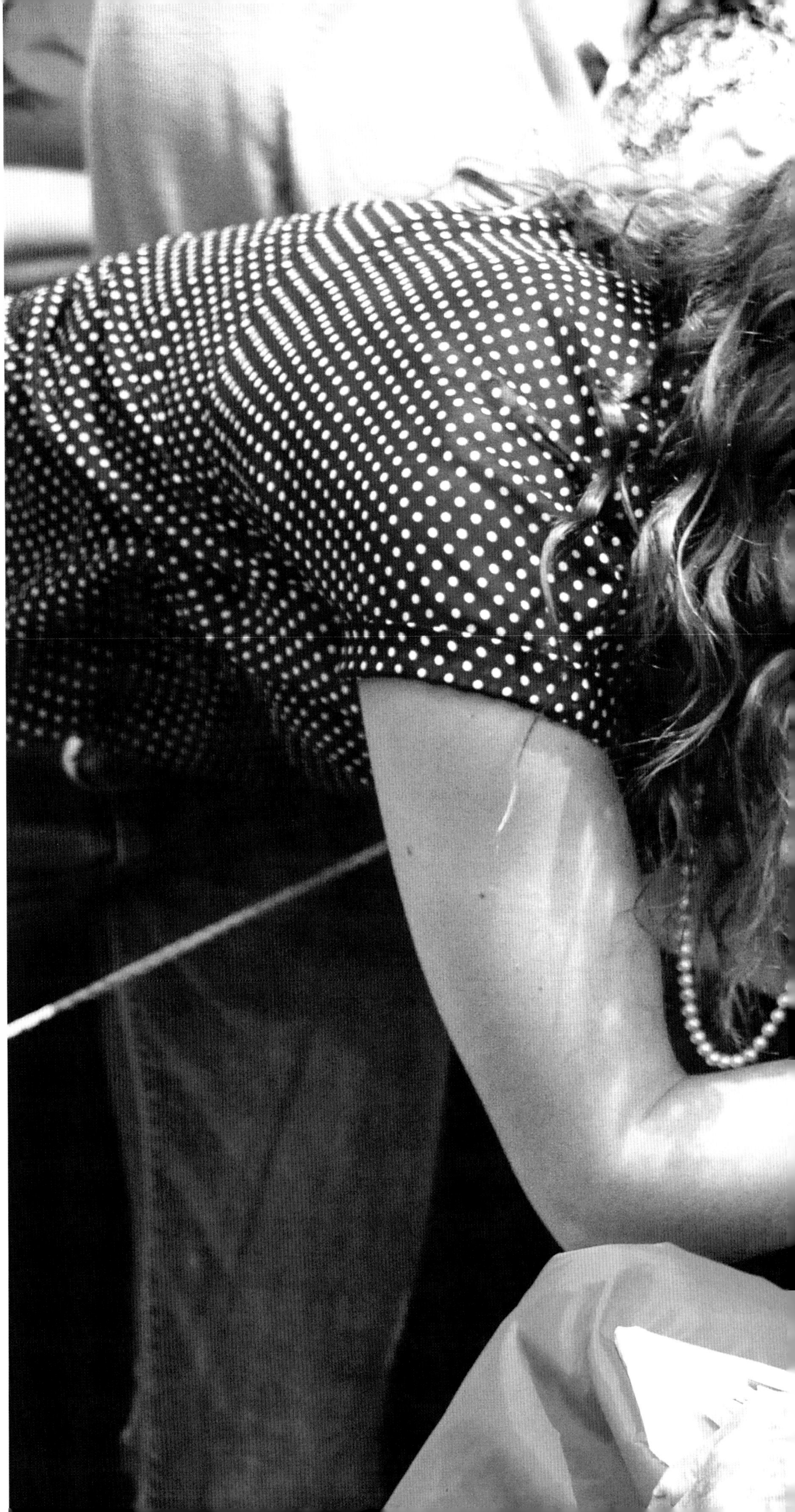

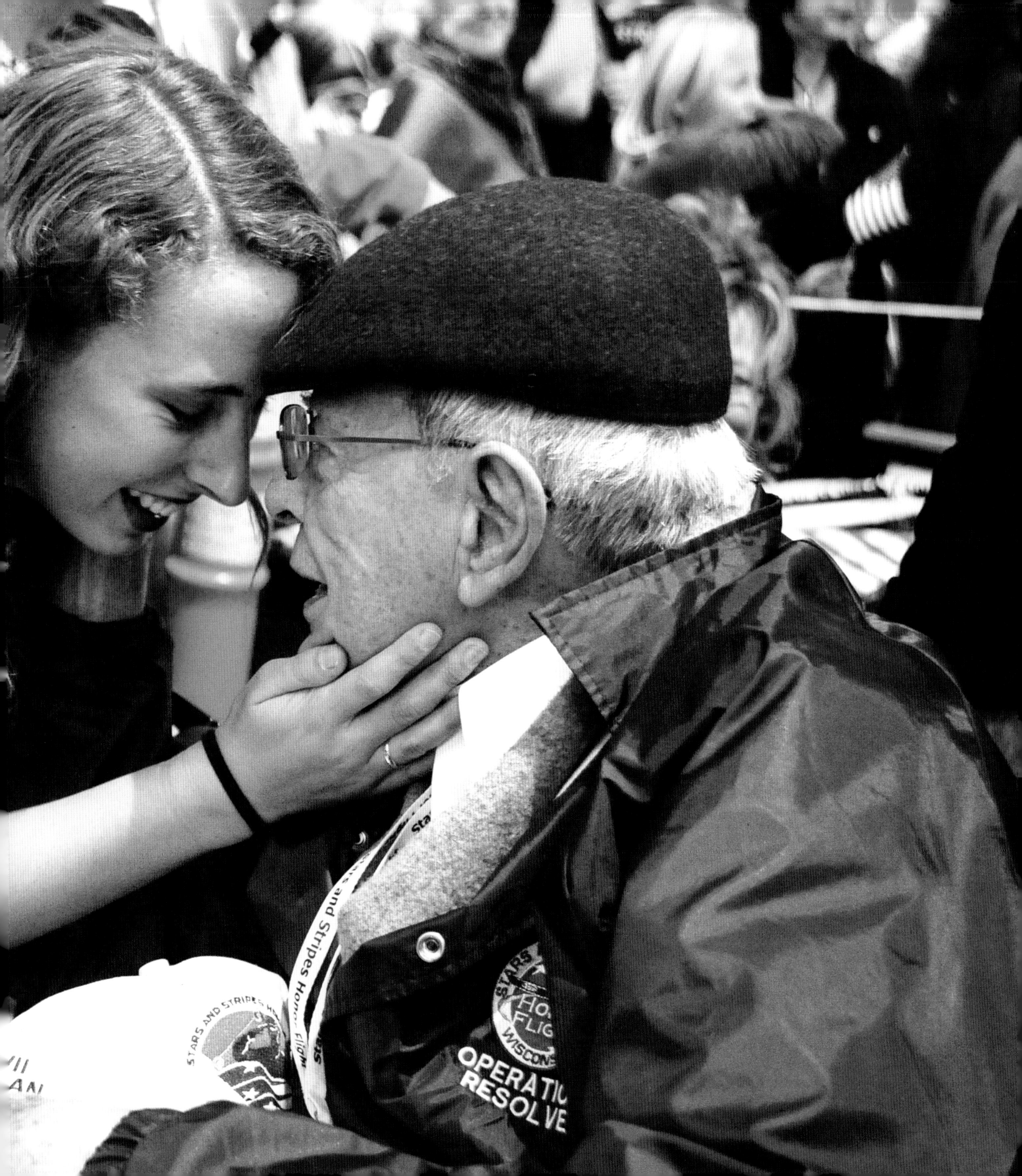
OPERATIO
RESOLVE

Happy Birthday DAD

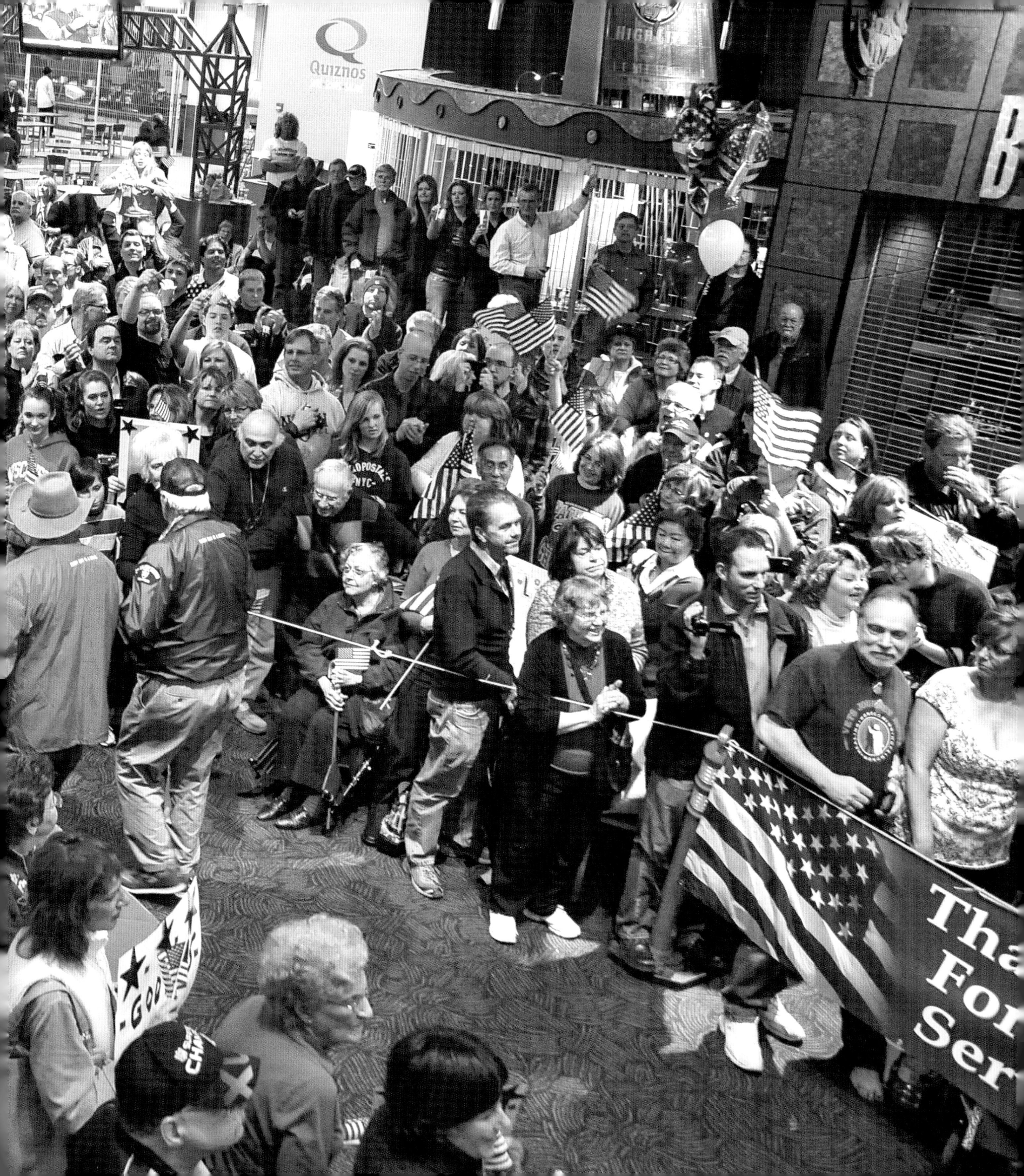
Quiznos

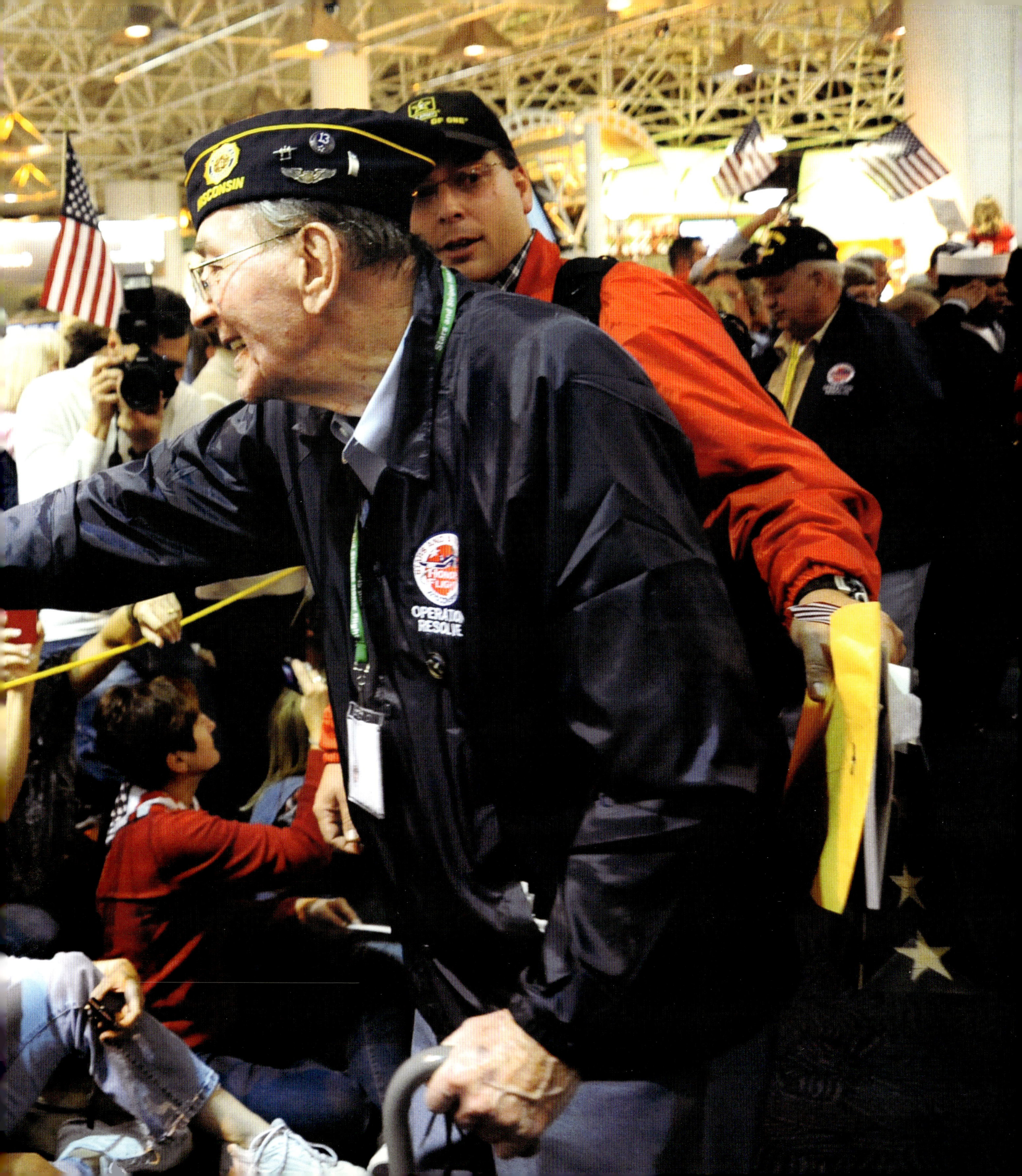

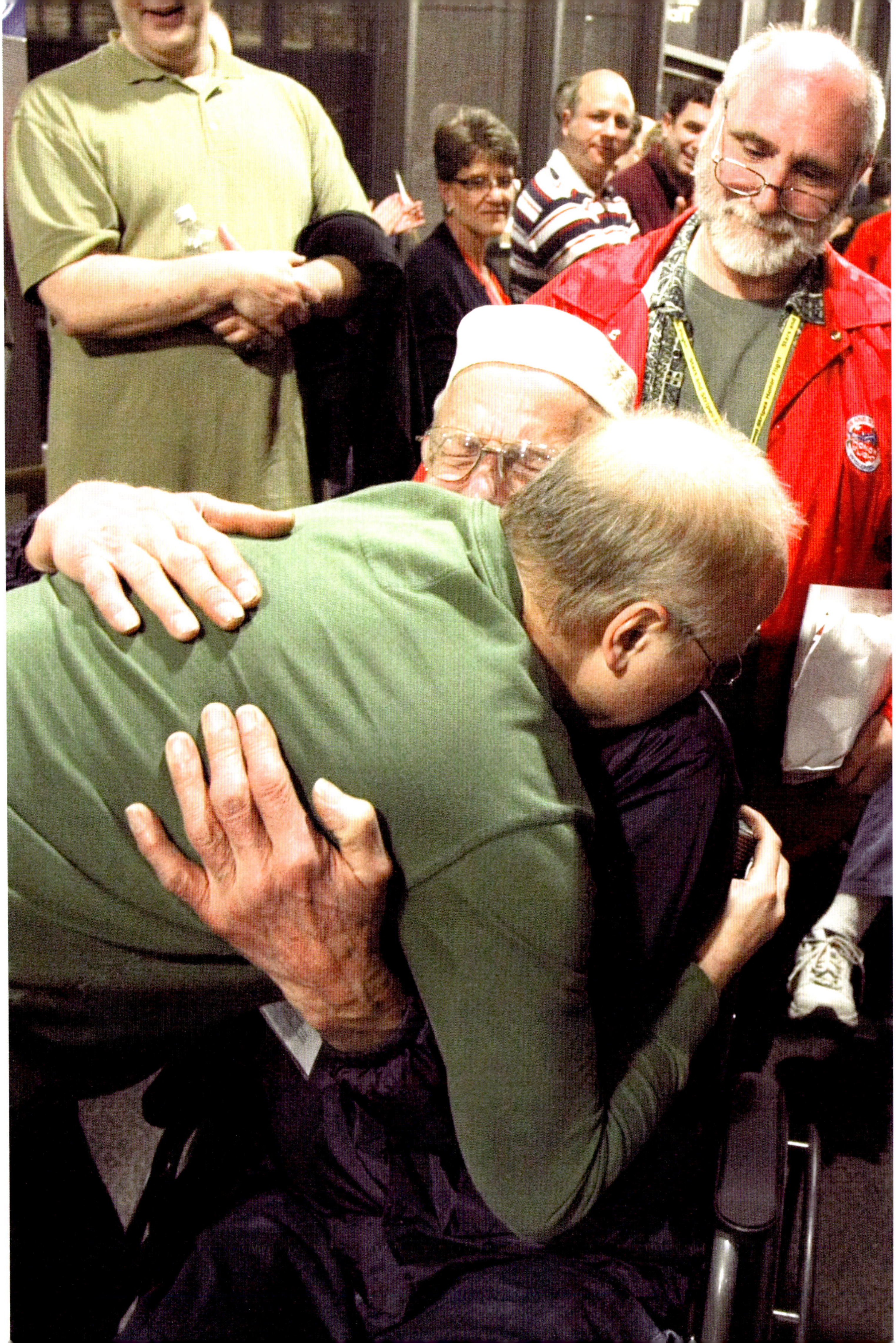

Honor Flight Homecomings can sometimes be the catalyst for very emotional reunions. WWII veteran Jim Bornemann was surprised at his Homecoming by his son, Steve, whom he had not seen in nearly a decade. After hearing radio talk show host Charlie Sykes talk about how meaningful the Homecoming celebration is to our veterans, Steve decided to go to the airport for the Homecoming, where he and his dad enjoyed an emotional reunion.

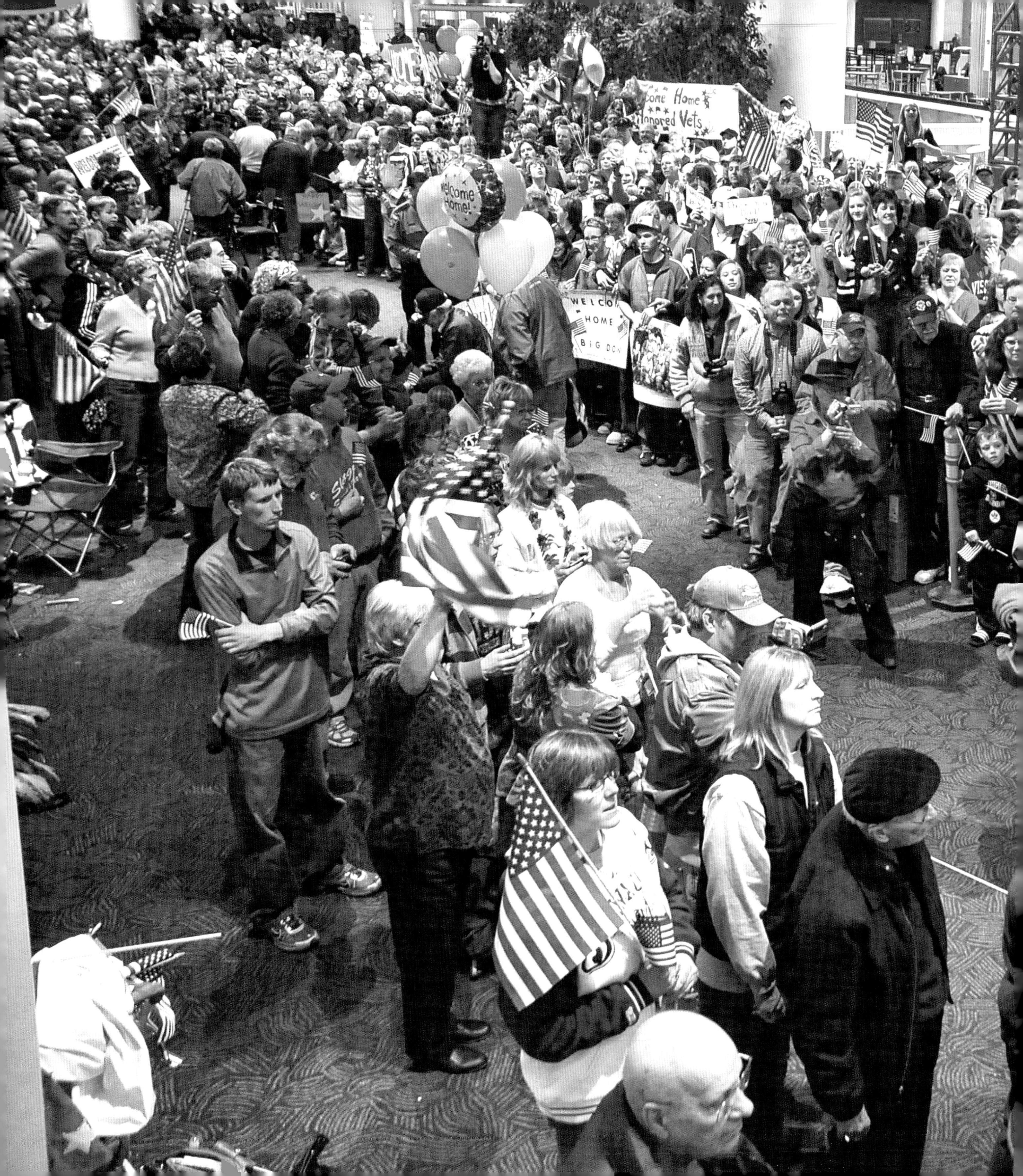
come Home
Honored Vets
Welcome Home!
WELCOM
HOME
BIG DON

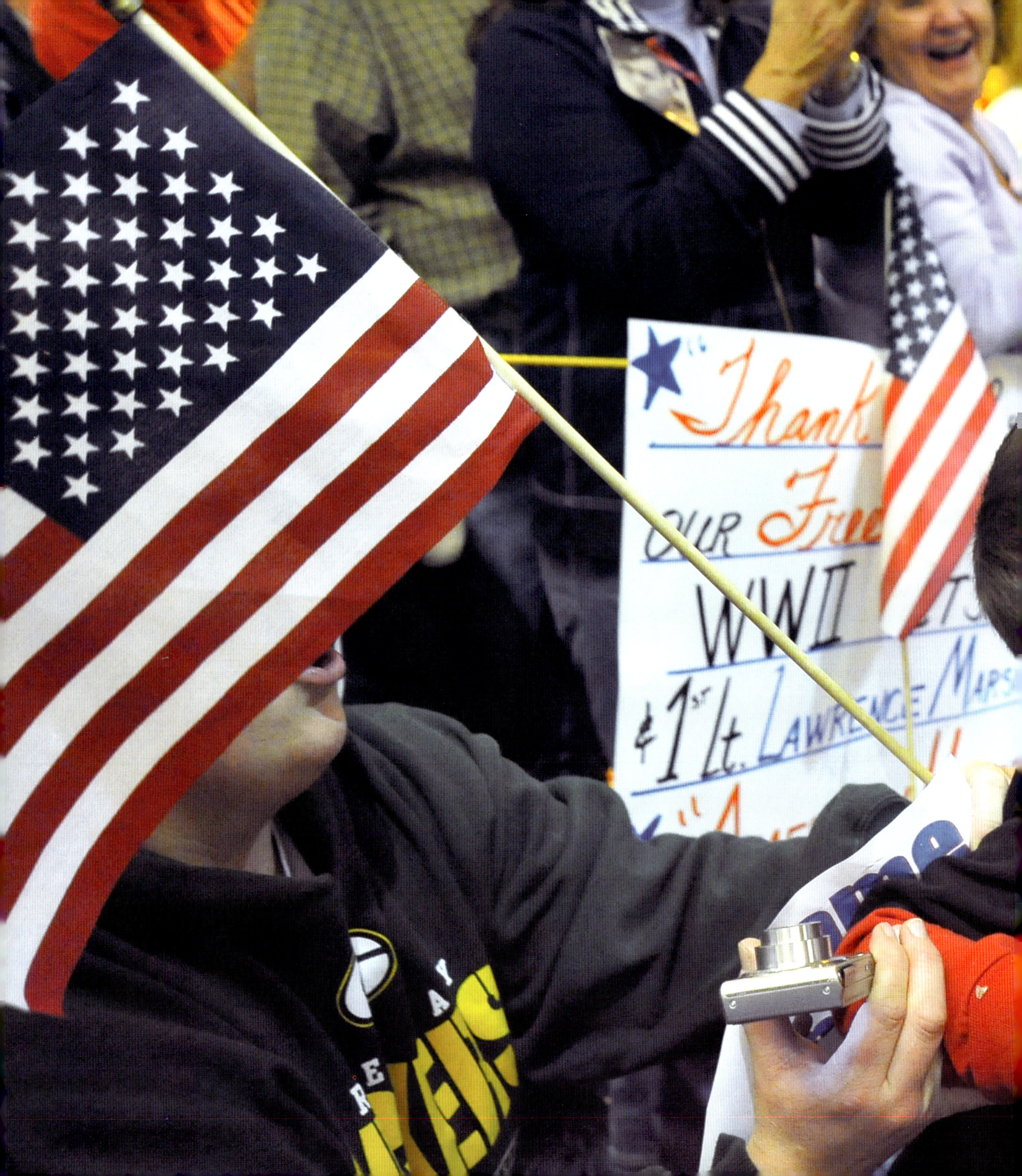
Thank
OUR
WWII
1st Lt. LAWRENCE

STARS AND STRIPES
HONOR FLIGHT
WISCONSIN
OPERATION
Richard A. Schauz
Stars and Stripes Honor Flight
Bravo 4

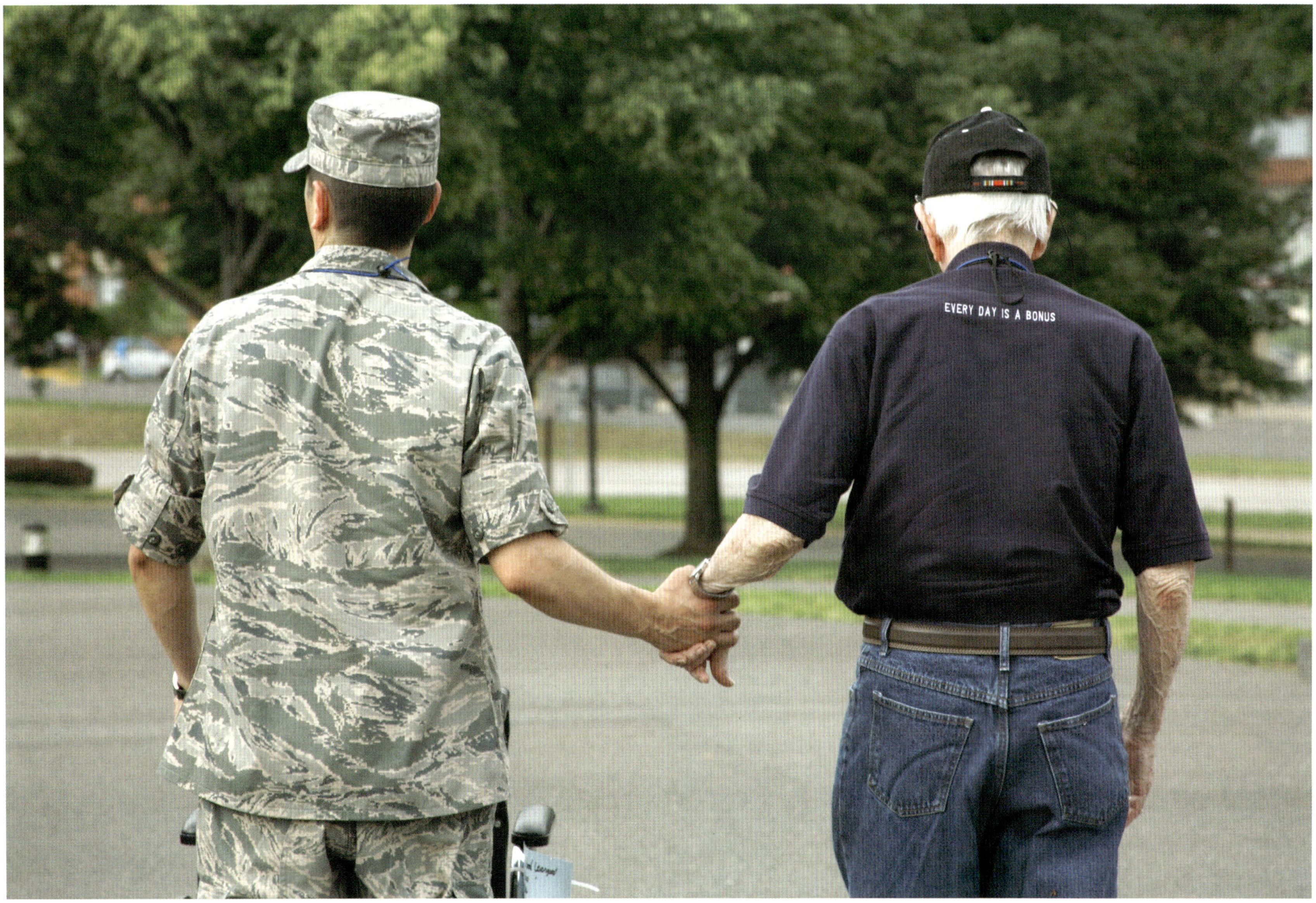
EVERY DAY IS A BONUS

EPILOGUE

The Stars and Stripes Honor Flight Homecoming has become a true community event, with thousands of family, friends and neighbors coming together to welcome home our heroes. So many people help us create this highly-charged, patriotic event, including hundreds of active duty and retired military personnel, local current and former policemen and firemen, Boy Scouts and Girl Scouts, community and high school bands and cheerleaders – and of course, our dedicated team of Stars and Stripes Honor Flight volunteers. We work to guarantee a proper homecoming as a demonstration of our gratitude for the sacrifices that our veterans and military personnel have made – and continue to make – for our country.

In this spirit of gratitude, Stars and Stripes Honor Flight has teamed with Fisher House Foundation, which caters to the millions of veterans and their families from our most recent conflicts. Half of the proceeds from the sale of *Honor Flight: A Visual Journey* will be used to help us continue our mission to fly our nation's veterans to see their memorials in Washington, D.C.

Together, we have learned along this journey. Never again should our veterans wait 70 years for a thank you or the knowledge that they have our support on the homefront. For this reason, the other half of the proceeds will go toward building a Fisher House Wisconsin, where families can stay free of charge while their loved one receives medical treatment. (Read more about Fisher House Wisconsin on the next page.)

We believe that the love and gratitude of family and community is good medicine. We believe this is more than a book. It's a mission. God bless our veterans past and present. Thank you for your support.

Sometimes Thank You is Not Enough

★ ★ ★ ★ ★

KEN FISHER
Chairman
Fisher House Foundation

They are called the "Greatest Generation" for a reason. And words do little to adequately explain the enormity of the debt we owe them for what they accomplished.

In the 1940s, they were young, some still teenagers. They stepped forward when their nation needed them and walked into the unknown for all the right reasons.

They stormed the beaches of Normandy, dodging bullets and mortar fire as they advanced. They parachuted behind enemy lines across Europe, into pitch-black darkness. They waged innumerable battles across the wide expanse of the Pacific, in the air and on the water. They fought, they bled, gave their limbs, their sight and in some cases, their whole existence to protect the values of our country and the lives of those at home.

With each victory, they took back territory from the enemy: one mile, one city and one country at a time, until they had vanquished an evil the world had never seen before. An enemy that was hell-bent on the enslavement or destruction of anyone who disagreed with its twisted world view.

These men and women made sure history was written differently. The United States – and indeed, the entire world – is free today because of the sacrifices that these veterans made. And they defined the values of service and honor for decades to come, followed by their brothers and sisters who served in Korea, Vietnam and Desert Storm.

above: Ken Fisher *(photo/courtesy of Fisher House Foundation)*
opposite: The Fisher House Foundation provides housing for families of veterans receiving medical treatment, making the healing process easier for all. *(photo/Craig Orsini, www.orsinistudio.com)*

337

FISHER HOUSE WISCONSIN

This 10,000-square-foot, 16-suite home will be built on the grounds of the Clement J. Zablocki VA Medical Center in Milwaukee, making it the first Fisher House in the state and one of the largest in the country. The Milwaukee VA anticipates about 8,000 inpatient admissions this year, with more than 9,500 returning soldiers from the wars in Iraq and Afghanistan receiving inpatient and outpatient care there. Fisher House Wisconsin will be able to accommodate more than 400 families annually – at no cost to them. The proposed budget for Fisher House Wisconsin is $6,000,000.

above: Artist's rendering of Fisher House Wisconsin *(photo/courtesy of Fisher House Foundation)*

> *Families are separated across time and geography, deployments last for months and years. Back on the home front, there are children who need to go to school, mortgages that have to be paid, and laundry to be done.*

Although the specifics may have changed, our military today fights a similar battle against a familiar enemy and its agenda of carnage, terror and domination. Although our modern fighting force – comprising warriors downrange, logistical support and domestic operations – is made up of less than one percent of the American population, they and their families make the same kinds of sacrifices as those who headed off to fight the Nazis and the Axis of Evil more than 70 years ago. Families are separated across time and geography, deployments last for months and years. Back on the home front, there are children who need to go to school, mortgages that have to be paid, and laundry to be done. Life doesn't stop, even though each day begins with the fear of a knock on the door bearing the worst possible news. These are the sacrifices – emotional and psychological – that the vast majority of Americans will never be able to fully comprehend.

As the beneficiaries of the hard work and sacrifice of our military and our veterans, it becomes our duty to ensure the world never forgets their accomplishment, and provide them with the support they need whenever they need it.

At Fisher House, we make sure every family that wants to be near a loved one receiving medical care has a place to stay, free of charge, for as long as they need. We see to it that we not only provide the bricks and mortar that make up a house, but the emotional, psychological and spiritual support system that creates a caring environment where families can pause, heal and draw strength from sharing their experiences.

In addition to its own work – such incredibly important and impactful work for our World War II veterans – we salute Stars and Stripes Honor Flight for its vital role in the creation of Fisher House Wisconsin, which will join a network of more than 60 other houses around the world. This campaign, to help bridge the gap between the veterans of yesterday and the veterans of today, is simply selfless.

So this book that you hold in your hands, that you will share with the people who enter your home, is the story of every veteran. It is an extension of the work we all do to help those families who need – and in fact, deserve – the best we can offer them.

On behalf of Fisher House Foundation, the Fisher family and all of the military families we serve, we thank Stars and Stripes Honor Flight for its work on behalf of veterans. And we thank you for your support of them.

WITH GRATITUDE TO:
Our World War II heroes and all our nation's veterans, past and present
Wisconsin Energy Foundation
Quad/Graphics

HONOR FLIGHT: A VISUAL JOURNEY
Editors: Renee Riddle, Kristen Scheuing
Design: Meghan Blaney   Essay Design: Jena Sher
Production Assistance: Michelle Janda   Editorial Assistance: Chris Dean-Miota
Photo research and selection: Courtney Lutz, Karl Boettcher, Jane Dean, Renee Riddle
Photography: Visual Image Photography www.vipis.com
VIP: Courtney Lutz, Karl Boettcher, Josh Pierringer, Mike Arndt, John Bryan, Holly Nelson, Brian Hurley
Other photos: pp. 41, 99: Freethink Media; p. 115: Jeremy Wilson; p. 130: Mark Lackovic;
pp. 132 (right), 144 (bottom left and right), 192, 234, 243, 311: Joe Dean; pp. 138, 249, 270: Deborah Foote;
p. 156 Brian McCutcheon; p.199: Shawn Gerrits; pp. 278-281, 295, 318: Jerry Luterman;
pp. 300, 306, 314: Ben Lorber; p. 310: Kelly Dzurick

www.honorflightbook.com
MojoWeb productions
The Scan Group

Stars and Stripes Honor Flight Board of Directors:
Joe Dean, Founder and Chairman
Liane Baranek; Barb Burja; Jane Dean; Steve Deutsch; Mark Grams, USMC GySgt (R); Brad Hoeft;
Amy Klapper; Jim Kliese; David Krause; Amy Luft; Dr. Michael Lischak; Dr. Doug McManus; Paula Nelson;
Peter Pochowski; Renee Riddle; Dan Toomey; Eileen Wilson

Board Members – Emeritus:
Ruth Auer, Rob Brooks, Ken Brown, Kathy Geracie, Roger Kirgues, Debbie Krueger, Dan Pelchen,
Chuck Skogland, Kathleen Schilling, Mike Shea, Dr. Michael Weber

342

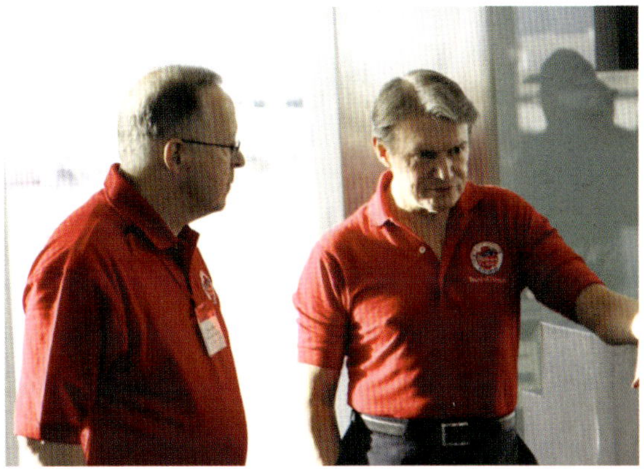
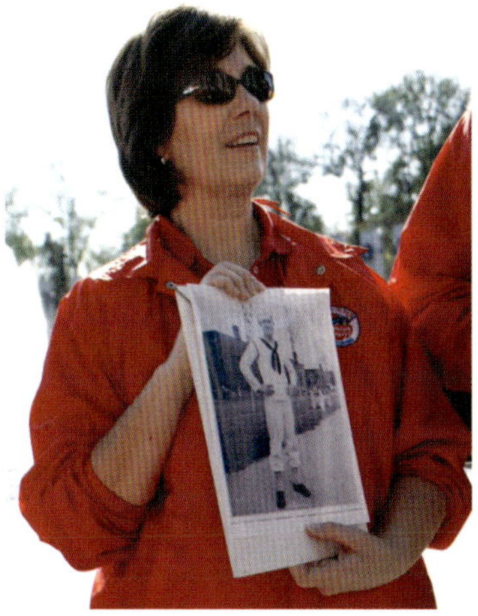
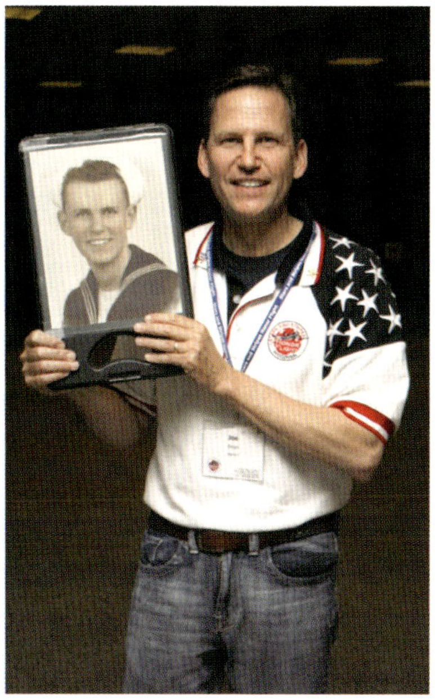
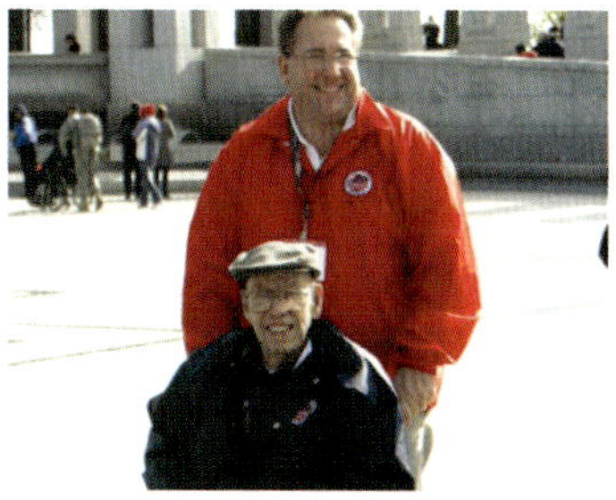
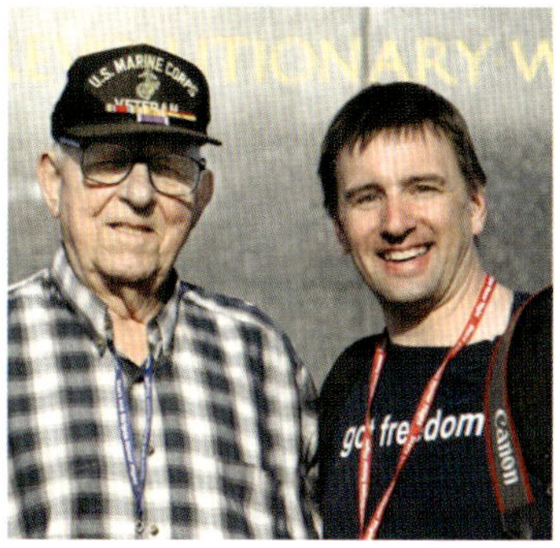

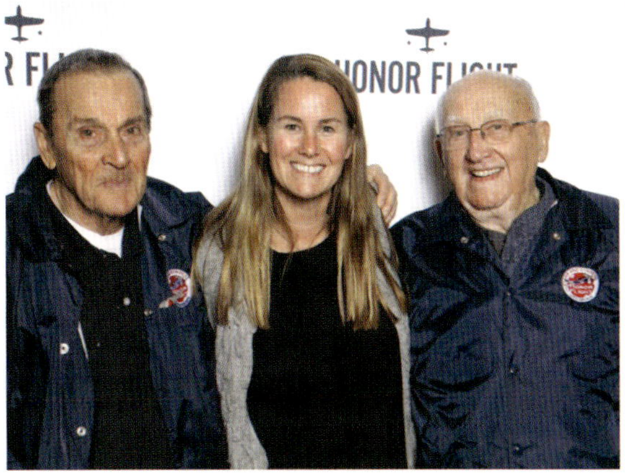
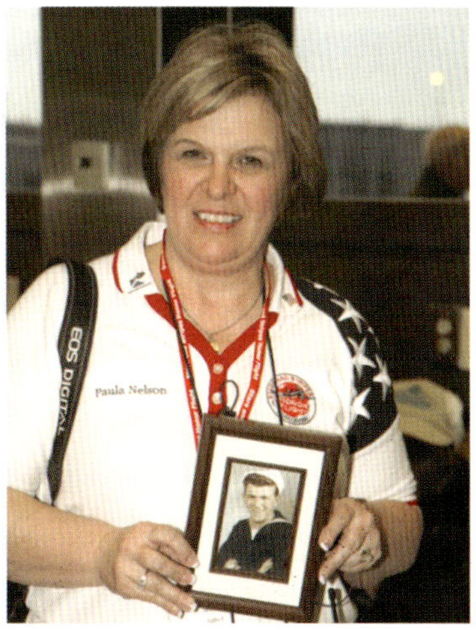

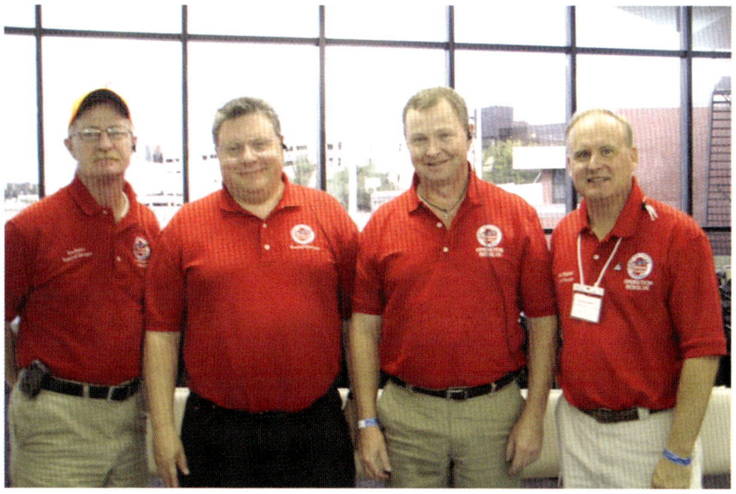
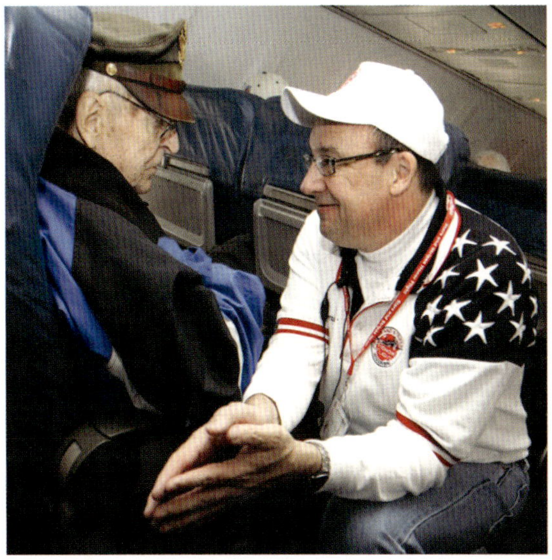
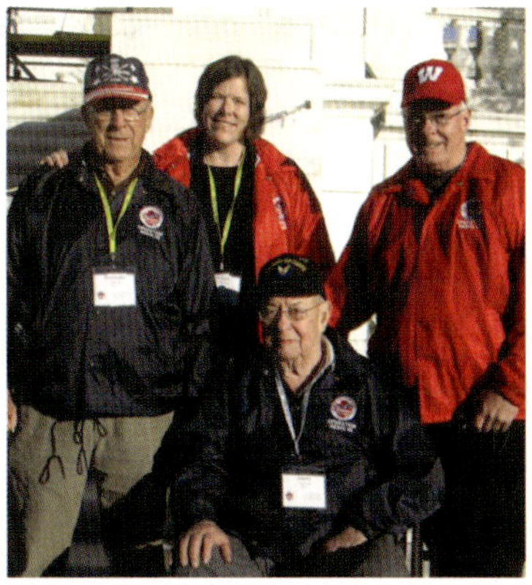
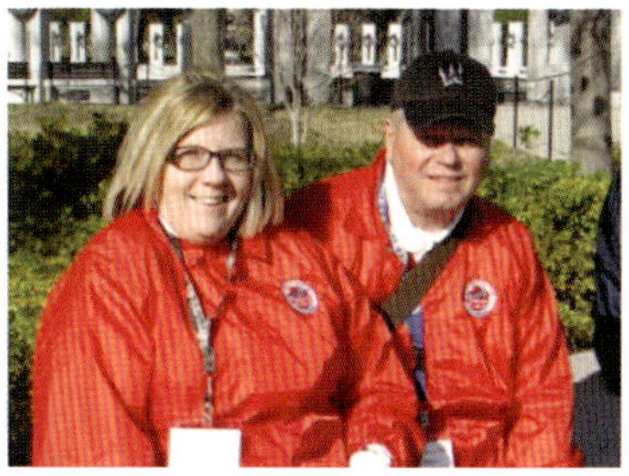
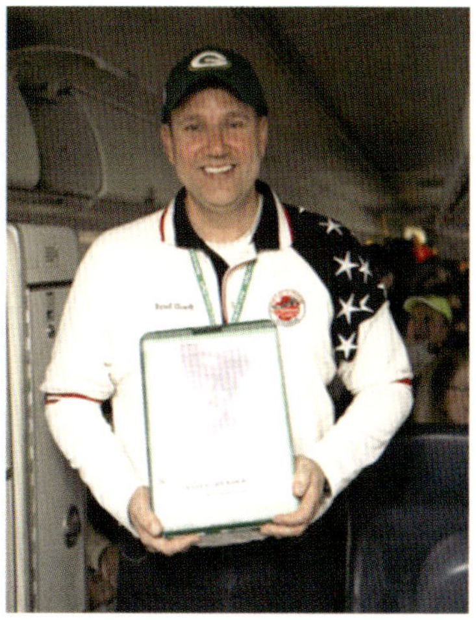
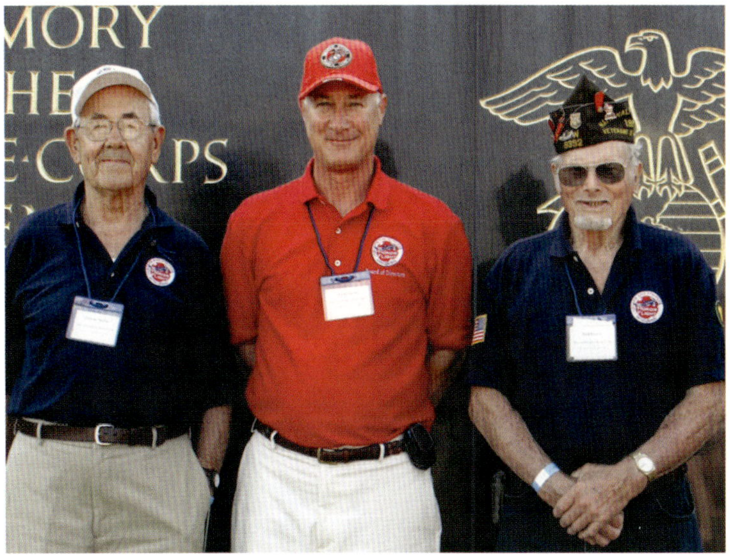
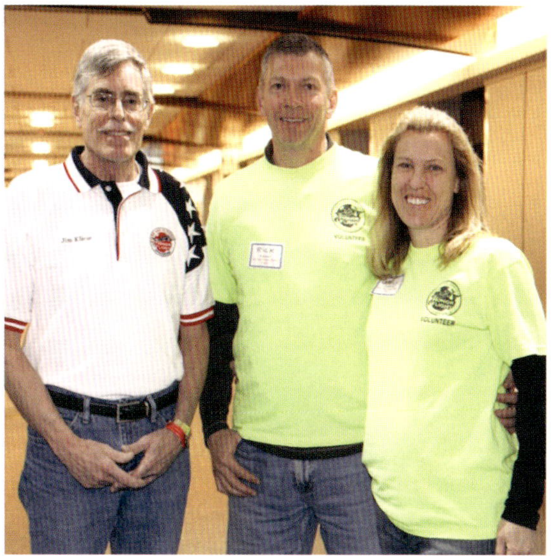

STARS AND STRIPES
HONOR FLIGHT
WISCONSIN

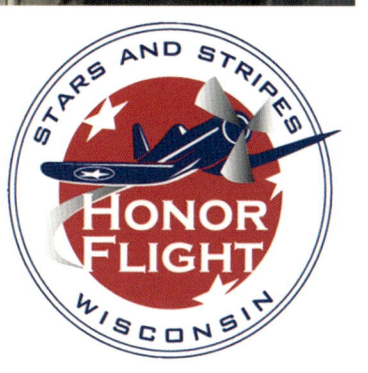